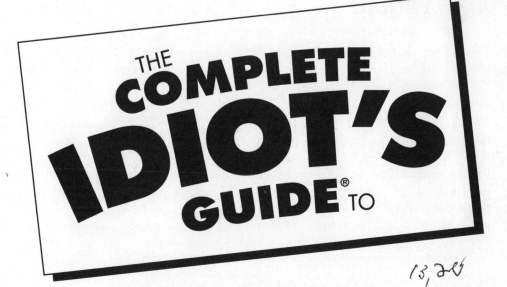

THE COMPLETE IDIOT'S GUIDE® TO

Writing Well

by Laurie E. Rozakis, Ph.D.

ALPHA

A member of Penguin Group (USA) Inc.

ALPHA BOOKS

Published by the Penguin Group

Penguin Group (USA) Inc., 375 Hudson Street, New York, New York 10014, U.S.A.

Penguin Group (Canada), 10 Alcorn Avenue, Toronto, Ontario, Canada M4V 3B2 (a division of Pearson Penguin Canada Inc.)

Penguin Books Ltd, 80 Strand, London WC2R 0RL, England

Penguin Ireland, 25 St Stephen's Green, Dublin 2, Ireland (a division of Penguin Books Ltd)

Penguin Group (Australia), 250 Camberwell Road, Camberwell, Victoria 3124, Australia (a division of Pearson Australia Group Pty Ltd)

Penguin Books India Pvt Ltd, 11 Community Centre, Panchsheel Park, New Delhi—110 017, India

Penguin Group (NZ), cnr Airborne and Rosedale Roads, Albany, Auckland 1310, New Zealand (a division of Pearson New Zealand Ltd)

Penguin Books (South Africa) (Pty) Ltd, 24 Sturdee Avenue, Rosebank, Johannesburg 2196, South Africa

Penguin Books Ltd, Registered Offices: 80 Strand, London WC2R 0RL, England

Copyright © 2000 by Laurie E. Rozakis, Ph.D.

International Standard Book Number: 0-02-863694-5
Library of Congress Catalog Card Number: Available upon request.

08   07   12

Interpretation of the printing code: The rightmost number of the first series of numbers is the year of the book's printing; the rightmost number of the second series of numbers is the number of the book's printing. For example, a printing code of 00-1 shows that the first printing occurred in 2000.

Printed in the United States of America

Publisher
Marie Butler-Knight

Product Manager
Phil Kitchel

Associate Managing Editor
Cari Luna

Development Editor
Joan D. Paterson

Production Editor
Christy Wagner

Illustrator
Jody P. Schaeffer

Cover Designers
Mike Freeland
Kevin Spear

Book Designers
Scott Cook and Amy Adams of DesignLab

Indexer
Tonya Heard

Layout/Proofreading
John Etchison
Michael J. Poor
Gloria Schurick

Contents at a Glance

Appendixes

Contents

Appendixes

Foreword

I always knew I was a writer. From the time I first learned to wield a pencil, I've been scribbling stories, driven by a passion to see my words on paper, cheered on by loving parents and teachers who assured me that yes, I certainly had talent and was sure to be a published author.

So years later, imagine how shocked I was when I carefully bundled up my first novel, sent it off to New York publishers, and promptly got back a rejection. And then another rejection. And another.

I am telling you about my sorry early years as a novelist to make a point: Raw talent and passion are not enough to make one a good writer. Most successful authors, if they are honest with you, will admit to some pretty shaky starts in their careers, some dark moments when they despaired of ever seeing their words in print. But with time and perseverance, these same writers eventually learned the art of stringing words together. They learned that writing well is not automatic, that even "born" storytellers must learn how to make their words sing.

Here is where this book comes in. Whether you are drafting a business report or composing a letter to a friend, whether a novel burns inside you or a deadline looms for a college term paper, the lessons on these pages will help you nurture your own writing skills. These skills will surely serve you well, both professionally and personally.

Through writing, our thoughts, our feelings, may endure. The spoken word fades at once into silence; the written word is meant to last. May we all learn to make our words sing.

Tess Gerritsen

Tess Gerritsen is the *New York Times* Bestselling author of the medical thrillers *Gravity, Bloodstream, Harvest,* and *Life Support.* She has been praised by critics around the world as "tops in her genre" (*USA Today*) and "the reigning champion of the medical thriller" (*San Jose Mercury*). She lives in Maine.

Introduction

"I'm just not a good writer," you say. "I'll master everyday writing when pigs fly." Hold on to your hats, ladies and gentlemen, because there will be pork in the treetops by the time you finish this book.

Mastering the types of writing you need in your daily life isn't as hard as you think. *The Complete Idiot's Guide to Writing Well* will help you learn the skills you need to write fine essays, letters, e-mail, and reports. You'll also learn how to express yourself in personal narratives, stories, letters of evaluation, recommendations, and journals.

Writing can change your life—and the lives of others around you. Writing can …

> ➤ Help you understand yourself more fully.
> ➤ Achieve the goals you've set for yourself.
> ➤ Enable you to sort the information that's thrown at you every day.
> ➤ Present ideas so other people will take your ideas more seriously.
> ➤ Move you up the ladder of success and prestige.
> ➤ Record your feelings and deepest thoughts in creative ways.

Writing can broaden your vistas by enabling you to communicate more effectively with people you may never have even met.

Despite the immense possibilities that writing offers, many people convince themselves that they can never learn to write because they think that when writing talent was handed out, they were at the back of the line. Unfortunately, it's all too easy to talk yourself into something that isn't true. It *is* true that some people write more easily than others because they have been encouraged by their teachers, parents, or peers. It's also true that some people seem to have a greater facility with words than others.

But this is most true of all: Writing is a skill that can be learned by anyone who is willing to take the time and trouble. Learning any new skill takes hard work, determination, and time, but this is one investment that's a sure thing.

You probably know a great deal more about writing well than you realize. However, you may not know how to use what you know to accomplish the many different kinds of writing you need. You may be discouraged by the sheer variety of writing you must do: letters, e-mail, notes, term papers, and reports. Perhaps you're a bit shaky on grammar, usage, and mechanics—all those commas, semicolons, and dangling modifiers. If so, then this book is for you.

The famous American wit Dorothy Parker (1893–1967) once said:

> *Four be the things I am wiser to know:*
> *Idleness, sorrow, a friend, and a foe.*
> *Four be the things I'd be better without:*
> *Love, curiosity, freckles, and doubt.*

I'll leave the decision about "love, curiosity, freckles" to you, if you'll let me have "doubt." By the time you've finished reading this book, you'll have no doubt that you can be a good writer. You'll be writing with skill, confidence, and even pleasure.

What You'll Learn in This Book

This book is divided into six sections that teach you the skills you need to write well. Together, they help you grasp each specific type of writing and the entire writing process. By the end of this book, you'll be sure of yourself as a writer.

Part 1, "**Write Now**," first explains why mastering the basics of good writing is important in your job and life. You'll also learn how writing developed, starting with the alphabet. I'll prove that writing is a skill that can be acquired, not an inborn trait. Next, I introduce the four types of writing: exposition, narration, argumentation, and description. Later in this part, you'll explore the essential elements of effective writing: logic, organization, unity, coherence, purpose, audience, tone, details, style, and word choice. We'll review phrases, clauses, sentences, and paragraphs, too.

Part 2, "**The Writing Process**," teaches the entire writing process, including planning, researching, shaping and drafting, revising and editing, and proof-reading. There's also a section on dealing with "writer's block." Next, you'll explore the different ways that you can organize the information in your writing. After you learn how to write great introductions, body paragraphs, and conclusions, you'll discover how to make your writing shine.

Part 3, "**Write for Success**," covers exposition, narration, persuasion, and description in detail. You'll also learn how to write for different subject areas, including natural sciences, social sciences, and the humanities.

Part 4, "**Just Shoot Me Now: Research Papers and Term Papers**," covers everything you need to know about research papers, from soup to nuts. This part opens with a chapter on generating subjects, narrowing them into suitable topics, and writing thesis statements. Then you'll enter "basic training" to review research methods. I'll also teach you how to evaluate and track your sources. The part concludes with a chapter on parenthetical documentation, endmatter, and frontmatter.

Part 5, "**More Big Deals**," copes with writing under pressure, including assignments that ask you to recall, analyze, evaluate, or synthesize. Then I'll teach you how to write fine speeches, effective personal and social letters, and resumés that work.

Part 6, "**Picture Perfect**," puts the finishing touches on your writing, starting with a crash course in grammar and usage. Then we'll review spelling rules, contractions, possessives, plurals, punctuation, and capitalization.

Last, there's an appendix of sample term papers and one of research paper documentation.

More for Your Money!

In addition to all the explanation and teaching, this book contains other types of information to make it even easier for you to learn how to write well. Here's how you can recognize these features:

Author! Author!

You could skip these tasty tidbits, but you won't want to because they're so interesting!

Word Watch

As with every skill worth knowing, writing has its own terminology. These definitions explain all those terms so you can talk the talk as well as walk the walk.

Writer's Block

These warnings help you stay on track and write your best.

Write Angles

Dazzle your family and friends by learning the little expert tips that give you that "extra edge."

Acknowledgments

Special thanks to Jessica Swantek for her brilliant research papers on calorie reduction and Irish step dancing/Appalachian clogging. Love and thanks to Charles Rozakis for his paper on Felix Mendelssohn. Jessica and Charles, in addition to being fine writers, you two are fine people.

Special Thanks to the Technical Reviewer

The Complete Idiot's Guide to Writing Well was reviewed by an expert who double-checked the accuracy of what you'll learn here, to help us ensure that this book gives you everything you need to know about writing well. Special thanks are extended to Sharon Sorenson.

Trademarks

All terms mentioned in this book that are known to be or are suspected of being trademarks or service marks have been appropriately capitalized. Alpha Books and Penguin Group (USA) Inc. cannot attest to the accuracy of this information. Use of a term in this book should not be regarded as affecting the validity of any trademark or service mark.

Part 1

Write Now

Did you know that …

> ➤ *A snail can sleep for three years.*

> ➤ *Polar bears are left-handed.*

> ➤ *The electric chair was invented by a dentist.*

> ➤ *Banging your head against a wall uses 150 calories an hour.*

> ➤ *You have the ability, intelligence, and determination to become a competent writer.*

In the following chapters, you'll learn how to get yourself in the "write" frame of mind. I'll also explain the four different kinds of writing, cover the essential information all writers need to know, and help you select the exact word you want—not its first cousin. In addition, you'll review the building blocks of all powerful poetry and prose: phrases, clauses, sentences, and paragraphs.

Chapter 1

Why Writing Matters

In This Chapter

➤ The advantages of writing over speech

➤ A writing quiz

➤ The importance of writing well

➤ Sumerian writing systems

➤ The development of the alphabet

➤ Writing as a symbolic method of communication

We live in a world of words. Without doubt, words are the lifeblood of all modern societies. And English is becoming the international language of technology, science, diplomacy, and business. About 350 million people speak and write English as their native language. An additional 350 million people speak and write English as their second language. More than half the world's books are published in English. About 80 percent of the world's computer text is in English.

Therefore, knowing how to express yourself in clear, concise, and correct written English is a key factor for success in the twenty-first century.

Writing with confidence and skill allows you to communicate your feelings, ideas, hopes, and fears. In this chapter, you'll explore why writing is so important, no matter who you are or what you do.

The Power of the Pen

We live in an age of touch-tone phones, cordless phones, and cell phones. There are still a few rotary phones plugged in, too. (I have one!) And let's not forget beepers. In a worst-case scenario, we can always hop in the car and speak to someone face to face. So why bother writing? Why can't we just say what we mean? Why does writing matter in an age of constant electronic yakking?

Author! Author!

Scientists have discovered that babies recognize elements of speech sounds very shortly after birth and they begin to copy the patterns of speech before they can form words. At one month, infants can distinguish certain features of spoken sound that will later represent vowels and consonants. Before a child is one year old, it is possible to tell Chinese-, French-, and English-speaking babies apart from tape recordings of their babbling.

Take this quiz to see whether you recognize writing's advantages. Answer True (T) if you think the statement is true or False (F) if you think I'm a liar.

Unlike speech, writing allows us to ...

True	False	
_____	_____	1. Mend fences, especially when it's hard to come out and say something to a person.
_____	_____	2. Tell a story that many people can share over time and down through the ages.
_____	_____	3. Create contracts and other legal documents.
_____	_____	4. Report scientific and technological findings.
_____	_____	5. Make guarantees that people can trust.
_____	_____	6. Sell products and services to a vast audience—even internationally!

True	False	
	___	7. Professionally state our qualifications for a position in a professional manner.
	___	8. Convince someone to hire us when talking just won't do the trick.
	___	9. Persuade someone to love us.
	___	10. Protect our reputations.
	___	11. Express our feelings fully.
	___	12. Record the story of our lives.
	___	13. Entertain others with our wit, humor, and descriptions.
	___	14. Help others through the power of our prose.
	___	15. Publish our opinions for others to share.
	___	16. Create convincing, entertaining, or persuasive speeches that can live through the ages.
	___	17. Express our thanks, sorrow, or appreciation in a way that people can read and reread.
	___	18. Communicate electronically via e-mail.
	___	19. Record the proceedings of a meeting.
	___	20. Acknowledge life's milestones such as births, weddings, and funerals.

Want to know your score?

Every item is true. And that's only the tip of the iceberg when it comes to the power of writing. Consider the following:

➤ More information has been produced in the last 50 years than in the previous 5,000 years.

➤ Currently, there are more than 100 million volumes in the Library of Congress.

➤ Fifty thousand books are published in the United States every year.

➤ Ten thousand magazines are currently published in the United States every year.

➤ Seven thousand scientific studies are written daily worldwide.

➤ Today, the amount of writing produced doubles every five years.

Captain of Your Fate

A mastery of writing is essential for anyone who wants to play an important role in society. Writing allows you to communicate with others efficiently, hold a responsible position, and earn a good salary. Companies want employees who can write clear memos and letters; telecommuters, freelancers, and other lone eagles must be able to sell their services in writing.

Write Angles

No one is born knowing how to write. Even the greatest writers made mistakes when they first learned to write. Writing is a skill that is acquired through study and practice. You can learn to write well—and even enjoy it!

Word Watch

Prose is any writing that is not poetry, such as letters, memos, biographies, autobiographies, e-mail, short stories, plays, and novels.

Writing helps you …

➤ **Get it right.** Putting down your thoughts on paper helps you say what you want the way you want. Because writing lets you think more carefully before you communicate, you can convey complex information in more detail. Writing has another great advantage over speech: It can be revised. Because you can go over and over your written words before you pass them on, you can polish your *prose* until it shines. This helps you say exactly what you mean. Clear writing helps you avoid miscommunication, because your words are down on paper rather than floating through the air where they can be misheard.

➤ **Do well in school.** Increasingly, your mastery of all subjects is being assessed in writing. With the tough new state education mandates sweeping the nation, multiple-choice tests have gone the way of the horse-and-buggy. Even the Scholastic Aptitude Test (SAT) now has a mandatory writing component. If you can write clearly and well, you'll be in a better position to ace your tests—whether you're in high school, college, or graduate school.

➤ **Get a good job.** Writing is one of the key skills for getting—and keeping—the plum jobs. That's because employers want people who can write, since they because people who can write help sell products, bring in clients, create goodwill, and make points clearly.

Author! Author!

There are more than 9,000 individual spoken languages—but fewer than 15 writing systems have been developed individually and independently. New languages continue to be discovered in remote corners of the globe. Another 1,000 languages, such as ancient Egyptian, are known but no longer used.

Today, the most widely spoken language is Chinese, used by more than one billion people. However, since Chinese has several dialects, we may be fudging to call it one language. The Mandarin dialect is used by more than 500 million Chinese and will probably become even more widespread now that it is taught in schools in China.

➤ **Save time.** Less than 5 percent of our reading time is spent moving our eyes across the page; the rest of the time is spent trying to understand what we're reading. Inarticulate, confusing writing takes longer to read and understand than clear writing. As a result, bad writing wastes a tremendous amount of time. If a document is clear, at least people can spend their time arguing whether they should adopt it, rather than wasting time trying to understand it.

➤ **Earn a good salary.** Being able to write well can help you get promoted. The higher you move up the ladder, the more money you're going to earn. (If not, you're on the wrong ladder.) At promotion time, the ability to write well can tip the scales in your favor.

➤ **Change the world.** As James Baldwin said, "Writing is a political instrument … a way to describe and control your circumstances."

If you write well, you can draft letters and petitions to improve conditions in your neighborhood, state, or even country. The Declaration of Independence and the Constitution are just two of the documents that have changed the world.

➤ **Express your ideas, plans, and feelings.** When North America was first settled, beavers grew to the size of bears. Like beaver size, some things change, but others remain constant. One of the constants is the usefulness of expressing yourself in writing. Writing comes in handy for winning sweethearts as well as sweet deals.

Writer's Block

Don't make the mistake of assuming that writing can solve all your personal and public problems. It can't. Sometimes the best response is none—especially none in writing. There are instances when the last thing you want to do is state something in writing, because it can come back to haunt you.

➤ **Create good will.** A very wise woman I know once said, "Don't start no mess, won't be no mess." Bad writing can make a big mess by causing hard feelings. Sticks and stones can break bones, but words can be equally powerful weapons—if not more so. Insulting expressions, misused words, and biased terms can shatter a relationship. Writing well, in contrast, can cement a personal friendship, family tie, business association, or civic alliance.

➤ **Protect your reputation.** Two kids were trying to figure out what game to play. One said, "Let's play doctor."

"Good idea," said the other. "You operate, and I'll sue."

We live in a litigious society. Unless your associates tape-record all your utterances, speech doesn't allow you to document events, players, and blunders. (And if they do get it all down on tape, you could end up doing a Watergate—not a pretty picture.) Writing, however, enables you to build a "paper trail." This trail can serve as protection in case a touchy situation escalates to a nasty one and ends up in a court of law.

If you've kept pertinent documents, you'll be less open to litigation. If a lawsuit does develop, you'll have the documentation you need to prove your side of the case.

➤ **Connect with others.** As you'll learn in Part 3, "Write for Success," people write for different purposes. For example, you can write to persuade others that your point of view deserves serious consideration. Or you might write to explain a process, trace a series of events, or express your feelings. In so doing, you're forging connections with others. Writing is a powerful means of discourse, especially for people who have been traditionally excluded from the mainstream.

➤ **Be all that you can be.** James Van Allen said, "The mere process of writing is one of the most powerful tools we have for clarifying our own thinking. I am never so clear about any matter as when I have just finished writing about it."

Writing encourages us to be organized, logical, and creative because it invites us to ask questions and to look critically at what other people say as well as what we ourselves believe.

There's a symbiotic relationship between writing and thinking. Just the act of writing can help you learn. When you arrange words in a logical order, you're developing ideas and making judgments. Further, writing helps you learn to analyze and evaluate what you experience firsthand and learn from others. Writing helps you to think with accuracy and order.

Now that you know why it's so important to write well, let's take a stroll down memory lane to see how this wonderful thing we call "writing" developed.

Write Angles

Many people fear writing because they haven't had much practice and they're afraid they'll make mistakes, especially with grammar and usage. Remember that making some mistakes is part of any learning process. You'll soon find that once you get your ideas down on paper, the grammar and mechanics will fall into place.

Take a Letter

People have been putting pen to paper (make that stone to cave wall) since the days of the real Flintstones. Pictures are the basis of the earliest known examples of writing. This "writing" was comprised of simplified pictures of objects, animals, and people, such as bison and hunters. People learned to "write" when they first understood that they could communicate by means of visible signs that were understood not only by the writer but also by others savvy to the system.

But writing as we know it is such a specialized form of human communication that it evolved relatively late in the evolutionary game. This evolution happened when these pictorial scripts gave way to writing in which the symbols came to stand for words themselves, rather than the things the words represented.

Author! Author!

Scientists estimate that Moses' tablets appeared about 3,250 years ago, which is a hop, skip, and a jump on the timeline of human development. The pre-Christian tribes had their own script, called runes, meaning "secret." The runes, a form of the Greek alphabet that the Vikings developed, seem to have been used mainly for magical charms and monuments rather than commerce.

Why did writing finally develop? It all had to do with goods and services—some of the same reasons why we need to write well today. If an ancient merchant sold a pile of wheat or a peck of pomegranates, it would be in his or her best interests to record the transaction. The first people to create a workable written language were the Sumerians of Mesopotamia, around 3000 B.C.E. Their solution was a word-and-picture combination, much like *rebus* puzzles today.

Author! Author!

A **rebus** is the representation of a word or phrase by pictures, symbols, and words. Here's a rebus for "I see the bee":

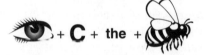

This type of "writing" has been found on clay tablets in parts of the Middle East and southeastern Europe. The pictures, such as a foot to show the concept of walking, were drawn on soft clay. The tablets were then baked in the sun to harden them. And what did people write about in this fashion? Tax accounts, land sales, and other business deals. After all, nothing is permanent but death and taxes.

Egyptian hieroglyphic writing developed about 100 years later. Similar writing systems developed in the Aegean area, Anatolia, the Indus Valley, and China. But writing as we know it didn't develop until the alphabet was created. And it was a good thing, too, because picture writing has its downsides, as the following story illustrates.

It's as Easy as A, B, C

According to the traditional story, Darius the Great, King of Persia, received a hieroglyphic message from his enemies the Scythians. The Scythians' message included a mouse, a frog, a bird, and an arrow. Darius interpreted this to mean the Scythians would surrender in the morning: The arrow meant they would give up their weapons, the mouse meant they would surrender their land, the frog meant they would surrender their water, and the bird meant they would soon fly away from the battlefield. Convinced he had read the message correctly, Darius headed for bed.

During the night, the Scythians sacked the camp. As they loaded the prisoners, the Scythians explained how they coded the message: The bird meant the Persians would never escape unless they could fly, the mice and frog meant that the only way they could escape was to burrow under the ground or hide in the swamps, and the arrows meant they would never escape the Scythians' sharp weapons.

Okay, I'll admit that this is an extreme example, but it does show that clear writing is essential. Picture writing just doesn't cut it, especially when lives are at stake.

Sometime around the eighth or ninth century B.C.E., the Greeks borrowed the Phoenician writing system and used it as the basis of the *alphabet* we use today. When the Greeks adopted this writing system, some symbols didn't correspond to any sound used in spoken Greek. The Greeks, a clever bunch, used the leftover symbols for the vowel sounds they needed for Greek. The rest of the letters were kept as consonants. The Greeks also standardized the direction of the lines to read from left to right. Voilà! A real alphabet was born, circa 800 B.C.E.

Write Angles

Arabic and Hebrew are still read from right to left; traditional written Chinese arranges the words in vertical columns rather than horizontal lines. The columns are read from top to bottom and right to left.

Word Watch

The word **alphabet** comes from the Hebrew names for the first two letters of the Semitic writing system: *aleph*, meaning "ox," and *beth*, meaning "house."

Phonemes are the sounds of a language.

The Romans knew a good thing when they saw it, and decided to use this writing system as well. By 700 C.E., the Roman alphabet was being used in Old English. The Greek alphabet also gave rise to the Cyrillic alphabet, devised by two Greek missionaries, St. Cyril and St. Methodius, in the ninth century C.E. This alphabet is still used in Eastern Europe and Russia. The North Semitic alphabet also gave rise to the Aramaic alphabet, which spread eastward to develop into the Asian alphabets, such as Hindi.

The creation of the alphabet revolutionized writing. Why was the alphabet such a great thing for writing?

➤ The alphabet can represent all the significant sounds, or *phonemes,* of a language with only a few characters.

➤ The alphabet was much easier to learn.

➤ The alphabet was much simpler to use than picture systems.

➤ The alphabet helped standardize written communication.

➤ The alphabet helped prevent tragic miscommunication.

People feel strongly about their alphabets. Any attempt to change the alphabet or our writing system in general has always met with great outcry; even today, attempts to reform spelling or eliminate inconsistencies in writing conventions meets strong resistance.

Break the Code

How good are your code-breaking skills? Although the same letter can look very different in different alphabets, every form can be traced back to a common ancestor. Here are the different ways the same letter is formed in different alphabets. See whether you can figure out what letter is being shown.

Write this way?

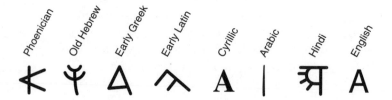

All writing is a kind of code, a system agreed upon by the writer and reader. The writer sends a message in a series of agreed-upon symbols. The reader interprets the symbols to decode the message. The process looks like this:

    writer — text — reader

Language, whether spoken or written, is a system of social interaction. Most people learn to speak from their mothers, fathers, siblings, and other relatives as a way of communicating with them. We often learn the basics of reading at home as well but acquire the foundation of writing in school.

However, the way we speak may be different because we grew up in a different part of the country, or we may be from another country and grew up speaking a different language. Further, we may have picked up words from television or radio, as well as from books.

Regardless of the way you acquired English, everyone who speaks and writes the same language learns to recognize certain patterns: what specific words mean when they're used a certain way, how words should be arranged to make a sentence meaningful, how sentences are linked to create paragraphs, and so on. This pattern of language makes communication possible and meaningful.

The connection between words and their meaning is always a symbolic one. And because symbols are always open to interpretation, words signify different meanings to different people. Your task as a writer is to find the words that convey your exact shade of meaning to best transmit your message.

As you write, consider all elements of communication: writer, reader, text, and the world around you.

Write Angles

There may be times when you deliberately wish to be ambiguous in writing. In those instances, you will select words that mask your meaning or leave it open to many different interpretations. More on this topic is covered in Chapter 4, "Words, Words, Words."

Author! Author!

Graphite, the material used in today's pencils, was used by the Aztecs for marking purposes centuries before Cortés landed in Mexico in 1519. It wasn't used in pencils until 1564, with the discovery of a commercial graphite mine in Cumberland, England. The mine was worked for over 250 years and contained the purest form of graphite ever found. The process used to make pencils today is essentially the same as the process developed by Nicholas-Jacques Conté in 1795.

The Least You Need to Know

➤ Writing has significant advantages over speech. Writing helps you to communicate with others efficiently, advance in your career, and earn a good salary.

➤ Writing is a political instrument, too, and can help you express your feelings, create good-will, protect your reputation, connect with others, and maximize your potential.

➤ The ancient Greeks adapted the Phoenician writing system as the basis of the alphabet we use today. The alphabet revolutionized writing.

➤ Writing is a kind of code, a system agreed upon by the writer and reader. The writer sends a message in a series of agreed-upon symbols. The reader interprets the signals to decode the message.

Chapter 2

The Write Way

In This Chapter

➤ Writing myths and realities

➤ The "write" attitude

➤ The advantage of writing models

➤ Reading and writing

➤ The four modes of discourse: exposition, narration, persuasion, and description

---

Imagine saying, "I think I'll spend a few hours writing, just for the fun of it." It's not something most people would say. Many people don't write unless they have to.

When was the last time you looked forward to writing?

If you're not wild about writing, don't worry—you have plenty of company. Why? It's natural to shy away from something we perceive as hard or tedious. Writing can also be time-consuming, and who has time to spare nowadays?

However, writing doesn't have to be difficult, boring, or time-consuming. Writing can be enjoyable, exciting, and even easy. In this chapter, you'll discover ways to make writing something you might even anticipate with pleasure. (I promise!)

First, you'll explore some myths and realities about writing to see what other people think about it. Then, I'll teach you how to approach writing to maximize your chances for success. Next, I'll show you the advantages of using writing models and how being a reader can help you be a good writer.

Finally, you'll learn about the four kinds of writing: exposition, narration, argumentation, and description.

Trick or Treat

Writing, unlike many other important life skills, has become shrouded in mystery. It's not uncommon to find people who think writers have secret handshakes, mystical amulets, and odd habits. (Okay, so maybe I'll give you the odd habits, but wouldn't you eat Chunky Monkey with pastrami and mustard if you could get away with it?)

Here are just a few of these writing-related these myths:

Myth: Writing is only for transmitting information.

Reality: Writing does indeed communicate facts and ideas, but it also entertains, expresses feelings, and persuades. The different types of writing are introduced later in this chapter and covered in depth in Part 3, "Write for Success."

Myth: Writing is an inborn trait, like the ability to curl your tongue or wiggle your eyebrows independently.

Reality: Writing is an acquired skill. Like any other skill, it can be taught and learned. Learning to write well takes time and much effort, but it can be done.

Write Angles

Writing is as much process as product. As a result, people often write to discover what they want to say. The process of writing can be an act of discovery, which means that you can start out not knowing where you're going and get there just fine.

Myth: If you don't write brilliantly from the get-go, you'll never learn to write.

Reality: Research has shown that writers improve with practice. Although some people may seem to have a gift for writing, virtually anyone can learn to write confidently enough to handle the writing tasks required in school, on the job, and in daily life.

Myth: If you haven't shown that you have the "write stuff" by the time you're in your 20s, odds are good that you'll never learn to write well.

Reality: Nonsense. The beloved children's book writer Laura Ingalls Wilder didn't put pen to paper until she was middle-aged (when she wrote newspaper articles on raising chickens and growing apples). Wilder published the first of her *Little House* books when she was in her mid-60s.

Myth: You have to be very well-educated to be a good writer.

Reality: British novelist Charles Dickens, nineteenth-century American icon Mark Twain, Russian writer Maxim Gorky, and Irish writer Sean O'Casey never finished elementary school. American novelist Jack London, American humorist Will Rogers, and American writer William Saroyan never finished high school.

This isn't to say that you'd better drop out of that MBA program right now if you want to learn to write. It is to say that you can still be a fine writer if you haven't had a chance to get as much education as you might want.

Myth: I'm not a real writer.

Reality: Everyone who has ever been to school has a history as a writer; perhaps you have also written reports or letters on your job. If you write, you're a writer.

Myth: Good writers can dash off a good paper in one try.

Reality: No way. Professional writers (the people who are paid for their words) prepare draft after draft after draft of their writing. Plato is said to have rewritten the first sentence of *The Republic* 50 times; Hemingway rewrote the last page of

Writer's Block

Don't fall into the trap of thinking that writing is a neat process. It's rather messy, like baking a cake. As you add each "ingredient," you stir the whole thing around a lot to blend it altogether. If your paper looks sloppy, you're probably on the right track!

A Farewell to Arms 39 times. Sinclair Lewis took 17 years to finish *Main Street;* Katherine Anne Porter worked on *Ship of Fools* for over 20 years. Virgil took 10 years to write the *Aeneid* and believed it still needed about three years' work when he died. And you think it's taking you a long time to finish the memo on the Schmendrick deal?

Author! Author!

The great American writer Thomas Wolfe was famous not only for the quality of his prose but also for its quantity. He had a brutally hard time cutting excess words from his drafts. "Although I am able to criticize wordiness and overabundance in others," Wolfe wrote to his editor Maxwell Perkins about his novel *Look Homeward, Angel*, "I am not able practically to criticize it in myself. The business of selection and revision is simply hell for me—my efforts to cut out 50,000 words may sometimes result in my adding 75,000." The first draft of *Look Homeward, Angel* came in at over 1,000 pages. Wolfe and Perkins did a nice job editing, however; the edition I have is around 750 pages.

Write Angles

School is a good place to learn to write, but it's far from the only place. You can also learn to write on the job, at home, and through community service.

Myth: Writers work in a vacuum, in total silence, friendless and isolated. Maybe they have a cat, but it's a solitary creature, too.

Reality: Writers aren't hermits. As the famous writer Truman Capote advised: "My point to young writers is to socialize. Don't just go up to a pine cabin all alone and brood. You reach that stage soon enough anyway."

Myth: Writing is a magical process.

Reality: Rubbish. Writing is the hardest job you can do that doesn't involve heavy lifting, but there's nothing magical about it.

Myth: Writing cannot be done to order.

Reality: You can learn to write when you need to, even if you're not feeling especially inspired. That's because writing is a skill, not a mystical form of divine inspiration. You can produce the document you need when you need it, with a little bit of training and practice. (Hey, that's why you bought this book.)

Cop an Attitude

Attitude is everything, especially when it comes to writing. With that in mind, let's take a closer look at your attitude toward writing. When you have to sit down and write, are you terrified or merely nervous? Would you describe yourself as untaught or traumatized? Are you convinced that writing is somewhere between an IRS tax audit and root canal—that is, excruciatingly painful and horribly unfair?

Answer each of the following questions to analyze your attitude toward writing. And don't worry; even if your eleventh-grade English teacher did a number on your head ("What is this thing you call a paper? Come to my office and we'll burn it ..."), you can still be a fine writer.

1. What are your most memorable writing experiences (good as well as not-so-good)?

   My piece for Sunfline, Ca.

2. What specific teachers come to mind when you think about your experiences as a writer? What makes you remember those teachers? What specific details do you recall about them?

   Whoever that was I had for English + grammar in the 7th + 8th grades.

3. What was your most successful writing? What made it a hit?

   *Surfline.com   It was well organized
   and flowed beautifully.*

4. What was your most disastrous writing? Which writing gave you the most trouble? Why?

   Can't remember one.

5. What aspects of writing do you enjoy the most? What aspects of writing do you enjoy the least (for example: getting started, doing research, editing)?

   *I like all aspects especially looking at the
   finished product.*

6. What types of writing do you like to write the most (for example: short stories, e-mail, poetry)?

   *Email, Web Web site content. I would
   like to do short stories.*

7. What types of writing do you like to write the least (for example: letters, memos, reports)?

   None come to mind.

8. What aspect of writing do you most want to improve (for example: spelling, grammar, usage, sentence structure, word choice, organization, logic)?

   All of the above

Study your answers and see what they reveal about your attitude toward writing. If you're terrified or traumatized, sit back and relax. Improving your writing won't hurt at all. (If you're eager and enthusiastic, you have half the battle won already.)

Author! Author!

Set your mind to it, and you can write from anywhere—even from prison. John Bunyan, Miguel de Cervantes, Daniel Defoe, and O. Henry all wrote masterpieces from behind bars. O. Henry (William Sydney Porter), for example, wrote a number of his short stories while serving three years and three months of a five-year sentence for bank embezzlement. Other literary prisoners include Eldridge Cleaver, Oscar Wilde, and Jawaharlal Nehru.

Model Behavior

Explaining how he learned to write, the famous nineteenth-century novelist and short-story writer Robert Louis Stevenson said …

> "I have played the sedulous ape to Hazlitt, to Lamb, to Wordsworth, to Sir Thomas Browne, to Defoe, to Hawthorne, to Montaigne, to Baudelaire, and to Obermann …. That, like it or not, is the way to learn to write."

Write Angles

Experts estimate that an astonishing 80 to 90 percent of the information we need comes from what we read. One sure way to become a better writer is to read more. Any type of reading will do: fiction, nonfiction, or drama. Try to read at least one hour a night.

Sedulous, from the Latin word *sedulus*, meaning "to be careful," means diligent attention to detail, so the phrase "sedulous ape" describes someone who slavishly imitates somebody else. Stevenson claimed that he learned how to write by studying the best writing available.

Think back, way back. How did you learn to ride a bike, throw a ball, and cook a meal? How did you learn to talk? To swim? To get that hole in one? You copied someone else, and then you practiced, practiced, and practiced some more. The same process works just as brilliantly when it comes to learning how to write well.

By studying the world's finest writers and then trying your hand at copying their style, you'll learn how to develop your own style. Here's what else this method can teach you:

➤ Which words work—and which ones don't

➤ How to make your sentences graceful

➤ The basic rules of grammar

➤ Where those itty-bitty punctuation marks go

➤ Spelling rules

➤ Various ways to organize your paragraphs

➤ Ways to achieve the correct tone

➤ How to arrange your material logically

➤ Methods for linking ideas

➤ Ways to use figures of speech

➤ The importance of details

➤ Why rhythm matters—even in prose

Be careful about aping a specific writer's style too closely. Your aim is to use models to help you form your own style. More on this later.

Reading to Write

"I always thought that if you want to be a writer, you've got literature; literature is all you need."

—Larry McMurtry, novelist

Each kind of writing has its own conventions and its distinctive features and content. Biographies, for example, tell a story, usually in chronological order. Business letters, in contrast, often present information in order of importance, from most to least important.

To learn the conventions of a specific genre, you need to read examples of that genre. At the same time, you should also practice writing in that genre.

➤ Want to write boffo business letters? Read a lot of them. Use the good ones as models of what you should do and the bad ones as models of what you should not do. In Chapter 24, "The Professional Edge: Writing on the Job," I've provided some good ones to make your job easier.

➤ Interested in penning a poem? Read as many poems as you can. See which ones appeal to you and which ones don't. This process will help you decide whether you wish to express your thoughts and feelings in conventional form or in *free verse,* for example.

➤ Need to create a term paper? Study models of successful papers. You'll find several in Appendix A, "Sample Term Papers."

➤ Have an urge to set the story of your life down in words? Read as many autobiographies as you can find. Study their form as well as content.

You get the idea: Good writers are avid readers. "Read, read, read …. Just like a carpenter who works as an apprentice and studies the master. Read!" said Nobel laureate William Faulkner.

Word Watch

Free verse is poetry without a regular rhythm and rhyme. Free verse closely attempts to mirror the cadence of everyday speech. Chapter 15, "Picture This: Description," has more information on this topic.

Write Angles

Do you SQR3 (Survey, Question, Read, Recite, Review)? First survey the passage by skimming the title, headings, illustrations, first paragraph, and last paragraph. Ask questions about the material and make predictions. Turn the title and headings into questions and look for answers. Then read the selection. Recite by summarizing what you've read; review by thinking back to your predictions and questions.

Color My World

"Reading is to the mind what exercise is to the body."

—Richard Steele, essayist

Reading is essential to writing. As you read examples of different kinds of writing, you begin to recognize the predictable patterns as well as possibilities for innovation. This is education, not imitation. Working with a specific genre or type of writing doesn't mean that your writing will be a word version of "connect-the-dots" or "paint-by-numbers." Each type of writing follows a broad set of reader expectations, but working within the framework will actually allow you to be more creative rather than less so. That's because once you know where the lines are, you'll be free to color inside them or outside them, depending on your audience, purpose, and tone. These considerations are covered in Chapter 3, "Pack the Essentials."

Four Play

I know what you're thinking: "Okay, Doc, you've convinced me that if I discard common writing myths, get the 'write' attitude, and read widely, I can learn to write well. But haven't you forgotten something? What about all the different kinds of writing that I have to do? How can I possibly learn all of them?"

Good point, Gentle Reader.

How many different kinds of writing or modes of discourse are there? Circle the best answer:

75–100

50–75

50

4

The answer is 4. That's all! They are exposition, narration, argumentation, and description. Let's look at them now.

Writing That Explains: Exposition

Exposition is writing that explains. The word *exposition* comes from the Latin word *exponere,* which means "to place out." When you write exposition, you try to place out or set forth specific information.

Exposition shows and tells by giving information about a specific topic. The topic can be anything: computers and the Internet, medicine, economics, social studies, history, math, science, or music. Different examples of expository writing that you may already be composing include:

➤ "How to" essays, such as recipes and other instructions
➤ Business letters
➤ Personal letters
➤ News stories
➤ Press releases
➤ Reports
➤ Scientific reports
➤ Term papers
➤ Textbooks
➤ Wills

Most of the writing you do in school and in life will be expository.

Word Watch

The four types of writing—**exposition, narration, argumentation,** and **description**—are often called the **four modes of discourse.**

Write Angles

You can remember that exposition is writing that explains by using this memory trick: Exposition equals explain. Both words starts with the same three letters, "exp."

23

Writing That Tells a Story: Narration

Scheherazade, the legendary queen of Samarkand, told her husband, Schariar, a story each night to keep him from killing her. By ending each story before the climax and thereby keeping his interest, Scheherazade won a delay of execution for 1,000 nights. On the 1,001st night, the king relented and granted her a pardon. And you thought storytelling didn't have a practical purpose!

Author! Author!

The Arabian Nights, also called *A Thousand and One Nights*, is a collection of stories, fairy tales, and fables gathered from Arabian and Indian folklore and passed down orally. Nearly 200 stories were compiled between 988 and 1011; about 250 tales appear in standard collections today. Well-known stories include "Aladdin," "Sinbad the Sailor," and "Ali Baba and the Forty Thieves."

Narration is storytelling—writing that contains plot, characters, setting, and point of view. Here are some different forms that narration can take:

➤ Anecdotes
➤ Autobiography
➤ Biography
➤ Novels
➤ Oral histories
➤ Short stories

Writing That Persuades: Argumentation

Persuasion is writing that appeals to reason, emotion, or ethics (the sense of right and wrong). Writing that appeals specifically to reason is often called *argumentation*. When you argue a point in writing, you analyze a subject, topic, or issue in order to persuade your readers to think or act a certain way. The Declaration of Independence is a persuasive essay; so is the letter to the editor you read this morning in the daily newspaper. Here are some other forms that persuasion can take:

➤ Critical review

➤ Editorials

➤ Job evaluation

➤ Job application letter

➤ Letter of recommendation

➤ Letters to the editor

➤ Resumé

You're probably already writing a great many persuasive essays, because they are common both on the job (recommendations, evaluations, resumés) and in daily life (letters to the editor).

Writing That Describes: Description

Hells Canyon

Hells Canyon is one of America's most dramatically beautiful places, a 130,000-acre scenic area extending for 22 miles along the Snake River. The Snake River writhes its way north, majestically separating the states of Oregon and Idaho. For some distance, this river flows through the deepest gorge on the North American continent, Hells Canyon. To the east, the Seven Devils Range in Idaho, volcanic in origin, towers 8,000 feet above the river. The western side of the canyon formed by the flat-topped ridge between the Imnaha and Snake Rivers rises a stunning 5,500 feet. Jutting out into the canyon are circular rock benches that give a spectacular observation point. From the crest of the ridges, a person can look for miles into Oregon, Washington, Idaho, and Montana, across a soft grassy plateau country and tumbling masses of mountains. On a clear day, a person can see into nine national forests. Higher up, the grass gives way to magnificent clear lakes and roaring waterfalls.

How does this writer help you visualize Hells Canyon? The writer uses *description*, which is details drawn from the five senses: sight, taste, touch, sound, and smell. The second sentence—"The Snake River writhes its way north, majestically separating the states of Oregon and Idaho"—appeals to sight. The phrase "a soft grassy plateau" appeals to touch; the phrase "roaring waterfalls" sparks the sense of hearing. See how many more descriptive details you can find in this passage.

Write Angles

You want to write well, so let's tilt the scales in your favor. First, recognize that you can succeed. Many people who weren't very good at writing have learned more than enough to get where they want to be. Second, realize that you're not going to become an outstanding writer instantly. It will take you some time to master the information you need.

Description often forms the basis for these two types of writing:

1. Journals
2. Poems

However, description is the only mode of discourse that's found in every other mode: you can't write narration or persuasion and exposition for that matter, without a description. Nonetheless, you'll often find elements of narration in exposition and persuasion, as when you open an explanation with a brief story. As a result, you'll often see that you incorporate more than one type of writing in your work.

The Least You Need to Know

➤ Writing is a skill that can be acquired, not an inborn trait. When it comes to writing, practice makes perfect.

➤ Analyze your attitude toward writing. If you're terrified or traumatized, sit back and relax.

➤ By studying the world's finest writers and then trying your hand at copying their style, you'll learn how to develop your own style—so read, read, and read some more.

➤ There are only four types of writing: exposition, narration, argumentation, and description. All the writing you'll ever do falls into one or more of these categories (since they often overlap).

Chapter 3

Pack the Essentials

In This Chapter

➤ The importance of logic

➤ Purpose in writing

➤ Audience analysis

➤ Tone in writing

➤ How to develop your own writing style

Question: What do you call a boomerang that doesn't work?

Answer: A stick.

Question: What do you call writing that doesn't work?

Answer: Boring, confusing, and annoying.

You know what makes a great boomerang, a great vacation, and a great date. No matter what the specific object or person, the essentials are the same. The same is true when it comes to writing. All four types of writing—exposition, narration, description, and argumentation—are distinguished by the same benchmarks. Therefore, no matter what you write, it must share these same qualities: logic, organization, unity, purpose, audience, tone, details, and style.

In this chapter, you'll learn what makes a great piece of writing, so you can make your writing great!

The People's Court

I set before you, ladies and gentlemen, two pieces of writing. They walk alike, they talk alike, but they're not at all alike. Why not? Because one is much better than the other one. Decide which one you like better and why.

Exhibit A:

> In conclusion, too official reference books on medicine oficialy recognized the medical value of allot of Native American drugs and plants. That's why every-one should use herbs today. Only really stupid people ignore herbs; I mean you gotta be a jerk to not take this stuff. Like the Indians theirselves, some white guys owed their life to a medicine mans neat stuff in many Native American tribes, the medicine man acted like an ceremonial preist, in other tribes, how-ever, the medicine mans' job was to help any one of his people whom got real sick. As a doctor, the medicine man carried a bag of real cool things to help you. I read in this book that a prince were cured of some real bad stuff buy the Indians.

Exhibit B:

> In many Native American tribes, the shaman, or medicine man, acted as a cere-monial priest. In other tribes, however, the medicine man's job was to treat any one of his people who became ill. In his role as a healer, the medicine man car-ried a bag of secret herbs and charms to rid the patient of his sickness. Among the tools of his trade were dried fingers, deer tails, drums, rattles, and tiny sacks of herbs. Different tribes used different herbs, depending on what was available in the area and through trading. The Dakotas, for example, relieved asthma with the powdered root of skunk cabbage; the Kiowas controlled dandruff with a shampoo made from the soaproot plant. The Cheyenne drank boiled mint to settle upset stomachs, and the Cree chewed the tiny cones of spruce trees to soothe a sore throat. Like the Native Americans themselves, some white fron-tiersmen owed their life to a medicine man's cure. In 1834, for example, Prince Maximilian was cured of scurvy by the Native American remedy, eating raw bulbs of garlic. Ultimately, two official reference books on medicine, the *U.S. Pharmacopoeia* and the *National Formulary,* officially recognized the medicinal value of 170 Native American drugs, including mint, yarrow, Indian turnip, and skunk cabbage.

Did you find yourself scratching your head as you read the first passage? Perhaps you had trouble following the ideas. Maybe you didn't know for whom the passage was written. Perhaps you were confused as the writer veered from informal language to formal language and back again.

The second passage is light-years better than the first one because it has a clear sense of purpose, logic, audience, and tone. The ideas are also more fully developed with details and facts. The words are spelled correctly, the sentences are complete, and the punctuation helps link related ideas. Let's look at each specific element of effective writing.

How's That Again? Logic

As you learned in Chapter 1, "Why Writing Matters," all writing is a kind of code, a system agreed upon by the writer and reader. The writer sends a message in a series of agreed-upon symbols. The reader then interprets the symbols (the letters and words) to decode the message. When the symbols aren't used correctly, the code cannot be read. The reader becomes confused and frustrated at the writer's lack of logic.

All writing must be logical, with examples that follow sensibly from one to another. Logical reasoning is sound reasoning. You can tell that an essay, letter, memo, or other writing is logical if it …

➤ Uses evidence to back up assertions.

➤ Distinguishes between facts and opinions.

➤ Analyzes cause and effect correctly.

➤ Makes sense.

Doctors take as their prime directive the oath, "First, do no harm." As a writer, take this as your prime directive: "First, make sense." Logical writing is characterized by a clear pattern of organization and unity. Let's turn to those two qualities now.

Write Angles

First and foremost, all writing must communicate its ideas clearly. If the selection doesn't get its point across, it's not good writing.

Writer's Block

Avoid logical fallacies, statements that sound reasonable but really aren't. In Exhibit A, the statement, "That's why everyone should use herbs today," is an example of a specific logical fallacy called an overgeneralization, a statement that can't be true because it's too broad. Logical fallacies are covered in detail in Chapter 14, "Why Not See It My Way?: Persuasion and Argumentation."

Organization

Organizing your writing involves coming up with a plan for arranging the information logically. As you'll learn in Chapter 9, "A Place for Everything, and Everything in

Word Watch

Unity results when every sentence in a paragraph is related to each other and the main idea.

Its Place," there are many different organizational plans you can choose from, depending on your purpose and audience. Here are some of the main ones:

➤ Order of time or chronological order

➤ Order of space (up to down, down to up, inside out, and so on)

➤ Order of importance (most to least important, least to most important)

➤ Order of impression (the order in which the details catch the writer's attention)

➤ Questions and answers

Unity and Coherence

People work together on teams, in classes, and in committees to get things done. When people cooperate with each other, they can achieve their goal more easily. In the same way, when all the sentences in a paragraph are on the same topic, the paragraph achieves its purpose. A paragraph has *unity* if all of its sentences support the same main idea. Unity is lost if the paragraph goes off the topic by including sentences that do not relate to the main idea.

The writer of the following paragraph achieved unity by linking every detail in the paragraph to the topic sentence, the first sentence in the passage:

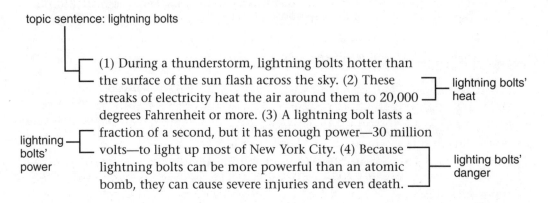

topic sentence: lightning bolts

(1) During a thunderstorm, lightning bolts hotter than the surface of the sun flash across the sky. (2) These streaks of electricity heat the air around them to 20,000 degrees Fahrenheit or more. (3) A lightning bolt lasts a fraction of a second, but it has enough power—30 million volts—to light up most of New York City. (4) Because lightning bolts can be more powerful than an atomic bomb, they can cause severe injuries and even death.

lightning bolts' heat

lightning bolts' power

lighting bolts' danger

The writer states the topic, lightning bolts, in the first sentence. Then, the writer gives three details to support the topic: the lightning bolts' heat, power, and danger.

Take Aim: Purpose

Imagine that you're going to write two very different pieces on the same topic: softball teams. The first piece is a memo to recruit employees for the office softball team. The other piece is an article for the local newspaper on the standings of the high school softball teams. How would the two pieces differ?

The memo would have an upbeat, positive tone to convince people that playing softball on the company team would be jolly fun. You'd use your facts and details to convince your readers that joining the team would help improve their health and be great for company morale and camaraderie.

Write Angles

A specific piece of writing can have more than one purpose, and often does. A fable, for example, amuses its readers as it teaches a lesson.

The newspaper article, in contrast, would have a direct, informative tone and be filled with statistics about hits, runs, and errors.

Your purpose for writing is your reason for writing. The four main purposes for writing are the same as the four types of writing you learned about in Chapter 2, "The Write Way": to persuade, to entertain, to explain, and to describe. The primary purpose of Exhibit B, the writing sample that opened this chapter, is to explain. It also entertains by using vivid details and examples.

Sometimes your purpose is defined by the task: A resumé, for example, always tries to persuade. A short story, however, would be designed to entertain. Keeping your purpose firmly in mind as you write helps you achieve your desired aim.

Crowd Control: Audience

People who need people are the luckiest people in the world. Repeat this as you write, and you'll be more likely to remember that no matter what you write, you always have a specific audience in mind. Your audience are the people who are reading your writing.

Look back to the beginning of this chapter. Exhibit A falls flat on its face in part because the writer didn't aim at a specific audience. Phrases such as "white guys," "neat stuff," and "real cool things" suggest an MTV audience. But "official reference books" and "ceremonial priest" suggest an older and more sophisticated readership. Exhibit B, on the other hand, is clearly aimed at educated readership. It has complex sentence structure and elevated diction and assumes a certain level of knowledge.

Sometimes you will have a clearly identified audience: your boss, your coworkers, the members of a service organization. I know that this book, *The Complete Idiot's Guide to*

Writing Well, is aimed at a general reading public. (That's you, Pinky!) You're part of an educated elite who frequently reads newspapers, books, and magazines. You attend

movies and concerts, too, and are culturally knowledgeable. You have some general information about the subject of writing, but you enjoy having a chance to learn something new or to see the topic from a different perspective.

Other times, however, your audience won't be as easy to identify. You may be sending a resumé and cover letter for a job identified only by the most general description and a post office box, for example. In these situations, it's even more crucial to get a handle on who will be reading your words.

Writer's Block

Don't assume that if you're writing for yourself you don't have an audience. You do—it's you.

Getting to Know You, Getting to Know All About You

To help you pinpoint your audience, ask yourself the following questions every time you prepare to write a document.

Audience Analysis

1. Who will be reading my work?

   _____

   _____

2. What is their age? Is their age likely to have a big effect on the way they approach my work? Why or why not?

   _____

   _____

3. What is their gender? Is this an important factor in my choice of organization and purpose?

   _____

   _____

4. Where do they live? Are they rural, suburban, or urban people?

   _____

   _____

---

5. What is their socio-economic status? How will this influence their approach to my writing?

   _____

   _____

6. Why are they reading my writing? To learn? To be entertained? To be persuaded?

   _____

   _____

7. How much do they already know about this topic?

   _____

   _____

8. How do they feel about my topic? Are they likely to be receptive, hostile, or somewhere in between?

   _____

   _____

Your writing is likely to have a primary and a secondary audience. The primary audience is the group of people to whom you are deliberately aiming and addressing your writing. The secondary audience is the rest of the people who are likely to read your writing as well.

Doing the Legwork

To streamline the analysis of the audience, you can make a quick chart like the one on the following page for each piece of writing you do. I've filled it out for someone writing e-mail in the office.

Question	Answer
Writing form?	E-mail
Purpose?	To inform
Audience?	Fellow managers
Organizational method?	Most-to-least important

Writing without identifying your audience is like sending e-mail without an address or buying a dress without trying it on. How do you know the writing will hit its mark? How do you know it will suit? You're nobody's fool, so I'm sure you'll always pinpoint your audience before you write a word.

Word Watch

Tone is the writer's attitude toward his or her subject and readers.

Writer's Block

When you write, it's especially important to stay cool when you're hot. Don't make the mistake of using inflammatory language, even if you're on fire. You'll accomplish your purpose far more effectively if you keep your writing cool.

Hitting the Right Note: Tone

Although you'll no doubt be called on to address many different audiences as you write, most of your work will be addressed from one adult to another. As such, you're expected to sound reasonable and moderate. The line "Only really stupid people ignore herbs; I mean you gotta be a jerk to not take this stuff" from Exhibit A would go over about as well as a poke in the eye with a sharp stick.

Your stance in writing is reflected in your *tone,* which is what you say and how you say it. Tone can be broadly described as *formal* or *informal.* Journals are informal; business letters are formal. Most audiences call for a tone somewhere between formal and informal, with some key exceptions:

➤ Always use a more formal tone when you're writing up—to supervisors or teachers, for example.

➤ Never write down by condescending to your audience. Always avoid name-calling, even if they deserve it (especially if they deserve it).

➤ Avoid overblown and artificial language. Putting on airs makes you sound phony. See Chapter 4, "Words, Words, Words," for ways to select words that help you create the tone you need.

What tone would you create with each of these words? Would it be positive or negative?

1. Sly
2. Cowardly
3. Craven
4. Stupid
5. Sneaky

6. Clever
7. Prudent
8. Cautious
9. Silly
10. Vigilant

Answers

1. Negative
2. Negative
3. Negative
4. Negative
5. Negative

6. Positive
7. Positive
8. Positive
9. Positive
10. Positive

Sentence structure can also influence your tone. Short, simple sentences tend to convey a childlike tone, while longer, more complex sentences tend to create a more mature and serious tone.

Details, Details, Details

I kept six honest serving men
They taught me all I knew
Their names are What and Where and When
And How and Why and Who

—Rudyard Kipling

Like the writer Rudyard Kipling, you can make your writing effective by adding specific details that answer the questions what, where, when, how, why, and who.

Word Watch

Details are small pieces of information that support the main idea by telling about people, events, things, time, objects, situations, or the way something happened. Use details to develop your ideas.

Writer's Block

All your writing must be error-free. This means no boo-boos at all. Exhibit A is riddled with mistakes in spelling, sentence structure, and word choice. To avoid this kind of tackiness, read the chapters in Part 6, "Picture Perfect."

Details fall into these six main categories:

➤ **Examples.** Writers often use models used to illustrate their point. Examples help a reader understand a general statement by giving specific information that represents one piece of the whole concept.

➤ **Facts.** These statements can be proven. For example, the statement "John F. Kennedy was the first Catholic president of the United States" is a fact because it can be verified and there are no reasonable arguments against it.

➤ **Statistics.** These numbers provide additional information.

➤ **Reasons.** These explanations tell why something happened. They may also explain the cause of someone's beliefs or actions.

➤ **Definitions.** These statements explain what something means.

➤ **Descriptions.** Words or phrases that tell how something looks, smells, tastes, sounds, or feels. Descriptions use sensory words to help readers visualize what they're reading.

Here are some examples of each type of detail:

Types of Details	Examples
Examples	Florida boasts many famous natives and residents, including the singer Gloria Estefan and the author Marjorie Kinnan Rawlings.
Facts	The capital of Florida is Tallahassee.
Statistics	Florida has 105 state parks with a total of 215,820 acres.
Reasons	Many people visit Florida to enjoy its great tourist attractions and warm weather.
Definitions	The name Florida comes from a Spanish word that means "feast of flowers."
Descriptions	The majestic palm trees swayed gently in the brilliant Florida sunshine.

Look back at Exhibit B. Which details did you find especially effective? Why?

Author! Author!

Ambrose Bierce, his pen dipped in wormwood and acid, had perhaps the most sardonic wit in the history of American letters. From his vitriolic pen came *The Devil's Dictionary* (1906), famous for its ironic definitions. Here are a few of the most famous ones:

alone	in bad company
love	a temporary insanity cured by marriage
marriage	a master, a mistress and two slaves, making in all, two
positive	mistaken at the top of one's voice
saint	a dead sinner, revised and edited

Simply Irresistible: Style

In 1946, Winston Churchill traveled to Fulton, Missouri, to deliver a speech and to be present at the dedication of a bust in his honor. After his speech, a rather attractive and well-endowed woman approached the wartime Prime Minister of England and said, "Mr. Churchill, I traveled over a hundred miles this morning for the unveiling of your bust." Churchill, who was known far and wide for his quick wit, replied, "Madam, I assure you, in that regard I would gladly return the favor."

Word Watch

Style is a writer's unique way of combining words to express ideas.

Churchill had style. So did Ernest Hemingway and Aldous Huxley. Even Dr. Seuss had style. And now you can, too.

A writer's *style* is his or her distinctive way of writing. All good writing has style. The specific style you select depends on these two main considerations:

1. Audience
2. Purpose

Writer's Block

Style is not something slapped on like a layer of pancake makeup or a dash of cologne. It is deeply embedded in the writing and so defines the piece as something worth reading.

Style is made up of elements such as word choice, sentence length and structure, punctuation, figures of speech, and tone. Writers often change their style for different kinds of writing and to suit different audiences. A business style is formal, authoritative, and knowledgeable; an informal style is often light, relaxed, and humorous.

As you learn more about writing, you'll discover ways to create your own writing style by experimenting with different words, sentences, and punctuation. Sharpen that sense now by looking back at Exhibit B: What makes its style pleasant to read?

The Least You Need to Know

➤ All writing must communicate ideas clearly. This is achieved through logic, a clear organizational plan, and unity.

➤ To create logic, organization, and unity, you must have a clear purpose or reason for writing in mind.

➤ Always identify and consider your audience, the people reading your writing.

➤ Select the most appropriate tone for your audience and purpose.

➤ Use details that develop your ideas fully.

➤ The specific style you select depends on your audience and purpose.

Chapter 4

Words, Words, Words

<table>
<tr><td colspan="2">

In This Chapter

➤ So many words; so little time!

➤ Beautiful words—in the eye of the beholder!

➤ Different types of words, including doublespeak, jargon, and buzzwords

➤ P.C. speech

➤ Formal and informal English

</td></tr>
</table>

Ever hear the old proverb "One picture is worth a thousand words"? Don't believe it; pictures aren't always as useful as we think. If you don't believe me, fall in a lake and pretend to drown. Instead of screaming "Help!" hold up a picture of yourself drowning. If someone pulls you out, you win.

Words are what counts when it comes to carefully written communication. In this chapter, you'll explore how to find the words you need to say exactly what you want as you write.

There's a Word for It

A student having trouble finding the right word once complained to me, "There are simply too many words in English!" Exactly how many words does English actually have? That's not such an easy question to answer.

Word Watch

The **Oxford English Diction-ary** is often called the **"OED"** for short (that's pronounced *oh-ee-dee*).

Living languages, like English, are always changing, so the word count shifts from day to day. The *Oxford English Dictionary,* the gold standard of dictionaries, contains over 400,000 words. That fills 22,000 pages, is bound in 20 volumes, and takes up 20 feet of shelf space. No lightweight, the *OED* weighs in at 150 pounds.

But linguistic scholars think that even this stupendous number represents barely half the total number of English words. The *OED* editors agree. For their 1999 online version, there are 10,000 new or revised entries.

The reason for this growth is that there are hundreds of dialects in English, each with many words that don't appear in a dictionary. Further, new words are constantly being created, especially in science, technology, and literature.

Author! Author!

Shakespeare had a large vocabulary, using 22,000 different words in his plays, compared to 6,000 different words used in the entire Old Testament. If you read the plays, expect to encounter these beauties: anon (until later), aroint (away), aye/yea (yes), bum (buttocks), enow (enough), and nay (no). Few people insult with Shakespeare's skill. Here's a tasty tidbit to throw at an enemy: "I do desire that we may be better strangers" (*As You Like It*).

As you'll learn in Chapter 27, "Spelling Ace," new words are coined every day. Some make the cut, but others get the ax. According to the *Merriam-Webster's Collegiate Dictionary, Tenth Edition,* the following words achieved enough currency in English to make the 1998 copyrighted revision of the dictionary. How many of these new words have you used—or even heard?

➤ **Bottom-feeder.** An opportunist who seeks quick profit, usually at the expense of others or from their misfortune.

➤ **Comfort food.** Food prepared in a traditional style having a nostalgic or sentimental appeal.

➤ **Ecoterrorism.** Sabotage intended to hinder activities that are considered damaging to the environment.

➤ **Edge city.** A suburb that has developed its own political, economic, and commercial base independent of the central city.

➤ **Trash talk.** Disparaging, taunting, or boastful comments, especially between opponents trying to intimidate each other.

But never fear—even highly educated people are likely to know fewer than 10 percent of the words that English boasts, and they are likely to use less than 10 percent of that number regularly in speech and writing—usually fewer than 10,000 words in all. According to several sources, 70 words make up 50 percent of our written language.

What does this mean for you? It suggests that you'll have no difficulty mastering the words you need to express yourself clearly and eloquently in writing. You'll be able to find the word you want and need.

Write Angles

To help you find the words you need, you can turn to specialized dictionaries as well as the garden-variety ones. Some of these specialized books include *Roget's Thesaurus of the English Language, Dictionary of Slang and Unconventional English, Dictionary of Word and Phrase Origins, Modern American Usage,* and the *Dictionary of American Regional English.*

Royal Words

According to *The Book of Lists,* edited by David Wallechinksy, Irving Wallace, and Amy Wallace, the 10 most beautiful words in the English language are …

Word	Meaning
10. tranquil	serene
9. murmuring	a soft, gentle sound
8. mist	water in the form of particles floating in the air
7. melody	a sweet arrangement of sounds
6. luminous	shining
5. lullaby	song sung to children to lull them to sleep
4. hush	quiet, calm
3. golden	containing gold, relating to gold
2. dawn	to begin to grow light as the sun rises
1. chimes	a set of bells or slabs of metal, stone, or wood that produce musical tones when struck

Carl Sandburg, the poet, disagreed. His choice for the most beautiful word in English was "Monongahela"; James Joyce weighed in with "cuspidor." The French writer Baudelaire chose "hemorrhoids." Go figure.

According to a poll taken by the National Association of Teachers of Speech, the 10 worst-sounding words in English are …

	Word	Meaning
1.	cacophony	disharmony
2.	crunch	bite, chomp
3.	flatulent	pretentious
4.	gripe	complain
5.	jazz	type of music
6.	phlegmatic	stoic, impassive
7.	plump	chubby
8.	plutocrat	member of the ruling class
9.	sap	tree juice
10.	treachery	treason

These words may be ugly, but they're also useful. If one of these babies is the word you need to convey your exact meaning, feel free to use it.

The fact that people stay up nights debating these issues shows the hold that words have on us. Words are the building blocks of effective written communication. The words you select can make—or break—your writing.

Author! Author!

Ghost words are words that never existed until someone mistook an error for a word. For example, *dord* (meaning density) began life as an error made in transcribing a card that read: "D or d, meaning a capital D or a small d—for 'density.'" The word appeared in the 1934 edition of the *Merriam-Webster Dictionary*, but it was eliminated from future editions.

And the Commoners

Following are the 20 most commonly used words. See if you can pick out the 12 we use most often.

a	and	are	around
before	computer	for	of
I	is	in	it
near	out	she	that
the	to	we	you

The envelope, please.

In order of use, the words most commonly used in English are ...

1. the	7. is
2. I	8. you
3. and	9. that
4. a	10. it
5. to	11. of
6. in	12. for

See, it's not so bad. English may have more words than you can shake a stick at, but you don't have to sift through quite as many as you think. Now, how can you pick the ones you need?

Words to Live By

Chefs use the freshest fruits, vegetables, and meats to make the best dishes. Artists use the finest colors and brushes to make beautiful pictures. What do writers use to communicate their ideas? Words! You've just learned how many words we have in English and how strongly people feel about words. So which words should you use? Your *diction* depends on these three considerations:

1. Purpose
2. Audience
3. Style

Word Watch

Diction is a writer's choice of words. Your diction affects the clarity and impact of your message.

In general, always use words that are precise, appropriate, and familiar. Here's why:

Precise words say what you mean.

Appropriate words convey your tone and fit with the other words in the document.

Familiar words are easy to read and understand. Using this type of words helps you communicate your message.

Your first consideration is the amount of detail the word offers, which depends on whether the word is concrete or abstract.

Concrete and Abstract Words

Words can be concrete or abstract. Abstract words refer to things that you can't perceive with your senses. Examples of abstract words include love, democracy, and sorrow. Concrete words refer to things that you can perceive with your senses, such as blue, spinach, and fire. To make your meaning clearer, use concrete words to help readers understand abstract concepts. This will make your meaning clearer.

Author! Author!

The famous writer and wordsmith Dr. Johnson silenced two readers who complimented him for the omission of "naughty words" in his great dictionary with the comment: "What! My dears! Then you have been looking for them."

Specific and General Words

What's the difference between the words in each of these pairs?

color   scarlet

place   Glassy Point, Idaho

44

some	a dozen
things	slippers
nice	gracious

The first word in each pair is general; the second word is specific.

General words, such as music, animal, and flower, relate to an overall group and describe big ideas and concepts such as music, animal, and flower. *Specific words* describe particular objects within the group, such as jazz, moose, and rose.

In almost all cases, use specific words rather than general ones to make your writing more descriptive. Specific words help communicate your meaning more clearly.

Try it now. Replace each of the following general words with one or more specific words.

Writer's Block

Avoid **substandard English,** which is words and phrases such as "irregardless," "ain't," and "theirselves" that are not considered part of standard written English. Other substandard phrases include being that (use since), had ought (use ought), this here (use this), like I told you (use as I told you), off of (use off), that there (use that), and kind of (use rather).

General Word	**Specific Word**
1. automobile	_____
2. place	_____
3. fish	_____
4. city	_____
5. move	_____
6. job	_____
7. building	_____
8. college	_____
9. article of clothing	_____
10. person	_____

Sample Answers

1. Chevrolet Caprice
2. Guam
3. carp
4. Toledo
5. amble
6. rocket scientist

7. Empire State Building
8. State University of New York College of Technology at Farmingdale
9. G-string
10. Moon Unit Zappa

The writer George Orwell once said, "Prose consists less and less of words chosen for the sake of meaning, and more and more of phrases tacked together like the sections

of a prefabricated henhouse." In general, replace vague, unclear words with specific, precise words that hit the meaning right on the head. Here are some vague words to avoid:

really	fine
nice	kind of
sort of	great

Write Angles

The sound of your words also influences the effect they create. Depending on your purpose and audience, you can use **ono-matopoeia,** words that suggest the sounds they describe, to make your writing more descriptive. Examples include woosh, buzz, and hoot.

Concrete language is not always preferable to abstract language, and specific language is not always preferable to general language, however. Effective writing matches the words to the purpose and audience. There are times when you'll want to be intentionally vague, especially on some business communication. In these instances, you will select words and craft sentences that leave the meaning nebulous to avoid placing blame—or assuming it.

More Than Meets the Eye: Denotation and Connotation

Denotation is a word's definition. When you look up a word in the dictionary to find out what it means, you are looking up its denotation. For example, the denotation of aggressive is "the action of a state in violating by force the rights of another state, particularly its territorial rights; an unprovoked offensive, attack, invasion, or the like."

All words have a denotation.

In addition, some words have a *connotation*. A word's connotation is its emotional overtones. For example, assertive and aggressive are close in denotation, but their connotations are worlds apart: *assertive* is positive, considered a desirable trait; *aggressive* has a negative connotation, conveying the impression of brutality, excessive force, or hostility.

Likewise, *slender* and *scrawny* both mean "thin," but *slender* makes you sound like a model; *scrawny* makes you sound like a plucked chicken. *Strong-minded* is positive; *stubborn* is negative.

Author! Author!

The verb "cleave" is the only English word with two synonyms that are antonyms of each other: adhere and separate.

Not all words have a connotation; some have just a denotation.

Recognizing a word's connotation helps you convey the exact shade of meaning you want. Connotation often comes into play when you think you have to use a word with the same meaning over and over to fit your topic. In these instances (as well as others), you'll want to use synonyms to prevent your reader from dozing off. Say you're using the word innocent. *Vindicated, exonerated,* and *pure* are all synonyms for *innocent*—but they don't all have the same connotation. *Vindicated* and *exonerated* suggest that the person was tried and acquitted, which means they were accused of a crime in the first place. *Innocent* and *pure* have no such connotation.

Writer's Block

A computerized thesaurus is a handy feature, but a thesaurus in book form is better. The books still contain more choices than their electronic cousins.

Complete the following chart to analyze the denotation and connotation of words. In the second column, write the word's denotation. In the third column, write a + if the word's connotation is positive, a – if the connotation is negative, or 0 if the word does not have a connotation.

Word	Denotation	Connotation
1. prestigious	_____	_____
2. notorious	_____	_____
3. economical	_____	_____
4. cheap	_____	_____
5. guru	_____	_____
6. pendant	_____	_____
7. diplomat	_____	_____
8. bureaucrat	_____	_____
9. resolute	_____	_____
10. stubborn	_____	_____
11. plump	_____	_____
12. fat	_____	_____

Answers

Each pair of words has the same denotation. All odd-numbered words have a positive connotation, however, while all even-numbered words have a negative connotation. Here's the scoop:

1. *Prestigious* means "celebrated." It's a good thing.
2. *Notorious* means "infamous." It's a bad thing.
3. *Economical* means "thrifty." Way to go.
4. *Cheap* means "parsimonious." What a Scrooge.
5. *Guru* means "teacher, a wise guide."
6. *Pedant* means "teacher, a bore."
7. *Diplomat* means "ambassador."
8. *Bureaucrat* means "official, a petty paper pusher."
9. *Resolute* means "determined."
10. *Stubborn* means "obstinate."
11. *Plump* mean "chubby."
12. *Fat* means "overweight."

How's That Again?

It's not nice to fool Mother Nature—or your readers.

Therefore, to avoid infuriating your audience, always try to use words they will know and understand. It's a great way to communicate clearly, your ultimate aim in writing. Further, Dr. Laurie suggests that you always avoid language that deceives your readers. Here are some examples:

Word Watch

Doublespeak is language designed to muddle meaning. It's also called **doubletalk.**

1. **Doublespeak.** Have you seen any "personal time control centers" advertised in the supermarket tabloids? Maybe you thought you couldn't figure out what was being sold because you were too busy loading toaster pastries onto the conveyer belt. It wasn't overwork or distraction; it was the language of the advertisement. A "personal time control center" is a watch. It's also an example of *doublespeak,* a convoluted phrase that deliberately hides meaning. Don't use doublespeak. Ever.

   Here are a few more examples of doublespeak:

Doublespeak	Meaning
personal manual databases	calendar
underground condominium	grave
unauthorized withdrawal	robbery
nonpositively terminated	fired
social expression products	greeting cards
learning facilitators	teachers

2. **Jargon.** Jargon is the specialized vocabulary of a particular group. As a result, jargon features words that an outsider unfamiliar with the field might not understand. As you write, consider your purpose and audience to decide whether a word is jargon in the context of your material. For example, if you're writing for engineers, you could use the technical words that engineers use since they would know and expect those words. The same technical words wouldn't be suited for an audience of accountants, for example.

3. **Buzzwords.** Buzzwords have been so overused that they have lost their meanings. Here are some examples:

quite	very	basically	really
central	major	field	case
situation	kind	scope	sort

type	thing	area	aspect
factor	quality	nice	central
major	good	excellent	fine

Try to avoid using buzzwords, because they hinder meaning. They're the linguistic equivalent of cotton candy because they take up space without filling you up.

Write Angles

Women comprised more than half the labor-force growth between 1985 and 1995, the most recent year for which statistics are available. Therefore, it's likely people of the female persuasion won't appreciate words that put them down by slighting their abilities and accomplishments.

Write Angles

Always use the title the person prefers, even if it's not politically correct. If a woman wishes to be addressed as "Miss" rather than "Ms.," that's her choice—not yours.

Use Nonbiased Language

Always use nonbiased language to avoid assigning qualities to people on the basis of their gender, appearance, age, race, or physical condition. Here are some guidelines to help you use fair and impartial language in all your writing.

1. Don't use *he* or *man* to refer to both men and women. An easy way to get around this issue is by using the plural form of the pronoun or the noun itself.

   Biased: Due to the extreme turbulence, she has a hard time serving the meals.

   Nonbiased: Due to the extreme turbulence, they (or flight attendants) have a hard time serving the meals.

2. Avoid expressions that exclude one sex.

   Biased: mankind

   Nonbiased: humanity, humankind, people

3. Use the correct courtesy title. Use Mr. for men and Ms. for women, but professional titles take precedence over Mr. and Ms. For example, when I'm teaching at the university, I am Dr. Rozakis rather than Ms. Rozakis.

4. Refer to a group by the term it prefers. Language changes, so be aware of the current preferred terms. Here's the latest buzz:

   ➤ "Asian" is preferred over "Oriental."

   ➤ "Inuit" is preferred over "Eskimo."

   ➤ "Latino" is the preferred designation for people with Central and Latin American backgrounds.

5. Focus on people, not their conditions.

   Biased: mentally retarded

   Nonbiased: people with mental retardation

Formal and Informal English

You wouldn't wear a long gown or a tuxedo to the beach, or shorts to a wedding in a banquet hall. (Okay, so maybe you would, but we won't go there.) You suit your clothing to the occasion. Similarly, you suit your language to your audience and purpose.

Author! Author!

Names are a special class of words. Many cultures believe that a person's name expresses his or her soul and should not be given or taken away. According to the *1999 World Almanac,* the five most common names for boys are Michael, Christopher, Matthew, Joshua, and Nicholas. For girls, it's Ashley, Sarah, Jessica, Kaitlyn, and Brittany.

English has two levels of word use: formal and informal. Formal English does not use contractions, such as can't and I'll. Formal English has more difficult words and longer sentences, too. As a result, formal English is used in academic writing such as legal papers, scholarly compositions, and college essays.

Informal English uses contractions, simpler words, and shorter sentences. Informal English is used in casual situations such as conversations with friends, newspaper stories, magazine articles, and informal letters. Informal English includes slang, the very informal language of a particular group. "What a snow job" and "He burned me again" are both examples of slang.

Write Angles

Writers often use informal dialogue in personal narratives, because it makes the dialogue sound real. Learn more about personal narratives in Chapter 13, "Tell Me a Story: Narration."

Culture Club

I present these examples for your consideration:

Exhibit A: Formal Diction

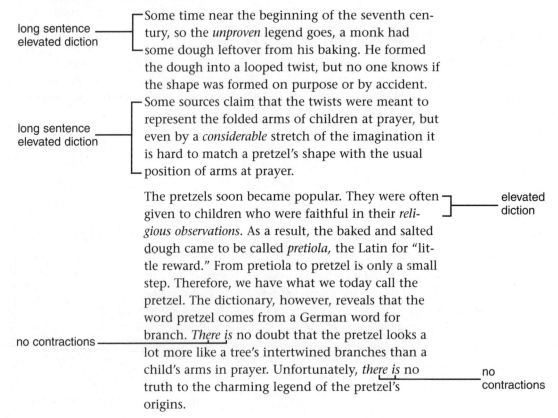

long sentence elevated diction — Some time near the beginning of the seventh century, so the *unproven* legend goes, a monk had some dough leftover from his baking. He formed the dough into a looped twist, but no one knows if the shape was formed on purpose or by accident.

long sentence elevated diction — Some sources claim that the twists were meant to represent the folded arms of children at prayer, but even by a *considerable* stretch of the imagination it is hard to match a pretzel's shape with the usual position of arms at prayer.

The pretzels soon became popular. They were often given to children who were faithful in their *religious observations*. — elevated diction

As a result, the baked and salted dough came to be called *pretiola,* the Latin for "little reward." From pretiola to pretzel is only a small step. Therefore, we have what we today call the pretzel. The dictionary, however, reveals that the word pretzel comes from a German word for branch.

no contractions — *There is* no doubt that the pretzel looks a lot more like a tree's intertwined branches than a child's arms in prayer. Unfortunately, *there is* no truth to the charming legend of the pretzel's origins. — no contractions

Author! Author!

A palindrome is a word or sentence that reads the same backward as forward. The first palindrome recorded in English is "Lewd did I live & evil I did dwel." More famous examples include "Madam, I'm Adam," "A man, a plan, a canal—Panama," and "Able was I ere I saw Elba." My personal favorite is this number: "Rise, sir lapdog! Revolt, lover! God, pal, rise, sir!"

Having the Last Word

Late one night a mugger wearing a ski mask jumped into the path of a well-dressed man and stuck a gun in his ribs. "Give me your money," he demanded.

Indignant, the affluent man replied, "You can't do this—I'm a U.S. Congressman!"

"In that case," replied the robber, "give me MY money."

See? Even the itty-bitty words count a lot.

The Least You Need to Know

➤ English has more than 400,000 words, but we tend to use only a fraction of that number—usually fewer than 10,000 words in all. Some scholars estimate that 70 words make up 50 percent of our written language.

➤ Your choice of words always depends on your purpose, audience, and style.

➤ Denotation is a word's definition; connotation is its emotional overtones.

➤ Avoid deceptive language such as doublespeak and buzzwords. Only use jargon if it suits your audience.

➤ Use nonbiased language, words that avoid assigning qualities to people on the basis of their gender, appearance, age, race, or physical condition.

➤ English has two levels of word use: formal and informal. Formal English is suitable for business letters, scholarly writing, and college essays; informal English is suitable for personal letters, short stories, and e-mail.

Clause and Effect

In the late 1800s, the man who was shot out of the cannon daily at the Barnum and Bailey Circus decided to quit because his wife had asked him to find a less risky career. P.T. Barnum hated to lose a good man, so he sent him a message, "I beg you to reconsider—men of your caliber are hard to find." Good sentence parts are just as hard to find, but you won't have to get shot out of a cannon to write some brilliant ones after you finish this chapter.

In Chapter 4, "Words, Words, Words," you learned all about word choice. Now you'll discover how to put all those words together into logical units of expression: phrases and clauses. The first half of this chapter covers the different phrases, including prepositional phrases, verbal phrases, and appositives. The second half of the chapter explores independent and dependent clauses, including adverb, adjective, and noun clauses. Recognizing these different kinds of phrases and clauses is the first step in knowing how to use these sentence parts to write clearly, gracefully, and effectively.

Going Through a Phrase: Phrases

What do all these examples have in common?

➤ Over the top

➤ With a hint of mint

➤ At the ant farm

➤ Trekking from pillar to post

➤ To lose 15 pounds

➤ Frolicking naked in the public fountain

➤ The breathtaking backdrop of the Dew Drop Inn

Word Watch

A **phrase** is a group of words without a subject and verb that serves as a single part of speech.

Each one is a *phrase,* a group of words that functions in a sentence as a single part of speech. Phrases do not have subjects or verbs. As a result, a phrase cannot stand alone as an independent unit. You use phrases in your writing to make your meaning more precise by describing, limiting, and expanding ideas.

Parts of Speech

Parts of speech are classified into eight categories: adjectives, adverbs, conjunctions, interjections, nouns, prepositions, pronouns, and verbs. Here's how it shakes down:

➤ *Adjectives* are words that describe nouns or pronouns. They tell what kind, which one, how much, or how many.

➤ *Adverbs* are words that describe verbs, adjectives, or other adverbs. They answer the questions when? where? how? or to what extent?

➤ *Conjunctions* connect words and show how they're related. *And, but, yet,* and *because* are just a few of the conjunctions available for your writing pleasure.

➤ *Interjections* are words that show strong emotion. *Oh, Wow,* and *Hey* are all interjections.

➤ *Nouns* name people, places, or things. *Book, essay,* and *best-seller* are all nouns.

➤ *Prepositions* link nouns or pronouns following them to other words in sentences. *To, by, over, in,* and *from* are prepositions.

➤ *Pronouns* are words used in place of a noun or another pronoun. *I, you, we,* and *they* are some of the most commonly used pronouns.

➤ *Verbs* name actions or describe states of being. *Jump, run, hire,* and *to be* are all verbs.

Variety Is the Spice of Life

There are eight different types of phrases: prepositional phrases, adjective phrases, adverbial phrases, verbal phrases, gerund phrases, infinitive phrases, participle phrases, and appositive phrases. These eight types fit into three main categories:

Write Angles

Unless you're writing a bodice ripper or airport fiction, use vivid adjectives and adverbs rather than interjections and exclamation points when you want to convey strong emotion.

➤ Prepositional, which includes adjective and adverb phrases

➤ Verbal, which includes gerund, infinitive, and participle phrases

➤ Appositive, which includes appositive phrases (go figure)

The following table explains each type of phrase. The phrase is in italics.

Type of Phrase	Definition	Example
Prepositional		
(All prepositional phrases function as either adjectives or adverbs.)		
Prepositional	Begins with a preposition and ends with a noun or pronoun	We sat *next to the blow-up doll.*
Adjective	Prepositional phrase that functions as an adjective	Lois ate a peach *with a fuzzy skin.*
Adverb	Prepositional phrase that functions as an adverb	The gambler toiled *at the craps table.*
Verbal		
Verbal	Verb form used as another part of speech	See the following examples.
Gerund	Verbal phrase that functions as a noun	*Dealing with incompetence* frayed their nerves.
Infinitive	Verbal phrase that functions as a noun, adjective, or adverb	*To eat a whole case of Yummy-Bars* is impressive.

continues

continued

Type of Phrase	Definition	Example
Participle	Verbal phrase that functions as an adjective	*Working quickly,* the executive soon resolved the matter.
Appositive		
Appositive	Noun or pronoun that renames another noun or pronoun	Laurie Rozakis, *a writer,* is both attractive and modest.

Word Watch

A **prepositional phrase** begins with a preposition and ends with a noun or a pronoun; for example: in the room, around the corner, near the door.

Write Angles

Long sentences commonly contain more than one prepositional phrase. Here's an example from Charles Dickens' *A Tale of Two Cities:* "There were a king with a large jaw and a queen with a plain face, on the throne of England; there were a king with a large jaw and a queen with a fair face, on the throne of France."

Prepositional Phrases

A *prepositional phrase* is a group of words that begins with a preposition and ends with a noun or a pronoun. The noun or pronoun is referred to as the object of the preposition. Like a screwdriver, cup of coffee, or toaster pastry, prepositional phrases are just one of those things you can't live without. Prepositional phrases are especially handy for showing spatial relationships.

In the following prepositional phrases, the prepositions are in italics:

➤ *Over* the rainbow

➤ *Into* the lion's mouth

➤ *Above* your line of sight

➤ *Below* the waterline

➤ *At* the end of your rope

Here's how prepositional phrases look in a sentence:

➤ The first novel ever written *on a typewriter* was Mark Twain's *Tom Sawyer.*

➤ Every time you lick a stamp, you're consuming $\frac{1}{10}$ *of a calorie.*

➤ The shin is a device for finding furniture *in the dark.*

➤ Fred and Wilma Flintstone were the first couple to be shown *in bed together on prime-time television*.

➤ Every day more money is printed *for Monopoly* than *for the U.S. Treasury*.

Adjective Phrases

An *adjective phrase* is a prepositional phrase that functions as an adjective and so describes a noun or a pronoun. To find out whether a prepositional phrase is serving as an adjective phrase, determine whether it answers the traditional adjective questions:

➤ Which one?　　➤ What kind?

➤ How much?　　➤ How many?

For example, look at these two sentences:

The toaster with the automatic setting delighted every member of the family.

The cost of the tummy tuck was a real bargain.

In the first sentence, the adjective phrase "with the automatic setting" describes the noun "toaster." In the second sentence, the adjective phrase "of the tummy tuck" describes the noun "cost."

Word Watch

An **adjective phrase** is a prepositional phrase that functions as an adjective in a sentence. For example: *The caption on the cartoon made them laugh.* The adjective phrase "on the cartoon" describes the noun "caption."

Adverb Phrases

An *adverb phrase* is a prepositional phrase that fulfills the functions of an adverb: It describes a verb, an adjective, or an adverb. To find out whether a prepositional phrase is functioning as an adverb phrase, determine whether it answers one of these questions:

➤ Where?　　➤ When?

➤ In what manner?　　➤ To what extent?

These sentences use adverb phrases:

The sun always seems brightest on Friday afternoons.

The tooth fairy arrived early in the morning.

In the first sentence, the adverb phrase "on Friday afternoons" describes the adjective "brightest." In the second sentence, the adverb phrase "in the morning" describes the adverb "early."

Verbal Phrases

A *verbal phrase* is a verb form used as another part of speech. There are three kinds of verbal phrases: gerunds, infinitives, and participles. Each type of verbal phrase fulfills a different role in a sentence:

➤ Gerunds serve as nouns.

➤ Infinitives serve as nouns, adjectives, or adverbs.

➤ Participles serve as adjectives.

Gerund Phrases

A gerund is not an upscale breakfast food, snazzy designer water, or flashy imported car. A *gerund* is a verb form that acts as a noun. A gerund phrase is a gerund with modifiers that together function as a noun.

Many of the words you think are nouns are gerunds. They're just verbs playing with your head by masquerading as nouns. Within a sentence, a gerund can function as a subject, direct object, indirect object, object of a preposition, predicate nominative, or appositive.

Find the gerund phrases in these sentences:

> Running out of ice cream after a bad hair day can be a horrible experience.

> P.J.'s favorite activity is cruising the Internet.

In the first sentence, the gerund "running" is part of the gerund phrase "running out of ice cream after a bad hair day." The whole kit and caboodle is the subject of the sentence. In the second sentence, the gerund "cruising" is part of the gerund phrase "cruising the Internet." In this case, the gerund phrase is working as a predicate nominative.

Infinitive Phrases

Infinitives are verb forms that come after the word *to* and act as nouns, adjectives, or adverbs. As with gerunds, infinitives can fill different grammatical functions within a sentence, as the following examples show:

Word Watch

An **infinitive** is a form of a verb that comes after the word *to* and functions as a noun, adjective, or adverb.

➤ To apologize often requires courage and humility.

In this sentence, the infinitive "to apologize" functions as the subject of the sentence.

➤ Afraid to move, he stared straight ahead.

In this sentence, the infinitive "to move" functions as the direct object.

Unlike gerunds, infinitives can also act as adjectives and adverbs. The following sentence shows an infinitive phrase serving as an adjective: *The head of the committee is the person to notify*. The infinitive phrase "to notify" modifies the noun "person." As an adverb: *Afraid to speak, she stared at her hands*. The infinitive phrase "to speak" modifies the verb "afraid."

The Grammar Police on Patrol

Some verbs must be followed by a gerund used as a direct object, as in the following examples:

➤ We considered *asking* (not *to ask*) for the check.

➤ We were having trouble *getting* (not *to get*) the server's attention.

Here are some of the most common verbs that must be followed by a gerund:

Verbs That Must Be Followed by a Gerund

acknowledge	admit	advise
anticipate	appreciate	avoid
complain about	consider	consist of
delay	deny	discuss
dislike	enjoy	escape
evade	favor	finish
give up	have trouble	imagine

61

include	insist on	keep on
mention	mind	object to
postpone	practice	put off
quit	recall	recommend
regret	resent	resist
risk	suggest	talk about
tolerate	understand	

Write Angles

Some verbs even change meaning depending on whether they come before a gerund or infinitive. For example, the sentence *We stopped eating* means the meal was over. But the sentence *We stopped to eat* means we took a break between activities to grab a meal.

Other verbs must be followed by an infinitive, as in the following examples:

➤ They wanted *to go* (not *going*) to the ant farm.

➤ Only one of us decided *to question* (not *questioning*) that decision.

Here are the most common verbs that must be followed by an infinitive:

Verbs That Must Be Followed by an Infinitive

afford	agree	aim
appear	arrange	ask
attempt	beg	cannot afford
care	claim	consent
decide	decline	demand
deserve	expect	fail
hesitate	hope	give permission
intend	know how	learn
like	manage	mean
offer	plan	prepare
pretend	promise	refuse
seem	struggle	tend
threaten	volunteer	vote
wait	want	

Participles and Participle Phrases

A *participle* is a verb form that functions as an adjective. There are two kinds of participles:

1. Present participles end in *ing* (snowing, burning, beating).

2. Past participles usually end in *ed, t,* or *en* (snowed, burnt, beaten).

These sentences use participles:

> The whining sound came from the engine.

> Confused, my friend could not follow my directions.

Word Watch

A **participle** is a verb form that functions as an adjective. For example: *The cracked ice looked like broken glass.* The participles are "cracked" and "broken."

In the first sentence, the present participle "whining" describes the noun "sound." In the second sentence, the past participle "confused" modifies the noun "friend."

Participle phrases contain a participle modified by an adverb or an adverbial phrase. Present participles look like gerunds—it's the function that identifies them. The entire phrase functions as an adjective, as these examples show:

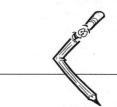

Write Angles

A participle phrase can be placed either before or after the word it describes.

> Our house, shaded completely by old trees, stays delightfully cool in the summer.

> Swimming slowly, we didn't notice the shark approaching up at an alarming speed.

In the first sentence, the participle phrase "shaded completely by old trees" describes the noun "house." The participle phrase "swimming slowly" describes the pronoun "we."

Appositive Phrases

An *appositive phrase* renames a noun or pronoun. Appositives are placed directly after the noun or pronoun they identify, as in the following examples:

➤ Sigmund Freud, the father of modern psychoanalytical theory, had a morbid fear of ferns.

In this sentence, the appositive "the father of modern psychoanalytical theory" renames the noun "Sigmund Freud."

➤ Dr. Seuss, the children's book writer, chose his name to rhyme with "rejoice."

In this sentence, the appositive "the children's book writer" renames the noun "Dr. Seuss."

Use an appositive to identify a person, especially the first time you mention him or her. Otherwise, your readers won't have a frame of reference. As they scratch their heads, they'll wonder, "Who is this writer talking about?"

Tighten Up

So how can all this stuff about phrases make your writing better?

➤ Because phrases add detail, they make your writing more descriptive and precise.

➤ Phrases can help you eliminate unnecessary words through combining sentences, which makes your writing more concise. People like concise writing because it gets to the point more quickly.

The following examples show how sentences can be improved with phrases:

Wordy: Laverne positioned the cream pie carefully. She threw it at the clown's face.

Concise: Positioning the cream pie carefully, Laverne threw it at the clown's face.

Wordy: You are given an open-book exam, which is likely to make you forget your book.

Corollary: You are given a take-home test, which is likely to make you forget where you live.

Concise: If you are given an open-book exam, you will forget your book.

Corollary: If you are given a take-home test, you will forget where you live.

Clause-ality

A *clause* is a group of words with its own subject and verb. Writers are very fond of clauses because clauses ...

➤ Add detail to a sentence.

➤ Help you combine ideas and reduce bulk.

64

➤ Sharpen meaning.

➤ Link related ideas.

➤ Show the relationship among ideas.

Clauses come in two flavors:

1. An *independent clause* is a complete sentence; it can stand alone.

2. A *dependent (subordinate) clause* is part of a sentence; it cannot stand alone.

The following table lists examples of each type of clause.

Write Angles

Here's one instance where length *doesn't* matter, because both dependent and independent clauses can be short or long.

Dependent Clause	Independent Clause
People who succeed in politics	must often rise above their principles.
If at first you don't succeed	destroy all evidence that you tried.
You never really learn to swear	until you learn to drive.

Let's look at each type of clause in greater detail, starting with dependent clauses.

Dependent Clauses

Dependent clauses add additional information to a main clause, but they don't express a complete thought. As a result, a dependent clause depends on its connection to an independent clause to make sense.

Independent Clauses

An independent clause contains a subject and a predicate. It can stand alone as a sentence because it expresses a complete thought. Here are some independent clauses divided into their subjects and predicates:

Write Angles

Dependent and independent clauses are linked with a subordinating conjunction. Examples of subordinating conjunctions include although, as, because, even though, if, because, so, though, where, when, unless, and until.

Subject	Predicate
Genetics	explains why you look like your father and if you don't, why you should.
Two wrongs	are only the beginning.
Coca-Cola	was originally green.
The hardness of the butter	is proportional to the softness of the bread.
The early bird	gets the worm, but what about the early worm?

Unite and Conquer

Remember how you linked related ideas and added detail with phrases? The same goes for clauses. Here are some examples of sentences made better with a little clause-ality because the sentences show cause and effect:

Blah: The car lurched into a pothole. The car cracked an axle.

Boffo: The car, which lurched into a pothole, cracked an axle.

Blah: Ralph's last name was hard to pronounce. Ralph decided to change his last name.

Boffo: Ralph wanted to change his last name because it was hard to pronounce.

Blah: Los Angeles and San Francisco are on opposite sides of the San Andreas Fault. They become 2.5 inches closer together each year.

Boffo: Because they are on opposite sides of the San Andreas Fault, Los Angeles and San Francisco become 2.5 inches closer together each year.

The Least You Need to Know

➤ A phrase is a group of words without a subject or a verb that functions as a single part of speech. Phrases cannot stand alone as independent units.

➤ Prepositional phrases begin with a preposition and end with a noun or pronoun. They can function as adjective phrases or adverb phrases.

➤ Verbal phrases contain verb forms used as another part of speech. Participles function as adjectives, gerunds function as nouns, and infinitives function as nouns, adjectives, or adverbs.

➤ Appositives rename another noun or pronoun.

➤ A clause is a word group that contains its own subject and verb.

➤ A dependent clause cannot stand alone; an independent (main) clause is a complete sentence.

Sentence Sense

"When it comes to language, nothing is more satisfying than to write a good sentence."

—Barbara Tuchman

You know that statement is true, but maybe you're not quite up to speed on the different kinds of sentences you can use. Perhaps you've been playing around with sentence variety and want to know why one type of sentence is more successful than another. Both on the job and in your personal life, you need to create sentences that convey your point with grace and power. You'll learn how to do exactly that in this chapter.

First, I'll explain what a sentence is and is not. Then you'll learn techniques for writing good sentences, including stressing the main point, being concise, and marrying related ideas. You'll also learn all about *voice* in writing and why the active voice is usually preferred over the passive voice.

Then I'll explain why (and how) you should eliminate expletive constructions. You'll discover the importance of maintaining parallel structure and varying the length and form of your sentences. Moving on to sentence errors, I'll show you how to revise choppy sentences and correct dangling modifiers, fragments, misplaced modifiers, and run-on sentences. The chapter concludes with a section on using the right word, not its first cousin.

I Know It When I See It

You've met a lot of sentences in your life. You've written a lot, too. So you know a sentence when you see it, but could you explain what exactly makes a sentence a sentence and not, say, a sandwich, sandcastle, or space shuttle?

To be a sentence, a group of words must …

1. Have a *subject* (noun or pronoun).
2. Have a *predicate* (verb or verb phrase).
3. Express a complete thought.

Here are some examples:

Not a sentence:	Zooms out of your mouth at over 600 m.p.h. (missing a subject)
Sentence:	A sneeze zooms out of your mouth at over 600 m.p.h.
Not a sentence:	More people killed annually by donkeys than die in air crashes. (missing a complete verb)
Sentence:	More people are killed annually by donkeys than die in air crashes.
Not a sentence:	Because every person has a unique tongue print. (not a complete thought)
Sentence:	Every person has a unique tongue print.

Superb Sentences

Given the wide variety of writing styles, it's surprising that all effective sentences share the exact same qualities: They are clear, complete, and correct. But maybe these qualities are not so surprising when you recall that every sentence you write is designed to communicate your ideas. The best way to do that is by giving your readers the information you want to convey in a form they will understand and enjoy. To write great sentences, remember these three points:

Write Angles

Dialogue is often written in incomplete sentences because that's the way people speak. Dialogue written in complete sentences can come out sounding artificial and stilted.

1. Effective sentences are clear.

   This sentence isn't clear: Eye drops off shelf.

   Does this mean that an eye fell off a shelf or that eye drops are no longer being sold in the store? Here's a clear revision: The eye drops have been taken off the shelf.

Author! Author!

What's the longest sentence on record? A book called *Gates of Paradise* by George Andrezeyevski (Panther, 1957) has no punctuation, so it might technically be called one long sentence. But I give Sylvester Hassell the nod for his 3,153-word sentence in *History of the Church of God* (circa 1884). Marcel Proust came close in *Cities of the Plain*, but his sentence contains only 958 words. Don't try this at home, kids.

2. Effective sentences are complete.

   This sentence isn't complete: Human bones can withstand stresses of 2,400 pounds.

   Is that 2,400 pounds per inch, foot, yard, or some other quantity? We need this information to understand the sentence. Here's the sentence with the missing information added: Human bones can withstand stresses of 2,400 pounds per square inch.

3. Effective sentences are correct.

   What's wrong with the following sentence?

   Three-year-old teacher needed for preschool students. Experience is preferred.

   This sentence isn't correct because it says that the teacher must be three years old. We assume that's not the case, but we have only the sentence to go by. Here's a correct version: Teacher needed for three-year-old preschool students. Experience is preferred.

Sentence Style

Sparkling sentences have style. In Chapter 3, "Pack the Essentials," you were introduced to the elements of style, including word choice, punctuation, and sentence length and variety. To create the sentence style that suits your topic, purpose, and audience, you must ...

➤ Emphasize the main point.

➤ Be concise.

➤ Link related ideas.

➤ Use the active voice.

➤ Eliminate expletive constructions.

➤ Maintain parallel structure.

➤ Vary sentences.

This section tells you how to do it.

It's What's Up Front That Counts

First impressions count in writing as well as in life, so put the most important information first in a sentence. This not only makes it easier for readers to find your point, but also creates a pattern that people can follow.

The following sentences all contain the same information, but notice how the meaning changes based on the information that's placed first:

➤ Our survey revealed that 44 percent of all Americans reuse aluminum foil. ("Survey" is the subject.)

➤ Forty-four percent of all Americans surveyed reuse aluminum foil. ("Forty-four percent" grabs your attention because it's first.)

➤ Reusing aluminum foil is done by 44 percent of all Americans surveyed. ("Reusing aluminum foil" is the subject.)

➤ Of all Americans included in the survey, 44 percent reuse aluminum foil. ("Of all Americans" gets top billing.)

Which version gets your vote? Make the choice by thinking about which fact is most important: The survey? The percentage of people? The foil itself? The sentence that puts that information first is most effective.

Author! Author!

Even the lowly period has its supporters, some of whom were quite eloquent. The period's greatest lover, however, was Russian author Isaac Babel, who was murdered by the Soviet secret police in 1939. He wrote: "No iron can stab the heart with such force as a period put at just the right place."

Lean, Mean, Writing Machine

You know how annoyed *you* get when you have to wade through waves of words to get to the point. All readers feel the same way. Wordy writing forces readers to clear away clutter before they can understand your message. This makes them impatient, if not downright cranky. To see what I mean, look at the following examples:

Wordy: If love is visually impaired, why do ladies' lacy undergarments continue to remain so well-liked at this point in time?

Better: If love is blind, why is lingerie so popular?

Write simply and directly. Be ruthless: Chop redundant words and phrases and combine sentences that repeat information. Start by replacing the following phrases with their concise counterparts. Do this every time you write, and your readers will be grateful.

Wordy	Pithy
honest truth	truth
past experience	experience
revert back	revert
foreign imports	imports
partial stop, complete stop	stop
free gift	gift
live and breathe	live
null and void	null (or void)
most unique	unique
cease and desist	cease (or desist)
at 8:00 A.M. in the morning	at 8:00 A.M.
sum total and end results	sum total
proceed ahead	proceed
kills bugs dead	kills bugs
repeat again	repeat
extra gratuity	gratuity
small in size	small
few in number	few
combine together	combine
final end	end

United We Stand, Divided We Fall

To make your writing more succinct, you can also combine related sentences. Focus on sentences that contain the same information and so logically belong together. Combine the sentences, rearrange words as desired, and eliminate unnecessary words. For example:

Windy: David Prowse was the actor in the Darth Vader suit in *Star Wars*. He spoke all of Vader's lines. He didn't know that he was going to be dubbed over by James Earl Jones. He was really surprised when he saw the screening of the movie and realized that his voice had been cut.

Good: David Prowse, the actor in the Darth Vader suit in *Star Wars*, spoke all of Vader's lines. He didn't know that he was going to be dubbed over by James Earl Jones until he saw the movie.

Better:	David Prowse played Darth Vader in *Star Wars,* but he didn't know he was going to be dubbed over by James Earl Jones until he saw the movie.

Which version do you select? It depends on your audience, purpose, and style.

Passive Aggressive

What's the difference between these two sentences?

➤ In 1936, a racehorse was beaten by American track star Jesse Owens over a 100-yard course, and a head start was given to the horse.

➤ In 1936, American track star Jesse Owens beat a racehorse over a 100-yard course, and the horse had a head start.

The first sentence is in the passive voice; the second sentence is in the active voice.

Verbs can show whether the subject performs the action or receives the action. This is called *voice.* A verb is *active* when the subject performs the action. A verb is *passive* when its action is performed upon the subject. The active voice creates a better writing style because it is less wordy and clearer than the passive voice.

To change a verb from the passive to active voice, make the agent ("by—") the new subject.

Passive voice:	Union dues are paid in Japan by robots.
Active voice:	Robots in Japan pay union dues.

Write Angles

Punctuation is a key style element because it determines the links between sentences. A period shows a full stop between ideas; a comma and a coordinating conjunction show addition, choice, consequence, contrast, or cause. A semicolon shows the second sentence completes the first sentence. Finally, a semicolon and a conjunctive adverb (a word such as nevertheless or however) show addition, consequence, contrast, cause and effect, time, emphasis, or addition.

Writer's Block

Don't make the mistake of assuming that the active voice is always better than the passive voice. It's not. Use the passive voice when you want to avoid placing blame ("A mistake was made" rather than "You made a mistake"). In addition, use passive voice in scientific writing to give prominence to the facts rather than the writer.

Word Watch

A **pangram** is a single sentence that uses all 26 letters of the alphabet. The best-known one, familiar to those of us who re-member how-to-type manuals, is "The quick brown fox jumps over the lazy dog." It has 35 letters. Can you think of a shorter sen-tence that contains all 26 let-ters?

Word Watch

Parallelism (or **parallel struc-ture**) calls for the use of match-ing grammatical forms to express ideas of equal importance.

Iron Man Writing

You can give your writing more strength by eliminat-ing *there* or *it* and a form of "to be" placed before the subject of a sentence. These *expletive constructions* just plug a hole when writers switch subject-verb word order. There's no need to plug the hole. Look for these openings:

➤ It is   ➤ There is

➤ There are   ➤ There were

Here's how the construction looks in sentence form:

     Blah: It was Friday that we skipped work.

     Better: We skipped work on Friday.

Parallel Play

Pick the winner:

➤ I've learned that true friendship and love that is true continue to grow, even over the longest distance.

➤ I've learned that true friendship and true love continue to grow, even over the longest dis-tance.

You're on to me now, aren't you? The second sentence is better because it's parallel. "True friendship" parallels "true love." Both are two-word phrases, with an adjec-tive (true) followed by a noun (friendship, love). Because the phrases match, the sentence sounds smoother and more logical. It has greater rhythm and flow.

Parallel structure means putting ideas of the same rank in the same grammatical form. You can have parallel words, phrases, clauses, and even sentences. Here are two more examples:

Not parallel:	Tyranny, like hell, is not easily conquered; yet we have this consolation with us, that the harder the conflict, the triumph will be even more glorious.
Parallel:	Tyranny, like hell, is not easily conquered; yet we have this consolation with us, that the harder the conflict, the more glorious the triumph (from "The American Crisis," by Thomas Paine).
Not parallel:	Whether expressed in a sit-in at lunch counters, a freedom ride in Mississippi, a peaceful protest in Georgia, or if we boycott buses in Montgomery, Alabama, it is an outgrowth of Thoreau's insistence that evil must be resisted and no moral man can patiently adjust to injustice.
Parallel:	Whether expressed in a sit-in at lunch counters, a freedom ride in Mississippi, a peaceful protest in Georgia, or a bus boycott in Montgomery, Alabama, it is an outgrowth of Thoreau's insistence that evil must be resisted and no moral man can patiently adjust to injustice (from "A Legacy of Creative Protest," by Reverend Martin Luther King Jr.).

Variety Is the Spice of Life (and Writing!)

Who can eat the same meal every day, watch the same shows, and wear the same clothes? (Don't answer that.) Variety makes life—and sentences—interesting.

Effective writing uses sentences of different lengths and types to create variety and interest. Craft your sentences to express your ideas in the best possible way. Start by varying the length of your sentences. The unbroken rhythm of the same length sentences can lull a reader into unconsciousness.

Sorry Sentences

You know when your car isn't working, when the washer heads south, and when the television is on the fritz. How can you tell when a sentence is falling down on the job? When your sentences aren't correct, clarity and communication break down. Here are six of the most common sentence errors, arranged in alphabetical order:

➤ Choppy sentences

➤ Dangling modifiers

➤ Fragments

➤ Misplaced modifiers

➤ Run-ons

➤ Wrong words

Let's see how these errors happen and how to fix them.

> **Write Angles**
>
> When your topic is complex or full of numbers, use short sentences to help your reader get your point. Save longer, more complex sentences to link easier ideas and avoid repetition.

Slice and Dice Choppy Sentences

Short sentences can be powerful because they create a rapid-fire, staccato rhythm, but too many short sentences can also be jerky and abrupt. They're often boring because they're repetitive. In addition, choppy sentences can subvert meaning because every sentence seems the same.

Choppy:	The brain is a wonderful organ. The brain starts working the moment you get up in the morning. It doesn't stop working until you get to work.
Coherent:	The brain is a wonderful organ: It starts working the moment you get up in the morning and doesn't stop until you get to work.

Missing in Action

What's wrong with this sentence?

Waiting at the corner, the bus passed me by.

As written, this sentence states that the bus was waiting at the corner, not the potential passenger. To convey the writer's meaning, the sentence should read: As I waited at the corner, the bus passed me by.

Fragments of Your Imagination

As its name suggests, a *sentence fragment* is a group of words that doesn't express a complete thought. Sentence fragments are created in three ways:

1. The sentence is missing a subject.
2. The sentence is missing a verb.
3. The sentence is not a complete thought.

You fix a fragment by adding the missing part or adding the fragment to another sentence as a subordinating clause. This example shows how to add what's missing:

Word Watch

Dangling modifiers result when a descriptive phrase isn't anchored to the subject.

> **Fragment:**   May your sports utility vehicle its resale value.
>
> **Sentence:**   May your sports utility vehicle hold its resale value.

If you add the fragment to a complete sentence, you'll likely have to add a subordinating conjunction, as the following example shows. The subordinating conjunction is in italics.

> **Fragment:**   Hershey's Kisses are called that. The machine that makes them looks like it's kissing the conveyor belt.
>
> **Sentence:**   Hershey's Kisses are called that *because* the machine that makes them looks like it's kissing the conveyor belt.

Lost in Space

For clarity, always place any describing words (modifiers) as close as possible to the words they describe. If the modifier is placed too far from the noun or pronoun it describes, the sentence won't communicate your meaning clearly. *Mis-placed modifiers* can also create humor, which is not a good thing when you're trying to be serious.

Word Watch

A **misplaced modifier** is an adverb, adjective, phrase, or clause placed too far from the word it describes.

| Misplaced modifier: | The two sisters were reunited after 18 years at the checkout counter. |

The sentence says that the two sisters spent 18 years at the checkout counter, not that they were apart for 18 years.

| Corrected: | After 18 years, the two sisters were reunited at the checkout counter. |

| Misplaced modifier: | Any time four New Yorkers get into a cab together, a bank robbery has just taken place without arguing. |

The sentence says that the New Yorkers robbed a bank without arguing, not that they're not arguing in the cab.

| Corrected: | Any time four New Yorkers get into a cab together without arguing, a bank robbery has just taken place. |

| Misplaced modifier: | Many hamsters only blink one eye at a time. |

The sentence says that the only thing that hamsters can do is blink one eye. Although not wildly talented animals, hamsters have been known to have a few other tricks up their furry little sleeves.

| Corrected: | Many hamsters blink only one eye at a time. |

Run-On and On and On

A *run-on sentence* is two incorrectly joined independent clauses. This muddies ideas or washes them completely down the drain. You can fix a run-on one of three ways:

1. Separate the run-on into two correct sentences with either a semicolon or a period.

2. Add a comma and a coordinating conjunction (and, nor, but, or, for, yet, so) to create a compound sentence. Leaving out the conjunction will result in a *comma splice*.

3. Add a subordinating conjunction to create a complex sentence.

Following are some examples of run-ons that have gone through the body shop.

Separate the run-on (in this case, a comma splice) into two complete sentences:

Run-on:	I'm not into working out, my philosophy is: No pain, no pain.
Sentences:	I'm not into working out. My philosophy is: No pain, no pain.

Add a coordinating conjunction:

Run-on:	I always wanted to be somebody I should have been more specific.
Sentence:	I always wanted to be somebody, but I should have been more specific.

Add a subordinating conjunction:

Run-on:	The grass is always greener you leave the sprinkler on.
Sentence:	The grass is always greener when you leave the sprinkler on.

America's Funniest Home Sentences

Sometimes, the sentence doesn't make sense because one word isn't right. Can you find the blooper in each of the following sentences?

1. I have a six-room hated apartment to rent.
2. We're selling eight puppies from a German Shepherd and an Alaskan Hussy.
3. Our experienced Mom will care for your child. Fenced yard, meals, and smacks are included.
4. Get rid of aunts. Zap does the job in 24 hours.
5. I saw a sign that read, "Great Dames for sale."

Writer's Block

Don't forget to add a comma before a coordinating conjunction. For example: Why is lemon juice mostly artificial ingredients, but dishwashing liquid contains real lemons?

Answers

1. Hated should be heated.
2. Hussy should be Husky.
3. Smacks should be snacks.
4. Aunts should be ants.
5. Dames should be danes.

This type of sentence error is easily fixed with some close proofreading. This is covered in detail in Chapter 11, "Personal Best: Revising and Editing."

The Least You Need to Know

➤ Emphasize the main point, be concise, and link related ideas.

➤ Use the active voice, eliminate expletive constructions, and maintain parallel structure.

➤ Vary sentences to achieve a strong and compelling style.

➤ Revise choppy sentences and ditch dangling modifiers.

➤ Repair fragments, misplaced modifiers, and run-ons.

➤ Use the right word to convey your meaning.

Chapter 7

Paragraphs Plus

In This Chapter

➤ Definition of a "paragraph"

➤ Parts of a paragraph

➤ Topic sentences, stated and implied

➤ Supporting sentences

➤ Concluding sentences

Ponder this ...

1. Before they created drawing boards, what did they go back to?

2. If all the world is a stage, where is the audience sitting?

3. If the #2 pencil is the most popular, why is it still #2?

4. If most car accidents occur within five miles of home, why doesn't everyone just move 10 miles away?

5. Before they invented paragraphs, how could you tell where one main point ended and another one started?

As far as we're concerned, the last question is the crucial one. Why? Because paragraphs are the essential building blocks of writing. So before we go any further, let's turn to paragraphs.

First, you'll learn about topic sentences, a necessary ingredient in successful expository and persuasive paragraphs. Then comes a section on supporting sentences, the workhorses of effective paragraphs. Finally, you'll discover how to create an effective concluding sentence for each of your paragraphs. By the end of this chapter, you'll be a paragraph pro.

Appearance vs. Reality

You know a paragraph when you see it: It's a group of sentences whose first word is indented. Yes? Not so fast, partner. If it was *that* easy, you wouldn't have bought this book.

Read each of the following models. One only is a paragraph. Decide which one it is—and why.

Exhibit A:

Japan is a very populated country. With so many big cities, natural disasters can be even more damaging. Have you thought yet about what it's like searching for a job? How do you think you will feel the first time you go on an important interview? Unruly fans have become a big problem in many major professional sports stadiums. Florida residents see alligators all the time, but not everyone welcomes these fascinating creatures. Acid rain is a problem all over the world; no country can escape its effects. Rain forests are incredibly rich in many forms of life. They are filled with an astonishing variety of plants and animals.

Exhibit B:

Long-time Boston residents still talk about the molasses flood that engulfed the city's north end on January 15, 1919. Many people were sitting near the Purity Distilling Corporation's 50-foot-high molasses tank enjoying the unseasonably warm day. The tank was filled with over two million gallons of molasses—and it was about to burst apart. First, molasses oozed through the tank's rivets. Then the metal bolts popped out, the seams burst, and tons of molasses exploded in a surge of deadly goo. The first wave, over 25 feet high, smashed buildings, trees, people, and animals like toys. Residents were carried into the Charles River, which was soon a gooey brown sludge. The molasses was not the only threat; sharp pieces of the tank sliced through the air, injuring scores of people. After the initial destruction, molasses continued to clog the streets for days. Many survivors had to have their clothing cut off: Dried molasses turned garments into cement. People were stuck to sidewalks and benches; molasses glued telephone receivers to ears and hands. The smell of molasses stayed in the air for months. The disaster left over 20 people dead and more than 50 seriously hurt.

As you can see, slapping together a group of sentences and indenting the first word does not a *paragraph* make. Exhibit A is a group of unrelated sentences. You can call it "Beanie," "Bernie," or "Banana," but you can't call it a paragraph because it's not one. Exhibit B *is* a paragraph.

What makes a group of sentences a paragraph is the relationship among them. Every sentence in a paragraph has to support the main idea. Paragraphs are a great invention because they allow you to divide your material into manageable parts that are connected by a common theme.

Word Watch

A **paragraph** is a group of sentences that all relate to a single main idea or central point.

What about paragraph length? Technically speaking, a paragraph can have as many sentences as you need to convey your ideas clearly. Practically speaking, however, most of the paragraphs you write will contain at least four sentences and no more than seven to eight. In expository or persuasive documents, these sentences include …

1. The topic sentence.

2. Supporting sentences (details).

3. A concluding sentence.

Here's a graphic representation:

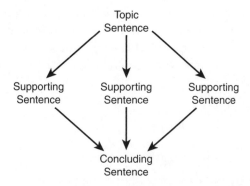

Narrative or descriptive paragraphs may or may not be arranged this way, depending on your purpose and audience. Paragraph organization of these modes of discourse is discussed in detail in Chapter 10, "Making Your Bones."

Now, let's look at each paragraph element in detail.

Don't Leave Home Without It: Topic Sentences

The topic sentence is the key sentence in any paragraph because it tells what the paragraph is about; it shapes the paragraph by limiting its contents. Including a topic sentence also makes it easier for you to write, because it helps you organize your material and stay on the point.

A topic sentence is *not* …

➤ An apology, as in: "I'm not sure this paragraph is what you want, but it's the only thing I could come up with."

➤ A public service announcement, as in: "In this essay, I am going to explain why mosquitoes are attracted to people who have recently eaten bananas."

➤ A gross generalization, as in: "A mind is a terrible thing to waste."

A topic sentence can be …

➤ A reworking of a question you have been given, as in: "What is the final test of maturity? I believe it is living with fear and not being overcome by it." The question was: "It has been said that to live with fear and not be overcome with it is the final test of maturity." This technique won't win you a Pulitzer Prize, but it's a great technique when you're faced with an essay test or writing deadline on the job.

➤ A statement of purpose.

➤ A sentence containing statistics.

Each of these methods is described in detail in Chapter 10.

Topic sentences please your readers because they announce the contents of the paragraph. This enables people to read faster, since they know *what* they'll be reading.

Your Place in the Sun

While most writers place their topic sentences first in a paragraph, you can also place it in the middle or end. To whit …

1. **First in line.** Placing your topic sentence first in a paragraph is especially useful when you're dealing with difficult or technical material, since it clearly states the subject matter. This leaves the reader free to focus on the details rather than trying to decode the topic.

    In addition, an effective topic sentence placed first in a paragraph grabs your reader's attention, urging them to read on.

2. **Middle man.** Placing your topic sentence in the middle of a paragraph allows you to support your topic before you actually state it. Since this method helps decrease reader resistance, use it when you think your audience will be unfavorable or hostile to your ideas.

    Placing your topic sentence in the middle also creates a sense of balance. Try to include the same number of details above and below the topic sentence to create even stronger symmetry.

3. **Last but not least.** Placing your topic sentence last creates suspense because you present the details before the topic. This helps create a dramatic effect, especially useful for advertisements and other forms of persuasive writing.

Author! Author!

The paragraph made its formal debut in the 1866 book *Composition and Rhetoric*, by Alexander Bain, a professor of rhetoric at the University of Aberdeen in Scotland. Bain defined a paragraph as a "collection of sentences with unity of purpose." Later, the paragraph came to be seen as a small-scale composition, a view we still hold today, due to the clear beginning, middle, and end that both share.

How can you learn to vary topic sentence placement? Experiment, using sample paragraphs as models. To that end, following are three paragraphs. The first paragraph has its topic sentences in the beginning, the second has its topic sentence in the middle, and the third has its topic sentence in the end (but you guessed that already, didn't you?). The topic sentence is underlined in each passage:

Topic sentence *first* …

> Given by the people of France to the people of the United States as a symbol of a shared love of freedom and everlasting friendship, the Statue of Liberty is the largest freestanding sculpture ever created. It weighs 450,000 pounds and rises 151 feet above its pedestal. More than 100 feet around, Ms. Liberty boasts eyes two and a half feet wide, a mouth three feet wide, and a nose four and a half feet long. Her upraised right arm extends 42 feet; her hand is nearly 17 feet long. Her fingers are close to 10 feet long. The statue has an interior framework of iron that keeps it from toppling over.

Topic sentence in the *middle* …

> Business people are dressed neatly—the women in suits or skirts and blouses and the men in jackets, ties, pressed pants, and stiffly starched shirts. The staff in the restaurants and shops are polite to tourists and residents alike. Children stand quietly by their parents, and rarely speak until they are spoken to. Almost all aspects of life on the island are polite and civilized, traceable to the residents' dignity and pride. People hold doors open for each other, wait to get into elevators until everyone has gotten off, and step aside to let those in a rush get by. At noon, the shops close and everyone goes home for a two-hour rest. But if you ask the shopkeepers to stay open a little longer, they will often gladly oblige.

Topic sentence *last* …

> The brown pelican, Florida's most popular bird, can often be seen perched on jetties, bridges, and piers. The state wetlands boast herons, egrets, wood ducks, and roseate spoonbills (often mistaken for flamingos). On the beach you can find sanderlings, plovers, and oystercatchers. Ospreys, white pelicans, and southern bald eagles call the Florida lakes, bays, and rivers their home. The state bird, the mockingbird, likes living in suburban neighborhoods. Offshore, cormorants, black skimmers, and terns look for their dinner. Florida's forests shelter quail, wild turkey, owls, and woodpeckers. In all, more than a hundred native species of birds have been found in Florida.

In Chapter 10, you'll learn the different forms that a topic sentence can take and how to make your topic sentences simply irresistible.

Hidden in Plain Sight

In addition, a topic sentence can be implied rather than directly stated. This technique works best when you want to draw your readers into your writing without directly stating the topic. When your point needs to be driven home, go with a stated rather than implied topic sentence.

Read the following paragraph. From the four choices that follow, select the one that best states the implied topic sentence.

> About 2,500 years ago there was a ball-kicking game played by the Athenians, Spartans, and Corinthians, which the Greeks called *Episkuros*. The Romans had a somewhat similar game called *Harpastum*. According to several historical sources, the Romans brought the game with them when they invaded the British Isles in the first century A.D. The game today known as "football" in the United States can be traced directly back to the English game of rugby, although there have been many changes to the game. Football was played informally on university fields more than a hundred years ago. In 1840, a yearly series of informal "scrimmages" started at Yale University. It took more than 25 years, however, for the game to become part of college life. The first formal intercollegiate football game was held between Princeton and Rutgers teams on November 6, 1869, on Rutgers's home field at New Brunswick, New Jersey. Rutgers won.

The implied topic sentence is best stated as …

1. The Romans, Athenians, Spartans, and Corinthians all played a game like football.

2. Football is a very old game; its history stretches back to ancient days.

3. American football comes from a British game called "rugby."

4. Football is a more popular game than baseball, even though baseball is called "America's pastime."

Writer's Block

Implied topic sentences are usually not the best choice for an unsophisticated audience. These readers are apt to lose patience with your subtlety.

Choices 1 and 3 are too narrow to state the topic; they're details rather than a general, overall statement. Choice 4 is also a loser because it contains information that isn't included in the paragraph. The winner is Choice 2, because it best states the main idea of the passage.

Try again.

> Egypt, a long, narrow, fertile strip of land in northeastern Africa, is the only place in the world where pyramids were built. Back then, all the water for the land and its people came from the mighty Nile River. Natural barriers protected the land from invaders. Around 300 B.C.E., when kings and other high Egyptian officials authorized the building of the first pyramids, these natural barriers protected the land from invaders. Deserts to the east and west cut off Egypt from the rest of the world; to the south, dangerous rapids on the Nile blocked invaders. Delta marshes lay to the north. This circle of isolation allowed the Egyptians to work in peace and security. In addition, great supplies of raw materials were needed to build the pyramids. Ancient Egypt had an abundance of limestone, sandstone, and granite, all quarried close to the banks of the Nile. Egypt's most precious resource—the great Nile River—provided the means to transport the rocks to the building sites.

1. The pyramids were built by the great kings around the year 300 B.C.
2. The pyramids were not worth the human cost, measured in enormous suffering, deprivation, and death.
3. Nature has made Egypt easy to defend from conquest.
4. Ancient Egypt's unique combination of resources helped make the pyramids a reality.

Choices 1 and 3 are out, because they're details, not the main idea. This makes them too narrow. Choice 2 is also incorrect, because the information it contains distorts the meaning of the paragraph. The best choice is 4, since it alone states the paragraph's focus.

Word Watch

Supporting details prove the assertion made in the topic sentence.

Build Me Up, Buttercup: Supporting Sentences

Okay, so you've stated your main idea in your topic sentence. Now, deliver the goods—the supporting sentences that make your point, explain your ideas, describe your subject, or tell your story. Without adequate support, a paragraph just goes around in a circle, saying the same thing over and over. In effect, it says nothing.

What distinguishes superb writing from shoddy writing is the quality of your supporting detail. It's the ability to move back and forth from generalizations (your topic sentence) to specific details (supporting sentences) that makes a paragraph effective communication. Here's an example:

Topic sentence:	The United States won 13 medals at the 1994 Winter Olympics, its best record ever.
Supporting sentence:	Bonnie Blair won four medals in speed skating.
Supporting sentence:	The U.S. also won four medals in Alpine skiing.
Supporting sentence:	Further, Nancy Kerrigan won a silver medal in figure skating.
Supporting sentence:	Finally, in the women's moguls, Liz McIntyre won a silver.

Remember, the type of supporting evidence you use depends on your purpose and audience. For example, if you're writing a persuasive essay for a hostile audience, you'll want to use statistics, facts, and examples rather than opinions. Such "hard" data is more likely to persuade a resistant reader than "soft," touchy-feely sentences.

Dig We Must

So where do you get all the details you need to create your supporting sentences? Most of the time it takes some research, since few of us can spout a fountain of relevant facts off the top of our heads. Fortunately, you don't have to dig your way through the stacks at the Library of Congress to get the detail you need—but you probably *will* have to look up the facts you need. Here are some great sources:

➤ Almanacs (*World Almanac* and *Information Please, Almanac* especially)

➤ Autobiographies (but balance these against unbiased sources such as newspaper articles and the reference books *Contemporary Biography* and *Who's Who*)

➤ Biographies

➤ Dictionaries

➤ Direct observation

➤ Encyclopedias (CD-ROM as well as text)

➤ Government documents

➤ Interviews

➤ Magazines

➤ Maps

➤ Newspapers

Write Angles

Paragraphs in newspapers are often one or two sentences long. Paragraphs in essays are far longer. Newspaper writers assume you're not going to read the article all the way through. They keep their paragraphs punchy to keep your interest. Essay writers assume you're in it for the long haul. They have the luxury of writing more discursive passages.

➤ Photographs

➤ Television documentaries and newsmagazines

➤ Textbooks

➤ Web sites on the Internet

Walk This Way

Here's an especially lovely little number I tailored just for you. As you read, decide which supporting sentences you find most interesting. Where do you think the writer got the information?

Born in 1833, John Styth Pemberton was a pharmacist who moved to Atlanta, Georgia, in 1869. To make a living, he created so-called "patent medicines," homemade remedies that were sold without a prescription. Fourteen years after settling in Atlanta, Pemberton registered a trademark for a medicine he called "French Wine Coca—Ideal Nerve and Tonic Stimulant." Soon after, Pemberton came up with a headache medicine he called "Coca-Cola." Nothing complex—he had taken the wine out of the French Wine Coca and added some caffeine. The medicine tasted so terrible that at the last minute he added some extract of kola nut and a few other oils. He sold it to soda fountains in used bottles. A few weeks later, a man with a terrible headache hauled himself into a drugstore and asked for a spoonful of Coca-Cola. Usually, druggists stirred such headache remedies into a glass of water. In this case, however, the person on duty was too lazy to walk over to the sink. Instead, he mixed the syrup in some seltzer water because it was closer to where he was standing. The customer liked the carbonated version better than the uncarbonated one and other customers agreed. From then on, Coca-Cola was served as a carbonated drink.

Writer's Block

Beware of Internet sources; some Web sites can be as unreliable as your ex. Learn all about authenticating online sites in Part 4, "Just Shoot Me Now: Research Papers and Term Papers."

Notice how all the supporting sentences serve to expand the implied topic sentence, which we can state this way: "Coca-Cola started out as a patent medicine and only accidentally developed into a carbonated beverage." The paragraph is well written because the topic is developed with specific supporting sentences.

In Chapter 9, "A Place for Everything, and Everything in Its Place," you'll learn different ways to arrange the supporting sentences in your paragraphs.

Sweet Endings: Concluding Sentences

A concluding sentence is like a good dessert: It draws together everything that has come before and leaves the reader with a sense of completion. A delicious concluding sentence also leaves your readers with a sweet taste in their mouths, as in, "What a good writer so-and-so is. I really enjoyed reading this paragraph. Yum."

A conclusion is *not* ...

> ➤ An announcement of what you've accomplished, as in: "In this composition, I have proven that penguins can jump as high as six feet in the air."

> ➤ A sweeping generalization, as in: "All lipsticks contain fish scales." (Actually, only some do.)

> ➤ An absolute claim, as in: "Never hold a dustbuster and a cat at the same time," or "Never wear polka-dot underwear under white shorts."

> ➤ An apology, as in: "Even though I may not have proven my point or been as eloquent as others, my paper did make some good points, I hope."

Write Angles

In writing, as in life, oftentimes *less is more.* You don't have to include every single detail you find. You're far better off selecting the examples that really make your case and suit your audience and purpose.

Writer's Block

Never introduce new ideas in your concluding sentence. Also avoid simply reworking your topic sentence—that's a cheap trick.

A conclusion may ...

> ➤ Restate the main idea, as in: "In these ways, we can all help preserve the wombat from extinction."

> ➤ State a decision, as in: "Tomorrow isn't soon enough; I intend to start dealing with the national debt today."

> ➤ Give your opinion, as in: "To err is human. To eat a muskrat is not."

> ➤ Call for action, as in: "Early to bed and early to rise is first in the bathroom."

Word Watch

The poetical equivalent of a paragraph is called a **stanza**.

➤ Use a transitional word that shows the paragraph is over, such as *in conclusion, to conclude, to summarize, ultimately, finally, at the end.* This is especially effective since it's the literary equivalent of your father putting on his pajamas at midnight to show that the party's over. (Hey, it always worked at our house.)

These techniques are covered in greater detail in Chapter 10, where you'll learn how to write complete essays, one paragraph at a time.

The following passage has an especially effective concluding sentence because it not only sums up the point of the paragraph but also ends on an appropriate tone for its purpose and audience.

> Most natural hazards can be detected before their threat matures. But seisms (from the Greek *seismos,* meaning "earthquake") have no known precursors, so they come without warning, like the vengeance of an ancient warrior. For this reason, they continue to kill in some areas at a level usually reserved for wars and epidemics—the 11,000 dead in northeastern Iran died on August 31, 1968, not in the ancient past. Nor is the horror of the lethal earthquake completed with the heavy death toll. The homeless living are left to cope with fire, looting, pestilence, fear, and the burden of rebuilding what the planet so easily shrugs away.

The Least You Need to Know

➤ A paragraph is a group of sentences that all relate to a single main idea or central point.

➤ In expository or persuasive documents, a paragraph includes a topic sentence (stated or implied), supporting sentences (details), and a concluding sentence.

➤ The topic sentence can be a reworking of a question you have been given, a statement of purpose, or a sentence containing statistics. It can be placed at the beginning, middle, or end of the paragraph.

➤ Supporting details prove the assertion made in the topic sentence.

➤ Your concluding sentence can restate the main idea, state a decision, call for action, or use a transitional word that shows the paragraph is over.

Part 2
The Writing Process

Want to bring your writing to life? In these chapters, I'll teach you how to use the writing process to plan, shape, draft, revise, and edit your documents. Then we'll focus on how you can create dazzling introductions, brilliant body paragraphs, and superb conclusions. By the end of this section of the book, you'll understand how to construct a lively essay from start to finish.

Write This Way

Humorist/writer Bennett Cerf claimed that he got his best ideas while sitting in the bathroom; Ernest Hemingway had to sharpen exactly 12 pencils before he stood up to write (after injuring his back in a nasty plane crash, he threw away his desk chair). Novelist Willa Cather had to read a passage from the Bible every morning before she started to write. Edgar Allan Poe perched his Siamese cat on his shoulder in preparation for writing a poem; Ben Franklin liked to write in the nude, in or out of the bathtub.

Are you upset because writing doesn't come easily to you? Are you ready to hide in the bathroom, stand up, sit down, sharpen pencils, take off your clothes, and grab a cat if it would make your writing easier? Are you jealous because it seems that "real" writers can pick up their pen (or sit down at their computer) and write effortlessly? Set aside your fears and your envy, partner, because writing doesn't flow magically for anyone. (And people who claim that it does are also the ones who say, "Oh, I never diet!" and "Yes, my hair has always been this color." Pish tosh.)

Research has shown that successful writers follow a specific process when they write. Learning the steps in this process can help you write more easily and effectively. That's what this chapter is all about. And don't worry: You can keep your clothes on the whole time.

Get the Big Picture

The writing process can be divided into a series of steps. While scholars bicker over the exact number, I'm going with five standard steps because they'll serve you best in all your writing situations. Knowing these five easy pieces can help you focus on one aspect of your writing at a time, so you can sidestep panic and procrastination to get the job done.

The five steps in "wRite with Rozakis" are ...

1. Planning
2. Researching
3. Shaping and drafting
4. Revising and editing
5. Proofreading

Here's what each step involves:

1. Planning

   ➤ Define your purpose.

   ➤ Analyze your audience.

   ➤ Select a topic.

   ➤ Narrow the topic.

   ➤ Choose a plan of organization.

   ➤ Establish a timetable.

2. Researching

   ➤ Gather facts.

   ➤ Find details.

   ➤ Tease out opposing viewpoints.

   ➤ Search the Web, hit the library.

   ➤ Take notes.

Write Angles

While writer's block, like the urge to shop, can strike any time, most people get the writing willies in the planning stage of the writing process. Knowing where the stress puppies bark at *you* can help you rein them in.

3. **Shaping and drafting**

  ➤ Outline.

  ➤ Write the first draft(s).

4. **Revising and editing**

  ➤ Add necessary material.

  ➤ Check length and format.

  ➤ Correct errors in spelling, grammar, punctuation, and capitalization.

  ➤ Cut unnecessary information.

  ➤ Get feedback from readers.

  ➤ Move parts around.

  ➤ Rewrite awkward or inaccurate statements.

Writer's Block

Don't get obsessive about the writing process: The steps don't have to be followed in this exact order. As you draft, you might find yourself doubling back and doing more research, for example. You may also skip some steps, depending on your audience, purpose, and time constraints.

5. **Proofreading**

  ➤ Correct typographical errors.

  ➤ Make sure no words are missing.

  ➤ Look for all sorts of bloopers.

  ➤ Make your writing letter-perfect.

Blueprint for Success: Planning

Question: What did the fish say when he hit the concrete wall?

Answer: "Dam."

Planning ahead pays off, whether you're swimming or writing. When you're swimming, always check for dams. When you're writing, always consider the big three elements:

1. **Purpose:** *Your reason for writing.* As you've already learned, there are four main purposes for writing: to tell a story, prove a point, explain, or describe.

2. **Audience:** *Your readers.* As explained in Chapter 3, "Pack the Essentials," your audience determines your tone and diction.

3. **Topic:** *Your subject.* Always be sure that you clearly understand the subject *before* you write. The matter of choosing a subject is covered in "Topic Time," later in this chapter.

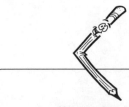

Write Angles

In addition to purpose, audience, and topic, you may also have other factors to consider. These include time constraints, length of the document, and writing in a group. Factor in these issues as you plan.

Word Watch

Your **subject** is the general theme; your **topic** is the specific focus of your paper.

In most writing situations, you'll be able to treat these three factors in this order, starting with purpose and ending with topic. Other times, however, you may have to consider them in a different sequence. For example, if you're writing in a school or office setting, you may be given the topic. In that case, the topic becomes your first consideration because it can't be changed. When in doubt, start with the element that's unalterable.

Your topic can be a cakewalk—without the cake, of course—when it's handed to you. But don't get too smug; a set topic can be tricky if you don't know much about that particular subject. Writing can also be challenging when you have to select the specific *topic,* especially if you're given a very broad subject. In these instance, you may have to select a *subject* and decide how to limit it. I'll show you how to do this now.

Topic Time

Unless you're a magician, you can't make a silk purse from a sow's ear. Similarly, even a professional writer shudders at the challenge of writing a good essay from an unsuitable topic. Topic choice is a crucial factor in the success of your writing.

Look for a topic that not only suits your audience and purpose but also your personality and interests. Want to see real panic? Check out someone who got halfway through a paper and suddenly realized the topic just doesn't suit. By then, it's often too late to select a new topic. To avoid being caught in this bind, spend the time finding a topic that works for you, every time you write. That said, how can you do it? Here are some proven methods.

1. **Read.** I read the following true story in the newspaper:

   Two men tried to pull the front off a cash machine by running a chain from the machine to the bumper of their pickup truck. Instead of pulling the front panel off the machine, though, they pulled the bumper off their truck. Scared, they left the scene and drove home … with the chain still attached to the machine, their bumper still attached to the chain, and their vehicle's license plate still at-tached to the bumper.

Author! Author!

Dame Edith Sitwell gets the nod for the strangest writing routine of all: She liked to lie in an open coffin for a while before beginning her day's work. English poet John Donne did the same thing every now and again, but claimed it was preparation for death, not work.

Want to find great topics? Check out newspapers and magazines. In addition to reports of amazingly stupid criminal wannabes, you'll find a wealth of topic ideas. Here are some additional topic sources to consider:

➤ Novels

➤ Plays

➤ Essays

➤ Short stories

➤ Nonfiction books

➤ Web sites on the Internet

2. **Make the scene.** Did you know that ...

➤ A duck's quack doesn't echo, and no one knows why.

➤ Camel's milk doesn't curdle.

➤ Murphy's Oil Soap is the chemical most commonly used to clean elephants.

➤ Nondairy creamer is flammable.

Isn't life grand? There are great ideas all around you. Try these sources:

➤ Television

➤ Theater

➤ Radio

➤ Travel

➤ Movies

➤ Museums

➤ Your friends

➤ Sports

Write Angles

Keeping a journal also helps you get into the habit of writing. Remember that writing, like any other skill, improves with practice.

3. **Keep a writer's journal.** Many writers keep a journal in which they jot down topic ideas for future writings. If you want to try this method, set aside about 15 minutes a day. You can also include newspaper and magazine clippings that spark your imagination. Use your journal as a quarry from which you can mine ideas. Journaling is so important to your development as a writer that I devote an entire section to it in Chapter 15, "Picture This: Description."

4. **Freewrite.** Some writers favor a technique called "freewriting," in which they write nonstop for several minutes. To get the most from this method, don't censor your thoughts or stop to correct writing errors. No revisions, edits, or cross-outs, either. After your allotted writing time, stop and read what you've written. Take the best ideas and move on. If necessary, repeat the process until you have enough to go with for your specific writing task.

5. **Brainstorm.** A type of free-association, "brainstorming" means listing all the ideas that come to mind on a specific subject. To get the best results, let your mind relax as you write down your ideas. Brainstorming works equally well when you have to come up with your own topic and when you already have a topic and want to consider what elements to include.

Narrowing Your Topic

Once you have a general subject, you may have to narrow it to fit your audience and purpose. In addition, you'll have to consider the length of your final writing and the time in which you have to do it. For example, the "Civil War" is a great topic if you're aiming to fill 25 volumes and devote a decade of your life to the project. On the other hand, it's a completely unworkable topic if you're allotted 350 words and a day in which to write your essay.

Say you want to write something on roller coasters. Here are your parameters:

Subject:	roller coasters
Purpose:	to explain
Audience:	general readers
Length:	one paragraph, about 200 words
Writing time:	several hours

Given these limits, you figure you can describe three roller coasters. Here's what you select: "The Big Bad Wolf" ride at Busch Gardens, "The Loch Ness Monster," also at Busch Gardens, and the "Cyclone" at Coney Island's Astroland in Brooklyn, New York. Your final draft might look like this one:

> Busch Gardens in Williamsburg, Virginia, has two thrilling roller coasters, "The Big Bad Wolf" and "The Loch Ness Monster." This first ride doesn't run on tracks the way most roller coasters do. Instead, each four-passenger car hangs from an overhead rail. "The Wolf" zooms at 48 miles per hour over rooftops, then plunges 80 feet to skim the river below. "The Loch Ness Monster" is just as exciting. It has three steep drops and two 360-loops. Riders zoom at more than 60 miles per hour along nearly 3,500 feet of track. The best part is the long, dark, twisting tunnel. Inside it, monsters shriek, strobe lights burst into the inky blackness, and water sprays from the walls. Both these rides are great, but nothing beats the "Cyclone." Located at Coney Island's Astroland in Brooklyn, New York, this is probably the most famous roller coaster in the world. In fact, roller-coaster fans come from all over the globe to ride its 2,640 feet of death-defying track. The "Cyclone's" first drop is the steepest of any roller coaster in the world. It's terrifying! From the top of the first hill, riders can't see the track that keeps them from flying into space—but they can see other terrifying highs, lows, and curves.

Having trouble narrowing your topic? Try these methods.

1. **Make a web.** This visual approach helps you generate subtopics. As your ideas branch off in new directions, you can see relationships, forge connections, and so limit your topic.

   Word Watch

   Webbing is also called "clustering" and "mapping."

   Make a web by drawing a circle in the middle of a sheet of paper. Add lines radiating out from the circle. If you wish, you can label each line with a major topic division.
   At the end of each line, draw a circle and fill it in with a subtopic. Following is a sample web for a writing on the Congressional Medal of Honor.

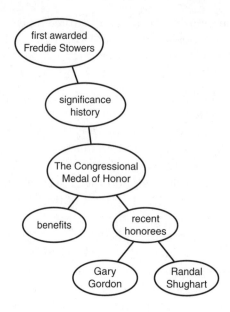

Based on this web, the paragraph has been narrowed to the following four subtopics:

a. Significance

b. History

c. Benefits

d. Recent honorees

Here's a sample paragraph, developed from this web:

Write Angles

Try turning off the computer monitor when you brainstorm or freewrite. This helps you focus on your thoughts without worrying about length or possible errors.

The Congressional Medal of Honor is the nation's highest military award for "uncommon valor" by men and women in the armed forces. It is given for actions that are above and beyond the call of duty in combat against an armed enemy. The medal was first awarded by the Army on March 25, 1863, and then by the Navy on April 3, 1863. In April 1991, President Bush awarded the Medal of Honor to World War I veteran Army Cpl. Freddie Stowers, posthumously. He was the first black soldier to receive the nation's highest honor for valor in either World War. Recipients of the medal receive $400 per month for life, a right to burial in Arlington National Cemetery, admission for them or their children to a service academy if they qualify and if quotas permit, and free travel on government aircraft to almost any where in the world, on a space-available basis.

President Clinton awarded the last medals to date posthumously in 1994 to two members of the ill-fated Delta Forces operation to capture warlord Gen. Aidid in Mogadishu on October 3, 1993. They are Master Sgt. Gary Gordon and Sgt. 1st Class Randall Shughart, who were killed trying to help wounded comrades.

2. **Create a chart.** Charting is another visual method you can use to generate ideas. While there are no restrictions on the charts you can design, the most common ones usually involve columns. Here's what a chart might look like as we narrow the Congressional Medal of Honor topic.

Topic: Congressional Medal of Honor

subtopics	details
significance	given for actions above and beyond the call of duty in combat
history	Army: March 25, 1863
	Navy: April 3, 1863
	April 1991: first black soldier honored (Army Cpl. Freddie Stowers)
benefits	$400 per month for life
	burial in Arlington National Cemetery
	admission to service academy, with qualifications
	free travel on government aircraft
recent honorees	1994: Master Sgt. Gary Gordon
	Sgt. 1st Class Randall Shughart

---

3. **Ask questions.** Asking the traditional *reporter's questions—Who? What? When? Where? Why?* and *How?*—as you plan forces you to approach a topic from several different vantage points. This helps you narrow your topic and focus your ideas.

Word Watch

The **reporter's questions** are also called the "5 Ws and H."

Author! Author!

If all else fails, desperate writers evoke the "Muse." We lump them altogether into one Super Muse, but according to Greek legends, there are actually nine Muses, the children of Zeus and Mnemosyne. The following chart describes the nine Muses. Call on the one most closely associated with your topic.

Muse	Symbols	Topics
Calliope	pen and scroll	epic poetry, eloquence
Clio	like Calliope	history, heroic deeds
Euterpe	double flute	lyric poetry, music
Thalia	comic mask	comedy
Melpomene	tragic mask	tragedy, song
Terpsichore	lyre (instrument)	lyric poetry, song
Erato	stringed instrument	erotic and love poetry
Polyhymnia	lyre	chants, hymns
Urania	wand, globe	astronomy

Getting the Facts: Researching

How can you make your writing entertaining, persuasive, and descriptive? What separates compelling prose from colorless prose? It's all in the details, chum. And how can you get the details? You check out a variety of reliable source materials.

As you research, you gather facts, statistics, expert opinions, and anecdotes. At the same time, you begin to shape your material by deciding what you'll include and what gets the old heave-ho.

Shaping and Drafting

Effective writing presents the ideas in an organized, logical manner. Shaping your writing involves *grouping similar ideas, eliminating nonessential ideas,* and *arranging ideas in a logical order.* Here's the scoop:

➤ **Group related ideas.** Sort your research into two categories: *general* and *specific.* Then place all the specific ideas under the general ones. Sorting ideas like this demonstrates that effective writing starts with general statements backed up by specific details.

➤ **Eliminate nonessential ideas.** If an idea doesn't fit, set it aside. Thanks to computers, you can safely stash the idea in another file and return to it later if you change your mind.

➤ **Arrange ideas in a logical order.** Decide what information to present first, second, third, and so on. There are several different ways you can order your ideas, including *chronological order* (order of time), *the order of importance* (most important to least important), or *spatial order* (left to right, right to left, and so on). In Chapter 9, "A Place for Everything, and Everything in Its Place," you'll learn each of these methods of organization, as well as others.

Writer's Block

Just because a source appears in print, in the media, or online doesn't mean that it's valid. As a result, you must carefully evaluate every source you find before you use it by reading critically and carefully. I cover this in Chapter 18, "Seek and Ye Shall Find."

Write Angles

Having a clear set of goals for each writing task and keeping your audience and purpose in mind makes it easier to write.

Outlines

Many writers—novices and pros alike—favor *outlining* to help them arrange their ideas in a logical sequence. Outlines are a great way to break big writing tasks (like this book!) into manageable chunks. Following is a general outline format you can use for your writing.

Title: _____

I. First main idea _____

_____

   A. Detail _____

      1. Reason or example _____

         a. Detail _____

         b. Detail _____

      2. Reason or example _____

         a. Detail _____

         b. Detail _____

   B. Detail _____

      1. Reason or example _____

         a. Detail _____

         b. Detail _____

      2. Reason or example _____

         a. Detail _____

         b. Detail _____

II. Second main idea _____

_____

   A. Detail _____

      1. Reason or example _____

         a. Detail _____

         b. Detail _____

      2. Reason or example _____

         a. Detail _____

         b. Detail _____

   B. Detail _____

      1. Reason or example _____

         a. Detail _____

         b. Detail _____

    2. Reason or example _____

        a. Detail _____

        b. Detail _____

Although it might seem that you spend most of your time drafting, studies have shown that only about one third of your time is actually spent at this stage. Nonetheless, people can still work up a serious sweat as they draft, leading to first-class procrastination. Stay tuned.

Big Night: Drafting

There's no one way to write, as long as you do it when you have to. If you're the life of the party, for example, you're unlikely to do much planning, preferring to work out your ideas as you write. On the other hand, if you're shy, you're far more likely to prepare detailed outlines before you get into writing actual sentences and paragraphs. No matter: Find the method that works with your personality and writing task.

> **Writer's Block**
>
> Understand that your first draft won't be perfect. Even when time is tight, you'll have to revise and proofread.

You can use your notes and outline as a framework for your first draft. Start at the beginning and work through everything. Try to write at a steady pace until you reach a natural breaking point, such as the end of a section or a meal. Most writers learn early to stop for a meal.

If you write without a net (any planning notes and outlines), look for links among ideas. Remember, you're not under any obligation to use all or even part of this first draft. This realization can free you to explore new directions.

No matter how you ultimately decide to create your first draft, set up a schedule and stick to it. It's tempting to put off writing, as with any tasks we find difficult or challenging. I'm cracking the whip, so get to it!

Spit and Polish: Revising and Editing

Jacqueline Susann wrote on colored paper, in this order: yellow for draft #1, blue for draft #2, pink for draft #3, and white for the final copy. Revision worked for *her,* sure enough.

Here's a hot tip: Your writing will *always* be better if you go over it with a critical eye. Revise and edit your drafts by cutting material, replacing material, adding material, and rearranging what's already there. Don't be shocked if your revised draft bears as much resemblance to the first draft as Arnold Schwarzenegger and Danny DeVito to each other.

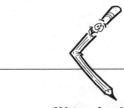

Follow these steps as you revise:

1. Let your draft "cool off" so you'll see where you want to make changes. Allow at least a day between drafting and revising.

2. First, read your draft once all the way through.

3. Decide whether you want to revise this draft or start again.

4. If you revise, focus on one issue at a time. For example, first read for organization, next for details, and so on.

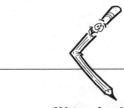

Write Angles

When you shop for feedback, look for readers who can be both objective and ruthless. For example, fiancés rarely make good editors because they're still smitten by your charms. Your teenagers can be superb editors because they're not afraid to tell the truth and they're usually ruthless with their parents anyway.

You don't have to fly solo here, so get someone to help. Select readers whose opinions you value and tell them exactly what you want them to look for in your document. For example, if you're seeking feedback on a first draft, you'll most likely want comments about organization and tone. By the second draft, however, you'll probably be looking for feedback on style rather than content. Try not to be defensive. If the feedback is negative, don't take it personally (even if it was intended that way).

The Proof's in the Pudding—and the Writing: Proofreading

You wouldn't leave the house without glancing in the mirror and patting that stray strand of hair in place. In the same way, you'd never turn in a piece of writing that hadn't been carefully proofread.

Writer's Block

Even if you're pressed for time, *never* skip the proofreading stage in the writing process.

When you proofread your writing, look for errors in spelling, punctuation, grammar, and usage. We're creatures of habit, so we're most likely to make the same writing mistakes over and over. For instance, your Waterloo might be run-ons, fragments, or spelling words with ie/ei. Check for these errors first—but don't neglect all the other wonderful typos that can slip right by like the years between 30 and 50.

Here are some tricks of the proofreading trade:

➤ First go-round, read the document for meaning. Check that nothing has been omitted.

➤ Second shot, look for typos.

➤ Double- and triple-check numbers, names, and first and last paragraphs.

➤ Read your document aloud while another person follows along on a typed copy.

➤ Have a friend proofread your paper—only after you've checked it, of course.

Brain Freeze

Writer's block, like hemorrhoids, is no laughing matter.

While most people who suffer from writer's block have the worst time moving from planning to drafting, people can get the writing willies at any stage in the process.

Write Angles

The larger the type, the more likely you are to assume that it's correct. Be extra careful with titles and headings; that's where some of the worst errors occur.

Not to worry; Dr. Mommy-the-Writing-Teacher is here. Try the following ideas if you've gotten bitten by the writer's block bug.

➤ Get something on paper. Brainstorming, freewriting, and the other planning techniques discussed earlier in this chapter work beautifully for this purpose.

➤ Schmooze with a friend—but only briefly. Tossing ideas around can sometimes get the creative juices flowing. Don't turn this into an all-day gab fest, however, even if it's a good buddy.

➤ Ignore factors such as line length or word count when you first start out. Concentrate instead on getting a draft in place.

➤ Write the draft out of order, starting with the parts you find easiest. For instance, no one says you can't start with the conclusion, move to the body, and end with the introduction.

➤ Vary your method of writing. If you usually keyboard, write longhand, and vice versa.

➤ Figure out what's keeping you from writing. Deal with the problem, and then go back to writing.

➤ Set aside a specific amount of time and make yourself write for all of it. Don't worry about the product.

➤ Set realistic goals, such as one paragraph or a page at a time, not an entire novel at one sitting.

The Least You Need to Know

➤ Writing is a process that can be mastered with instruction, practice, and con-centration.

➤ The writing process includes planning, researching, shaping and drafting, revis-ing and editing, and proofreading.

➤ Planning involves determining your purpose, audience, and topic. Find topics by reading, experience, keeping a writer's journal, freewriting, and brain-storming.

➤ Narrow your topic by webbing, charting, and asking questions. Then research to get the facts you need to support your thesis.

➤ Be sure to revise, edit, and proofread your writing.

➤ There are effective techniques for dealing with writer's block and procrastina-tion.

Chapter 9

A Place for Everything, and Everything in Its Place

In This Chapter

➤ Expose with exposition

➤ Plan persuasive essays

➤ Order in the essay: chronological order, order of importance, Q and A format, and spatial order

---

You know some of the big lies: "I never inhaled" and "We can still be good friends." Here's the biggest lie of all:

> One size fits all when it comes to organizing your paragraphs.

Okay, so maybe it's not the biggest lie *of all,* but it's one of the biggest lies when it comes to writing. That's because there are actually many different ways to organize your paragraphs, depending on your purpose, audience, type of writing, and topic. In this chapter, you'll learn all about the different organizational plans. Then you'll be equipped to select the one you need for each specific writing task.

Special Delivery

You know how to sort your shirts, groceries, and lovers. Some methods work better than others, but as long as you can find your black turtleneck, a jar of mayo, and the right sweetie for each occasion, you're home free. In a similar way, each piece of writing you do must be organized so your readers can find the information they need.

Write Angles

Reader expectation is a powerful factor when you select an organizational plan, but also consider your material and purpose. Some topics are better suited to specific methods of organization.

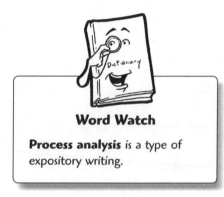

Word Watch

Process analysis is a type of expository writing.

When you choose an organizational plan for your writing, you decide how to best present your information. No one plan fits all types of writing, but certain plans often fit best with specific types of writing. For example, an informative essay is often arranged from *main ideas to supporting details*. The following outline shows how this plays out. (Each roman numeral stands for a major division within the essay, one or more paragraphs. Capital letters stand for sentences.)

The Main Event

An informative essay is *expository* writing, since it explains, shows, and tells. Here's how many expository essays are structured:

Informative Essay Structure

    I. Introduction

        A. Topic sentence

        B. Summary of points to follow

        C. Transition or lead-in sentence to the next paragraph

   II. Background information (if necessary)

  III. Your first main point

  IV. Your second main point

   V. Your third main point, etc.

 VI. Conclusion

The following informative essay is organized according to this plan:

Let's Hear It for TV!

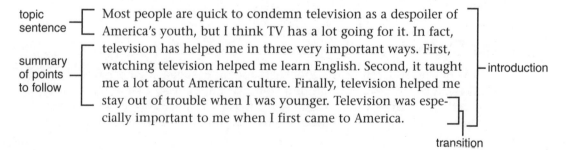

topic sentence — Most people are quick to condemn television as a despoiler of America's youth, but I think TV has a lot going for it. In fact,

summary of points to follow — television has helped me in three very important ways. First, watching television helped me learn English. Second, it taught me a lot about American culture. Finally, television helped me stay out of trouble when I was younger. Television was especially important to me when I first came to America.

— introduction

transition

first main point — Most important, watching television helped me learn English. When I came to the United States, I spoke only a few words of English. Since I was 12 years old, I was placed in the seventh grade. I was the same age as every other student in the classroom, but I could not communicate with a single person. When I got home from school every day, I did not have anything to do since I did not have any friends. To pass the time, I watched cartoons and the local news. As I gradually learned more English, I started watching sitcoms and soap operas. My English improved rapidly. As a result, I was able to communicate more easily with my classmates and teacher and so did much better in school. I made some good friends, too, and felt more at home in my new country.

second main point — Television also helped me learn about American culture. I found out from watching television that life in America is very different in some regards from life in my birthplace, Korea. In Korea, for example, most of the television commercials are about education. In America, however, most of the commercials are about cars, food, and clothing. This suggested to me that Americans are encouraged to be materialistic. I probably would have learned this eventually without television, but watching TV helped me realize what American life is like much more quickly.

third main point — Finally, watching television helped me stay out of trouble. As you have already realized, I watched a great deal of television when I was a child. Some of the commercials were public service announcements about drug and alcohol abuse. These commercials were very slick and persuasive. As a result, they helped me realize the importance of staying straight. In addition, I rarely hung out at night because I preferred to be inside watching my favorite shows, especially movies.

conclusion — As an immigrant, I found television an invaluable way of learning English. Thanks to TV, I quickly mastered the rudiments of the language and learned a great deal about American culture. Television also helped me avoid drug and alcohol abuse and even gangs. So don't be so quick to criticize TV; for many of us, it's a lifeline.

Author! Author!

All English isn't the same. British English, used not only in Great Britain but also in India, the West Indies, and parts of Africa, uses some words and phrases differently from American English. For example, here are some common British words and their American equivalents: *lorry* (truck), *lift* (elevator), *bonnet* (car hood), *chips* (French fries), *crisps* (snack chips), *flat* (apartment), *barrister* or *solicitor* (attorney or lawyer), *nappy* (diaper), *mate* (buddy), *sweets* (candy).

My Way or the Highway?

A persuasive essay, in contrast, is likely to be arranged this way:

Persuasive Essay Structure

I. Introduction

   A. Topic sentence

   B. Summary of points to follow

   C. Transition or lead-in sentence to the next paragraph

II. Background (if necessary)

III. Opposition (one to two points)

IV. Your side of the argument (two to four points)

V. Conclusion

Or

Persuasive Essay Structure

I. Introduction

   A. Topic sentence

   B. Summary of points to follow

   C. Transition or lead-in sentence to the next paragraph

II. Background (if necessary)

III. Your first main point

    A. Opposition

    B. Your side

IV. Your second main point

    A. Opposition

    B. Your side

V. Your third main point, etc.

    A. Opposition

    B. Your side

VI. Conclusion

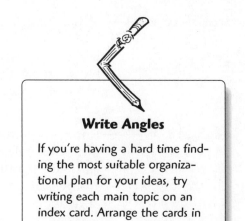

Write Angles

If you're having a hard time finding the most suitable organizational plan for your ideas, try writing each main topic on an index card. Arrange the cards in various ways to see which arrangement makes the most sense, given your purpose and readers.

Here's a model persuasive essay organized the second way. Notice how smoothly the writer deals with the opposition within each paragraph.

Luck of the Draw?

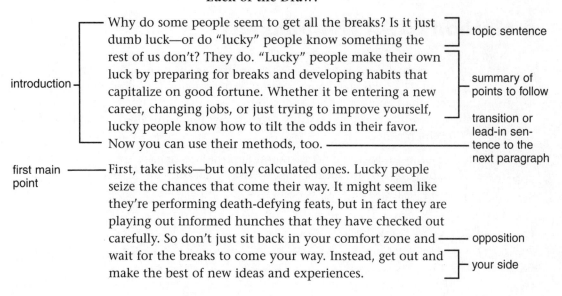

introduction — Why do some people seem to get all the breaks? Is it just dumb luck—or do "lucky" people know something the rest of us don't? They do. "Lucky" people make their own luck by preparing for breaks and developing habits that capitalize on good fortune. Whether it be entering a new career, changing jobs, or just trying to improve yourself, lucky people know how to tilt the odds in their favor. Now you can use their methods, too.

— topic sentence

summary of points to follow

transition or lead-in sentence to the next paragraph

first main point — First, take risks—but only calculated ones. Lucky people seize the chances that come their way. It might seem like they're performing death-defying feats, but in fact they are playing out informed hunches that they have checked out carefully. So don't just sit back in your comfort zone and wait for the breaks to come your way. Instead, get out and make the best of new ideas and experiences.

— opposition

— your side

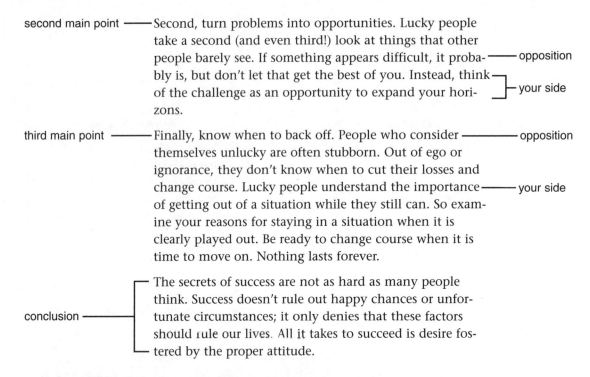

second main point ——Second, turn problems into opportunities. Lucky people take a second (and even third!) look at things that other people barely see. If something appears difficult, it proba- —— opposition bly is, but don't let that get the best of you. Instead, think of the challenge as an opportunity to expand your hori- ⊢ your side zons.

third main point ——— Finally, know when to back off. People who consider ——— opposition themselves unlucky are often stubborn. Out of ego or ignorance, they don't know when to cut their losses and change course. Lucky people understand the importance—— your side of getting out of a situation while they still can. So examine your reasons for staying in a situation when it is clearly played out. Be ready to change course when it is time to move on. Nothing lasts forever.

conclusion ———— The secrets of success are not as hard as many people think. Success doesn't rule out happy chances or unfortunate circumstances; it only denies that these factors should rule our lives. All it takes to succeed is desire fostered by the proper attitude.

A Method to All This Madness

Sometimes a piece of writing seems to fall easily into a certain structure, the way a tall glass of lemonade and sandals go with summer and hot cocoa and fuzzy slippers go with winter. That's because some types of writing are better suited to one organizational pattern than another. Other times, however, more than one organizational pattern will work with a particular writing project. The following chart presents some of the most useful parallels.

The third column shows the most common applications of each specific organizational plan, but that's by no means the only way each one can be used. Use the chart as a guide, not an ironclad set of rules you must obey.

118

Organizational Plan	Definition	Types of Writing
Chronological order	order of time	autobiographies
		biographies
		narrative poems
		novels
		process analysis
		short stories
Order of importance	rank	business letters
		business e-mail
		expository writing
		memos
		persuasive essays
		reports
		term papers
Question and answer	alternating Q's and A's	expository writing
		interviews
		persuasive essays
Spatial order	order of space	descriptive essays
		poems

Now, let's examine each method of organization in detail, starting with chronological order.

Time Marches On: Chronological Order

Chronological order presents details and events in time-order. A great way to show a series of events or a process unfolding, chronological order also allows you to jump ahead or back to fill in gaps in the narrative. A *flash forward* is a future event out of sequence; a *flashback* is a scene that breaks into the story to show an earlier part of the action. Flash forwards and flashbacks help fill in missing information, explain the characters' actions, and advance the plot.

Word Watch

Chronological order means arranging the events of a story in time order from first to last.

119

Write Angles

To be sure you've included all the details in the correct order when you write a piece in chronological order, make a flow chart or timeline as part of your prewriting.

When you use chronological order ...

➤ Check that the sequence of events will be clear to your reader.

➤ Add transitional words to help readers track time.

➤ Shift verb tenses if you break chronological order with a flashback or flash forward.

Here's a biographical essay I wrote for inclusion in a reference text about well-known authors. Since I was describing my development as a writer, I used chronological order, tracking my life from childhood to the present.

One Writer's Life

shows early part of story — In retrospect, I suppose that I've always been a writer, scribbling loopy crayon messages as a toddler, writing gossipy notes as a teenager, and typing dense letters in college. English was my best subject, but I never imagined making writing a career: I had never met a "real" writer and couldn't believe that people actually made a living as wordsmiths.

date signals time passing — My writing remained purely epistolary until 1981, when I was home for four months from teaching after the birth of my first child. Casting about for something to fill the time between burping and bathing my son, I decided to write a review book for the Advanced Placement Exam in English. I wish I could recount exactly when the lightning bolt hit, but I can't remember any one moment of illumination. Most likely, someone had passed an offhand remark in the teachers' room about the need for such a book. With the boundless confidence of the novice, I created a Table of Contents, resurrected and updated my resumé, wrote a cover letter, and sent the bundle to every single possible publisher listed in *Literary Market Place*.

Who bought the manuscript? ARCO—the very first name on the list. My editors at this test-prep division of Macmillan, especially the brilliant Linda Bernbach, proved both patient and kind, gently initiating me into the mysteries of the book biz.

transition signals ——— But, back to our story! I returned to teaching in September
end of flash forward of 1981, and writing was far back on the burner as I taught, completed my Ph.D., and took care of home and hearth. In 1984 the earth shifted once again, as I was laid off from the high school due to declining enrollment. I finished my Ph.D. and birthed our second child, a daughter. Although a year later I took a job teaching English in the State University of New York, I began to feel an almost physical need to write. Suddenly, letters weren't enough; I needed to write something solid to sink my teeth into. The contacts I had made with ARCO helped me begin to publish more and in greater variety, as did some friendships I had made with a handful of extraordinarily talented and generous writers. Soon, I was doing a wide variety of self-help and educational materials. My career had begun.

It's What's Up Front That Counts: Order of Importance

With this organizational plan, you draw attention to your key ideas by placing them first. This method is often used in persuasive writing, as the writer begins with the strongest ideas to create the most convincing argument. It's also a winner with expository writing, as the following essay shows:

Friend or Foe?

most
important ——— Described as a "swimming and eating machine without
ideas peer," the shark is considered an evolutionary success story, having changed little over 60 million years. Sharks are models of efficiency with their boneless skeletons, simple brains, generalized nervous systems, and simple internal structures. Their hydrodynamically designed shapes, razor-sharp replaceable teeth, powerful jaws, and voracious appetites make them excellent marauders. Through scavenging and predation, the 250 species of sharks perform a valuable service in maintaining the ecological balance of the oceans. Their well-developed sensory systems enable them to detect extreme dilutions of blood in water, low-frequency sounds of splashing made by a fish in distress, and movements and contrasts in water.

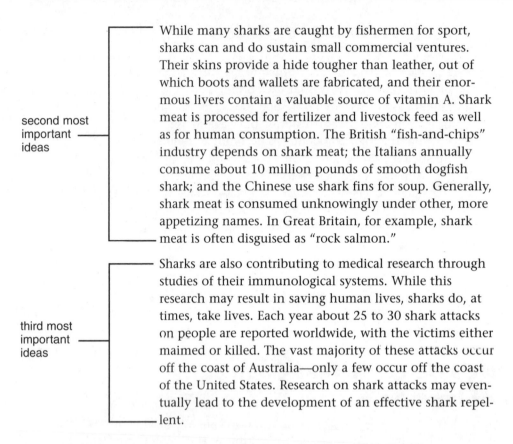

second most important ideas

While many sharks are caught by fishermen for sport, sharks can and do sustain small commercial ventures. Their skins provide a hide tougher than leather, out of which boots and wallets are fabricated, and their enormous livers contain a valuable source of vitamin A. Shark meat is processed for fertilizer and livestock feed as well as for human consumption. The British "fish-and-chips" industry depends on shark meat; the Italians annually consume about 10 million pounds of smooth dogfish shark; and the Chinese use shark fins for soup. Generally, shark meat is consumed unknowingly under other, more appetizing names. In Great Britain, for example, shark meat is often disguised as "rock salmon."

third most important ideas

Sharks are also contributing to medical research through studies of their immunological systems. While this research may result in saving human lives, sharks do, at times, take lives. Each year about 25 to 30 shark attacks on people are reported worldwide, with the victims either maimed or killed. The vast majority of these attacks occur off the coast of Australia—only a few occur off the coast of the United States. Research on shark attacks may eventually lead to the development of an effective shark repellent.

Asked and Answered: Question and Answer

As you've already learned, starting with an intriguing question grabs your readers' interest. You can continue this method by arranging your entire essay in a "Q and A" format. The following consumer pamphlet is arranged this way. You'll see that it conveys a great deal of information clearly and concisely.

Know Your Rights

You have rights as a consumer. Knowing and exercising those rights can save you money. Here are the three questions we are asked most often. The answers may surprise you.

Am I entitled to a refund when I return merchandise?

Say you've gotten a birthday present from a favorite nephew. While you appreciate his thoughtfulness, leopard-print thigh-high boots aren't really your style. No problem—just return the boots to the store and exchange them for something more subdued.

But you may have a problem after all! Contrary to what many consumers think, stores are not under any obligation to accept returns. If merchandise is defective, some state laws require that the seller replace the item with a comparable product; even then, however, there is no obligation for the merchant to issue a refund. When the item is something you simply don't like—whether it was a gift you received or something you bought yourself and then changed your mind—neither state nor federal law requires the seller to take it back.

What can I do with a credit slip if the store goes out of business?

You returned those boots and the merchant willingly gave you a credit slip when you couldn't find anything else you liked. Six months pass and the store has gone out of business. What do you do now?

Unless the store reopens under new ownership and that owner chooses to honor your credit slip (there's no obligation to do so), you are probably out of luck.

Can I get a discount for paying cash?

As things stand now, stores are not allowed to place a surcharge on credit purchases; they may, however, be given permission to do so. Stores *are* allowed under federal law to offer discounts to cash customers, as long as the discount is offered to all customers and a notice that a discount is given is clearly posted. Don't be afraid to get the information you need to make important consumer decisions.

To make the questions and answers pop out of the text, you can set them off with italic or boldface type. This is done very often in technical and business documents. In addition, the questions can be set off with numbers or letters, as in 1. or a).

Space, the Final Frontier: Spatial Order

"I've looked at love from both sides now," the tune goes, and the same can be said for your topics. You can describe a scene in the following ways:

➤ Right to left or vice versa

➤ Top to bottom or vice versa

➤ Inside out or vice versa

➤ Foreground to background or vice versa

➤ Around in a circle, starting and ending at the same place

As you read the following essay on cats, figure out how the writer arranged the details.

Top Cats

Cats are possibly the most beautiful and graceful of all animals. They are sleek, with fine fur that is often strikingly marked with spots or stripes. Although cats can vary in size from the familiar house cat to the huge Siberian tiger, they look alike, act alike, and are built alike.

Moving from the inside out, a cat's skeleton, consisting of about 250 bones, provides a rigid framework for the body's soft parts, allowing the cat to move with grace and agility. In both large and small cats, the skull is highly specialized for killing prey and eating it in the shortest possible time, an important feature for survival. There are seven neck vertebrae, as in most mammals, but they are compressed, making the cat's neck shorter in comparison to the rest of its body.

The cat's eyes are large and round, which allows a wide field of vision. Moving outward, we come to the cat's teeth. They are very sharp, because cats do not chew their food. Rather, they bolt it down. Since they don't gnaw bones as dogs do, cats do not need as many teeth as their canine cousins.

A cat's fur coat has many uses. It keeps the animal warm, acts as camouflage, and carries the animal's scent. It also acts as an organ of touch by means of each hair's sensitive roots. All wild cats have a two-layered coat: an undercoat of fine soft wool and an outer coat of coarser, longer hairs. The hairs of the outer coat carry the fur's spotted or striped pattern.

Author! Author!

For the last 3,000 years, since they were first revered as sacred animals by the ancient Egyptians, cats have played a major role in the folklore of many countries. For example, the Birman is the sacred cat of the Myanma (formerly Burma). According to legend, a Burmese temple was attacked and the high priest killed. His favorite white temple cat jumped on the priest's head and was transformed into a Birman. Where the paws touched the priest, the fur remained white, a symbol of goodness. This miracle encouraged the remaining priests to resist the invaders.

The writer moves from inside out, starting with the cat's skeleton, moving to its eyes and teeth, and finally to its coat. This spatial order lets readers get to know the cat "inside out"!

Life is full of difficult decisions. Fortunately, choosing an organizational plan for your writing doesn't have to be one of the nail-biters. Any arrangement that shows a clear and logical relationship among ideas will suit the bill. In every case, one idea should build on the previous one in a natural and sound way. When you select an organizational plan, remember to consider your purpose, audience, type of writing, and topic.

Write Angles

There's also the **order of impression,** in which the writer provides information according to the way each detail catches the writer's eye. Most often used in descriptive essays and personal narratives, this method helps readers grasp the writer's main idea and unique point of view.

The Least You Need to Know

➤ There are many different ways to organize your paragraphs, depending on your purpose, audience, type of writing, and topic.

➤ Informative essays are often arranged from main ideas to supporting details.

➤ Persuasive essays present the opposition before the writer's points or alternate each point and the opposition. This helps show the weaknesses in your opponent's arguments.

➤ Chronological order, the order of time, is a useful way to show a series of events or a process.

➤ Order of importance draws attention to your key ideas by placing them first.

➤ Question and answer format works well with expository writing, especially technical and business documents.

➤ Spatial order is well suited to descriptive pieces.

Chapter 10

Making Your Bones

> ## In This Chapter
>
> ➤ Super starts
>
> ➤ Introductions that use statements of purpose, anecdotes, jokes, quotations, questions, descriptions, or statistics
>
> ➤ Paragraphs that elaborate with statistics, facts, sensory details, examples, quotations, and anecdotes
>
> ➤ Sweet endings
>
> ➤ Conclusions that summarize and restate, offer an opinion, or call for action

You know good writing when you see it, no matter what the topic or type. That's because good writing holds your attention and makes you want to read on. How can you make *your* writing interesting? Great writing starts with great bones—the introduction, body, and conclusion.

In this chapter, you'll first learn how to write boffo beginnings that suit your audience and purpose. Then we'll move onto the body paragraphs, and I'll show you how to elaborate on your ideas with details, especially numbers, facts, sensory details, examples, quotations, and anecdotes. You'll learn how to flesh out your ideas with effective and engaging information. You'll put some solid meat on those great bones.

Finally, you'll discover the importance of a strong finish. I'll show you how to craft conclusions that summarize and restate, offer an opinion, or call for action. So let the fun begin!

Start at the Very Beginning: Introductions

First impressions matter, whether you're meeting someone new or opening an essay. If you can win over friends at the beginning, they'll probably stick with you over the long haul. It's the same with readers—catch 'em early, and they're yours for the duration.

There are many different ways to open your writings, depending on your audience, purpose, and genre. Stay tuned: more on that later. Right now, let's discuss your options. You can open your writing with one or more of the following seven techniques:

1. Statement of purpose
2. Anecdote
3. Humor
4. Quotation
5. Question
6. Description
7. Statistics

Here's how to master the magnificent seven, one at a time.

Write Angles

Study opening paragraphs in newspaper and magazine articles. You might be surprised to discover that topic sentences such as statements of purpose often appear in the middle and end of paragraphs as well as in the beginning.

Just the Facts, Ma'am

If you want to begin a composition, essay, or article clearly and directly, you can't go wrong with a straightforward statement of purpose. In fact, the majority of your writing—especially expository essays, e-mails, and business letters—will start this way. A direct opening is also well suited for the following types of writing:

➤ Essay tests
➤ Letters to the editor
➤ News stories
➤ Process analysis essays ("how to" do something)
➤ Research reports

Three different factual openings you can use as models for your own writing follow. Notice how each writer states all the relevant information right up front.

From a business letter …

Dear Ms. Algieri:

I am writing in response to your advertisement for a Production Manager which appeared in the *LA Times* on Sunday, February 28, 1999. After speaking with your assistant, Justin Tyme, I decided to fax my resumé to you. As it shows, my experience and background very closely match the requirements for this position.

From an essay test …

Market socialism is a system of economics based on the principle of government regulation and/or ownership of the means of production and property. The "founder" of this system was John Maynard Keynes, an English economist. During Keynes' time, the predominant idea was Free Capitalism—that the government should have no control over the economy.

From a research report …

Web pages shape people's lives with their enormous amount of rich information, the most up-to-date news, and of course, dazzling Web graphics. The two main formats widely used for Web graphics are GIF (Graphics Interchange Format) and JPEG (Joint Photographic Experts Group).

Once Upon a Time …

Do you yearn to build suspense in your writing? Do you want to have your readers hanging on the edge of their seats? If so, you'll want to open your writings with an *anecdote,* a brief story that illustrates your point. Few things hook your readers as well as a brief story, well told.

Anecdotes make great openings for the following types of writing:

➤ Autobiographical essays

➤ Biographical writing

➤ Humorous pieces

➤ Informative essays

➤ Oral histories

➤ Personal narratives

➤ Research or term papers

➤ Speeches

Word Watch

An **anecdote** is an illustrative story that serves to introduce your topic and grab your reader's attention.

Writer's Block

Keep your opening anecdotes short—no more than one to two paragraphs—or you run the risk of losing the thread of your narrative. An anecdote that overstays its welcome is worse than no anecdote at all.

Select an anecdote that sets the tone or mood of the writing. To be successful, the anecdote must *directly* relate to the topic you'll be discussing.

Here's an anecdote that opened personal narrative about a woman who learned that she is a survivor. The anecdote is the first two paragraphs.

> At the age of 20, I was a headstrong young woman who thought, "I know everything." I did not realize my naiveté and lack of common sense until I found myself in tears, on the New Jersey Turnpike, with $15 in my pocket, driving a 1969 Volkswagen death-trap with no floorboards and rotting brakes.

Following is an anecdotal opening from a term paper. The paper argues that Prozac's side effects may outweigh its benefits:

> Melissa Ryder was suffering from depression. To relieve her symptoms, her doctor prescribed Prozac. "After only six days on Prozac, I was in far worse shape than I had ever been before," she said in an interview. The bizarre side effects of the medication included uncontrollable trembling, urges to stab herself, and thoughts of killing her children. Melissa Ryder is no longer using Prozac and her condition has improved greatly (Bower 24).

> Despite Prozac's tremendous global popularity, some serious issues are being raised about its negative side effects. Prozac's many side effects can do more damage than the makers of the drug could ever have imagined, as Melissa Ryder's case illustrates. While Prozac can help some people suffering from depression and other mental disorders, it should only be used with great care.

How about one more model for good measure? Following is an anecdotal opening from an informative essay about vinegar (yes, vinegar) for a newspaper essay:

> Cleopatra, queen of Egypt, made history when she made a bet that she could eat at one meal the value of a million sisterces. One million sisterces was many years' wages for the average worker. Everyone thought that her wager was impossible. After all, how could anyone eat so much at a single meal?

> Cleopatra was able to eat a meal worth so much by putting a million sisterces worth of pearls into a glass of vinegar. Then she set the goblet aside while the dinner was served. The vinegar dissolved the pearls. At the end of the meal, when it was time for her to fulfill her gamble, she simply drank the dissolved pearls. Cleopatra won her bet because she knew that vinegar would dissolve pearls. Vinegar has many practical uses as well.

Author! Author!

"The most important sentence in any article is the first one," writer William Zinsser claims. "If it doesn't induce your reader to proceed to the second sentence, the article is dead. And if the second sentence doesn't induce the reader to continue to the third sentence, it is equally dead. Of such a progression of sentences, each tugging the reader forward until he is safely hooked, a writer constructs that fateful unit: the opening paragraph" (*On Writing Well*).

Hit the Funny Bone

As with an anecdotal opening, a humorous opening can be an effective way to spark your reader's interest as you introduce your topic. Humor works best in "lighter" writings, such as …

➤ Autobiographical writings

➤ E-mail

➤ Personal and informal letters

➤ Speeches

➤ Oral histories

➤ Personal narratives

➤ Short stories

Following is a humorous opening for an essay about dealing with "empty-nest syndrome," when the kids grow up and move away, leaving Mom and Dad alone.

Writer's Block

Few things can explode with the force of a bad joke. Only use humor in your writing if you and your audience are comfortable with it—and others have said that you're a joke meister.

> Seymour Schwartz was a good, deeply religious man. When Seymour passed away, he was greeted at the Pearly Gates by the Lord himself. "Hungry, Seymour?" asked the Lord.

> "I could eat," Seymour replied. So the Lord opened a can of tuna and added a chunk of fresh rye bread. While eating his humble

meal, Seymour looked down into Hell and saw the inhabitants devouring huge steaks, lobsters, pheasants, pastries, and fine wines. Curious but deeply trusting, Seymour stayed quiet.

The next day the Lord again invited Seymour to join him for a meal, and again the Lord served tuna and rye bread.

Once again looking down, Seymour could see the denizens of Hell enjoying caviar, champagne, lamb, truffles, and chocolates. Still Seymour said nothing.

The following day, mealtime arrived and another can of tuna was opened. Seymour could contain himself no longer. Meekly, he said, "Lord, I am grateful to be in Heaven with you as a reward for the pious, obedient life I led. But here in Heaven all I get to eat is tuna and a piece of rye bread and in the Other Place they eat like emperors and kings! Forgive me, O Lord, but I just don't understand."

The Lord sighed, "Seymour, for just two people, does it pay to cook?"

Quote/Unquote

Opening an essay with a quotation is an old standby, and with good cause—it's a sure-fire winner when used correctly. Someone else's wise or witty comment can make your point and spark your reader's interest. Of course, the quotation must fit your point to be relevant and suitable.

Open with a quotation to give your writing weight and authority. This works especially well when you're writing …

➤ Essay tests
➤ Letters to the editor
➤ News stories
➤ Persuasive essays
➤ Research reports
➤ Speeches

Write Angles

Always be sure to give complete and accurate credit for every quotation you use, whether you use the quotation in the introduction, body, or conclusion of your writing.

For example, more than one movie reviewer has opened an assessment of a new flick with this quote from Shakespeare's *Hamlet:* "A hit, a very palpable hit."

The following quote from poet T.S. Eliot quite nicely opened a letter to the editor about senior citizens:

"The years between fifty and seventy are the hardest. You are always being asked to do things, yet you are not decrepit enough to turn them down."

But even quotations from less-famous sources can engage your readers' interest. One clever best man toasted the bride and groom with this gem from the famous and prolific writer "Anonymous":

> "May your joys be as deep as the ocean
> And your misfortunes as light as the foam."

Ask a Question

Ask a question to grab your readers by the ears and pull them into your prose. Few readers can resist the lure of offering their two cents, even if they don't know much about the topic.

Opening your introduction with a question is an especially handy technique to use if you are a student writing essay tests—just turn the prompt into a question and you're home free. For example, let's say the prompt asks you to take a side on this issue:

> "Recently, many American educators have proposed that students be required to become competent in a foreign language. Students, they insist, should be able to speak, read, and write a second language. In a 350-word article for your local newspaper, state your opinion for or against this proposal."

Turn the prompt into a question, such as "Should students be required to learn to speak, read, and write a second language?" From there, briefly present your arguments and make sure your conclusion is complete.

You can also open with a question when you're drafting the following types of writing:

➤ Expository essays (cause-effect, classify and divide, comparison-contrast, and so on)

➤ Oral histories

➤ Personal narratives

➤ Letters to the editor

➤ Research papers

Following is an example of an introduction that opens with a question. It's taken from a scientific research paper on homeotic genes:

> Why is an arm an arm? Why is a leg a leg? Arms develop differently from legs due to the action of special genes. Every organism is designed with specialized structures. For example, human arms and legs are both made of muscle and

bone, but the overall shape and the details of the two types of limbs are different. These genes, which determine how parts of the body are shaped, or patterned, are called homeotic genes.

Describe It

A vivid, detailed description can effectively begin many types of writing. That's because the colorful words and strong images set the scene and spark the reader's imagination.

Descriptions work particularly well with the following types of writing:

➤ Eyewitness accounts

➤ Feature stories

➤ Oral histories

➤ Personal narratives

➤ Stories

Following is a description that opens a feature story on one of the oddest toys ever created:

> It stretches, snaps, and shatters when hit with a heavy object. If you press a blob of it against a comic book or newspaper, it picks up the image—even the colors. It can be used to build strength in a person's hands and remove lint from clothing. It's out of this world—literally. Astronauts use it to hold tools to space capsule surfaces during the weightlessness of space travel. What is it?

That's the question James Wright asked himself in the early 1940s when he created the odd stuff. By 1949, the odd stuff—now called Silly Putty—had become a best-selling toy, showing that Wright's accident has real staying power.

The Numbers Game

Statistics, like quotations from authorities, give your writing power and establish you as a credible author. Openings that use statistics suggest that you've done your homework so you're someone who can be trusted.

Statistics are especially useful to open ...

➤ Essay tests

➤ Letters to the editor

➤ News stories

➤ Persuasive essays

➤ Research reports

➤ Speeches

Following is a sample opening from a news story about the damage caused by major storms. Notice how the writer used statistics to help readers grasp the extent of the damage:

> Every year, storms kill and injure thousands of people around the world and cause billions of dollars worth of damage. Storms account for nearly all the most expensive America disasters. The costliest disaster in American history is Hurricane Andrew, the storm that ravaged Florida and Louisiana in 1992. Hurricane Andrew left $15.5 billion in damage. The Xenia tornadoes that occurred in 1974 in the Midwest left $1.3 billion in damage. Tsunamis have also caused considerable damage.

> The worst floods of the century struck the Midwest in 1993. At times, as much as one inch of rain fell every six minutes. Floodwaters rose up and down the Mississippi River basin. Missouri, Illinois, and Iowa were the hardest hit. Thousands of families were forced to flee their homes. More than eight billion dollars worth of property was damaged.

So many choices, so little time! How can you decide which type of opening to select? Your choice goes back to the basics you learned in Chapter 3: *audience* and *purpose*. As you plan your opening, always keep your audience and purpose firmly in mind.

Consider your audience: For example, are you writing a letter to the editor or a science paper? Each offers a different set of possibilities. You might open a letter to the editor with a statement of the situation or a question, but you're more likely to open a science paper with a set of statistics or the thesis.

Consider your purpose: For example, do you want to inform your readers, persuade them, or entertain them? Each purpose calls for a different type of introduction.

Body Talk

What makes the following paragraph so interesting? Read it to find out:

> The film industry changed from silent films to the "talkies" in the late 1920s, after the success in 1927 of *The Jazz Singer*. Mickey Mouse was one of the few "stars" who made a smooth transition from silent films to talkies. In November 1928, Mickey made his first sound cartoon, *Steamboat Willie*. Walt Disney (1901–1966) drew Mickey as well as used his own voice for Mickey's high-pitched tones. Within a year, hundreds of Mickey Mouse clubs had sprung up all across America. By 1931, more than a million people belong to a Mickey Mouse club. The phenomenon was not confined to America, however. In

London, Madame Tussaud's famous wax museum placed a wax figure of Mickey alongside its statues of other famous film stars. In 1933, according to Disney Studios, Mickey received 800,000 fan letters—an average of more than 2,000 letters a day. To date, no "star" has ever received as much fan mail as Mickey Mouse.

For a change, it's not the economy. When it comes to writing, the focus is on details, the words that *elaborate* on the writer's ideas. By describing the topic more fully, the details make it come alive for readers. Elaborate on your ideas to help your readers form vivid mental pictures and understand your point.

What types of details can you use in your writing? They fall into five main categories. Here are the Fab Five:

1. Statistics and facts
2. Sensory details
3. Examples
4. Quotations
5. Anecdotes

Let me show you how to use each method of elaboration to make your ideas come alive on the page.

Stats It!

Use *statistics* and *facts* to add information to your writing. Statistics are especially useful when you're writing a persuasive essay or any of the following types of writing:

➤ Business letters

➤ Cause-and-effect essays

➤ Definition essays

➤ News stories

➤ Process analysis ("how to" papers)

The following passage contains both facts and statistics to explain the history and impact of one of America's most popular games:

Word Watch

Elaboration is adding details to writing to make your words more precise, descriptive, and evocative.

Write Angles

Remember that **facts** are statements that can be proven true through direct observation, experimentation, or through a reference source. **Statistics** are facts expressed as numbers.

A world-wide economic Depression in the 1930s left many people unemployed. One such person was Charles Darrow of Philadelphia, Pennsylvania, who had lost his job as a heating engineer. To try to make a living, Darrow invented a board game he called "Monopoly." It made him a millionaire, although not at first. Initially, Darrow tried to sell his idea to the leading game manufacturer in America, Parker Brothers. The company turned the game down because they felt it was too complicated to play. No one could be bothered reading all the directions, they argued. In desperation, Darrow used his own money to have 5,000 games made by a small company. He sold the games himself and the craze spread. Seeing the success of the game, Parker Brothers changed its mind and purchased the game for manufacturing and distribution. In 1975, twice as much Monopoly money was printed in the United States as real money. In most years, the face value of the Monopoly money is much more than the face value of the entire U.S. Treasury's output. All told, nearly 100 million Monopoly sets have been sold since 1935.

Detailed Work

Want to make your writing sizzle? Kick the details up a notch and make them appeal to one of the five senses: appearance, feels, tastes, smells, and sounds. This creates *sensory details,* which work particularly well in the following types of writing:

➤ Journals

➤ Personal essays

➤ Poems

➤ Observations and descriptions

Following is an excerpt from a story about Matthew Henson and Robert Peary, the first explorers to reach the North Pole. The sensory details are so vivid that you're going to want to snuggle back under the covers!

Writer's Block

Don't be misled by the four examples listed here; they're just to give you an idea of how to use sensory details. Actually, you can't write *anything* without including sensory details.

Far, far north of the Earth, a small band of men struggled against icy blasts of wind. The shrieking Arctic gales shot needles of ice into their faces. The bitter east wind was like a piercing blade, slicing right through their thick fur parkas. It was 60 degrees below zero, so cold that if the men spilled a cup of hot coffee, it vanished before hitting the ground. The extreme cold turned the water into tiny crystals of ice, too small to see. It was so cold that the men's noses, cheeks, and toes could turn black with frostbite in seconds. Their brandy was frozen solid. Even the petroleum jelly was frozen. Like plastic, it was hard and white. But these men were determined to complete their journey. Robert Peary and Matthew Henson were going to be the first people to reach the North Pole—or die trying.

Let's Make an Example of It

You paint the broad strokes with generalizations and fill in the spaces with examples. Examples make your writing clear by offering specific instances. Here's a handful of writing types that just cry out for examples:

➤ Comparison-contrast essays

➤ Definition essays

➤ E-mail

➤ Letters to the editor

➤ Research reports and term papers

➤ Problem-solution essays

➤ Writing about literature

➤ Writing across disciplines

The following passage gives examples of how meteorologists forecast the weather:

Ever hear the phrase: "Everybody always talks about the weather, but no one ever does anything about it"? Well, we do talk about the weather a lot, because it affects almost everything that we do. Of course, forecasters don't just look out the window to prepare the weather report you see on television. Rather, they use a sophisticated weather information network located all over—and above—the planet. Over a dozen weather satellites orbit the earth constantly. Other weather satellites remain in fixed positions 22,000 miles above the equator. Their rotating cameras can photograph the entire earth, except for the North and South Poles. The North and South Poles are photographed by additional satellites, which follow north-south and south-north routes. Airplanes and balloons make daily ascents to gather data. Weather stations in almost every country on earth contribute information for forecasters to use.

Quote Me

Quotations function in the opening paragraph to establish the writer's credibility. The same is true in the body of the writing. That's because including quotations from credible sources marks you as a writer who can be trusted. Use quotations to your advantage in these types of writing:

➤ Cause-and-effect essays

➤ Problem-solution essays

➤ News stories

➤ Critical reviews

➤ Research reports

Write Angles

Don't forget to give full credit to all sources you use in your writing. Otherwise, you'll be guilty of **plagiarism**—literary theft. This is covered in detail in Part 4, "Just Shoot Me Now: Research Papers and Term Papers."

Here's a sample from a research paper on the writer Edith Wharton. The source quoted is Louis Auchincloss, a well-known and well-respected literary critic who specializes in Wharton's life and work. Notice how the writer used the quotation to back up the main idea of the passage:

> In 1910, when she was 48 years old, Wharton and her husband sold their home and moved permanently to France. As the noted literary critic and Wharton specialist Louis Auchincloss remarks, "Wharton had at last found a world where everything blended: beautiful surroundings, intellectual companionship, a society that combined a respect for the past with a vital concern for the present. London was within easy reach, and she could be in constant touch with writers whose conversation was as polished and civilized as their prose—James, Bourget, Lubbock, and Sturgis" (Auchincloss, 26). These writers, and their influence on Wharton's life and work, also reveal her concern with English mores and manners.

Story Time

You learned earlier in this chapter that anecdotes (brief stories) can help you craft interesting opening paragraphs. Anecdotes can also help you make your point clearer in the body of your writing. Anecdotes work especially well with personal narratives, oral histories, biographies, and stories.

Here's an example from a professional writer, Rudolph A. Anaya, from his essay "A Celebration of Grandfathers":

> I remember once, while hoeing the fields, I came upon an anthill, and before I knew it I was badly bitten. After he had covered my welts with the cool mud from the irrigation ditch, my grandfather calmly said, "Know where you stand."

End Game: Conclusions

Never can say good-bye? All good things must come to an end, and a piece of writing is no exception. Concluding a piece of writing involves more than just slapping on a final paragraph, however. An effective conclusion must fulfill these three functions:

1. Pull together all your ideas.
2. Leave your readers feeling satisfied.
3. Prompt readers to continue thinking about your writing after they've finished reading it.

All endings are not created equally. As with introductions, the ending method you select depends on your purpose, audience, and *genre*. For example, you might end a story with the final event in the narrative. Or, you could delight your readers with a surprise ending. An essay, in contrast, most often ends with a summary or a recommendation. Since most everyday writing involves nonfiction, let's focus on ways to write conclusions for essays, compositions, reviews, and e-mail.

Word Watch

A **genre** is a type of writing: short stories, novels, plays, biographies, autobiographies, and nonfiction, for example.

Summarize and Restate

The vast majority of essays and business letters (especially letters to the editor and letters of complaint and inquiry) conclude with a synopsis of the main points you've presented in the body.

Going back over the main idea in your conclusion helps your audience remember your most important points. To use this method, restate the main idea in your first sentence. Then summarize each of the key points you made. Be sure to restate your ideas in a way that is different from your essay. This will help you avoid repetition and so make your essay more effective.

The following article on the original Mr. Blue Jeans, Levi Strauss, concludes with a summary and restatement:

Author! Author!

"The perfect ending should take the reader slightly by surprise and yet seem exactly right to him. He didn't expect the article to end so soon, or so abruptly, or to say what it said. But he knows it when he sees it. It is like the curtain line in a theatrical comedy. We are in the middle of a scene (we think) when suddenly one of the actors says something funny, or outrageous, or epigrammatic, and the lights go out. We are momentarily startled to find the scene over, and then delighted by the aptness of how it ended.

—William Zinsser, *On Writing Well*

This is the story of how a rugged American symbol was born by a sudden inspiration. In 1850, 21-year-old Levi Strauss traveled from New York to San Francisco. A peddler, Strauss took needles, thread, pots, pans, ribbons, yarn, scissors, buttons, and canvas across the country to sell to the gold miners. The small items sold well, but Strauss found himself stuck with the rolls of canvas because it was not heavy enough to be used for tents. While talking to one of the miners, Strauss learned that it was almost impossible to find sturdy pants that would stand up to the rigors of digging. On the spot, Strauss measured the man with a piece of string. For six dollars in gold dust, Strauss had a piece of the leftover canvas made into a pair of stiff but rugged pants. The miner was delighted with the results, and word got around about "those pants of Levi's." Business was so good that Levi Strauss was soon out of canvas. He wrote to his two brothers in New York to send more. He received instead a tough brown cotton cloth made in Nimes, France, called *serge de Nimes*. Almost at once, the foreign term was shortened to *denim*. Strauss had the cloth dyed a rich blue color called "indigo," which became a company trademark. These were the humble beginnings of a fashion that would take the world by storm.

State an Opinion

To conclude your writing with an opinion, first briefly summarize the topic and then share your feelings on the issue. This method is especially effective for a letter, critical review, and persuasive essay where your opinion colors the reader's attitude and provides a sense of closure. Check out the following example. How do you feel about the writer's opinion?

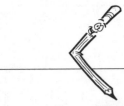

Write Angles

Notice that I said "state *an* opinion" rather than "state *your* opinion." While the opinion in your conclusion will normally be something you believe in, it doesn't have to be. You're free to take whatever side you want—even if you don't strictly believe it.

One of the many problems the welfare system faces is long-term participation. While welfare was designed to provide *temporary* financial relief, it usually turns to be a major income provider for poor families. The current system discourages work because, most of the time, work that is available pays minimum wage and is physically straining. Minimum wage is only a small amount of money over what the welfare check would provide for no work at all.

Call for Action

You've laid out the problem or situation in the body of your writing. Now, in the conclusion, tell your audience what you want them to think or do. The recommendation can be in the form of a suggestion, demand, or plea—or any combination of these proposals—to move readers to action. Here's an example on the same theme of welfare reform:

It is obvious that the current welfare system must be reformed. I believe the first step toward meeting that objective is to terminate any public financial aid that is shown to be based on the applicants' deception. The next step is to instill better values in children and newly formed families. Schools should focus on family issues and family life and structure. Children should be taught to be responsible for their own actions. These methods can help us successfully re-work an untenable and destructive system and so help *all* Americans.

Author! Author!

Talk about great conclusions: When the famous grammarian Dominique Bouhours was dying, his last words are reported to have been: "I am about to—or I am going to—die. Either expression is used." And here's a sorry conclusion: According to legend, the Greek playwright Aeschylus was killed when an eagle dropped a tortoise on his bald head, mistaking it for a rock. Ouch.

The Least You Need to Know

➤ Introductions matter, so craft them carefully, suiting the method to your purpose and audience.

➤ Your introduction can be a statement of purpose, an anecdote, a joke, a quotation, a question, a description, or a statistic.

➤ In the body of your paper, elaborate on ideas with details. These can take the form of statistics, facts, sensory details, examples, quotations, and anecdotes.

➤ Effective conclusions pull together all your ideas, leave your readers feeling satisfied, and move them to continue thinking about your writing.

➤ Your conclusion can be a summary and restatement, opinion, or call for action.

Chapter 11

Personal Best: Revising and Editing

In This Chapter

➤ The revising and editing stage in the writing process

➤ Revise by deleting, elaborating, punctuating, and rewording

➤ And don't forget to revise for unity!

Producer Russel Crouse asked the award-winning playwright Eugene O'Neill if he would cut some passages in *Ah, Wilderness* to make the play shorter. O'Neill was adamant about not cutting a single word from any of his plays, but he finally agreed to trim a bit. The next day O'Neill called Crouse and told him, "You'll be happy to learn I cut 15 minutes."

"How?" Crouse ecstatically replied. "Where did you do it? I'll be right over to get the changes."

"Oh, there aren't any changes in the text," O'Neill explained, "but you know we've played this in four acts. I've decided to cut out the third intermission."

Some people find revision more difficult than others.

Chapter 9, "A Place for Everything, and Everything in Its Place," taught you how to organize your ideas; Chapter 10, "Making Your Bones," how to write your first drafts. In this chapter, you'll learn how to improve your writing by editing and revising. First, I'll explain why revision is so important. Then, you'll learn to revise by deleting unnecessary words, phrases, and information.

Next, you'll discover how to make your writing buff by bulking up the details and examples. I'll show you how to make your writing better by revising the punctuation and rewording, too. Finally, you'll learn how to improve your drafts by using transitions to connect related ideas.

Word Watch

Revising and editing are evaluating your writing to find ways to make it better. The process involves deleting, adding, replacing, and moving words, sentences, and passages in the text.

Judgment Day

Revising and editing are part of the creative process of writing. As you learned in Chapter 8, "Write This Way," when you come to this step in the writing process, you evaluate your document to see what needs to be deleted, added, and moved to make your message and style more effective. Revision isn't one-stop shopping, however: Expect to rethink your writing several times before you're satisfied with it. As you make each round of improvements, you again assess your writing to see if it suits your audience and purpose.

Revising and editing, like exercise and oat bran, is good and good for you. It doesn't mean that you didn't do a fine job on your rough draft or that you're not a good writer. In fact, just the opposite is the case. The finest writers tend to do the most revising. The very word *revise*, meaning "to see again," shows that this process involves judging and rethinking your first thoughts to make improvements.

Stand Back!

It's also important that you step back from your work and see it with a fresh and impartial eye. As the anecdote that opened this chapter shows, writers tend to be an anal-compulsive bunch. We like to hold on to each and every one of our words, those little pearls of wisdom, all so carefully chosen. Don't go over to the dark side, Luke. As you revise and edit, try to be objective about your work, to judge it as others would.

I'm Ready for My Close-Up, Mr. DeMille

As you begin to revise your essay, think about your *audience* and *purpose* for writing. Remember that your *audience* is the people who will read your essay. To meet their needs, ask yourself, "What does my audience know about my topic?" Recall that your *purpose* is your reason for writing. To focus on the purpose, ask yourself, "What am I trying to accomplish in my essay?" The four main purposes are:

1. To entertain (narrative)

2. To prove a point (persuasive)

3. To explain an issue (expository)

4. To describe something (descriptive)

Of course, your writing can—and usually will—have more than one purpose.

Author! Author!

Thinking of asking a friend or lover to read your drafts to help you edit them? It's a great idea from your standpoint, but your reader may not be as enthusiastic. British Prime Minister and writer Benjamin Disraeli (1804–1881) had a standard reply unmatched for diplomatic ambiguity for people who sent him unsolicited manuscripts to read: "Many thanks; I shall lose no time in reading it."

Next, revise the form and content of your work. *Form* is the shape of the writing. For example, the form of your writing may be a story or a poem. Adjust your draft until it meets the requirements for that specific type of writing. Plays, for instance, tell the story through dialogue, so your final version of a play will likely be virtually all conversation.

Content is what you're saying. When you revise for content, you make sure that each part of your draft is clear and logical.

Once you understand how the revision and editing process works, you'll find the process relatively painless and even interesting. It's actually my favorite part of writing because it's like a puzzle, as I try to see how each piece fits best. Let's start by seeing how deleting material can often make your writing stronger.

Less Can Be More: Revise by Deleting

A university creative writing class was asked to write a concise essay containing these four elements:

1. Religion

2. Royalty

3. Sex

4. Mystery

The prize-winning essay read:

"My God," said the Queen. "I'm pregnant. I wonder who did it?"

Okay, so sometimes we get carried away when it comes to revision. Good things often come in small packages, but never fear: You don't have to cut to the bone to improve your writing.

As you learned earlier in this chapter, revision also involves deleting material that's off the topic or repeats what you've already said. As you revise, look for ways to tighten your sentences by removing extraneous material that clogs your writing. The following table provides some examples.

Look For	Revision
Repetition	*Cut the unnecessary material*
Bring it to *final* closure.	Bring it to closure.
Filler	*Cut the fluff*
The point that I am trying to make is that you should never miss a good chance to shut up.	Never miss a good chance to shut up.
Unnecessary modifiers	*Select the best modifier*
The *big, huge, massive* cloud *completely* covered *over* the sun.	The massive cloud covered the sun.
Passive voice	*Active voice*
Falling asleep is done by the average person in seven minutes.	The average person falls asleep in seven minutes.

Give it a shot with the following passage. See how much unnecessary material you can cut to improve this anecdote.

Write Angles

Don't automatically revise the passive voice into the active voice. The passive voice is preferable if you don't want to assign blame or don't know who is doing the action.

Sherlock Holmes and Watson were camping in the wooded forest. They had gone to bed and were lying beneath the dark night sky. Holmes said, "Watson, look up to the sky. What is seen by you?"

"Thousands and thousands and thousands of bright, shining, glittering stars are seen by me."

"And what do all those thousands and thousands and thousands of bright, shining, glittering stars mean to you?" Holmes asked.

"What I mean to say is that of all the stars, celestial bodies, and planets in the giant universe, we are truly fortunate and lucky to be here on Earth.

In light of the fact that we are tiny, small, and little in God's eyes, we should struggle every day to be worthy of our blessings. To get to the point, in a meteorological sense, it means a bright and sunny day will be had by us tomorrow. What does it mean to you, Holmes?"

"To me, it means our tent has been stolen by someone."

Here's a possible revision. Notice how eliminating the extra words and revising the passive voice into the active voice makes the writing much stronger.

> Sherlock Holmes and Watson were camping in the forest. They had gone to bed and were lying beneath the night sky. Holmes said, "Watson, look up. What do you see?"
>
> "I see thousands of stars."
>
> "And what does that mean to you?" Holmes asked.
>
> "Of all the planets in the universe, we are truly fortunate to be here on Earth. We are small in God's eyes, but we should struggle every day to be worthy of our blessings. In a meteorological sense, it means we'll have a sunny day tomorrow. What does it mean to you, Holmes?"
>
> "To me, it means someone has stolen our tent."

Write Angles

Be ruthless with these windy fillers: *as a matter of fact, because of the fact that, for the purpose of, in a very real sense, in light of the fact that, to get to the point, and what I mean to say.* Cut them all from your writing!

All Dressed Up and Ready to Go: Revise by Elaborating

As you learned in Chapter 10, effective writing uses relevant support to bring your topic to life, prove your point, and engage your readers. This "support" can be details, facts, definitions, examples, statistics, and quotations. Adding them to a draft is called *elaboration*.

Word Watch

Elaboration is adding details to support your main idea.

149

As you read your draft, see where you need to add more detail to make your writing come alive. Use the following table to help you focus your exploration.

Look For	Revision
Unclear topic	*Audience analysis*
	Never assume that your audience has your level of knowledge about a topic—especially if you've done research or work in the field.
Facts missing	*Add hard data*
	Persuasive and expository writing especially will often require specific facts, dates, examples, and expert opinions to make your case or explain fully.
Lack of sensory details	*Add details on five senses*
	Focus on things you can see, smell, touch, taste, and hear.

Following is the first draft of a paragraph about the legendary baseball player Jackie Robinson. The writer assumed readers knew more about the topic and so didn't add enough elaboration. As a result, we're left in the lurch. As you read, think about what else you would like to know about the topic.

> The color barrier that had kept major league sports white-only did not fall in baseball until Branch Rickey brought up Jackie Robinson from the minor leagues. Facing down hostility and prejudice with dignity and superb playing, Robinson was named Rookie of the Year. The way was opened for black athletes who have since enriched professional sports. Nonetheless, it was not until years later that an African-American became the coach of a major United States professional sports team. The man was Bill Russell, and his team won the NBA championship with Russell as player-coach.

Here's the revised paragraph. What new information did the writer add? How did the elaboration improve the passage?

> The color barrier that had kept major league sports white-only did not fall in baseball until 1947, when Branch Rickey of the Brooklyn Dodgers brought up Jackie Robinson from the minor leagues. Facing down hostility and prejudice with dignity and superb playing, Robinson was named Rookie of the Year. The way was opened for black athletes who have since enriched professional sports. Nonetheless, it was not until 1966 that an African-American became the coach of a major United States professional sports team. The man was Bill Russell, and

the team was the Boston Celtics of the National Basketball Association. In 1968 and 1969, the Celtics won the NBA championship with Russell as player-coach. As a full-time player, the six-foot nine-inch center led the Celtics to eight straight NBA championships from 1959 to 1966. He was voted the league's most valuable player five times.

> **Write Angles**
>
> There's such a thing as too much elaboration. You're under no obligation to include everything you found. Don't beat the topic to death.

Little Things Matter a Lot: Revise Punctuation

A panda walked into a restaurant and ordered a sandwich and a drink. When he finished, he pulled out a pistol and shot up the place, scaring customers and breaking dishes, glasses, and liquor bottles before turning to leave.

Shocked, the manager said, "Hey, where are you going?"

The panda glanced back over his shoulder and said, "I'm a panda—look it up," before disappearing out the door.

The bartender pulled out a dictionary and thumbed through it until he found an entry for PANDA. The definition read, "A tree-dwelling animal of Asian origin characterized by distinct black-and-white markings. Eats shoots and leaves."

Sometimes you'll have to add punctuation to make your meaning clear. As the previous anecdote illustrates, there's a big difference between "eats, shoots, and leaves" and "eats shoots and leaves." Add a comma here, take one out there, and you might radically alter your meaning. Punctuation creates meaning just as words do.

Try it yourself on the following letter by adding the punctuation you think is necessary. (You'll have to add capitalization, too, to show the start of a new sentence.)

Dear John,

I want a man who knows what love is all about you are generous kind thoughtful people who are not like you admit to being useless and inferior you have ruined me for other men I yearn for you I have no feelings whatsoever when we're apart I can forever be happy will you let me be yours

Mary

Here are two variations. See how the change in punctuation drastically alters the meaning in each case.

Version #1:

Dear John,

I want a man who knows what love is all about. You are generous, kind, thoughtful. People who are not like you admit to being useless and inferior. You have ruined me for other men. I yearn for you. I have no feelings whatsoever when we're apart. I can forever be happy—will you let me be yours?

Mary

Version #2:

Dear John,

I want a man who knows what love is. All about you are generous, kind, thoughtful people, who are not like you. Admit to being useless and inferior. You have ruined me. For other men, I yearn. For you, I have no feelings whatsoever. When we're apart, I can forever be happy. Will you let me be?

Yours,

Mary

So don't neglect the little guys—commas, periods, semicolons, and colons—as you focus on revising the words, phrases, and sentences in your writing.

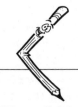

Write Angles

If you edit on your computer, be sure to print out every version. Don't just save it to your hard drive or floppy; it's too easy to lose a version by copying over it accidentally.

Come Again? Revise by Rewording

Other times, you'll have to select new words to get your meaning across. When you revise by rewording, you replace words and revise sentences to make your writing accurate and fresh. Here's how to do it:

➤ Look for words that you used too often.

➤ Replace repeated nouns with pronouns.

➤ Substitute other repeated words with synonyms.

➤ Ditch empty, overused adjectives such as *excellent* and *nice*.

➤ Sharpen your words by finding the precise word you want, not a close relative.

The following paragraph needs a little help from the Edit Meister. Smooth its rough edges by using the suggestions you just learned.

> There have been many controversial World Series, but the most controversial World Series was certainly the thrown World Series of 1919. Even though the White Sox were favored five to one, about two million dollars had been bet on the Cincinnati Reds to win. Sensing a nice thing, Jack Doyle, the head of a New York City betting ring, fixed the controversial World Series. Actually, the World Series seemed okay, with the Reds winning it five games to three. For this reason, very few people suspected the excellent players had been bought. Nevertheless, the next day sportswriter Hugh Fullerton said that something was not quite right. As a result of Fullerton's suggestion, the owner of the White Sox, Charles Comiskey, offered money to anyone who could prove a problem. It took almost a year for three men—Lefty Williams, Eddie Cicotte, and Joe Jackson—to sign confessions admitting the series had been changed and they were in on it. But just before the trial was supposed to start, the confessions esoterically vanished from the office of the Illinois State Attorney. When the case was finally tried, the three men denied having made any confessions and having been involved in any way in the rigging scheme because there was no proof against the three men.

Here's my trim. See how the passage snaps to life with a little judicious editing:

> There have been many controversial World Series, but the most infamous was certainly the thrown World Series of 1919. Even though the White Sox were favored five to one, about two million dollars had been bet on the Cincinnati Reds to win. Sensing a sure thing, Jack Doyle, the head of a New York City betting ring, rigged the series. Actually, the series seemed quite respectable, with the Reds winning it five games to three. For this reason, very few people suspected the players had been bought. Nevertheless, the next day sportswriter Hugh Fullerton suggested that something was not quite right. As a result of Fullerton's suggestion, the owner of the White Sox, Charles Comiskey, offered a cash reward to anyone who could prove a fix. It took almost a year for three men—Lefty Williams, Eddie Cicotte, and Joe Jackson—to sign confessions admitting the series had been fixed and they were in on it. But just before the trial was scheduled to start, the confessions mysteriously vanished from the office of the Illinois State Attorney. When the case was finally tried, the three men denied having made any confessions and having been involved in any way in the rigging scheme because there was no proof against them.

It's a Lock: Revise for Unity

As you learned in Chapter 6, "Sentence Sense," to make your writing more succinct, you can also combine related sentences. When you revise for unity, also look for sentences that are off the topic. The following paragraph, for example, contains two sentences that ravage the *unity* because they have nothing to do with the topic. See if you can find them.

(1) Even though a tornado is one of the smallest of all types of storms, it is one of the most dangerous of all storms because of its swiftly spinning winds and unpredictable path. (2) All tornadoes have one common characteristic—the rapidly rotating winds that cause them to spin like a fierce top. (3) Hurricanes can also be very dangerous storms, and they are very common in my neighborhood.

(4) Little accurate information on the speed of winds in a tornado is available, but estimates place them often at more than 300 miles per hour. (5) When nearby, a tornado usually sounds like the roaring of hundreds of airplanes. (6) A tornado's whirling winds toss thousands of pounds of debris like matchsticks and smash down on other property, causing even more damage. (7) There was a tornado in my neighborhood last year, but luckily we were away at the time.

Betcha got it: Sentences 3 and 7 are off-topic.

Word Watch

Unity, a single effect, is often linked to coherence, the logical arrangement of ideas within a passage.

Word Watch

A **transition** is a word or phrase that links related ideas. Examples include *also, in addition, for example, specifically,* and *on the other hand.*

Crazy Glue Your Sentences: Transitions

If your ideas don't cling together like teenagers in love, you can add *transitions.* A transition can be a word (such as *also*) or a phrase (such as *for example*) that shows how ideas are related. Each transitional word and phrase indicates a slightly different shade of meaning, so choose your transitions as carefully as you choose your peaches.

The following table shows the most common transitions and their meanings. I've lumped related transitions together, but you should tease out their gentle shades of meaning. For example, *and* joins two equal things, but *also* indicates something has been added to the mix.

Transitions	Meaning
and, also, besides, finally, further, furthermore, in addition, moreover, next, too, then	addition
as a result, because, consequently, for that reason, therefore, since, so, thus	cause and effect
for example, for instance, namely, specifically	example
different from, in comparison, in contrast, in the same way, like, likewise, on the one hand, same as, similarly, unlike	comparison
certainly, granted, naturally, of course, to be sure	concession
however, in contrast, on the contrary, on the other hand, nevertheless, nonetheless, still, yet	contrast
better, best, finally, first, last, least important, more important, most of all, second	importance
above, across, adjacent, at the side, below, beside, here, in the distance, in the back, in the front, near, nearby, next to, there, where	location
accordingly, as a result, consequently, due to this, so, therefore	result
as a result, finally, hence, summary, in brief, in conclusion, in short, in summary, on the whole	summary
after, at length, before, currently, during, eventually, finally, first, immediately, in the future, later, meanwhile, next, now, second, secondly, soon, subsequently, then, third	time order

Combining sentences isn't always the way to go. Sometimes, you'll want to keep your sentences short and crisp to get a staccato rhythm going, as this Rodney Dangerfield joke shows: "Once when I was lost, I saw a policeman and asked him to help me find my parents. I said, 'Do you think we'll ever find them?' He said, 'I don't know, kid. There are so many places they can hide.'"

Smooth as Silk

Here's an example of sentences revised for unity, thanks to a handy transition or two:

Flabby:	The Vikings consumed a bucket or two of vibrant brew they called "aul" (ale). The Vikings headed fearlessly into battle often without armor or even shirts. The term *berserk* means "bare shirt" in Norse. The term took on the meaning of their wild battles.
Fit:	<u>After</u> consuming a bucket or two of vibrant brew they called "aul" (ale), the Vikings would head fearlessly into battle, often without armor or even shirts. The term *berserk* means "bare shirt" in Norse, and <u>eventually</u> took on the meaning of their wild battles.

A Master at Work

A final word on revision: Like all other worthwhile endeavors, it's messy and time-consuming. If you edit by hand, you'll be doing a lot of crossing out, writing in, and arrow-drawing. If you edit on a computer, expect a lot of cut and paste.

Here's how the famous Romantic British poet John Keats edited *The Eve of St. Agnes*. This is one of the most famous of all manuscripts. Notice how many changes Keats made.

JOHN KEATS
From The Eve of St. Agnes

[*Stanza 26*]

But soon his heart revives—her prayers said
She ~~lays aside her heel~~   pearled
                strips her hair of all its ∧ wreathes pearl
~~Unclasps her bosom jewels~~
~~And twist it in one knot upon her head~~

                                        ~~soon~~
But soon his heart revives—her praying done,
    Of all its wreathed pearl she strips her hair
Unclasps her warmed jewels one by one
            ~~her bursting~~
    Loosens ~~the boddice from her~~
            ~~her Boddice lace string~~
            ~~her Boddice, and her bosom bar~~
            her

[HERE KEATS BEGINS A NEW SHEET]

Loosens ~~her fragrant boddice and doth bare~~
~~Her~~

                    26

    Anon
~~But soon~~ his heart revives—her praying done,
                                    frees:
    Of all its wreathe'd pearl hair she ~~strips~~
Unclasps her warmed jewels one by one

                                        by degrees
                            ~~to her knees~~
    Loosens her fragrant boddice: ~~and down slips~~
Her sweet attire ~~falls light creeps down by~~
                    creeps rusteling to her knees
                    Mermaid   in sea weed
Half hidden like ~~a Syren of the Sea~~
~~And more melodious~~
                    dreaming
She stands a while in ∧ thought; and sees
                        on
In fancy fair Saint Agnes ~~in~~ her bed
But dares not look behind or all the charm is ~~fl~~ dead

[*Stanza 30*]

            But
~~And still she slept:~~
And still she slept an azure-lidden sleep
        In blanched lined, smooth and lavender'd
    While he from frorth the closet brough a heap
                fruits
        Of candied ~~sweets sweets, with~~
                    apple Quince and plumb and gound
                            creamed
    With jellies soother than the ~~dairy~~ curd
                    tinct
    And lucent syrups ~~smooth~~ with ciannamon
    ~~And sugar'd dates from that oer Euphrates fard~~
                ~~in Brigantine transferrd~~
        Manna and daites in ~~Bragtine transferrd~~
                    ~~and manna wild transferrd~~
    ~~And Manna wild and Bragantine~~
                        sugar'd dates transferred
    ~~In Brigantine from Fez~~
        From fez—and spiced danties every one
            ~~glutted~~
From ~~wealthy~~ Samarchand to cedard lebanon
            silken

argosy

157

The Least You Need to Know

➤ Revising and editing involve deleting, adding, replacing, and moving words, sentences, and passages in the text.

➤ Consider your audience, purpose, form, and content as you revise and edit.

➤ Revise by deleting irrelevant material and adding necessary elaboration.

➤ As you revise, use punctuation to make your meaning clear.

➤ Revise for unity by combining related sentences, deleting sentences that are off-topic and adding transitions.

Part 3
Write for Success

I love being a writer. What I can't stand is the paper work.
—Peter De Vries

No one can deny there's a lot of that! This part of the book zeroes in on the four types of writing introduced earlier: exposition, narration, persuasion, and description. You'll learn how to construct effective explanations, fascinating stories, convincing arguments, expressive journals, and memorable poems. The last chapter in this section explores writing across the curriculum. I'll guide you through the conventions of writing in the social sciences, natural sciences, and humanities.

Chapter 12

You Got Some 'Splaining to Do, Lucy: Exposition

In This Chapter

➤ Cause and effect

➤ Classify-divide

➤ Comparison-contrast

➤ Definition

➤ Process analysis

As you learned in Chapter 2, "The Write Way," *exposition* is writing that instructs, explains, shows, or tells. Most of the writing you do in school and in life is expository. Exposition is writing that shows, explains, and tells by giving information about a specific topic. In this chapter, you'll discover the different forms that exposition can take: cause and effect, classify-divide, comparison-contrast, definition, and process analysis. By the time you finish this chapter, you'll be equipped to organize the information in your expository letters, memos, e-mails, essays, and reports to best suit your topic, purpose, and audience.

The Perfect Couple: Cause and Effect

Question: Why are there so many Smiths in the phone book?

Answer: They all have phones.

A perfect example of a cause-and-effect relationship. The cause is *why* something happens; the effect is *result, what happens* due to the cause. Therefore, cause-and-effect essays establish a relationship between events.

Cause and effect usually (but not always) happen in time order: The *cause* comes first, creating an *effect*. The following chart shows this order of events:

Cause	Brings About	Effect
door slams	brings about	picture falling

But with complex relationships, you'll likely be dealing with multiple causes and effects. An effect may have more than one cause, as the following diagram shows:

Cause 1		
Cause 2	bring about	effect
Cause 3		
people skills		
ability to network	bring about	a job in real estate
professional license		

A cause may also have more than one effect. For example:

		Effect 1
Cause	results in	Effect 2
		Effect 3
		Tim misses the train.
Tim oversleeps	results in	He's late for work.
		The 9:00 meeting is off.

The cause *always* takes place before the effect: Something happens, which leads to a result. But the cause and effect don't have to be presented in time order in the passage. The effect may be presented first, even though the cause occurred earlier.

Check It Out

How can you make sure you're on target when you write cause-and-effect papers? Use this checklist:

❏ I've shown a clear cause-and-effect relationship between events.

Just because one event occurred before the other doesn't mean that causality exists. Perhaps there's another explanation for the events—coincidence, accident, and so on. Here's false causality: "24 hours in a day … 24 beers in a case … coincidence?" The answer is, yes, it is. Don't push the envelope; if there's no causality, don't invent it.

❏ The cause-and-effect relationship I describe is valid.

Just because something happened once doesn't mean that true causality exists. For the relationship to be valid, it has to be repeated. That's why you wait at least a week before you take that toilet-trained toddler out of diapers.

❏ I've included all relevant causes and effects.

Look beneath the surface to find every factor that affects your analysis. When you omit one or more pertinent causes and effects, you weaken your writing (but you do keep your readers busy poking holes in your thesis).

Write Angles

An **immediate cause** is an event that comes directly before an effect and helped bring it about. A **underlying cause** is not immediately apparent; a **remote cause** is distant from the effect.

Chain Gang

As you learned in Chapter 11, "Personal Best: Revising and Editing," writers often use *transitions* to signal specific relationships among ideas. Following are the transitions most often used to signal cause and effect relationships. Like well-timed flowers and candy, the right transitions can help you cement relationships.

as a result	because
consequently	due to
for this (that) reason	for
if … then	nevertheless
since	so
so that	therefore
thus	this (that) is how

As you read the following passage about the *Titanic,* see if you can find the causes and effects. Then fill in the chart that follows:

A Night to Remember

Just before midnight on April 14, 1912, one of the most dramatic and famous of all maritime disasters occurred, the sinking of the *Titanic.* The *Titanic* was the most luxurious ship afloat at the time, with its beautifully decorated staterooms, glittering crystal chandeliers, and elaborate food service. In addition, it was supposed to be the safest ocean liner ever built. The hull of the 46,000 ton White Star liner was divided into 16 supposedly watertight compartments. According to the ship's manufacturer, four of the 16 compartments could be flooded without threatening the ship's buoyancy. That April, the majestic ocean liner was on its first voyage ever, traveling from Southampton, England, to New York City. The evening of April 14, the ship was sailing 95 miles south of Newfoundland when it collided with a gigantic iceberg. No one saw the iceberg until it was only about 500 yards away, a distance the ship would travel in 37 seconds. The ship sank because the iceberg ruptured five of the 16 watertight compartments. The "unsinkable" *Titanic* vanished under the water at 2:20 A.M., April 15. There were about 2,200 passengers aboard, and all but 678 died. The tragedy was made even worse by the crew's futile rescue attempts. Since there were not enough lifeboats, hundreds of people died who could have survived.

Cause	Effect	Signal Word
1.		
2.		

Author! Author!

Beware of "conventional wisdom," or what everyone says, when you construct cause-and-effect relationships in writing. Sometimes popular opinions are correct, but not always. A generation ago, for example, red meat, butter, and whole milk were considered healthy foods.

Did you get these answers?

Cause	Effect	Signal Word
1. The iceberg ruptured five of the 16 watertight compartments.	The *Titanic* sank.	because
2. Not enough lifeboats	Hundreds of people died who could have survived.	since

Here's another model. As you read it, notice the multiple effects from a single cause.

A Tragic Crop

The potato has had a major historical impact on Ireland. In the eighteenth and nineteenth centuries, the average Irish citizen planted potatoes and ate about 10 pounds of potatoes a day—and little else. Potatoes are nourishing: On this diet, the Irish population nearly tripled from the middle of the eighteenth century to just about the middle of the nineteenth century. But depending on only one food was dangerous. When the potato blight hit Europe in 1845, the results were devastating in Ireland. There, the potato famine meant more than starvation that year. It meant no seed potatoes to use to grow the next year's crop. It meant that the pig or cow that would usually have been sold to pay the rent had to be slaughtered, because there was nothing to fatten it on. No pig or cow meant no rent. No rent meant eviction. As a result, homelessness and disease followed on the heels of hunger. Almost a million Irish people died as a result of the potato blight. Another million moved to the United States.

Now, let's turn to another type of exposition, the classify-divide method of organization.

Neat and Tidy: Classify-Divide

Question: What do the following sentences have in common?

➤ In California, it is illegal to set a mouse trap without a hunting license.

➤ It is illegal to use a lasso to catch a fish in Tennessee.

➤ If a man is wearing a striped suit, you cannot throw a knife at him in Natoma, Kansas.

➤ Unless you have a doctor's note, it is illegal to buy ice cream after 6 P.M. in Newark, New Jersey.

➤ In Minnesota, it is illegal to tease skunks.

Answer: They are all laws. Or, they are all very *strange* laws. If you realized this, you have the basic strategy for classify-divide essays.

Writer's Block

A classification system is useless if the categories overlap.

When you *divide,* you separate items from one another. When you *classify,* you group things in categories of similar objects. For example, a bookseller would classify *The Complete Idiot's Guide to Writing Well* with *The Complete Idiot's Guide to Grammar and Style* because both deal with English and writing. *The Complete Idiot's Guide to Shakespeare* would go on a different shelf, however, because its distinguishing features are different. It describes one particular writer and his works, rather than instructing readers on the basics of writing.

Here's the basic rule for a valid classify-divide essay: *The classification system must serve a larger purpose other than just making piles of things.* Otherwise, it's just an empty exercise. You might as well clean your garage, walk the dog, or call your mother. (So, what are you waiting for?)

The following essay divides and classifies dolphins according to their characteristics. As you read the essay, see if you agree with the method of classification. What does it suggest about the author's purpose?

A Whale of a Tale

There is a great deal of confusion over what the 40 different species that belong to the family *Delphinidae* are called. For example, is a small cetacean a "dolphin" or a "porpoise"? Some people distinguish a *dolphin* as a cetacean having a snout or beak, while a *porpoise* usually refers to one with a smoothly rounded forehead. The larger members of this porpoise and dolphin fam-

Write Angles

Each classification system will vary, depending on the person creating it. When you're writing a classify-divide essay, any system is valid, as long as it is logical, sensible, and instructive. Division is also called "analysis."

ily are called "whales," but they nonetheless fit the same characteristics as their smaller relatives. The number of different names for these creatures reflects the confusion of long-ago sailors as they tried to classify them. Unfortunately, identifying them in their home in the sea is not easy, for the main differences between members of the species is in their skeleton structure.

The size of the bottlenose dolphin varies considerably from place to place. The largest on record are a 12.7-foot male from the Netherlands and a 10.6-foot female from the Bay of Biscay. The heaviest dolphin on record weighed in at 1,430 pounds. A newborn calf, in contrast, is 38.5 to 49.6 inches long and weighs between 20 and 25 pounds.

They are mainly fish-eaters. In the wild, the bottlenose feeds on squid, shrimp, and a wide variety of fishes. In some waters, the bottlenose have gotten in the habit of following shrimp boats, eating what the shrimpers miss or throw away. They often hunt as a team, herding small fish ahead of them and picking off the ones that don't stay with the rest of the group. And they eat a lot! A United Nations report claims that a group of dolphins off the California coast eat 300,000 tons of anchovies each year, whereas commercial fishermen take only 110,00 tons.

There has been a great deal of discussion about the intelligence of these creatures. Whales have the largest brains—over 20 pounds—of any species, but does this mean they are smart? All cetaceans can "read" vibrations that flood their watery home. Thanks to this skill, they can recognize what kind of fish they are chasing and the shape of the ocean floor and objects on it. In turn, they can give off signals of various kinds, sometimes called "voices" or "songs." These sounds enable cetaceans to "talk" to each other. In a laboratory, dolphins have been trained to crudely imitate the trainer's speech.

Alike and Different: Comparison and Contrast

The Short History of Medicine

2000 B.C.	Here, eat this root.
1000 A.D.	That root is heathen. Here, say this prayer.
1850 A.D.	That prayer is superstition. Here, drink this potion.
1940 A.D.	That potion is snake oil. Here, swallow this pill.
1985 A.D.	That pill is ineffective. Here, take this antibiotic.
2000 A.D.	That antibiotic is artificial. Here, eat this root.

The more things change, the more they stay the same, eh? When you *compare,* you show how things are alike. When you *contrast,* you show how they are different. Comparison and contrast is a useful way to organize many term papers, research reports, and feature articles.

Comparison-contrast essays can be organized two ways: *point-by-point* or *chunk.* In a *point-by-point* structure, you deal with each point in turn. In a *chunk* structure, you discuss one point completely before moving on to the next one. For example:

Point-by-Point	Structure	Chunk Structure
taxes: Town A, Town B		Town A: taxes, education, recreation, jobs
education: Town A, Town B		
recreation: Town A, Town B		Town B: taxes, education, recreation, jobs
jobs: Town A, Town B		

Use these transitions to emphasize similarities: *like, likewise, similarly, in the same way, also, as, just as, both.* Use these transitions to emphasize differences: *instead, rather than, unlike, on the other hand, in contrast with, however, but.*

How is the following passage structured, point-by-point, or chunk?

Build We Must

Western architecture traces its descent from the major public buildings in ancient Greece. Some earlier structures were built with an eye for proportion and striking decoration, but they had little influence on the evolution of building design. The Greek and Roman buildings bear some striking similarities as well as differences.

From 750 to 30 B.C.E., the Greeks created impressive temples, *stoas* (covered colonnades), theaters, and amphitheaters. The temples, built in marble and lime-stone, retained the post-and-lintel construction of the wooden originals. The temples had painted decorations and low-pitched wooden roofs. Columns had ornamental capitals—the top of the column—in one of three designs. The simplest, Doric, consisted of columns with plain molded capitals and no base. Ionic capitals were decorated with a pair of scrolls, known as *volutes*. Corinthian capitals, the most ornate, were decorated with an inverted bell-shaped arrangement of leaves. Prime examples include the Parthenon and Erectheum, in Athens.

From 100 B.C. to A.D. 365, the Romans, like the Greeks, built many magnificent buildings, including temples, baths, basilicas, theaters, amphitheaters, bridges, aqueducts, and triumphal arches. The materials, however, differed. The Romans used brick, stone, and concrete. Further, the Romans developed the arch and devised two other classical styles for columns, adding to the three used in ancient Greece. The Roman contribution included the Tuscan order, a plain column derived from the Greek Doric column; and the Composite, which combined Ionic scrolls with Corinthian leaves. Examples of Roman architecture include the Coliseum in Rome and the Pont du Gard in Nimes, France.

Although both the Greeks and Romans erected magnificent buildings, the Greeks used marble and limestone; the Romans, more homely materials. The Greeks created three columns; the Romans added two more. These beginnings paved the way for the development of many other styles of architecture, including the Byzantine (a combination of Roman and Eastern influence) and the Romanesque.

The chunk organization allows the writer to concentrate first on one topic and then the other. Notice how the writer used transitions to show points of similarity ("like") and difference ("however").

You Could Look It Up: Definition

The Greek philosopher Plato defined man as "a featherless biped." When his rival, the philosopher Diogenes, heard Plato's definition, he displayed a plucked chicken and observed, "Here is Plato's man." Quick on the draw, Plato added "having broad nails" to his original definition. Plato's blunder can help us today: If your definition doesn't set the objects off from others in the same class, refine the characteristics until they do.

You can tell whether a definition is valid if it's true when reversed. In Plato's case, for instance, all broad-nailed featherless bipeds *are* men or women (and not plucked chickens).

Here are some ways to construct a definition passage or essay:

➤ List characteristics of a thing beyond what you need to just identify it.

➤ Define the whole by naming its parts.

➤ Define the object by tracing its origins.

➤ Give synonyms for the concept or object being defined.

The following paragraph uses the history of "Melba toast" to define the term:

Toast of the Town

Have you ever wondered how Melba toast got its name? It was named after Nellie Melba, a famous Australian soprano of the late nineteenth and early twentieth century. The prima donna was staying at the Savoy Hotel in London and following a stringent diet. According to the legend, she was living on almost nothing but toast. Normally she was served her meals by the famous French chef and food writer Auguste Escoffier, but on one particular occasion the master chef was busy elsewhere, so the great lady's toast had to be prepared by one of the sous chefs. Probably more used to preparing timbales than toast, the assistant bungled the job. When the hapless waiter served the toast to Nellie Melba, the head steward rushed forward to offer his heartfelt apologies at the debacle. But before the head steward could reach her, Nellie exclaimed, "How clever of Escoffier! I have never tasted such lovely toast!" Ever since then, these crisp, thin slices of toast have been known as "Melba toast."

Author! Author!

Here's how the nineteenth-century American poet Emily Dickinson defined **hope**:

"Hope" is the thing with feathers—
That perches in the soul—
And sings the tune without the words—
And never stops—at all—
—"Poem 254"

"How to" Essays: Process Analysis

Take the following snap quiz (it's easy—there's only one question):

What, in your opinion, is the most reasonable explanation for the fact that Moses led the Israelites all over the place for 40 years before they finally got to the Promised Land?

- A. He was being tested.
- B. He wanted them to really appreciate the Promised Land when they finally got there.
- C. He refused to ask for directions.

Write Angles

If you're describing a circular process, such as the circulation of blood, break into the process at a logical point and follow it around to that point again. In the case of blood, for instance, it's reasonable to start and end with the heart.

Process analysis essays are directions. They explain how to do something, how something works, or how something happens. These essays present the steps in the process in chronological order, from first to last. Be sure to define any unfamiliar terms or concepts.

As you revise process analysis essays ...

1. Check the order of the steps to make sure you haven't skipped or repeated any.
2. Add any necessary transitions, such as *first, second, next, then, after, later,* and *finally.*
3. Try to sum up the results or benefits of the process.

The following process analysis essay explains how beer is made. What clues does the writer provide to make the steps easier to follow?

Bottom's Up

"Beer here! Get your ice-cold beer here!" You probably heard that shouted the last time you were at the ball park. At a ball game, a party, a barbecue, or a fishing trip, people enjoy an ice-cold beer. Throughout the world, people drink 22 billion gallons of beer annually. Americans alone consume 24 gallons of beer per person every year. Few people know how beer is produced, however. The basic brewing process has five steps.

The first step is mashing. Cereal grains, usually barley and hops, are mixed with water. The mixture, called "wort," is heated to about 150 degrees and stirred constantly. When the mixture is allowed to settle, the solids settle and the liquid passes through it.

Then comes boiling and hopping. During these steps, dried flowers from the hop vine are added, about three quarters of a pound of hops for every 31 gallons of wort. The hops prevent spoiling and give the beverage flavor. The mixture is boiled for about two hours.

Next comes the fermenting stage in the process. The brewer uses yeast to cause fermenting, adding about one pound per 31 gallons of wort. Alcohol and carbon dioxide form during fermentation. The mixture is kept at 38 degrees Fahrenheit and completes fermentation in about a week or two.

The final step is called "finishing." Here, the brewer compresses and stores carbon dioxide from the beer wort. Stored in huge metal vats for three to six weeks, the beer continues to settle and clear. Then the beer is carbonated and passes through a pressure filter to be packaged.

Perhaps the next time you have a beer, you'll appreciate it more. Even if you're not a beer drinker, you'll realize the work that went into producing one of the world's best-selling products.

The Least You Need to Know

➤ When you write cause-and-effect essays, be sure causality really exists. Also, include all relevant causes and effects.

➤ When you write classify-divide essays, any classification system is valid, as long as it is logical, sensible, and instructive.

➤ When you write comparison-and-contrast essays, you can use a point-by-point or a chunk structure.

➤ When you write definition essays, list characteristics of a thing beyond what you need to just identify it, define the whole by naming its parts, define the object by tracing its origins, or give synonyms for the concept or object being defined.

➤ When you write process analysis essays, give directions that explain how to do something, how something works, or how something happens.

Chapter 13

Tell Me a Story: Narration

In This Chapter

➤ Story basics: plot, characters, setting, theme, and point of view

➤ Good things come in small packages: short stories

➤ Writing from the heart: personal narratives

Seized with a determination to learn to read, at any cost, I hit upon many expedients to accomplish this desired end. The plea which I mainly adopted, and the one by which I was most successful, was that of using my young white playmates, with whom I met in the street, as teachers. I used to carry, almost constantly, a copy of Webster's spelling book in my pocket; and, when sent on errands, or when play time was allowed me, I would step, with my young friends, aside, and take a lesson in spelling. I generally paid my tuition fee to the boys with bread, which I also carried in my pocket. For a single biscuit, any of my hungry little comrades would give me a lesson more valuable to me than bread.

—Frederick Douglass, *My Bondage and My Freedom* (1855)

Narration is writing that tells a story. Like coffee, narration comes in different flavors. Narration that tells about real events includes *autobiographies, biographies,* and *personal narratives,* such as the excerpt you just read from Douglass's autobiography. Narration that deals with fictional events includes *short stories, myths, narrative poems,* and *novels.* In this chapter, you'll learn the basics for writing stories and personal narratives.

Narrative Building Blocks

Autobiographies and oral histories are both narratives, but they have distinct differences. The same is true of fairy tales, fables, and feature stories. You can tell a novel from a short story, too, even when you're bleary-eyed from staying up until 3:00 to find out whodunit. So what makes these diverse types of narration similar? All narratives contain the following elements:

➤ Plot

➤ Speaker

➤ Characters

➤ Setting

➤ Theme

➤ Point of view

Let's start with the first element on the list, plot.

Author! Author!

When a person is surrounded by disciples, Oscar Wilde remarked toward the end of his life, there is always "a Judas who writes the biography."

Word Watch

Plot is the arrangement of events in a story. Plots include the **exposition, rising action, climax,** and **denouement (resolution).**

The Plot Thickens: Plot

All narratives center around a *plot,* the arrangement of events. Plots have a beginning, middle, and end. The writer (that's you!) arranges the events of the plot to keep the reader's interest and convey your message about life. In most stories and novels, the events of the plot can be divided as follows:

➤ **Exposition.** Introduces the characters, setting, and conflict.

➤ **Rising action.** Builds the conflict and develops the characters.

➤ **Climax.** Shows the highest point of the action.

➤ **Denouement or resolution.** Resolves the story and ties up all the loose ends.

Here's the classic diagram of plot structure. Why not use this plot map as you brainstorm ideas for *your* stories?

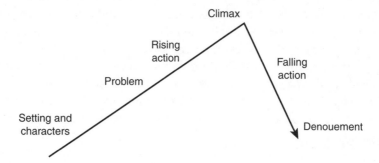

What about the person telling the story? Find out about the *speaker* now.

Who Was That Masked Man? The Speaker

The *speaker* (also called the *personae*) is the personality the writer assumes when telling a story. For example, you can tell the story as a young girl, an old man, or a figure from history. You can be anyone you want to be when you tell a story. You can change size, shape, age, gender, and even species.

When you become the speaker, you're donning a mask that allows you to reveal—and conceal—as you will. Don't confuse the speaker with the writer. Even when you're telling the story as yourself, you're wearing a mask.

Author! Author!

Many famous writers adopt pseudonyms that mask their identity, even to the extent of changing their gender on paper. Some of the most famous examples include the female writers Acton Bell (Anne Brontë), Currer Bell (Charlotte Brontë), Ellis Bell (Emily Brontë), George Eliot (Mary Anne or Marian Evans), and P.D. James (Phyllis Dorothy James). Going in the other direction, we have Edith Van Dyne (L. Frank Baum).

175

And then we have the figures who animate your stories, the *characters*. Learn how to create them now.

Invasion of the Body Snatchers: Characters

> He had changed little since his New Haven years. Now he was a sturdy straw-haired man of thirty with a rather hard mouth and a supercilious manner. Two shining arrogant eyes had established dominance over his face and gave him the appearance of always leaning aggressively forward. Not even the effeminate swank of his riding clothes could hide the enormous power of that body—he seemed to fill those glistening boots until he strained the top lacing, and you could see a great pack of muscle shifting when his shoulder moved under his thin coat. It was a body capable of enormous leverage—a cruel body.
>
> —F. Scott Fitzgerald, *The Great Gatsby*, Chapter 1

A *character* is a person or an animal in a story. *Main characters* have important roles in the narrative; *minor characters* have smaller parts. They usually serve as a contrast to the main character or to advance the plot.

Characterization is the different ways a writer tells readers about characters. Sometimes you may wish to describe the characters directly by naming their traits. Here's an example of direct characterization:

> John Reed was a schoolboy of fourteen years old; four years older than I, for I was but ten; large and stout for his age, with a dingy and unwholesome skin; thick lineaments in a spacious visage, heavy limbs and large extremities. He gorged himself habitually at table, which made him bilious, and gave him dim and bleared eyes and flabby cheeks.
>
> —Charlotte Brontë, *Jane Eyre*, Chapter 1

Author! Author!

The first woman to earn her living as an author seems to have been Aphra Behn (1640–1689), who wrote a number of popular poems, plays, and novels, including the romantic novels *The Fair Jilt*, *The Rover*, and *The Amours of Philander and Sylvia*. When not busy writing, Behn served as a spy for Charles II.

Other times, writers let readers reach their own decisions about the characters by showing the comments, thoughts, and actions of the other characters. For example:

> I unwound his long scarf and helped him out of his coat. As I got him settled in his desk, Mother arrived with my other brown shoe. I jammed my foot into it with all the children watching.
>
> —Jean Little, *Stars Come out Within*

From this excerpt, you can infer that the speaker, Jean Little, is kind and helpful. You might also have figured out that there's something different about her, since all the children are staring at her. In fact, she is blind.

Write Angles

If you're writing a novel, you've got the room for a shipload of characters, but in a short story, space is at a premium, so keep the guest list short.

The Curtain Rises: Setting

> I lay there in the grass and cool shade thinking about things and feeling rested and ruther comfortable and satisfied. I could see the sun out at one or two holes, but mostly it was big trees all about, and gloomy in there amongst them. There was freckled places on the ground where the light sifted down through the leaves, and the freckled places swapped about a little, showing there was a little breeze up there. A couple of squirrels set on a limb and jabbered at me very friendly.
>
> —Mark Twain, *The Adventures of Huckleberry Finn,* Chapter VIII

The *setting* of a story is the time and place where the events unfold. You can establish the setting directly or suggest it from details in the story. In this excerpt from *Huck Finn,* you can infer that Huck is outside from these details: "grass and cool shade," "big trees," and "little breeze." You can also provide clues to the setting in the characters' speech, clothing, or means of transportation. Huck's speech—words such as "ruther" (for "rather") and "there was freckled places" (for "there were …")—suggests that Huck is a country lad in the mid-nineteenth century.

The setting is more than a mere backdrop to the action. Rather, it serves to underscore the action and theme.

In some narratives, the setting can even function as a character, as in Twain's *The Adventures of Huckleberry Finn.* The Mississippi River may not say anything, but it's as important as any of the characters with speaking roles! Consider your settings carefully when you plot a short story or other narrative.

Writer's Block

Don't confuse the **theme** with the **topic;** the former is a broad statement about reality; the latter, the subject of the narrative. A theme might be "War is hell"; the subject, World War II.

The Meaning of Life: Theme

Effective narratives do more than entertain; they often suggest a truth about life, a *theme*. This observation touches a cord within your readers and makes your story memorable. It can even help lift your writing to the level of Art.

Here are some sample themes:

➤ People are capable of great heroism when put to the test.

➤ Beauty is in the eye of the beholder.

➤ The world is a lonely and bitter place.

➤ You can't recapture the past.

➤ It's a dog-eat-dog world.

You can state the story's *theme* directly in the story, or have readers infer it from details about plot, characters, and setting. The choice is yours.

I Spy: Point of View

In narration, the point of view is controlled by the grammatical *person* in which an author chooses to write. You have three choices: *first-person point of view, third-person omniscient point of view,* and *third-person limited point of view.* Here's the run-down:

➤ **First-person point of view.** The narrator is one of the characters in the story and explains the events through his or her own eyes, using the pronouns *I* and *me.* Unless the narrator is Carnack the Magnificent, he or she doesn't know the other characters' thoughts.

➤ **Third-person omniscient point of view.** The narrator is not a character in the story. Instead, the narrator looks through the eyes of all the characters. As a result, the narrator is omniscient or "all-knowing." The narrator uses the pronouns *he, she,* and *they.*

➤ **Third-person limited point of view.** The narrator tells the story through the eyes of only one character, using the pronouns *he, she,* and *they.*

Each point of view has its advantages. Your choice depends on the Big Three: audience, purpose, and topic. For example, if you use the first-person point of view for your narrative, readers see the experience through your eyes and your eyes only. As a result, the first-person point of view allows an immediacy and intimacy absent from the third-person point of view. Ben Franklin chose the first-person point of view for his *Autobiography* (1771), as the following excerpt shows. Notice his slightly mocking tone, as he pokes fun at the earnest adolescent he had been.

> It was about this time I conceived the bold and arduous project of arriving at moral perfection. I wished to live without committing any fault at any time; I would conquer all that either natural inclination, custom, or company might lead me into.

The third-person points of view, in contrast, allow the writer to achieve distance and some measure of objectivity. Henry Adams decided on the third-person point of view for his classic autobiography, *The Education of Henry Adams* (1918). Notice how much more formal and distant the tone is from Franklin's writing:

> As the boy grew up to 10 or 12 years old, his father gave him a writing-table in one of the alcoves of his Boston library, and there, winter after winter, Henry worked over his Latin Grammar and listened to these four gentlemen discussing the course of politics.

Which point of view should you select? Your choice depends on your subject, aim, and readers. For example, if you want to achieve some distance from your topic, the third-person point of view is a good choice. If you want to give the readers the feeling of "you are there," try first person. Here's the basic rule: Be consistent. You can't switch from first person to third person in midstream. Your readers will be confused and your narrative shattered.

Write Angles

Truman Capote invented a hybrid between fiction and non-fiction, which he called the "nonfiction novel." This genre starts with a true story (the non-fiction aspect) and adds elements of fiction (such as invented dialogue and details). Capote's finest example is *In Cold Blood*, the gripping tale of a pair of murderers on a Midwestern killing spree.

Write Angles

If your writing stalls, try switching the point of view. Laura Ingalls Wilder, for example, originally wrote the first novel in her famous *Little House* series in the first-person. It didn't allow her the distance she needed, however, so on the advice of her editor, Wilder retold the story from the third person. This change in point of view transformed memories into story.

Get Cookin'!

When you write a short story or other narrative, you can rework an incident from your own life, come up with something completely fictional, or create a hybrid of fact and fantasy. Easier said than done, eh? Here are a few hints to get you started:

Writer's Block

Just because something happened in real life doesn't mean that you have to include it in your plot—even if you're writing an autobiography or a narrative based on a true event. Instead, select the details and events that work toward a single effect. Remember: Art is life transformed.

➤ **Create the plot.** Use the brainstorming techniques you learned in Chapter 8, "Write This Way," or the plot diagrams included in this chapter to help you create an interesting scenario.

➤ **Give birth to a character.** Friend or foe, insider or outsider, familiar or foreign: Story ideas often start with a memorable character. Who has made an impression on you? Why? Why not use this person as the inspiration for a fictional creation?

➤ **Jump into a setting.** Sometimes a place sparks a story, so think about what a familiar place might be like at another time, a strange place at any time, or a place that holds special meaning for you.

➤ **Get the meaning.** Successful stories do more than entertain: They give us insights into the meaning of our existence. These themes reverberate long after we've put the story down. Consider building your plot around a statement about life that holds special meaning for you.

The following story chart is an enjoyable and effective way to plot your ideas:

Setting		Characters		Plot
		Name		Problem
		Traits		Complications
		1. _____		1. _____
		2. _____		2. _____
		3. _____		3. _____
				Conclusions

The earliest stories we read are fairy tales, fables, legends, and myths. You can start your own story by modeling it on a fable, such as this one by Aesop:

The Man, His Boy, and the Donkey

A man and his son were going with their donkey to market. As they were walking along the donkey's side, a countryman passed them and said, "You fools! What is a donkey but for you to ride upon?"

So the man put the boy on the donkey and they went on their way. But soon they passed a group of men, one of whom said, "See that lazy youngster; he lets his father walk while he rides."

So the man ordered his boy to get off, and got on himself. But they hadn't gone far when they passed two women, one of whom said to the other, "Shame on that lazy lout to let his poor little son trudge along."

Well, the man didn't know what to do, but at last he took his boy up with him on the donkey. By this time they had come to the town, and the passersby began to jeer and point at them. The man stopped and asked what they were scoffing at. The men said, "Aren't you ashamed of yourself for overloading that poor donkey of yours—you and your hulking son?"

The man and the boy got off and tried to think what to do. They thought and they thought, till at last they cut down a pole, and tied the donkey's feet to it, and raised the pole and the donkey to their shoulders. They went alone amid the laughter of all who met them till they came to Market Bridge, when the donkey, getting one of its feet loose, kicked out and caused the boy to drop his end of the pole. In the struggle, the donkey fell over the bridge and, his forefeet being tied together, he drowned.

"That will teach you," said an old man who had followed them.

Moral: Please all and you will please none.

Use the same moral (or one of your own) and create some new characters to act out the plot.

Write Angles

In a fable, the theme is stated outright at the end in the form of a **moral.**

Word Watch

Autobiographies and biographies are types of **personal narratives.**

Life Line: Personal Narratives

The great American showman and circus impresario Phineas T. Barnum was near death in 1891 when an editor of a New York newspaper contacted his agent to see if Barnum would enjoy having his obituary published while he could still read it. Never one to refuse a little free publicity, Barnum told his agent he thought it was a fine idea. The next day, P.T. Barnum read a four-column story about his own life and death—and loved it.

Okay, so maybe you haven't scaled K2, plundered the *Andréa Doria,* or started your own circus. "My life is about as exciting as watching paint dry," you think. Wrong. Your life is actually tremendously exciting. That's because even mundane events are fascinating in the hands of a good writer. And that's *you,* buddy.

When you write a *personal narrative,* you relate a meaningful incident from the first-person point of view. The story might describe a conflict that you untangled, a discovery that you made, or an experience that moved you in some way, for instance.

A personal narrative has the same elements as a short story—plot, speaker, characters, setting, theme, and point of view. But when you write a personal narrative, you're not creating these elements from your imagination. Rather, they come from your own experience. Consider interviewing family, friends, and neighbors about the incident you wish to describe. Considering their recollections can help shed light on your memories and enable you to view the incident from several different vantage points.

Author! Author!

James Boswell's *The Life of Samuel Johnson, L.L.D.,* published in 1791, is the greatest biography in English and a treasure chest of in-your-face erudition. It's like a talk show with a great guest and a host smart enough to keep quiet and listen. You should be so lucky.

Many people use the following process as they write their personal narratives:

➤ Jot down the main events in the narrative.

➤ Arrange the events in chronological order, from first to last. A flow chart can help you straighten out the time tangle.

➤ Decide if you wish to use a flashback, flash forward, or straight chronology.

➤ Draft the narrative, writing in the first-person point of view.

➤ Show, don't tell. Don't just make claims; instead, provide your readers with specific details and images that make your point.

➤ Weave in figures of speech, sensory details, and dialogue to spice up your story.

➤ As you revise and edit, make sure that your personal narrative has a clear focus. The nature of the experience itself may naturally indicate the focus, or you may wish to show the effects of the experience to underline its importance.

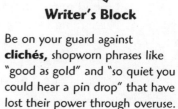

Writer's Block

Be on your guard against **clichés,** shopworn phrases like "good as gold" and "so quiet you could hear a pin drop" that have lost their power through overuse. Replace these hackneyed expressions with fresh comparisons.

Here's a personal narrative about a key incident in the writer's life. Notice the sparkling detail, engaging dialogue, and clear theme.

I Will Survive

At the age of 20, I was a headstrong young woman who thought, "I know everything." I did not realize my naiveté until I found myself in tears on the New Jersey Turnpike, with $15 in my pocket and half a tank of gas, driving a decrepit 1969 Volkswagen death trap with no floor boards or brakes.

Against my father's strong advice, I had left my home in Kentucky to work as a live-in nanny in Chatham, New Jersey. Without so much as an interview, I had been hired. My father said it would never work, but what did he know? He had no faith in me. He wanted to dominate me. He didn't even know me!

"You'll be home within six weeks," he said. He was wrong. I lasted eight weeks, and didn't know how to get home. With echoes of "I told you so" ringing in my ears, I had to make a decision. Should I call my father, ask for money, and crawl the 856 miles back home with my tail between my legs—or drive to New York City and take my chances? Filled with fear, I drove through the Holland Tunnel, hoping to find food, faith, and strength on the other side.

"What do I have to lose?" I half-asked, half-told myself. I spent the next week riding the subway, trying to think of a plan. After many long, silent summer days in the nauseating stench of urine and the sweat of human sardines commuting in the heat, I thought there must be a better way. So I returned to my car and drove across the bridge to the beach, to Long Island.

I found public showers at the beach, and there were crowds of happy people, peaceful and serene, unlike the sardines of the subway, mashed into the E-train, bogged down with the baggage of tension, and oppressed by the heat. Here I could think and plan.

It was day nine that I blended into a company picnic. The tantalizing aroma of free hot dogs called me, and the crowd was large. No one would recognize me as an outsider. And if they did, what was the worst they could do? Take away my hot dog? Tell me to leave? Have me arrested? It was a risk I would have to take.

After successfully caging four hot dogs, I felt brave. I had been silent for days, lonely and scared. I began talking, first to children, then to the clown hired to entertain them. Finally, I approached some adults.

The following week, I reported to this company for work. I thought I would work a few weeks to earn enough money to get home. That was eight years ago. I am still at the same company, I have married, and I still live on Long Island.

I view this as the most positive experience of my life. Although I was frightened, hungry, and insecure, I learned that I am a survivor. I can do anything I set my mind to, and with faith, I will always get through.

The Least You Need to Know

➤ Narration is writing that tells a story.

➤ Autobiographies, biographies, and personal narratives are factual narratives; short stories, myths, narrative poems, and novels are fictional narratives.

➤ All narratives contain the following elements: plot, characters, setting, theme, and point of view.

➤ A personal narrative relates a meaningful incident from the first-person point of view.

Chapter 14

Why Not See It My Way?: Persuasion and Argumentation

Rhetoric, the art of argument, developed in the fifth century B.C.E. in Sicily to help everyday people argue that they should be entitled to recover property seized by a tyrant. See? Real estate has always been "location, location, location"—or lack thereof.

This chapter will take you step by step through the process of writing convincing arguments, whether they're letters of application, essays, editorials, letters to the editor, critical reviews, or job evaluations. That's because the process for all persuasive writing is essentially the same, as you'll discover here.

First, you'll learn how to write a persuasive document that appeals to reason, using a business letter and an excerpt from the *Declaration of Independence* as models. Next, we'll explore appeals to emotion, using part of Thomas Paine's incendiary pamphlet *Common Sense* as a model. Then, I'll show you how to write a persuasive essay based on an appeal to ethics. You'll also discover how to disarm the opposition, a key strategy for constructing any effective argument. The chapter concludes with a discussion of *logical fallacies,* so you can make sure you won't make any of these blunders as you write.

It Won't Be Greek to You

Persuasive writing moves readers to action or belief.

Aristotle, the Big Greek Daddy of Persuasion, believed that argument meant discovering all the available ways of persuasion in a situation where the truth was up for grabs.

Aristotle settled on three ways that people could convince others to adopt a certain point of view or approve a course of action. Broadly stated, he identified these three elements as ...

1. **Logos.** The appeal to the audience's reason

2. **Pathos.** The appeal to the audience's emotions

3. **Ethos.** The degree of confidence that the speaker's character or personality inspires in readers.

Writer's Block

Today, the term "rhetoric" has gotten a bum rap, like the labels "liberal" and "conservative." We think of rhetoric as an attempt to deceive through tricky or windy language, but it wasn't always this way.

The goal of these three appeals is the same, although each one takes a different approach. Each appeal can be used separately, or they can be combined to increase the persuasive mojo. When you argue a point in writing, you analyze a subject, topic, or issue in order to persuade your readers to think or act a certain way.

Let's start with the first appeal on Aristotle's hit parade, the appeal to reason.

A + B = C: Appeal to Reason

Whether our argument concerns public affairs or some other subject, we must know some, if not all, of the facts about the subject on which we are to argue. Otherwise, we can have no materials out of which to construct arguments.

—Aristotle, *Rhetoric*

Word Watch

Writing that appeals specifically to reason is often called **argumentation.**

Appeals based on reason rely on facts rather than on emotion. In turn, each logical argument in your essay must be supported by evidence: facts, statistics, expert testimony, or details about the argument. The basic organization for a persuasive essay or letter developed on a logical argument looks like this:

➤ **Introduction.** Catches the reader's attention and states your argument. Includes a concise statement of your position on an issue that will interest your readers.

➤ **Body.** States each logical argument by presenting supporting evidence. Disarms the opposition, establishes the writer's credibility, and sets an effective tone.

➤ **Conclusion.** Restates your argument and summarizes your main points.

Here's an example of a logical argument constructed this way. It's in the form of a cover letter to accompany a resumé.

---

3 Covered Bridge Road
Los Angeles, CA 90039

April 4, 2000

Mr. Juan Perez, Manager
Fox Hollow Inn
1414 Jericho Turnpike
Los Angeles, CA 90039

Dear Mr. Perez:

I am writing in response to the advertisement you placed in Sunday's Los Angeles *Times* for a part-time maître d'hôtel at the Fox Hollow Inn. Next year, I will receive my degree in Restaurant Management from the Culinary Arts Institute. I believe that both my education and experience are directly related to your needs.

As a junior, I have taken many courses in Restaurant Management and have earned a B+ average in my major. As a result, I have a great deal of formal instruction in running a restaurant efficiently. I can perform most dining room procedures skillfully, especially serving as a welcoming and efficient host. Last month, I was named "Junior Man of the Year" for Restaurant Management, in recognition of my hard work and accomplishments.

Besides taking courses in this field, I have years of hands-on experience. For the past two years, I have been working at the campus restaurant, the Fireside Lounge. In this capacity, I have been a line cook, server, and maître d'hôtel. This year, I organized the annual Wine and Cheese Party (a benefit for the Heart Fund) as well as staffing dozens of major receptions and parties.

I would welcome the opportunity to join your staff because you enjoy a reputation for helping students gain experience in the industry. I am enclosing my resumé and am available for an interview at your convenience.

Sincerely,

Matt Ling

enc.

Logical arguments are developed in two basic ways: *inductively* or *deductively*.

Specific to General: Inductive Reasoning

Inductive reasoning draws a logical conclusion from specific facts. It depends on drawing inferences from particular cases to support a generalization or claim. Many of our everyday conclusions are based on inductive reasoning. For example, if three people whose judgment you respect tell you that a particular movie is worth seeing, you'll conclude that the movie is most likely something you'll enjoy. It might even be worth the $8.50 ticket (not counting the popcorn and soda).

Write Angles

Remember that a persuasive essay doesn't have to prove a point beyond a shadow of a doubt; it need only convince your readers that your viewpoint is valid and deserves serious consideration.

Therefore, the success of an essay built inductively depends on the strength of your examples. When it comes to examples in argumentation, more is often better, but space is always a consideration. As a result, you're better off presenting a handful of examples in detail than a pile of proof without much backing. When in doubt, stick with the magical number three: introduction, three examples, conclusion. This gives you a balanced, five-paragraph essay or letter and meets reader expectations.

General to Specific: Deductive Reasoning

Word Watch

A **syllogism** is a pattern of logical thinking used in deductive reasoning. It has three parts: a major premise, a minor premise, and a conclusion.

Deductive reasoning moves in the opposite direction, from a general premise to particular conclusions. Sometimes, it depends on a logical structure called a *syllogism*. Here's an example:

Major premise: All men are mortal.

Minor premise: Herman is a man.

Conclusion: Therefore, Herman is mortal.

If you accept the major premise that all men will eventually kick the bucket and the minor premise that Herman is a man, then you have to accept the conclusion. Most written arguments collapse because the major premise isn't true. The rest of the argument, built on a rickety frame, is bound to crash. Here's an example from *Alice in Wonderland*:

"Very true," said the Duchess: "flamingoes and mustard both bite. And the moral of that is—Birds of a feather flock together."

"Only mustard isn't a bird," Alice remarked.

"Right, as usual," said the Duchess. "What a clear way you have of putting things!"

However, a *syllogism* can be valid but not true, as in this example:

Write Angles

Rarely will a writer lay out a deductive argument this neatly, however. In most cases, for example, the first statement will be implied rather than stated.

Major premise: Ten chefs can cook faster than one chef.

Minor premise: One chef can make a soufflé in an hour.

Conclusion: Therefore, 10 chefs can make a soufflé in six minutes.

To use deductive reasoning correctly, first make sure that the major premise is true. If it isn't valid, the rest of the argument will bomb. Then craft a minor premise that logically follows the first one. Finally, decide if the conclusion is sound.

It's not likely that you'll be using formal syllogisms in your writing, but you *will* be using this method of thinking when you construct an argument deductively. The following excerpt from the *Declaration of Independence* relies on a deductive pattern to make its argument. See if you can find the major premise. (Hint: It's in the very beginning.)

> When in the course of human events, it becomes necessary for one people to dissolve the political bands that have connected them with another, and to assume among the powers of the earth, the separate and equal station to which the laws of nature and of nature's God entitle them, a decent respect to the opinions of mankind requires that they should declare the causes which impel them to the separation.
>
> We hold these truths to be self-evident: that all men are created equal; that they are endowed by their Creator with certain unalienable rights; that among these are life, liberty, and the pursuit of happiness; that to secure these rights, governments are instituted among men, deriving their just powers from the consent of the governed; that whenever any form of government becomes destructive of these ends, it is the right of the people to alter or abolish it, and to institute new government, laying its foundation on such principles and organizing its powers in such form, as to them shall seem most likely to effect their safety and happiness.
>
> —Thomas Jefferson, *Declaration of Independence* (1776)

Take the High Road: Appeal to Ethics

Ethics is our moral sense, our sense of right and wrong.

The credibility and persuasiveness of your claims is in direct proportion to your reader's view of you as a person of good sense, good moral character, and good intentions—your ethics. Your trustworthiness arises from the quality of your proof and your ability to take the high ground. Cheap shots weaken your argument, especially if they intentionally deceive your audience.

The following argument is especially strong not only because it draws on solid examples and ethics, but also because the writer is not afraid to admit his own culpability.

The Blame Game

"Yes, I did it, but it wasn't my fault." Yes, it was your fault. Today, it has become common to disavow our actions. This practice is used in many situations, such as the Menendez brothers' defense, Joel Rifkin's defense, and my own defense. It is time for everyone to accept responsibility for their actions and deal with the consequences.

On the night of August 20, 1989, the Menendez brothers, 21-year-old Lyle and 18-year-old Erik, brutally murdered their parents by shooting them 15 times with a 12-gauge shotgun. The brothers claimed that their parents, Jose and Kitty, abused them physically, mentally, and sexually. When Jose and Kitty were gunned down, they were quietly watching television. To be acquitted of the murders, the Menendez brothers had to prove that their lives were in imminent danger. I cannot understand how they could claim this, but Laurie Levenson, a former prosecutor, said, "It was probably their only defense." The trial lasted five months. When it was over, the brothers were acquitted of murder. By denying responsibility for their actions, the Menendez brothers were able to get away with murder.

Another example of denying responsibility is Joel Rifkin's defense. Accused of strangling 17 women, Rifkin failed in his first attempt to be exonerated. On June 8, 1994, Rifkin was sentenced to 25 years to life in prison. But as the saying goes, if at first you don't succeed, try, try again. For his next trial, Rifkin tried a variation of the insanity defense called the "adopted child syndrome." Rifkin's lawyer, Martin Efman, argued that the trauma of being separated from his mother led Joel to strike back at women he identified with her. Dr. David Bordzinsky, a professor of law at Rutgers University, called the defense "a bunch of malarkey." Fortunately, the jury agreed.

People don't have to be murderers to deny responsibility for their actions. On July 30, I was driving to Cleveland, Ohio, when a police officer pulled me over and informed me that I was driving 70 miles per hour in a 55 mile per hour zone. He then issued me a summons for speeding. Even though I knew I was

190

speeding, I wouldn't admit it. On October 9, I went to the Mt. Olive Municipal Court in an attempt to shirk my guilt. However, I was convicted and fined $100.

It doesn't matter if people succeed in escaping responsibility for something they have done. The fact that they tried to escape responsibility is wrong. Until we realize this, I think we are likely to see more cases similar to those of the Menendez brothers, Joel Rifkin—and me.

Tug the Heartstrings: Appeal to Emotion

I Will Fight No More Forever

Tell General Howard I know his heart. What he told me before, I have in my heart. I am tired of fighting. Our chiefs are killed. Looking Glass is dead. Toohoolhoolzote is dead. The old men are all dead. It is the young men who say yes and no. He who led on the young men is dead. It is cold and we have no blankets. The little children are freezing to death. My people, some of them, have run away to the hills and have no blankets, no food: no one knows where they are—perhaps freezing to death. I want to have time to look for my children and see how many I can find. Maybe I shall find them among the dead. Hear me, my chiefs. I am tired; my heart is sick and sad. From where the sun now stands I will fight no more forever.

—Chief Joseph, 1877

Chief Joseph uses emotion to persuade his audience that he will never again fight a battle. The stately sentences, simple diction, and poignant details combine to create a tragic tone that convinces readers of his sincerity—and his heartbreak.

Author! Author!

Chief Joseph (1840?–1904), leader of the Nez Perce tribe originally from Oregon, was one of the finest Native American generals. After the government broke their treaties, the Nez Perce, led by Chief Joseph, mounted a resistance that aroused even the respect of their enemies. The tribe was hopelessly outnumbered, however, and forced to retreat. On October 5, 1877, after being defeated in a battle in the Bear Paw Mountains of Montana, Chief Joseph surrendered. The tribe moved first to a reservation in Oklahoma and then to Washington.

An effective essay can draw its strength from facts and reasoning, but logic can carry you just so far with certain readers. Depending on your audience and topic, you're going to want to pour on some feeling. You do this by appealing to your reader's needs:

➤ **Physical needs** (food, water, sleep, air, protection from injury and harm)

➤ **Social needs** (status, power, freedom, approval, belonging, fitting in)

➤ **Psychological needs** (love, affection, security, self-esteem, respect)

Following is an example of a persuasive appeal that relies on emotion. It's from Thomas Paine's *The Crisis*. Paine's essay was so effective that it propelled the colonies into the Revolutionary War.

Writer's Block

Don't use appeals to emotion in place of solid arguments or to stir up feelings that are dangerous or harmful.

Write Angles

When you're addressing an audience that doesn't agree with your argument, search for **common ground,** or areas of agreement. If you can get readers to agree with you on one point, they're more likely to be persuaded by your other points.

These are the times that try men's souls. The summer soldier and the sunshine patriot will in this crisis shrink from the service of his country; but he that stands it NOW deserves the love and thanks for man and woman. Tyranny, like hell, is not easily conquered; yet we have this consolation with us, that the harder the conflict, the more glorious the triumph. What we obtain too cheap, we esteem too lightly; 'tis dearness only that gives everything its value. Heaven knows how to put a proper price upon its goods; and it would be strange indeed, if so celestial an article as FREEDOM should not be highly rated. Britain, with an army to enforce her tyranny, has declared that she has a right (*not only to TAX*) but "to BIND us in ALL CASES WHATSOEVER," and if being *bound in that manner* is not slavery, then there is no such thing as slavery upon earth. Even the expression is impious, for so unlimited a power can belong only to God …

—Thomas Paine, *The Crisis, Number I* (1776)

The Moment of Truth

Which persuasive strategy do you use? Use reason, emotion, and ethics (or some combination of these) based on the following considerations:

➤ What kind of persuasion is most likely to sway your readers as you deal in an open and honest manner?

➤ What objections, if any, are they likely to have to your argument?

➤ How strong is your case? (Use more examples, facts, statistics, and other "hard" proof if your argument is weak.)

My Way or the Highway: Acknowledging the Opposition

As much as you might like to, you can't ignore the arguments against your opinion. Think of it like the dog next door—you know, the one who barks all night, no matter how much you moan. Sometimes, you just have to take action.

You can deal with the opposition by ...

➤ Identifying the main arguments against your side.

➤ Acknowledging the arguments in your writing.

➤ Countering the opposition.

With the barking dog next door, you're on your own.

Start by considering your audience. The more information you have about your readers, the easier it will be for you to anticipate possible opposition. This table lays it all out:

Type of Audience	Type of Opposition
neutral	likely very little
friendly	none
hostile	a great deal
unknown	up for grabs

There are three main ways that you can deal with the opposition to decrease its force. These methods are ...

1. Show the opposition is wrong.

2. Show the opposition has some merit, but give a point of your own that is just as convincing.

3. Show the opposition has merit, but your point is stronger.

Let's look at each strategy in turn.

Writer's Block

Don't give the same space to the opposition as you do to your points. Devote more space to *your* argument or place it last in your essays so readers will understand that it's crucial.

Method #1: Show the Opposition Is Wrong

The following passage acknowledges the opposition straight away and then sets about disproving it.

> Very few people claim to really like television commercials. Most people say that television commercials are annoying and insulting. The best that people can say about television commercials is that they give us time to get something to eat. But this view is unfair, since TV commercials have many advantages.

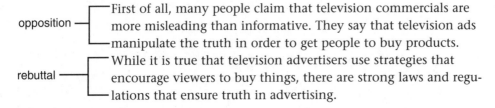

opposition — First of all, many people claim that television commercials are more misleading than informative. They say that television ads manipulate the truth in order to get people to buy products.

rebuttal — While it is true that television advertisers use strategies that encourage viewers to buy things, there are strong laws and regulations that ensure truth in advertising.

Effective persuasive writing uses specific support, not vague references to unidentified studies and sources. You can't evaluate "many important experiments" or "recent clinical studies" unless you know how they were undertaken, by whom, and where the results were published.

Method #2: Show the Opposition Has Some Merit, but Your Point Is Just as Good

Here's another paragraph from the same essay. See how the clever writer dealt with the opposition by presenting a point that's equally convincing. Use this technique if you can't come up with a point that's stronger.

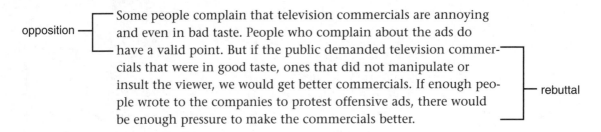

opposition — Some people complain that television commercials are annoying and even in bad taste. People who complain about the ads do have a valid point. But if the public demanded television commercials that were in good taste, ones that did not manipulate or insult the viewer, we would get better commercials. If enough people wrote to the companies to protest offensive ads, there would be enough pressure to make the commercials better. — rebuttal

Method #3: Show the Opposition Has Merit, but Your Point Is Stronger

For a whizbang argument, acknowledge the other side, but rebut with your own point—and make it a real humdinger. Here's how one writer did it:

> Second, television commercials inform viewers of new products such as no-fat snack foods. They also show us new uses for old products. For example, baking soda ads on TV show us how to use the product to take odors out of the refrigerator and carpets, not just for baking. There are some people who say that people can learn about products and services in other ways—through magazine and newspaper ads, for example. To some extent this is true. ⎤— opposition
>
> rebuttal —⎡ However, a person would have to buy and read many, many newspapers and magazines to get as much information from print as we ⎣ do from television. Who has time to read all these newspapers and magazines? It is clear that television commercials are a much more efficient way to get information about products.

Now, time to look at some of the errors that writers make in logic when they construct a persuasive essay. After you read this section, I can rest assured that you'll never make any of these errors. (Promise?)

How's That Again? Logical Fallacies

While driving to his next performance, a juggler was stopped by the police. "What are those knives doing in your car?" asked the officer.

"I juggle them in my act."

"Oh yeah?" says the cop. "Let's see you do it."

So the juggler starts tossing and juggling the knives.

A guy driving by sees this and says, "Wow, am I glad I quit drinking. Look at the test they're making you do now!"

Faulty logic—like the example here—can demolish the most carefully constructed persuasive essay. It's one of the surest ways to lose your readers. Following are the most common *logical fallacies*, errors in reasoning. They are arranged in alphabetical order.

> ➤ **Ambiguity.** Deliberately using expressions that are confusing because they have more than one meaning.

> ➤ **Argument to the person.** Attacking the person rather than the topic.

195

➤ **Begging the question.** Circular reasoning that offers the argument itself as proof.

➤ **Bogus claims.** The writer promises more than he or she can deliver.

Author! Author!

"Well-known" information is another form a bogus claim can take. Be wary of sources that tell you that "Everybody knows that ..." or "It is a well-known fact that ..."

➤ **Card stacking.** Ignoring evidence on the other side of the issue.

➤ **Either-or fallacy.** Offering only two choices when other valid ones exist.

➤ **False analogies.** Misleading comparisons.

➤ **Guilt by association.** Attacking a person's beliefs because of the person's associations.

➤ **Jumping on the bandwagon.** Suggesting that something is right because everyone else does it.

➤ **Hasty generalization.** Generalizing from inadequate evidence, such as stereotyping.

➤ **Irrelevant argument.** A conclusion that does not relate to the premise.

➤ **Loaded terms.** Slanted or biased terms, especially those with strong connotations.

➤ **Misrepresentation.** Outright lies or other deliberate misrepresentation.

Write Angles

Loaded terms are sometimes used in inflammatory essays that deal with politics.

➤ **Oversimplifying the issue.** Twisting the truth by presenting too narrow a range of possibilities.

➤ **Post hoc ergo propter hoc.** Latin for "after this, therefore because of this," it is the mistake of confusing after with because.

➤ **Red herring.** Diverting the issue with an unrelated topic.

➤ **Self-contradiction.** Arguing two premises that cannot both be true.

➤ **Taking the issue out of context.** Distorting the issue by taking it out of context.

These are sneaky little critters, so be especially vigilant. Reread your papers to make sure that every point you make is valid and logical. And while you're at it, check that you haven't built your entire argument on a fallacy. If that happens, even the best prose won't save the day.

The Least You Need to Know

➤ Persuasive writing moves readers to action or belief. Effective persuasive writing relies on appeals to reason, emotion, and/or trust.

➤ Inductive arguments draw a logical conclusion from specific facts; deductive arguments move from a general premise to particular conclusions, often through a syllogism.

➤ Emotional appeals build on your readers' physical, social, and psychological needs.

➤ Disarm the opposition by acknowledging the main arguments against your side and countering the opposition.

➤ Errors in logic can destroy an argument.

Picture This: Description

This Is My Letter

This is my letter to the world
That never wrote to me—
The simple news that Nature told
With tender majesty.

Her message is committed
To hands I cannot see;
For love or her, sweet countrymen,
Judge tenderly of me.

—Emily Dickinson (1830–1886)

Only seven of the more than 1,700 poems Emily Dickinson wrote were published during her lifetime. We write for many reasons: to define something, explain a process, inform others, pass on news, solve problems, tell a story, make money, persuade others—and to express our feelings. In this chapter, we'll explore writing that describes and reveals our deepest thoughts and feelings.

The chapter starts with a look at writing journals and ways they can help your writing—and your life. Next, you'll learn all about *descriptive* writing, essays that use vivid images to paint a word picture of a person, place, scene, object, or emotion.

Then I'll show you how to express yourself in poetry. You'll learn why writing a poem is among the most satisfying kinds of writing you can do, for poetry lets you express your ideas and emotions as your language soars. After I define poetry, we'll survey the different types of poems, poetic elements, and figures of speech. The chapter concludes with some concrete guidelines to help you start writing poetry *now*.

Help Is on the Way!

Last year, Louise was at her wit's end because she was being pulled in too many directions. A full-time systems analyst, mother, wife, and self-styled "soccer mom," Louise managed quite well until her boss handed her still more responsibility. "I just couldn't take it anymore," she said. "I felt totally strung out. There was no way I was going to get everything done," she explained.

Write Angles

Some psychologists encourage their clients to keep journals to supplement therapy. Career counselors often suggest job seekers write in journals to work out anger and despair over job loss and anxiety over career changes.

For comfort, Louise turned to her journal. It's a simple black marble notebook, the kind she used in elementary school. Louise has long kept a journal, "the one thing I do for myself," she notes. In her journal, Louise was able to face her fear and come up with productive ways of dealing with it. "What is most important? What is least important?" she wrote. "How do I define success? What do I have to accomplish to feel good about myself?" She figured out a way to arrange her tasks, which ones had to be perfect and which ones could just be done. She also realized that she didn't have to do it all to have it all.

For many people, journals have become the equivalent of a trusted confident. Keeping a journal can help just about everyone to confront issues in their lives, resolve some of the "big" questions, and become better writers.

Professional writers have long known the value of journals. They're always searching for topics to explore and details to develop. Writers use journals as idea books to record what they read, heard, saw, or experienced. The nineteenth-century New England philosopher Ralph Waldo Emerson, for example, filled more than 10 volumes of journals.

Keeping a journal also helps you become an interactive reader. If you get into the habit of responding to an outside stimulus in writing, you'll be more likely to write when you have something important to say. This might take the form of a letter to the editor, a memo to a colleague, or an e-mail to a service organization, for example. This helps you become a leader in your community and on the job.

For this purpose, many writers carry a pocket-sized notebook and pen with them all the time. Try it; you'll like it!

Make a Deposit in the Idea Bank

Whether you keep a journal to help you express your feelings or gather ideas for your writing, the very act of journaling will help you become a more skilled and confident writer. Here's how:

Writer's Block

Under no circumstances should you keep your personal journal on your office computer; increasingly, courts are upholding the rights of employers to read any writing done on office time and even to use it in court cases.

1. The more you write, the better your skills become. Practice *does* make perfect.

2. The more productive you are, the better you'll feel about your progress as a writer. Success engenders more success.

3. Keeping a journal helps you learn to observe things, people, and ideas closely. The more you delve into a subject, the more you'll learn—and the more you'll be able to express on paper.

4. Experimenting on paper when it doesn't count, as in a journal, takes a lot of the anxiety out of writing.

5. A journal is a great place to store ideas for later writings.

As you can tell, keeping a journal offers even more benefits than exercising—and you don't have to break a sweat to become a fine journal writer! Stay tuned; here's how to make journals work for you.

Journals vs. Diaries

A journal is not the same as a traditional diary. Journal writing is generally used to spark self-reflection, to get in touch with your deepest feelings, and to sort out your emotions. This is what makes journal writing, when done often, such a powerful tool.

Diaries, in contrast, are used to record the day's events—sort of a super Filofax or Day Timer.

Word Watch

A **journal** is an idea book, a record of your thoughts, emotions, and reflections. A **diary,** in contrast, is a record of your activities.

201

Diaries are not used for reflection or experimentation. As such, they don't help you improve your writing skills while you grapple with life issues. A diary can help you make it to that 10:00 meeting on Tuesday, however.

Don't Go There

So far, journals sound like the best thing since sliced bread. After all, they can help you become a better writer as you're dealing with the stress of everyday life. But journaling isn't for everyone.

Writer's Block

If you decide to keep your journal in electronic form, on a laptop or PC for example, be sure to back up each entry on a disk. I also recommend that you print each entry so you have a hard copy in case the computer crashes.

Write Angles

If you don't want people to read your journal, put it in a secure place, or write a note on the first page for people who might open your journal, accidentally or on purpose. For example: "This is my personal journal. Please respect my privacy and return the journal to me without reading it."

Journal writing may *not* be for you if …

➤ You are obsessive, because the technique itself could become an obsession. In that case, you would get little benefit from the writing, since you're not doing it to explore technique or content but rather just for the sake of doing it.

➤ You are coping with a terrible loss. For some people in a tragic situation, writing in a journal becomes a substitute for taking action.

Take the Plunge

So, you've decided that keeping a journal is for you. Here's how to get started and get the maximum benefit as a writer:

1. **Day tripper.** Try to write every day. If that's not possible, try to write at least three days out of every week. Keeping a journal is like any beneficial pastime; the more often you do it, the easier it is and the more you'll get from it.

2. **The write stuff.** Use the type of writing material that makes you feel most comfortable, no matter what anyone says. If you're comfortable with pen and paper, go for it. Consider spiral notebooks, loose-leaf notebooks, or even plain pads of paper. Some people like fancy leather- or cloth-bound books. If you're a keyboarder like me, jot down your ideas on a computer. The important thing is to get into a routine with writing materials that feel comfortable to you.

3. **Time to write.** If possible, try to write at the same time every day. This makes writing a priority in your life and shows your commitment to improving. For many people, writing in their journals is a good way to start the day, while others use it at night to decompress.

4. **Free to be me.** Write freely. Remember that a journal is for you and you alone. Don't worry about spelling, punctuation, or grammar.

5. **Experiment with topics.** Here are some ideas to get you started: You can write your reactions to local and national events, responses to books you've read and movies you've seen, memories of past events, plans for the future, ideas for poems and stories.

6. **Burn, baby, burn.** Don't censor your ideas, either. If you're using your journal to blow off steam or express ideas that you really don't want anyone else to ever see, you can always destroy those pages right after you write them.

Author! Author!

If you decide to use your journal to express your ideas as well as practice your writing, I recommend *The Artist's Way: A Spiritual Path to Higher Creativity*, by Julia Cameron and Mark Bryant (Tacher Putnam, 1992), and *Opening Up: The Healing Power of Expressing Emotions*, by James W. Pennebaker (The Guilford Press, 1997). There's also *How to Keep a Spiritual Journal: A Guide to Journal Keeping for Inner Growth* and *Personal Recovery*, by Ronald Klug (Augsburg Fortress Publications, 1993). I also liked *Writing to Grow: Keeping a Personal-Professional Journal*, by Mary Louise Holly (Heinemann, 1989). For the younger set, we have *A Book of Your Own: Keeping a Diary or Journal*, by Carla Stevens (Clarion Books, 1993). Get those pens poised, ladies and gentlemen, because journaling is sizzling!

Remember: A journal can become an extension of your thinking. By writing in a journal, you're taking the ideas out of your head and putting them down on paper.

Color My World

Suddenly there shot along the path a wild light, and I turned to see whence a gleam so unusual could have issued; for the vast house and its shadows were alone behind me. The radiance was that of the full, setting, and blood-red moon, which now shone vividly through that once barely discernible fissure, of which I have before spoken as extending from the roof of the building, in a zigzag direction, to the base. While I gazed, the fissure rapidly widened—there came a fierce breath of the whirlwind—the entire orb of the satellite burst at once upon my sight—my brain reeled as I saw the mighty walls rushing asunder—there was a long tumultuous shouting sound like the voice of a thousand waters—and the deep and dank tarn at my feet closed sullenly and silently…

—Edgar Allan Poe, "The Fall of the House of Usher"

Word Watch

Descriptive writing uses vivid images to illustrate a specific experience, person, or place.

As you can see from this passage from Poe's short story, *descriptive writing* uses sensory details to paint a word picture of a person, place, scene, object, or emotion. Descriptive writing is an important part of any writing—even technical pieces. That's because in addition to helping readers grasp emotions, feelings, and characters, effective descriptive writing helps explain and persuade.

You can use descriptive writing in the following ways:

➤ To make scenes realistic and memorable

➤ To help readers experience an emotion

➤ To share your feelings more clearly

➤ To bring characters to life

➤ To convey key ideas, especially complex ones

➤ To help readers feel like they're on the scene

Write Angles

Descriptive writing is more than scattering a few adjectives and adverbs like rice at a wedding. Rather, it means using vivid words and images to convey meaning.

So Write, Already

Follow these guidelines when you write descriptive pieces:

1. Start by deciding on a method of organization. Spatial organization, for example, works especially well if your details are mainly visual. If you're describing an incident, consider chronological order.

2. Then select a point of view, the vantage point from which you will relate events or details.

3. Clearly identify the subject (no guessing games, please).

4. Use details to create a strong mood or feeling about the subject.

5. As you write, draw on all five senses: sight, touch, hearing, taste, and smell.

6. Consider including *figures of speech,* those imaginative comparisons that evoke feelings in your readers. Figures of speech (or figurative language) is covered later in this chapter.

A Master at Work

The following passage describes a pivotal scene from George Orwell's famous essay "Shooting an Elephant." Orwell, the pen name of Eric Blair (1903–1950) is famous not only for his grim novels *Animal Farm* (1945) and *1984* (1948), but also for his passionate defense of the integrity of the English language. "Shooting an Elephant" focuses on the use and abuse of power. Notice how Orwell draws on the sense of touch and hearing as well as sight:

> When I pulled the trigger I did not hear the bang or feel the kick—one never does when a shot goes home—but I heard the devilish roar of glee that went up from the crowd. In that instant, in too short a time, one would have thought, even for the bullet to get there, a mysterious, terrible change had come over the elephant. He neither stirred nor fell, but every line of his body had altered. He looked suddenly stricken, shrunken, immensely old, as though the frightful impact of the bullet had paralyzed him without knocking him down. At last, after what seemed a long time—it might have been five seconds, I dare say—he sagged flabbily to his knees. His mouth slobbered ....

Many novice writers rely most heavily on sight when they're writing a descriptive essay or poem, but smell and taste are actually far more evocative.

Music to the Eyes

Writing a poem is among the most gratifying kinds of writing you can do, for poetry lets you express your ideas and emotions as your language soars. Poetry can also help improve your prose writing, since it teaches you to handle language with skill and precision. So even if you're not a poet, writing some poetry can help you create better letters, memos, reports, and essays.

A poem should be palpable and mute
As a globed fruit ...

A poem should be wordless
As the flight of birds ...

A poem should not mean
But be.

—Archibald MacLeish

205

What Is a Poem?

Poem:

Do not go gentle into that good night,
Old age should burn and rave at close of day;
Rage, rage, against the dying of the light.

—Dylan Thomas

Not a poem:

Turn off the light and put out the cat before you come to bed, Dylan.

—Mother Thomas

Word Watch

Poetry is a type of literature in which words are selected for their beauty, sound, and power to express feelings.

The word *poem* comes from an ancient Greek word meaning "to make, to compose." The implication is important; poetry is made and the poet is the maker. The word *made* suggests materials; the word *maker* suggests effort. There's nothing mysterious about poetry. Like any other kind of writing, it requires a knowledge of the genre, time, effort, and practice.

To make sure we're all starting on the same page, *poetry* is a type of literature in which words are selected for their beauty, sound, and power to express feelings. The poet uses vivid and expressive language to provide a fresh, unexpected way of looking at things.

Author! Author!

Edgar Allan Poe believed that poetry was "the rhythmical creation of beauty"; to Robert Frost, poetry was "a reaching out toward expression, an effort to find fulfillment." Percy Bysshe Shelley wrote that "Poetry is the record of the best and happiest moments of the best minds, the very image of life expressed in its eternal truth."

In "Loveliest of Trees, the Cherry Now," A.E. Housman (1859–1936) uses a commonplace tree to provide a breathtaking insight into the swift passage of time. What emotions does this poem evoke in you?

Loveliest of trees, the cherry now
Is hung with bloom along the bough,
And stands about the woodland ride
Wearing white for Eastertide.

Now, my threescore years and ten,
Twenty will not come again,
And take from seventy springs a score,
It only leaves me fifty more.

And since to look at things in bloom
Fifty springs are little room,
About the woodlands I will go
To see the cherry hung with snow.

Did you feel the beauty of the cherry tree, the clear red against the stark white snow? Did this poem leave you with the urge to seize the day and appreciate the beauty around you? Emotion + Language = Poetry.

Something for Everyone

Poetry takes all life as its subject matter. To embrace life's diversity, poetry has many different forms. This variety gives you free reign to select the type of poem that best suits your purpose, audience, topic, and personality.

Following are some of the traditional poetic forms and an explanation of each one. If you can't make up your mind which variety to try, try expressing the same idea in different forms to see which one(s) work best for you. (This is the same concept as ordering a triple-decker ice-cream cone to see which flavor you like best. Ain't life grand?)

➤ **Ballad.** A story told in song form, with a strong rhythm, repetition, and simple words.

➤ **Epic.** A long story poem written in an elevated style, presenting high-born characters in a series of adventures that portray key events in the history of a nation.

➤ **Haiku.** A three-line poem with a total of 17 syllables. The first and third lines have five syllables each; the second line has seven syllables. Haiku creates a distinct emotion and suggests a spiritual insight, often through images from nature.

➤ **Limerick.** A humorous five-line poem. The first, second, and fifth lines rhyme, and the third and fourth rhyme. Most limericks are ribald.

➤ **Lyric poems.** A brief, musical poem that presents a speaker's feelings.

➤ **Narrative poems.** A poem that tells a story, either through a story or through a dramatic situation.

➤ **Sonnet.** A lyric poem of 14 lines written in *iambic pentameter*. In "Italian" sonnets, the first eight lines rhyme *abba, abba,* and present the problem; the concluding six lines rhyme *cde, cde,* and resolve the problem. In "English" sonnets,
the poet describes the problem in the first 12 lines, which rhyme *abab, cdcd,
efef,* and resolves it in the final two lines, which rhyme *gg.*

Tools of the Trade

Traditionally, poems had a specific rhythm and rhyme, but modern poetry such as
free verse doesn't have regular beat, rhyme, or line length. Before you start your
poems, let's review the different tools you have to work with: poetic elements and
figures of speech. Pick and choose from these elements to create the poem that
expresses your soul.

Word Watch

Iambic pentameter is a
rhythm scheme with five accents
in each line.

Write Angles

Use rhyme to create a musical
sound, meaning, and structure in
your poems.

Poetic Elements

As with any other skill worth knowing, poetry has its
own lingo. Here are some of the most commonly used
terms:

➤ **Blank verse.** Unrhymed poetry. Many English
poets wrote in blank verse because it captures
the natural rhythm of speech. Now, you can,
too.

➤ **Couplet.** Two related lines of poetry, which
often rhyme.

➤ **Foot.** A group of stressed and unstressed syllables in a line of poetry.

➤ **Free verse.** Poetry without a regular pattern of
rhyme and meter.

➤ **Meter.** The beat or rhythm in a poem, created
by a pattern of stressed and unstressed syllables.
The most common meter in English poetry is
iambic pentameter.

➤ **Refrain.** A line or a group of lines that are repeated at the end of a poem. Refrains serve to
reinforce the main point and create musical
effects.

➤ **Rhyme.** The repeated use of identical or nearly identical sounds. End rhyme
occurs when words at the end of lines of poetry have the same sound. Internal
rhyme occurs when words within a sentence share the same sound, as in "Each
narrow cell in which we dwell."

➤ **Rhythm.** The pattern of stressed and unstressed syllables that create a beat, as in music. The meter of a poem is its rhythm.

➤ **Stanza.** A group of lines in a poem, like a paragraph in an essay.

Yes, I know I packed a lot in here, but let's just take it slow. First, read the list over a few more times. Then look back at some of the poems I've included in this chapter, some of your own favorites, and some you've written yourself. See how many of the elements listed here you can find in the poems. Finally, try using some of these elements when you write your own poems.

Figures of Speech

Figurative language, words and expressions not meant to be taken literally, uses words in fresh, new ways to appeal to the imagination. Figures of speech include *alliteration, hyperbole, image, metaphor, onomatopoeia,* and *simile.* Let's look at them now:

➤ **Alliteration.** The repetition of initial consonant sounds in several words in a sentence or line of poetry. Use alliteration to create musical effects, link related ideas, stress certain words, or mimic specific sounds.

➤ **Hyperbole.** An exaggeration used for a literary effect such as emphasis, drama, or humor. Here is an example: "I'm so hungry, I could eat a horse."

➤ **Image.** A word that appeals to one or more of our five senses: sight, hearing, taste, touch, or smell.

➤ **Metaphor.** A comparison between two unlike things, without the words "like" or "as." "My heart is a singing bird" is a metaphor.

➤ **Onomatopoeia.** The use of words to imitate the sounds they describe, as in crack, hiss, and buzz.

➤ **Simile.** A comparison between two unlike things, using the words "like" or "as" to make the comparison, as in "A dream put off dries up like a raisin in the sun."

Remember that figures of speech are usually appropriate in any of the four kinds of writing. The right figure of speech can enhance *everything* you write—not just poetry.

An Affair to Remember

Poetry is a special kind of writing, for it allows you to say things you can't say in prose. Writing poetry gives you a chance to fall in love all over again—with life, language, and literature.

Here are some ideas to get you started writing poetry:

1. Try an acrostic poem from your name. Run the letters of your first or last name vertically down the page. Then write a line for each letter that describes your personality, hopes, and dreams.

2. Since poetry is based on sound, collect some pleasant-sounding words and use them to spark ideas for a poem.

3. Write a poem in list form that names or describes things. Include as many specific details as you can. Check Whitman's "I Hear America Singing" for a model.

4. Write a poem that directly addresses someone or something. Perhaps describe some unfinished business you have with that person or why that person is so special. Address the subject directly, by name, to help you keep the focus.

5. Take a narrative, perhaps something you wrote in Chapter 13, "Tell Me a Story: Narration," and retell the story as a poem.

6. As you write your poem, say each line out loud. Pay attention to the words and the feelings they evoke. This will help you select the precise word you need.

Revise your poems by sharpening the language. Add specific words and vivid images. Condense draggy lines by eliminating unnecessary adjectives and adverbs, too. You might have to rearrange stanzas to make your meaning clear or emphasize the mood. Then publish your poem by sharing it with a friend, relative, or colleague. You might want to join a writers' group (check your local library or adult education for a list). If your community doesn't have a writers' group, why not start your own?

The Least You Need to Know

➤ Keeping a journal is a win-win situation, because it can help you gather ideas for writing topics, be a better reader, and practice your writing skills.

➤ Descriptive writing uses vivid images to illustrate a specific experience, person, or place.

➤ Poetry is a type of literature in which words are selected for their beauty, sound, and power to express feelings.

➤ There are a wide variety of poetic forms and styles; feel free to express yourself—but learn the techniques and forms that best suit your purpose, audience, topic, and personality.

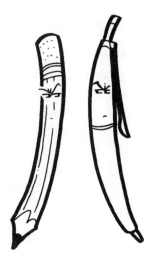

Writing Across the Curriculum

"You can write about anything, and if you write well enough, even the reader with no intrinsic interest in the subject will become involved," claims Tracy Kidder, an award-winning nonfiction writer.

He's right. Occasionally, you'll have the luxury of selecting your topic, so you can make it a honey. Most often, however, the topic will be given to you, like a soggy tuna fish sandwich. Ditto on your audience. Then, you'll have to work your writer's magic to make something marvelous from something mediocre—while making sure you exactly target your readers.

In this chapter, you'll explore the writing styles and slants of various subjects you'll likely have to write about in school, on the job, and in your community work. These include business, humanities, social sciences, and natural sciences. After we compare and contrast the writing tasks common to the various subjects, I'll teach you effective techniques for writing across the curriculum. Next comes a section on documenting sources in the different disciplines. The chapter concludes with a discussion of collaborative writing, a common writing method in many curricula.

Different Strokes for Different Folks

Write Angles

What happens if you have to cover two or more different subject areas in the same document? Which audience should you write for? If you try to satisfy everyone, you'll satisfy no one, so play the numbers and aim for the primary audience.

Every area of study has its own way of looking at the world, and that is how it should be. For example, a musician and a nuclear physicist look at sound very differently; a chemist and a cook rarely regard a pot roast in the same light. To prove my point, here's the same topic as approached by writers in two different areas. The first writer is an historian; the second writer, a geologist.

From the pen of the historian:

Earthquakes can be so deadly that entire cities can be eradicated from the face of the earth. That's exactly what happened in A.D. 365 on the Mediterranean island of Cyprus, when an earthquake measuring 7 on the Richter scale destroyed the city of Kourion and much of Cyprus. The destruction was so massive that the remains of the city were not even discovered until 1934, more than 1,500 years after the event had taken place. That year, the American archaeologist J.F. Daniel unearthed the remains of a Roman house. He found structural remains, debris, and skeletons. The massive earthquake hit at sunrise, before most people had awakened. It was followed by an enormous tsunami, traveling at about 500 miles per hour. Thousands of residents of the city of Kourion appear to have been killed instantly.

From the pen of the geologist:

The intensity of an earthquake can be measured quantitatively on one of two scales. The more common is the Richter scale, which measures the energy released at the focus of a quake. A logarithmic scale, it runs from 1 to 9; a magnitude 9 quake is 10 times more powerful than a magnitude 7 quake, 100 times more powerful than a magnitude 4 quake, and so on. An estimated 800 earthquakes of magnitude 5 to 6 as measured on the Richter scale occur annually, in comparison to about 50,000 earthquakes of magnitude 3 to 4 and only one earthquake of magnitude 8 to 9. The other scale, introduced at the turn of the twentieth century by the Italian seismologist Guiseppi Mercalli, measures the intensity of the shaking with gradations from I to XII. The Mercalli rating assigned to an earthquake depends on the site of the measurement, since seismic surface effects diminish with distance from the focus of the earthquake. An earthquake of intensity I is felt by few people; intensity XII, in contrast, denotes catastrophic earthquakes. Events measured I to II are roughly equivalent to earthquakes of magnitude 3 to 4 on the Richter scale, while earthquakes that measure XI to XII on the Mercalli scale correlate to earthquakes in the 8 to 9 range on the Richter scale.

As you can see, the same subject can vary greatly when written for a different audience. The first paragraph concentrates on the impact of an earthquake on one ancient city. The second paragraph, in contrast, centers on two ways to measure the impact of an earthquake. In the second passage, there's no mention of any specific human involvement, since the writer focuses on quantifying the experience.

Author! Author!

Concern for audience (and propriety) reached absurd heights during the Victorian era, when the author of *Lady Gough's Book of Etiquette* advised Victorians with a home library to avoid placing books by married male authors next to those by female authors, and vice versa.

Border Disputes

Further, many types of writing blur the boundaries between curriculum areas. Henry David Thoreau's classic guide to good living, *Walden,* could be considered social science, humanities, and botany. The following excerpt might fall into all these categories and economics, too. How would *you* classify the passage?

But to be more particular, for it is complained that Mr. Coleman has reported chiefly the expensive experiments of gentlemen farmers, my outgoes were,

For a hoe	$0 54
Ploughing, harrowing, and furrowing	7 50 Too much.
Beans for seed	3 12 $\frac{1}{2}$
Potatoes	1 33
Peas	0 40
Turnip seed	0 06
White line for crow fence	0 02
Horse cultivator and boy three hours	1 00
Horse and cart to get crop	<u>0 75</u>
In all	$14 72 $\frac{1}{2}$

Thoreau follows this balance sheet with a list of his income and a calculation of his profit.

It's plain that the four types of writing—exposition, narration, argumentation, and description—still apply to writing across the curriculum. See? Writing across the curriculum isn't anything very new from what you've already learned. In addition, it's often a matter of format and vocabulary that shapes writing across the curriculum, not a different kind of writing.

Let's look at techniques you can use as you write across the curriculum, starting with establishing a bond with your audience.

One Size Doesn't *Fit All!*

As you've learned, each subject area has its own specific writing style and slant; however, all subjects overlap to some degree. The following table shows some of the similarities and differences among the various curricula.

Alike	Different
Has set purpose	Follows rules of subject area
Aimed at a specific audience	May follow specific format
Has a clear thesis	Uses specialized language
Is well-organized	Tone suits specific subject
Uses details and examples	May use passive voice (science)
Has an effective style	Uses correct documentation style

Mix 'n' Match

So what types of writing will you be called on to produce? Here's the run-down on each subject area and the most common writing tasks:

Subject Area	Common Writing Tasks
Business	e-mail
	flyers, brochures
	letters
	memos
	performance appraisals
	press releases
	recommendations
	reports
	resumés and cover letters

Subject Area	Common Writing Tasks
Humanities (literature, language, philosophy, religion, etc.)	reaction papers term and research papers literary interpretations
Social Sciences (sociology, political science, psychology, education, economics)	term and research papers case studies
Natural Sciences (medicine, engineering, geology, physics, computer science, astronomy, biology, chemistry)	reports critical reviews

Playing with the Big Kids

When you're an expert in a specific subject, you have the inside track. Your audience will often give you the benefit of the doubt automatically, since you have the reputation to back up your claims.

Writer's Block

Don't pretend to be something you're not, and never, *ever*, lie to your readers.

For example, you believe I can teach you how to write well, since I've published over 100 books, have a doctorate in English and writing, and am a tenured university professor. But would you be so quick to believe me if I tried to teach you how to replace a hard drive, whip up a perfect crème brûlée, or bungee-jump off the Empire State Building? I think not. That's where my skill as a writer comes in. I have written very successful books in subjects not specifically in my area. Now you can, too. Here's how.

➤ **Establish trust.** Build a rapport with your audience by establishing your relevant credentials and experience. Either method (or both) will reassure your readers that you're qualified to write about the specific subject—even if it *is* out of your field.

➤ **Know your stuff.** Do your research. For example, while writing *Roots* and trying to imagine how it felt to be shipped to America aboard a slave boat, Alex Haley boarded a freighter from Africa to the United States. He even got permission from the captain to spend every night stretched out naked on a plank in the cold, black ship's hole.

You don't have to go this far, but no matter how qualified you appear to be, it won't wash in print unless you have a firm grasp on the topic. You can achieve this by making sure you're up on the latest in your field and speaking to experts.

Author! Author!

Writers can get carried away when it comes to getting the facts. It's reputed that in 1972, Frederick Forsyth and a dozen friends attempted to oust the government of Equatorial Guinea by kidnapping President Francisco Marcias Nguema. Forsyth's plan failed, setting him back more than $200,000. Fortunately, art doesn't have to imitate life. Two years later, Forsyth published *The Dogs of War,* which describes a band of mercenaries who overthrow an African government by killing its president. In the book, the plot was a success.

➤ **Be logical.** Make sense. Even if you're not trained in the field you're writing about, you'll make a more convincing case if your writing is well-organized, unified, and coherent.

➤ **Use sufficient details and examples.** You don't have to bury your readers in minutiae. You *do* have to provide the fabric to fill in the framework of your thesis. In this book, for instance, I've provided a lavish number of model essays, both student and professional examples. These serve to prove my point and give you models for your own writing. I also give you specific examples, hints, and warnings.

Write Angles

You can find technical experts by contacting professional organizations, universities, and trade organizations. Don't forget alumni associations and civic groups, too. Treat the task as you would any other networking contact.

➤ **Check and double-check your facts.** Since you're not an expert in the field, make an extra effort to get it right. For example, I've written a number of science books for children, even though my field of expertise is humanities. I always do every experiment and demonstration I write to make sure it really does work. No exploding chemical volcanoes from *my* books!

➤ **Hire a technical editor.** It's always a good idea when you're writing for a specialized audience to have a technical editor in that field look over the document. The majority of the *Complete Idiot's Guides* are checked by an outside technical editor. (You can find the credit in the frontmatter.)

➤ **Fit the format.** Documents in every subject area follow a slightly different style. For example, lab reports have a special format: Title, *Abstract,* Introduction, Method and Materials, Results, Discussion, Conclusion, and References. Case studies in the social sciences, in contrast, start with information about the person or group being studied, followed with a history, observations, and conclusions. Case studies often end with a recommendation. You can find format and style information for each discipline in the subject area guides listed later in this chapter.

Word Watch

An **abstract** is a brief summary, usually no more than 125 words.

➤ **Use jargon.** Yes, I know that I advised you earlier in this book (in Chapter 4, "Words, Words, Words," to be exact) that jargon should be avoided like stiletto heels and spandex. Here's the prime directive: *Always* use the language that suits your audience and purpose. When you're writing papers in a specific subject area, use the technical words you need to convey your precise shade of meaning. This means you'll be dealing with some jargon.

➤ **Suit the tone to the subject and audience.** Papers in engineering and science are impersonal, even dry, for example. Before you start to write, read a number of documents in the field to catch the tone. You can find models in technical journals, books, and monographs.

➤ **Consider voice.** The active voice is usually preferable to the passive because it is more vigorous and concise. However, many science papers are written in the passive voice to place the subject in the foreground and the writer in the background. Often, business documents are written in the passive voice for the same reason (and to avoid having to take the fall for a deal that goes south).

Writer's Block

Warning: Don't cite too many outside experts when you're writing outside your area of expertise. This diminishes the trust you've built with your readers.

Using some or all of these suggestions can help you produce brilliant writing no matter what the subject. Start small, with perhaps one or two ideas at first. Then experiment with other ideas to see which ones work best for you.

Full Credit

You must *document* or credit any information you pick up that's not common knowledge. Usually, this is done in footnotes, endnotes, bibliographies, and Works Cited pages.

Of course, life would be too easy if every field used the same method of documentation. No, different fields of study embrace their method of documentation with all the passion of newlyweds. And like the ad wars, each curricula is stalwart in its defense of its own method of documentation. The "tastes great/less filling" argument has been replaced with "easy to use/gives a more complete citation" debate. Here's a list of the standard documentation reference guides in major fields:

Area of Study	Documentation Method
Biology	Council of Biology Editors. *Scientific Style and Format: The CBE Manual for Authors, Editors, and Publishers.* New York: Cambridge University Press, 1994.
Business Publishing	*Chicago Manual of Style.* Chicago: University of Chicago Press, 1993.
Chemistry	American Chemical Society. *The ACS Style Guide: A Manual for Authors and Editors.* Washington: ACS, 1985.
Engineering	Michaelson, Herbert B. *How to Write and Publish Engineering Papers and Reports.* Phoenix: Oryx, 1990.
English	Gibaldi, Joseph. *MLA Handbook for Writers of Research Papers.* New York: Modern Language Association, 1999.
Geology	United States Geological Survey. *Suggestions to Authors of the Reports of the United States Geological Survey.* Washington, GPO, 1991.
Government	Government Printing Office. *Style Manual.* Rev. ed. Washington: GPO, 1984.
Law	*The Bluebook: A Uniform System of Citation.* Comp. Editors of Columbia Law review, et al. Cambridge: Harvard Law Review, 1991.
Linguistics	Linguistic Society of America. *LSA Bulletin.* December issue, annually.
Mathematics	American Mathematical Society. *A Manual for Authors of Mathematical Papers.* Providence: AMS, 1990.

Area of Study	Documentation Method
Medicine	Iverson, Cheryl, et. al. *American Medical Association Manual of Style*. Baltimore: Williams, 1989.
Music	Holoman, D. Kern, ed. *Writing About Music: A Style Sheet from the Editors of 19th Century Music*. Berkeley: University of California Press, 1988.
Physics	American Institute of Physics. *AIP Style Manual*. New York: AIP, 1990.
Psychology	American Psychological Association. *Publication Manual of the American Psychological Association*. Washington: APA, 1994.

Two's Company, Three's a Crowd— Unless You're Writing

Essay tests are solo events, novels are written in lonely garrets, and we don't want to get into poetry and pain. When you write across the curriculum, however, you're likely to be called upon to do some collaborative writing.

Collaborative writing involves several people working together to create a document. The participants may be working in the same place, different places, at the same time, or at different times. Increasingly, collaborative writing is being done electronically, through e-mail.

You'll most likely be asked to write collaboratively in situations such as these:

➤ You're conducting a scientific experiment in a class or laboratory.

➤ A grant application has to be completed.

➤ On the job, the writing task is too big, important, or complex for one person to complete alone. This is true with government bids, for example.

➤ It is important to reach consensus and have a group viewpoint.

➤ You're a government official, lawyer, or physician preparing a document for publication.

It's plain to see that group writing is here to stay. Even if you haven't been involved in this method of composition yet, I guarantee that it's on your horizon.

Point/Counterpoint

Writing in groups has its advantages and disadvantages. Here are the two sides in a nutshell:

Pro:	Many hands make light work.
Con:	Too many cooks spoil the broth.
Pro:	Two heads are better than one.
Con:	A camel was a horse designed by a committee.

As these clichés show, some people think collaborative writing is the greatest thing since sliced bread; others consider it in the same class as spiders, sky-diving, and snarling dogs. Even if you're a member of the latter group, remember that even the finest writers can benefit from some judicious editing.

Group writing can also help relieve some of the tension you may have about writing, since it takes part of the burden from your shoulders by spreading the task. Writing with a partner or in a group also helps you ...

➤ Consider the issue from different sides.

➤ Appeal to a wider audience.

➤ Complete the task more quickly.

➤ Pick up writing tips from others.

➤ Experiment with different styles.

Write Angles

People write well in groups when they are flexible, respect others, confident, able to accept criticism, and deal well with conflict.

All Together, Now

Try these suggestions to make collaborative writing as successful and painless as possible.

1. Start by defining the task clearly.

2. Identify the audience and purpose from the outset.

3. Set a timetable.

4. Always build in extra time. A few extra days can make the difference between a merely acceptable document and a superb one—as well as between failure and success.

5. Try to allocate tasks as fairly as possible: Don't let anyone be a martyr or a shirker.

6. Don't assume that everyone knows what you mean or how you feel. State your points clearly and if necessary, in writing.

7. Keep the meetings brief and on task.

8. Try to be flexible.

9. Make the time to build group cohesion and loyalty. Group members will work harder and better if they're united and feel invested in the project.

10. Have one group member proofread the entire document for errors in spelling, grammar, mechanics, and usage.

Author! Author!

Close to 90 percent of all business executives write in teams at least some of the time. About half of those surveyed found collaborative writing productive. Since half of the executives did not find group writing worth the time or trouble, you can tell that collaborative writing isn't everyone's cup of tea. However, when it comes to writing many kinds of documents across the curriculum, you may have to share your toys.

The Least You Need to Know

➤ Every area of study has its own way of looking at the world, but some writers blur the boundaries between curriculum areas.

➤ All subjects overlap to some degree.

➤ To write successfully across the curriculum, you should establish trust, know your stuff, be logical, use sufficient detail, double-check your facts, hire a technical editor, fit the format, consider diction, suit the tone to the subject and audience, and consider voice.

➤ Use the correct method of documentation for each subject area.

➤ Collaborative writing, common in many subject areas, involves several people working together to create a document.

Part 4

Just Shoot Me Now: Research Papers and Term Papers

Question: *Why do people dread writing research reports and term papers?*

Laurie Rozakis: *Got me. It's actually fun.*

In this part, I'll prove my point by taking you step by step through the research and writing process. We'll start with an explanation of the different types of reports and move on to managing your time, selecting a topic, and writing a thesis statement. Then I'll show you how to find the information you need, evaluate and document sources, and integrate the material you found. By the end of these chapters, you'll be writing research papers like a pro!

Chapter 17

Paper Chase

> ## In This Chapter
>
> ➤ The importance of research papers and term papers
>
> ➤ Research papers vs. term papers
>
> ➤ Writing schedules
>
> ➤ Research paper subjects
>
> ➤ Research paper topics
>
> ➤ Thesis statements

In a research paper …

    They write: It is clear that much additional work will be required before a complete understanding …

    They mean: I don't get it.

By the end of this chapter, you *will* get it, all of it. That's because writing a research paper is easy when you take it step by step, which is what you'll learn here. First, I'll explain the difference between a research paper and a term paper, the two major types of investigative reports. Then you'll learn the first crucial steps in the process: selecting a subject, narrowing it to a specific topic, and writing a thesis statement.

Inquiring Minds Want to Know

Parent: "What do you want to be when you grow up, Billy?"

Child: "A researcher, of course."

Yes, every child dreams of becoming a researcher. Not very likely, eh? However, the odds *are* great that every child will do hard time in the library or in cyberspace hunting for the facts they need. They'll be standing right next to every adult in town, too. That's because research is essential to our lives.

Whether you're looking for information about a van's safety record, a town's schools, or a company's stocks, you'll need to know how to gather, sort, and track the facts and opinions available to you.

Author! Author!

In America, research papers were first assigned in schools in the 1870s. By the turn of the century, most universities required seniors to write a research paper as a prerequisite for graduation. These essays were four to 12 pages long. Realizing that they had stumbled upon a good way to prepare students to be critical thinkers and responsible citizens, instructors decided to require underclass students to churn out a research paper as well. By the 1930s, high school students were writing term papers, too. Now, students as young as the first grade are learning the basics of writing a research paper. You can run, but you can't hide.

Employees in the public as well as private sector are often required to write research papers, especially in hot fields where information is flying around at dizzying speeds. The logic is strong: If you can gather the facts in a readable format, then you've got the power to make logical decisions and reasonable judgments. That's why you need to know how to write a research paper.

The facts you gather can be presented in two forms: as a *research paper* and as a *term paper*. The two types of writing are confused more often than Patty and Cathy, partly because there are no fixed differences between them regarding length, topic, format, or citations. Let's see how they're the same and different.

Meet the Research Paper

A *research paper* presents and argues a *thesis,* the writer's hypothesis, theory, or opinion. Therefore, a research paper is an analytical or persuasive essay that evaluates a position. When you write a research paper, you'll use outside evidence to persuade your readers that your argument is valid or at least deserves serious consideration.

Because your thesis will be original and creative, you won't be able to merely summarize what someone else has written. Instead, you'll have to synthesize information from many different sources to create something uniquely your own.

As you reach your own conclusions about the topic, you'll persuade readers that you're onto something good.

In brief, a research paper ...

> ➤ Argues a point.
> ➤ Formulates a thesis.
> ➤ Argues/persuades.
> ➤ Evaluates.
> ➤ Considers *why* and *how.*

Word Watch

A **research paper** is persuasive, as it argues a thesis. A **term paper** is expository, as it shows or tells.

And Here's the Term Paper

A *term paper* doesn't argue a point or try to convince readers to think or act a certain way. Rather, a term paper is a summary of information from one or more sources. When you write a term paper, you're serving as a conduit, reporting what others have said.

Don't treat the term paper as a dowdy country cousin, however. Term papers are a great way to present a lot of data in an organized and easy-to-use form. That's why government employees often write term papers with information on the economy, demographics, transportation, and so forth.

In brief, a term paper ...

> ➤ Presents data.
> ➤ Reports what others said.
> ➤ Explains or describes.
> ➤ Summarizes.
> ➤ Considers *what.*

We're going to focus on research papers here, because they require more analytical thinking and original thought. As a result, they're more challenging to write.

Writer's Block

I'm presenting the steps of the writing process in chronological order, but remember that writers compose differently. You may double-back, combine two steps, or even omit a step or two. That's okay.

Time Flies When You're Having Fun

You don't have enough time to do the laundry (how *does* it pile up so fast?), so how are you going to find the time to write your research paper? Here's the brutal truth: You *won't* have the time you need. No one ever does, so why should you be different? Nonetheless, the task has to get done—and within a set time frame. That's why it's especially important that you plan the task from the get-go. So let's get going.

Here are the steps you'll complete as you write a research paper:

1. Select a topic
2. Narrow the topic
3. Write the thesis statement
4. Research material
5. Take notes on material
6. Outline paper
7. Draft rough copies
8. Find more sources, if necessary
9. Integrate source materials
10. Document sources
11. Do Works Cited page
12. Write frontmatter, backmatter, title page
13. Revise, edit, proofread
14. Keyboard
15. Deal with catastrophes

That last step is a dilly, so it's crucial that you build in time to deal with it. Computers crash; the dog eats your rough draft. Sometimes the *one* book you really need isn't available from the library; more than one Web site has been known to mysteriously vanish into the Bermuda Triangle of cyberspace.

I've worked out some time allocation plans you can follow as you prepare your research paper. Each plan includes some "air," that crucial extra time, so your back won't be up against the wall as the deadline looms.

In the following spaces provided, note the day you started and completed each step. You may want to photocopy these plans so you can use them again as you write different research papers.

Write Angles

Using a laptop computer can shave days off the time it takes to write a research paper. It's especially helpful for taking notes and organizing information.

A Month in the Country

If you have one month (20 days) in which to complete a research paper, allocate your time this way:

Task	Days	Date Started	Date Ended
1. Select topic	½	_____	_____
2. Narrow topic	½	_____	_____
3. Do thesis statement	½	_____	_____
4. Research	2	_____	_____
5. Take notes	2	_____	_____
6. Outline	½	_____	_____
7. Draft	3	_____	_____
8. Find more sources	2	_____	_____
9. Integrate materials	1	_____	_____
10. Document	½	_____	_____
11. Do Works Cited	½	_____	_____
12. Write frontmatter	1	_____	_____
13. Revise, edit, proof	3	_____	_____
14. Keyboard	1	_____	_____
15. Extra time	2	_____	_____

See Results in Six Weeks!

If you have six weeks (30 days) in which to complete a research paper, allocate your time this way:

Task	Days	Date Started	Date Ended
1. Select topic	1	_____	_____
2. Narrow topic	1	_____	_____
3. Do thesis statement	1	_____	_____
4. Research	3	_____	_____
5. Take notes	3	_____	_____
6. Outline	1	_____	_____
7. Draft	4	_____	_____
8. Find more sources	3	_____	_____
9. Integrate materials	2	_____	_____
10. Document	1	_____	_____
11. Do Works Cited	1	_____	_____
12. Write frontmatter	1	_____	_____
13. Revise, edit, proof	4	_____	_____
14. Keyboard	2	_____	_____
15. Extra time	2	_____	_____

Author! Author!

We have Ben Franklin to thank for the library, since he started the first one back in 1731. The idea spread fast: By the time America became independent from Great Britain, there were 29 libraries in the 13 colonies. By the turn of the century, there were 49 libraries, holding 80,000 books. Today, the Library of Congress alone has over 70 million items in its collection (over 16 million books and 30 million manuscripts).

Forty Days (but Not Forty Nights)

If you have eight weeks (40 days) in which to complete a research paper, allocate your time this way:

Task	Days	Date Started	Date Ended
1. Select topic	2	_____	_____
2. Narrow topic	2	_____	_____
3. Do thesis statement	1	_____	_____
4. Research	4	_____	_____
5. Take notes	5	_____	_____
6. Outline	1	_____	_____
7. Draft	7	_____	_____
8. Find more sources	3	_____	_____
9. Integrate materials	3	_____	_____
10. Document	1	_____	_____
11. Do Works Cited	1	_____	_____
12. Write frontmatter	1	_____	_____
13. Revise, edit, proof	4	_____	_____
14. Keyboard	2	_____	_____
15. Extra time	2	_____	_____

Around the Library in Sixty Days

If you have two months in which to write a research paper, don't get too comfortable. With that much time, it's human nature to get a little complacent. "This paper will be a walk in the park," you might think. Not so fast, friend.

With a long lead time, it's tempting to leave the assignment to the last minute. After all, you do have *plenty* of time. But "plenty of time" is relative, like "losing a *little* hair." Time, like hair, goes faster than you think.

Now that you've been warned, if you have two months in which to write a research paper, why not use it this way:

Write Angles

In many instances, it's actually easier to have *less* time in which to write a research paper, because you know that you're under pressure to produce.

Task	Days	Date Started	Date Ended
1. Select topic	3	_____	_____
2. Narrow topic	2	_____	_____
3. Do thesis statement	1	_____	_____
4. Research	8	_____	_____
5. Take notes	8	_____	_____
6. Outline	2	_____	_____
7. Draft	10	_____	_____
8. Find more sources	4	_____	_____
9. Integrate materials	3	_____	_____
10. Document	2	_____	_____
11. Do Works Cited	1	_____	_____
12. Write frontmatter	2	_____	_____
13. Revise, edit, proof	6	_____	_____
14. Keyboard	3	_____	_____
15. Extra time	5	_____	_____

Now that we have our timetable in place, let's move on to the first step in the process of writing a research paper, *selecting a subject.*

Subject to Change

Some of us have greatness thrust upon us; the rest of us have to settle for subjects. If you're given the subject of your research paper (a common occurrence in business and government jobs), you're all set. If not, the ball is in your court.

Writer's Block

Don't forget: A research paper isn't a laundry list of your findings. Rather, it's a unified argument that incorporates all relevant information.

The right subject can make your paper; the wrong one can break it. How can you tell if you've picked a stinker? Unsatisfactory subjects …

➤ Can't be completed within your time frame.

➤ Can't be researched since the material doesn't exist.

➤ Don't argue a point.

➤ Are inappropriate, offensive, or vulgar.

Understand that nearly every subject *can* be researched, but not every subject *should* be researched. After all, why waste your time finding information about a subject that's been done to death? Banal and boring subjects often lead to banal and boring research papers. Give yourself (and your readers) a break by starting with an original subject or an original way of looking at an old subject.

One Percent Inspiration + Ninety-Nine Percent Perspiration = Great Subjects

"I don't have anything to write about," you moan. Quit your kvetching; you know far more than you think you do. Besides, Dr. Laurie's here now. So take two of these ideas and thank me in the morning.

Top Ten Ways to Get Great Research Paper Ideas

1. **Read subject headings.** You can skim the multi-volume *Library of Congress Subject Headings* (a reference text), leaf through a *Readers' Guide to Periodical Literature,* or even check the subjects listed on your Web browser.

2. **Browse through encyclopedias.** Skim online, book, or CD-ROM encyclopedia headings for a rich list of topics.

3. **Stroll the stacks.** Walk around the shelves and see what topics catch your eye. Or, let your fingers do the walking by skimming the library's book catalog.

4. **Consider textbooks.** Pick a field that intrigues you and check out a few textbooks in that area. Read the table of contents; leaf through the pages. Find an idea that piques your interest and delve into it.

5. **Tap into your journal.** As you learned in Chapter 15, "Picture This: Description," your journal can be a place to store fabulous writing ideas. Make a withdrawal now.

Write Angles

If you've been assigned a subject you detest, see if you can find an aspect of the subject that you like. Nearly all topics can be tweaked a bit here and there. Of course, always clear those "tweaks" with the person who assigned the topic.

Writer's Block

Warning: Your teacher may make selecting and narrowing a subject part of the research paper process itself. As a result, you may be assessed on how well you choose and focus the subject of your paper.

6. **Make a list and check it twice.** If you've been assigned the paper in a class, jot down all the ideas linked to the subject of the class. For example, if you're taking a sociology class, you might list *working women, divorce laws, immigration regulations,* and *eating disorders.* One of these might make a good paper.

7. **The medium is the message.** Create a visual, as you learned in Chapter 8, "Write This Way." Many writers find that charts, webs, graphs, and other pictures help them generate a slew of ideas.

8. **Ask questions.** Use the five Ws and H (*who, what, when, where, why,* and *how*) to help you consider all sides of an issue.

9. **Talk the talk.** Speak to people who have written research papers: teachers, parents, and professionals. Doctors, lawyers, accountants, real estate salespeople, computer programmers, and other business people are all excellent sources for ideas.

10. **Read, listen, and watch.** Read anything and everything: newspapers, magazines, journals, critical reviews, essays, and matchbook covers. Watch TV, listen to the radio, go to the movies. Inspiration is all around; just tap into it.

Time to Squeeze the Tomatoes

So now you have some ideas for subjects—how can you tell if they're keepers? Ask yourself these questions as you evaluate your catch:

1. **How much time do I have?** The amount of time you have to write a research paper is vital since it's all too easy to get caught up in your research and make it a career choice. So choose a subject that you can complete in the time you've been allotted.

2. **How long must my paper be?** When it comes to subjects for research papers, length matters. It will obviously take you much longer to write a 50-page research paper than it will to write a 10-page one. Weigh this consideration as you select a subject. The shorter the paper and the longer you have to write, the more leeway you'll have to select a challenging subject that will require more research.

3. **What type of research must I do?** As you'll learn in Chapter 18, "Seek and Ye Shall Find," there are two main kinds of sources: primary sources and secondary sources. Primary sources include firsthand material such as letters, interviews, and eyewitness accounts. Secondary sources include almanacs, biographies, and encyclopedias. Sometimes, you'll have to use a specific type of source, or a mix. If that's the case, factor it into the subject/choice equation.

Writer's Block

Never select a subject that condescends to your readers, offends them, or panders to them. Don't try to shock them, either—it *always* backfires.

4. **What are my reader's expectations?** Some subjects play better than others. You don't want to parrot back the reader's own words, but neither do you want to deliberately antagonize your reader. I'm always astonished at the number of times I explain, "I'm fed up to *here* with papers on gun control, euthanasia, and the death penalty"—and I still get papers on gun control, euthanasia, and the death penalty. I crave papers on new topics, such as cloning, filtering the Internet, and a flat tax. Heck, I'd even be delighted to receive a paper that argues the merits of artificial turf over natural grass ... rather than another research paper on gun control, euthanasia, and the death penalty.

You can stint on many things, but not when it comes to selecting the topic for your research paper. Judge your topic harshly; you don't want to end up picking a stinker.

Judge and Jury

You shouldn't pick a subject just like that, but you're not going to have time to dally. If you're stuck in third gear, try these suggestions to get your engine revving:

1. **Remember that your purpose is to persuade.** With a research paper, you're arguing a point. If you can't slant the subject to be persuasive, toss it back.

2. **Select a subject you like.** If you have a choice, try to select a subject that interests you. You'll be living together a while, so why not make it pleasant?

3. **Be practical.** Look for topics that have enough information available, but not so much information that you can't possibly dig through it all. Writing a research paper is challenging enough without shooting yourself in the foot.

4. **Beware of hot subjects.** "Hot" subjects—very timely, popular issues—often lack the expert attention that leads to reliable information. The books, articles, and interviews on such subjects have often been produced in great haste. As a result, they're not carefully fact-checked.

5. **Recognize that not all questions have answers.** Some questions invite informed opinions based on the evidence you've gathered from research. Dealing with questions that don't have definitive answers can make your paper provocative and intriguing.

You *can* pick a winner, fellow writer. After all, you had the wisdom to invite *me* to guide you on the path to better writing. That's how I know you're an intelligent, sophisticated judge of character.

Subjects vs. Topics

So now you have a subject, and it's a lulu. The only problem is size—this baby's as big as a 747. So you *narrow the subject into a topic* by finding smaller aspects of the topic within the subject area to use as the basis of your research paper. First, let's make sure we're all on the same page when it comes to subjects and topics.

Word Watch

A **subject** of a research paper is the general content. A **topic** is the specific issue being discussed.

Write Angles

Your teacher likes your topic, your parents like your topic, your buddies like your topic. Even your dog likes your topic. The problem? You don't like your topic. So get a new topic!

A *subject* of a research paper is the general content. Subjects are broad and general. For example:

➤ Health

➤ Television

➤ Stocks and bonds

➤ Travel

The *topic* of a research paper, in contrast, is the specific issue being discussed. Here are some possible *topics* for a research paper developed from the previous subjects:

➤ **Health**

assessing fad diets

arguing the merits of AIDS testing of health care workers

➤ **Television**

arguing for or against the V-chip in televisions

taking a side in the cable wars

➤ **Stocks and bonds**

showing that day trading is profitable (or not)

persuading readers to use e-trades rather than brokers (or vice versa)

➤ Travel

arguing that surcharges for solo travelers are unfair

arguing the merits of e-tickets

Consider all facets of your subject as you develop topics. You may wish to speak to other people about the subject or just let your mind free-associate. Let those ideas bubble up!

Cut Down to Size

To get that beast of a subject tailored to an appropriate size, try phrasing the subject as a question. You can also list subdivisions of the subject to create topics. Can't find subtopics? Consult card catalogues, reference books, and textbooks for ideas. Here are some examples:

Subject	Topic
space exploration	Should the space program be drastically cut back?
social services	Is workfare working?
violence	Do violent video games, movies, and songs influence children to commit violence?
antidepressants	Are antidepressants being over-prescribed?
intelligence	Is intelligence determined by nature or nurture?

Goldywriter and the Three Bears

So the porridge is too hot, the porridge is too cold. How can you make sure the porridge—and your topic—is just right? Try this checklist:

❑ **Is my topic still too broad?** Check your sources. How many pages do they devote to the topic? If it takes other writers a book to answer the question you've posed, your topic is still too big.

❑ **Is my topic *too* limited?** Is the topic perfect for a 350- to 500-word essay? If so, it's too narrow for the typical research paper.

❑ **Is my topic tedious?** Been there, done that, got the T-shirt. If your topic bores you before you've even started writing, you can bet it will bore your audience.

❑ **Is my topic too controversial?** If you're afraid you're going to offend your audience with your topic, don't take the risk. Start with a new topic that suits both your audience and purpose.

❑ **Is my paper one-sided?** If there's only one opinion about your topic or the vast majority of people think the same way as you do, there's no point in arguing the issue. Save your breath to cool your porridge.

Here's where the rubber meets the road, you driving machine. You can't cut corners with this stage; answer all the questions to make sure you're on the right track.

The Heart of the Matter: Writing a Thesis Statement

Once you've narrowed your topic, it's time to turn your attention to your *thesis statement*, what you're proving in your research paper.

Word Watch

The **thesis statement** is the central point you're proving in your research paper.

Write Angles

Research may lead you to revise your thesis, even disprove it, but framing it at the very beginning of your research will focus your thinking.

An effective thesis statement states your main idea, reveals your purpose, and shows how your argument will be structured. As you draft your thesis statement, consider what you want to prove.

Here are some terrific thesis statements:

➤ Much of the conflict between men and women results from their very different way of using language.

➤ Fairy tales are among the most subversive texts in children's literature.

➤ The brief economic boom of the 1920s had a dramatic impact on the U.S. economy.

➤ The computer revolution has done more harm than good.

➤ Everyone wins with a flat tax: government, business, accountants, and even consumers.

Try several variations of your thesis statement until you have one that says all you need to say. Don't panic: Remember that you're very likely to revise your thesis statement several times as you research, draft, and revise your paper.

The Least You Need to Know

➤ A research paper is persuasive. It argues a thesis, the writer's hypothesis or opinion.

➤ A term paper is expository. It summarizes information from various sources.

➤ Start your work by setting up a timetable. Then stick to it.

➤ There are many ways to find good research paper subjects, including reading subject headings, browsing through encyclopedias, and tapping into your journal.

➤ Select subjects by considering time constraints, the length of your paper, the type of research you must do, and your reader's expectations.

➤ Choose a subject you like. Be practical, shun overly timely subjects, and recognize that not all questions have answers (but that's okay).

➤ Narrow your subject into a topic that fits the assignment. Then write a thesis statement, a sentence that explains what you're proving in your research paper.

Chapter 18

Seek and Ye Shall Find

In This Chapter

➤ The thrill of the (research) hunt

➤ Talk the talk: interviews and surveys

➤ Your tax dollars at work: government documents

You've got your subject, you've narrowed it to a topic, and you've written your thesis statement. Now it's time to get the facts you need to prove your thesis. In this chapter, we play *Dragnet* and get the facts, ma'am.

All the information you need is available—but you have to know how to find and sort the treasures from the trash. Let's plunge right in by exploring the different reference sources available.

Basic Training

Before you even thumb through the card catalog or turn your computer on, try the following ideas to make your search as easy and enjoyable as possible.

1. **Use key words.** List the key words for your topic, using the title, author, and subject to direct your thinking. For example, key words for a research paper on the poem "Howl" might include ...

   ➤ Title: "Howl"

   ➤ Author: Allen Ginsberg

   ➤ Subject: The Beats

2. **Include related words.** Brainstorm synonyms to expand or narrow your search. For example, if you're writing on overcrowding in national parks, here are some possible synonyms:

➤ Environmentalism

➤ National monuments

➤ Federal lands

➤ Wilderness

➤ Conservation

➤ Government lands

3. **Learn the lingo.** Nearly every research tool has an abbreviation—or two. The *World Wide Web,* for example, is abbreviated as *WWW; Something About the Author* is called *SATA.* You can learn the abbreviations for print sources by checking the introduction or index. For online sources, check the Help screen.

4. **Know your library.** They *are* the latest and the greatest, these libraries. Ask your reference librarians (a.k.a. "media specialists") what special services the library offers, their cost (if any), and the time involved. Find out from the start what extra help is available.

5. **Consult reference librarians.** I'll teach you how to find nearly every reference source you need on your own, but you might hit a research roadblock. That's why we have reference librarians. Don't be afraid to ask these marvelous experts for help; that's why they work in the library and not in the DMV.

Now, it's time to learn how to use libraries and library catalogs efficiently so you can get the primary and secondary sources you need.

Book Learning

Books are "user friendly"—they're light, easy to use, and familiar. They can't crash as computers can, either. Best of all, since it takes time to write and publish a book, they tend to be reliable sources, but more on that in Chapter 19, "Cast a Critical Eye." Right now, you'll learn how to find the books you need to complete your research.

Write Angles

Scan the *Library of Congress Guide to Subject Headings* for help finding synonyms or related terms for your research topic.

Word Watch

Primary sources, such as auto-biographies, diaries, eyewitness accounts, and interviews, are created by direct observation. **Secondary sources,** such as biographies, almanacs, encyclopedias, and textbooks, were written by people with indirect knowledge. Effective research papers often use a mix of both primary and secondary sources.

Since libraries have a lot of books—a university library can have over a million volumes, a community library over 100,000 tomes—*classification systems* were created to track the volumes. Knowing how these systems work can help you find the books you need to complete your research. It's all based on the concept of *call numbers*.

Books are divided into two broad classes: *fiction* and *nonfiction*. Fiction is catalogued under the author's last name. Nonfiction books, however, are classified in two different ways: the *Dewey Decimal* classification system and the *Library of Congress* classification system. The systems use completely different sets of letters and numbers, as you'll learn.

Word Watch

The Dewey or Library of Congress classification designation for a book is its **call number.**

Dewey Decimal Classification System

Melvil Dewey (1851–1931) had a thing for order, which may have made life at home somewhat tense, but it *did* revolutionize libraries. Before Dewey came along, many libraries filed books by color or size, a chaotic system at best. Dewey's classification system, published in 1876, divided nonfiction books into 10 broad categories:

Write Angles

Be sure to copy down the call number *exactly* as it appears in the card catalogue. Otherwise, it will be tough—if not impossible—to find the book.

000–099	General works such as encyclopedias
100–199	Philosophy
200–299	Religion (including mythology)
300–399	Social sciences (including folklore, legends, government, manners, vocations)
400–499	Language (including dictionaries and grammar books)
500–599	Pure science (mathematics, astronomy, chemistry, nature study)
600–699	Technology (applied science, aviation, building, engineering, homemaking)
700–799	Arts (photography, drawing, painting, music, sports)
800–899	Literature (plays, poetry)
900–999	History (ancient, modern, geography, travel)

Each category is further divided. For example, 500–599 covers "pure" science, including mathematics. The math books are shelved from 510–519; geometry is listed under 513. There are finer and finer categories. Dewey's system works so well that today it's used by most elementary schools, high schools, and small public libraries.

Library of Congress Classification System

The Library of Congress Classification system, in contrast, was designed for just one library—you guessed it, the Library of Congress. Since the Library of Congress system allows for finer distinctions than the Dewey system, it's been adopted by nearly all large college and university libraries. Here's how it works.

Each Library of Congress classification call number starts with a letter, followed by a number, ending with a letter/number combination. For example, here's the call number for Jack London's *The Sea Wolf:* PS3523.046S43.

The Library of Congress classification system has 20 classes, as follows:

A	General Works
B	Philosophy and religion
C	History
D	History and topography (except America)
E–F	American history
G	Geography, anthropology, folklore, manners, customs, recreation
H	Social sciences
J	Political sciences
K	United States law
L	Education
M	Music
N	Fine arts
P	Language and literature

Q	Science
R	Medicine
S	Agriculture
T	Technology
U	Military science
V	Naval science
Z	Bibliography and library science

As with the Dewey system, each category in the Library of Congress system can be divided into subclasses.

Author! Author!

Library call numbers don't work like the Celsius and Fahrenheit temperature systems, so there's no magical formula you can use to convert the call numbers in one system to the call numbers in the other system. To save yourself hours of extra work, choose one library system—either university or public—and stick with it.

Hunt and Peck

Whether you use an online card catalogue (even though there's no actual "card" involved) or a paper catalogue, there are three different ways that you can locate material in books:

➤ Subject search

➤ Title search

➤ Author search

Your topic determines how you search for a book. Since most research papers deal with topics and issues, you'll likely be searching by subject. Nonetheless, you'll probably have to check titles and authors as well. Consider all three ways to find information as you look through the card catalog.

Bargain Books

In addition to specific books on your topic, here are some general reference sources to consider:

➤ **Almanacs.** These handy, easy-to-use reference guides are a great source for statistics and facts. *The World Almanac* and *The Information, Please Almanac* are the two best-known almanacs. They're updated every year.

Write Angles

Other reference sources include archival materials (rare books, charts, etc.), atlases, audio-visual materials, government documents, indexes, interviews, book reviews, TV shows, surveys, and yearbooks.

Writer's Block

Danger, Will Robinson: CD-ROM encyclopedias with video and sound often sacrifice text to make room for these multimedia bells-and-whistles. As a result, for serious research, print encyclopedias are usually a better bet. The exception is *Britannica*, which is now available free online. It's the gold standard for encyclopedias.

➤ **Bibliographies.** You'll save time if you find a *bibliography*, a list of books, articles, and other documents on a specific subject area. Well-known bibliographies include *Guide to the Literature of Art History, Communication: A Guide to Information Sources, Science and Engineering Literature,* and *Social Work: A Bibliography.*

➤ **Books in Print.** This annual listing of books currently in print or slated for print can tell you if a book is still being issued by the publisher. If so, the library can order a copy of the book or you can buy one yourself at a book store. If not, well … let's not go *there.*

➤ **Encyclopedias.** There are general encyclopedias (*World Book, Britannica, Colliers, Funk and Wagnalls*) as well as technical ones. Both types can give you a reliable overview of your subject and topic.

➤ *Guide to Reference Books.* Published by the American Library Association, this useful guide has five main categories: general reference works; humanities; social and behavioral sciences; history and area studies; and science, technology, and medicine.

➤ *Who's Who in America.* Are you researching a famous person? If so check *Who's Who,* because it includes biographical entries on approximately 75,000 Americans and people linked to America. *Who Was Who* covers famous dead people.

Mags and Rags

For more timely information, check out *periodicals,* material that is published on a regular schedule, such as weekly, biweekly, monthly, bimonthly, four times a year, and so on. Newspapers, magazines, and journals are classified as *periodicals.*

Back in the good old days, when a dollar was worth a dollar, when kids trudged five miles to school uphill in the snow, etc., periodicals were indexed in print. To get the actual article, you had to jot down the bibliographic citation, ask a clerk to retrieve the magazine, and then read it. If the periodical was on microfilm or microfiche, you had to jimmy it into a machine to read.

In today's technological age, a dollar isn't worth a dollar, it rarely snows and no one walks, and many libraries use *computerized databases* in place of printed indexes. Some databases include only periodicals; others include books, media, and much more. No matter what information is indexed, each entry provides the title, author, and sometimes, a summary. You can read the entire article from the screen, print it, or e-mail it to your home computer. This is a wonderful thing.

Every library has different periodical databases. Here are some of the best ones:

Word Watch

Periodical literature is published on a regular basis, such as newspapers, magazines, and journals.

Write Angles

When you're dealing with research, more is better, so try to collect more material than you think you need.

➤ *DataTimes* is an online index to local newspapers.

➤ *DIALOG* is an extensive, well-regarded database.

➤ *ERIC* (Educational Resources Information Center) and Education Index are the place to be for information on education.

➤ *InfoTrak* lists more than 1,000 business, technological, and general-interest periodicals, including *The New York Times* and the *Wall Street Journal.*

➤ *LEXIS/NEXIS* affords access to thousands of full-text articles.

➤ *MEDLINE* is a very well-respected source for information on medical topics.

➤ *MILCS* is a database of all the holdings of academic and public libraries in specific regions.

➤ *OCLC First Search* lists all the periodicals, media, and books in the United States and Canada. It has many indexes.

➤ *PAIS*, the Public Affairs Informational Service, is great for economics. Ditto for *EconLit*.

➤ *ATLA* Religion Database covers religion.

➤ *VU/TEXT* is a newspaper database.

➤ *WILSONSEARCH* is an online information sys-tem containing the Wilson databases not on CD-ROM, such as the *Education Index* and the *Index to Legal Periodicals*.

While more and more libraries are replacing their print indexes with online and CD-ROM sources, many libraries still maintain their print indexes, so you'll have to check both sources. In addition, the CD-ROM or online databases may not reach back far enough to include the sources you need, especially if you're doing historical research. Therefore, you're probably going to have to use both print and online indexes.

Researching on the I-Way

I do so love my modem, because it lets me access information from around the world—including text, graphics, sound, and video—without ever getting up from my

comfy chair. If you're linked to the Internet, you can view masterpieces from the Louvre Museum in France, take an aerial tour of Bali, or dissect a virtual frog. You can search databases at the Library of Congress and read electronic newsletters—without ever leaving your home. This makes the Internet an invaluable source of information as you prepare your research papers.

The *World Wide Web* is made of documents called *Web pages,* which can combine text, pictures, and sound. The "home page" is the entry point for access to a collection of pages. Specific words, pictures, or *icons* (special places to click) act as links to other pages. It doesn't matter where the other pages are located—even if they're on the other side of the world, the computer programs will retrieve them for you.

Author! Author!

The **Internet** is an expanding global information computer network comprised of people, hardware (computers), and software (computer programs). Each regional network is linked to other regional networks around the world to create a network of networks: the Internet. The Internet dates back to the 1960s, when scientists used it to collaborate on research papers. It's not owned or funded by any one organization, institution, or government. The Internet is directed by the Internet Society (ISOC), a group of volunteers. There's no president or CEO.

"Wait a minute, Rozakis," you mutter, "there has to be a catch." Actually, there is (isn't there *always?*). The Web isn't like a library where information is arranged within an accepted set of rules. It's more like a really big garage sale, where similar items are *usually* grouped together—but not always. Further, Web sites come and go without warning. Even if they stay put, the good ones are updated often so the material changes.

So how can you search the Web for information to use in your research paper? There are several different ways, each of them surprisingly easy. Here's how they work.

Search Engines

Search engines, which work with *key words,* help you locate Web sites. You type in a key word and the search engine automatically looks through its giant databases for matches.

The more precise the phrase, the better your chances of finding the information you need. Here are some of the most popular search engines and their Internet addresses.

AltaVista	www.altavista.digital.com
Cyberhound	www.thomson.com/cyberhound/
Excite	www.excite.com
HotBot	www.hotbot.com
InfoSeek	www2.infoseek.com
Inference Find	www.inference.com/ifind/

Lycos	lycos.cs.cmu.edu/
WebCrawler	webcrawler.com
Yahoo!	www.yahoo.com

Some search engines, such as *Yahoo!,* also let you search the Web by categories. For example, here's the opening subject list on the *Yahoo!* screen:

Arts and humanities	News and media
Business and economy	Recreation and sports
Computers and Internet	Reference
Education	Regional
Entertainment	Science
Government	Social sciences
Health	Society and culture

Writer's Block

Beware: The Web is addictive, like potato chips. You start a search, find interesting sites, and suddenly three hours have passed. So be sure to set aside ample time to search and roam through cyberspace.

Click on any of these categories and you get loads of subcategories. Most provide links to current news programs and online chat rooms, too.

Since not all search engines lead to the same sources, you should use more than one. Bookmarks or hot lists (accompanying each search engine) help you mark sources to which you want to return.

URLs

If you already have the address for a Web site, the *URL* (Uniform Resource Locator), you can type it in. URLs are made of long strings of letters. For example, here is the address for the World Wide Web Virtual Library subject catalogue:

www.w3.org/pub./DataSources/bySubject/Overview.html

It's crucial that you type the address *exactly* as it appears. Pay special attention to periods, capital letters, and lowercase letters. If you're even one letter off, you won't reach the site. So if you're not getting anywhere with your search, check your typing for spelling and accuracy.

WAIS

Pronounced *ways* and standing for "Wide Area Information Service," *WAIS* enables you to search for key words in the actual text of documents. This increases the likelihood that a document you've identified has information on your topic. You can use WAIS to search Web documents.

News Groups

News groups are comprised of people interested in a specific topic who share information electronically. You can communicate with them through a *Listserv,* an electronic mailing list for subscribers interested in a specific topic, or through *Usenet,* special-interest news groups open to the public.

These sources allow you to keep up with the most recent developments in your area of research and may also point you to useful information and resources you might not have found on your own.

Author! Author!

During the Middle Ages, the clergy were the only people who could read, so almost all libraries were church-owned. By our standards, these libraries were modest, housing perhaps a few hundred books each. Naturally, most of the magnificent illuminated manuscripts (all hand-written) concerned theology and the classics, with a smattering of medical, legal, and historical works. Around 1300, universities began their own libraries by printing small, portable books.

Help Me, Rhonda

One of the best strategies to find a subject on the Internet is to use a *Boolean search.* It uses the terms *and, or, not,* and the symbols + and – to expand or restrict a search. Here's how Boolean search works:

➤ **"and"** Link two key words with *and* to narrow your search to *only* those sources in which *both* terms appear. For example: Laurie and Rozakis.

➤ **"or"** Link two terms with *or* to get all sources that contain *either* term. For example: Laurie or Rozakis.

➤ **"not"** Link two key words with *not* to get all sources about the first term except those mentioning the second term. For example: Laurie not Rozakis.

➤ **"+" or "–"** Some search engines use + for "and" and – for "not." Place the symbols directly before the word, as in +Clinton–Impeachment–Health Care.

No matter how you search the Internet, there is help available electronically. Look for introductory screens, welcome messages, or files with names like ...

➤ About ...

➤ FAQ (Frequently Asked Questions)

➤ Formulating a search with ...

➤ Readme

➤ ?

For a Good Time, Call ...

Following are some useful places to visit on the Web as you begin your research. (Note: Every care has been taken to make this list timely and correct. But just as people move, so do Web sites, and the Web site may have moved since this book was published. In that case, there may be a forward link. If not, use "key word" to find the new site.)

Write Angles

In addition to raindrops on roses and whiskers on kittens, here are a few of my favorite things: www.nytimes.com (*The New York Times*), www.cnn.com (CNN Interactive), and www.savers.org/wash_times (*Washington Times*). For a big fat list of online newspapers, hit www.yahoo.com/News_andMedia/Newspapers.

➤ **Guide to the Web.** www.hcc.hawaii.edu/guide/www.guide.html

➤ **Internet Resources.** www.ncsa.uiuc.edu/SDG/Software/Mosaic/MetaIndex.html

➤ **Library of Congress.** www.lcweb.loc.gov

➤ **List of Web Servers.** www.info.cern.ch/hypertext/DataSources/WWW/Servers.html

➤ **Newspaper Links.** www.spub.ksu.edu/other/journal.html

➤ **Nova-Links.** www.nova.edu/Inter-Links

➤ **Sports.** www.atm.ch.cam.ac.uk/sports/sports.html

➤ **U.S. Federal Agencies.** www.lib.lsu.edu/gov/fedgov.html; www.fedworld.gov

➤ **Virtual Tourist World Map.** www.wings.buffalo.edu/world

➤ **Who's Who on the Internet.** www.web.city.ac.ik/citylive/pages.html

You're Not Done Yet

Not so fast, partner! There are lots of other places to look. And here they are:

1. **Interviews.** There's a lot to be said for first-hand information. Discussing your subject with an expert adds credibility and immediacy to your report. You can conduct interviews by telephone, by e-mail, or in person.

   Call and confirm the interview, prepare a series of questions well in advance of the interview, and later write a note thanking the person for his or her time. Get the person's permission *beforehand* if you decide to tape-record the interview. Obtain a signed release for the right to use their remarks on the record.

Writer's Block

Include only respected people in the field. Don't waste your time with cranks and people with their own agendas to further.

2. **Surveys.** Surveys can help you assess how a large group feels about your topic or a significant aspect of it. On the basis of the responses, you draw conclusions. Such generalizations are usually made in quantitative terms, as in "Fewer than one third of the respondents said that they favored charter schools." To get fair and unbiased data …

   ➤ Survey a large number of people.

   ➤ Avoid loaded questions that lead people toward a specific response.

   ➤ Make the form simple and easy.

3. **Government documents.** The government publishes *tons* of pamphlets, reports, catalogs, and newsletters on most issues of national concern. Government documents are often excellent research sources because they tend to be factual and unbiased. To find government documents, try these CD-ROM and online indexes:

   ➤ *Monthly Catalogue of the United States Government Publications*

   ➤ United States Government Publications Index

Write Angles

Consider audiovisual sources, too. These include records, audio-cassettes, videotapes, slides, and photographs. AV materials can often be borrowed from your library as you would books, magazines, and other print sources.

4. **Special collections.** Many libraries also have restricted collections of rare books, manuscripts, newspapers, magazines, photographs, maps, and items of local interest. They're usually stored in a special room or section of the library and you'll probably need permission to access them.

The Least You Need to Know

➤ Start your research by brainstorming key words and synonyms on your topic. Familiarize yourself with your library; remember that reference librarians are there to help you.

➤ Nonfiction books are classified by either the Dewey Decimal system or the Library of Congress classification system. The systems use completely different call numbers.

➤ Also consult almanacs, bibliographies, Books in Print, encyclopedias, and other reference texts.

➤ Periodicals offer timely information and can be accessed by databases or printed indexes.

➤ Use search engines to access the Internet. Use URLs, WAIS, news groups, and Boolean search methods, too.

➤ You can also gather information through interviews, surveys, government documents, and the library's special collections.

Chapter 19

Cast a Critical Eye

In This Chapter

➤ Checking the authority, origin, and timeliness of a reference source

➤ Finding a source's bias and purpose

➤ Discovering if a source is appropriate to your topic, audience, and purpose

➤ Creating a working bibliography

➤ Fitting sources to your thesis

Four guys went on a cross-country road trip. They were from Idaho, Iowa, New York, and Florida. Two hours into the trip, the man from Idaho rolled down his window and started tossing potatoes out of the car. The guy from Florida said, "What are you doing?"

"We have too many potatoes in Idaho," he replied, "and this is a great way to get rid of some."

An hour later, the Iowan rolled down his window, opened his duffle bag, and began tossing out ears of corn. The New Yorker said, "Now what are you doing?" The Iowan replied, "Well, we have far too much corn in Iowa, so I figured this would be a great chance to get rid of some of it."

About two hours later, the Floridian rolled down his window and tossed out the man from New York.

We make evaluations on a daily basis; some are valid, while others may be a bit hasty. Nonetheless, in life and in writing, sometimes you have to be ruthless in your judgments. In this chapter, you'll learn to evaluate and track the material you use in your research paper to make sure you select only reliable sources.

An Embarrassment of Riches

Evaluating sources is nothing new; writers have always had to assess the reference material they find. But courtesy of the new electronic search techniques and burgeoning Internet resources, the task has taken on a new urgency.

In the good old days, a writer only needed to consider the quality of books, magazines, and journal articles; now, printed matter is just the beginning of the information available to the researcher. Further, in the past, editors, publishers, and librarians chose much of the material we could expect to find. Today, however, most online sources haven't been evaluated at all, so it's all in our hands. Besides, you can access everything online from the comfort of your own home. As a result, much of what you see won't even make it to the library's shelves.

Author! Author!

The average professional (that's *you!*) is required to read about four million words a month—that's 50 million words a year. In the medical profession alone, more than 10 thousand professional journals are published yearly.

Writer's Block

Just because a source appears in print, in the media, or online doesn't mean it's valid.

What does this mean for you? It means that before you decide to use any source, you have to judge its reliability, credibility, and appropriateness. Here's how to do it.

As you gather your sources, give them all the once over—and more than once. Use the following criteria as you determine whether a source is valid for inclusion in your research paper:

1. Authority
2. Source

3. Timeliness

4. Bias

5. Purpose

6. Appropriateness

Let's look at each criterion in detail.

Who's the Boss?: Authority

Don't believe that all sources are created equal, because it's just not so: Some sources are more equal than others. That's because they were prepared with greater care by experts in the field and have been reviewed by scholars, teachers, and others we respect for their knowledge of the subject.

Don't be afraid to make value judgments about the source materials you find. Some sources *are* more reliable than others. As a result, they carry greater authority and will help you make your point in your research paper. You can use the following checklist to weigh the authority of the material you're contemplating using:

❑ Is the author named? Unless you're working with an encyclopedia article or an editorial, the author should be credited in a by-line.

❑ Are the author's credentials included? Look for an academic degree, an e-mail address at a college or university, and/or a list of publications.

❑ Based on this information, can you conclude that the writer is qualified to write on this subject?

❑ For example, is the person an expert or an eyewitness to the events described in the source?

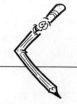

Write Angles

There are a growing number of review tools for online materials. Among the best are *Webcrawler's Best of the Net, Lycos Top 5%,* and *Gale's Cyberhound Guide.*

❑ In addition, does the person have a good reputation in this field?

❑ Was the source well-reviewed by other recognized authorities in the field? (Was the source even reviewed at all?)

❑ Is the source complete, or have certain facts been cut for their controversial nature or for space limitations?

❑ Does the author document his or her claims with other source materials? Are these sources credible?

Be especially suspicious of sources that claim to have the "secret" or "inside track" on a subject. If you can't find the same information in other sources, the material doesn't hold up to scrutiny. Give it the boot.

Now think about the source of the source.

What's Behind Curtain #3?: Source

As you evaluate the materials you located, consider where the source comes from, its sponsoring agency, publisher, and so on. For example, *portable sources,* such as CD-ROMs and encyclopedias, are like printed books—they have credited writers and publishers. In addition, they change only when a new version is issued. As a result, you can determine their value as you would a book.

Online sources, in contrast, may be published anonymously, so you can't evaluate the writer(s). Also, they can be updated and revised without notification, which means there could be a lot of fingers in that pie. Most frustrating of all, the Web site may vanish without warning. This makes it difficult to evaluate its reliability as well as its origin. It's tough to work with something invisible.

Ask yourself these questions as you consider the source of a reference piece:

➤ Can I find the source of this reference piece? If not, it gets the heave-ho.

➤ Is the source reputable? The best sources are well known; they appear on lists of "recommended" books or sites.

➤ Does the piece come from a place known for its authority, such as a reputable publisher or sponsored Web site? If the answer is yes, you've likely got a keeper. If the answer is no, throw the source overboard—or consider it with a leery eye.

The Web *is* a fabulous reference source (as well as a great place to hang out when there's nothing on TV), but it requires special evaluation. It *is* tempting to judge all online sources as equally valid, but you're too smart for that. Remember: Be very sure that any online source you locate is valid and reliable before you use it in your writing (or for anything else).

It's All Relative: Timeliness

As we learned from Uncle Albert years ago, time is relative. If you're writing a research paper on a very current topic, the date of publication or posting is crucial, since you're going to need some contemporary data. But you're also likely to include some traditional, "classic" reference materials to give your paper the weight and authority it needs. As a general rule of thumb, go for a mix of time-honored and recent reference materials. This helps balance your outlook, tempering the current with the classic.

Timeliness is a crucial issue with Web sites, since cyberspace is cluttered with piles of outdated sites. Sometimes people post the information and move on to something new. The site hangs out there, forgotten and woefully outdated. Always check the dates on any Web sites to find out when the material was posted and last updated.

Write Angles

To find reference materials that have withstood the test of time, ask academic librarians or follow the discussion in an academic MOO or Listserv. You'll hear the same titles and authors coming up over and over.

Find the Hidden Agenda: Bias

Every source is biased, because every source has a point of view. Bias is not necessarily bad, as long as you recognize it as such and take it into account as you evaluate and use the source. For example, an article on hunting published in *Field and Stream* is likely to have a very different slant from an article on the same subject published in *Vegetarian Times.*

Bias in reference sources can take many forms. First, a writer or speaker can lie outright. Or, a writer may be more subtle, inventing false data that masquerade as "facts." In addition, dishonest writers often twist what their opponents have said. To misrepresent this way, they reduce a complex argument to ridicule or skip over an important element. These problems all result from *oversimplification.*

Sometimes you can evaluate the bias of an online source by its suffix, the last part of its URL. Here's the crib sheet:

Word Watch

Reducing a complicated argument to mockery is called **oversimplification.**

Suffix	Meaning
.com	Commercial (business or company)
.edu	Education (academic site)
.gov	Government
.int	International organization

continues

continued

Suffix	Meaning
.mil	Military organization
.net	Internet administration
.org	Other organizations, including nonprofit, nonacademic, and nongovernmental groups
.sci	Special knowledge news group

Each site has its own bias. A business site is going to have a different slant from a university site, for example. Any intelligent business will want to sell you a product or a service, while the university is probably seeking to disseminate knowledge. As a result, knowing the source of the site can help you evaluate its purpose and assess any possible bias.

Bias has another aspect when it comes to the Web. Books don't have ads, and most of us skim the magazine ads. (Except for my husband—the ads bother him so much that he rips them out before he reads the magazine. Gotta love a man like that.)

But Web sites can have commercial intrusions. Not only are some Web sites filled with ads, but the ads can also flick on and off in search engines. This makes them hard to ignore, and there's no way to rip them out.

These ads reflect the commercial nature of some Web sites. What you see on the screen may reflect who's footing the bill. This bias is subtle but nonetheless important.

Author! Author!

Outside the United States, domain names often end with an abbreviation for the country of origin. For example, .au is Australia, .ca is Canada, and .uk is the United Kingdom. Another common abbreviation is .edu. It stands for an educational institution, all the way from elementary schools to universities. These are often very reliable sites because they post only verifiable information.

260

How can you avoid being misled by biased reference materials? Here are some issues to consider as you evaluate a print or online text for misrepresentation:

➤ Is someone quoted out of context?

➤ Are facts or statistics cited in a vacuum?

➤ Does the quotation reflect the overall content of the source, or does it merely reflect a detail?

➤ Has key information been omitted?

To protect yourself against biased sources and your own bias, select reference materials that reflect opinions from across the spectrum.

Writer's Block

The name "junk mail" says it all; when it comes to reference sources, junk mail doesn't make the cut because it is largely comprised of advertisements.

Take Aim: Purpose

Different sources are written for different reasons. The following table summarizes some of the most common purposes you'll encounter. I've arranged the source in a loose hierarchy from most to least reliable, but stay tuned for more on that.

Source	Purpose	Authors	Reviewed
scholarly books and articles	advance knowledge	experts	yes
serious books and articles	report information	experts; professional writers	yes
newsstand magazines	report facts	professional writers; reporters	yes
newspapers	report news	reporters	yes
sponsored Web sites	report facts; sell products	varies	sometimes
personal Web sites	varies	experts to novices	rarely
Listservs	discuss topics	anyone	no
Usenet newsgroups	discuss topics	anyone	no

The most reliable sources are written by experts and have been reviewed by equally reputable readers. However, these sources alone may not be enough to make your point in print. Read on, partner.

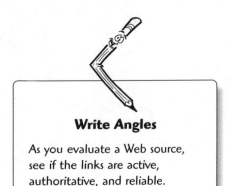

Write Angles

As you evaluate a Web source, see if the links are active, authoritative, and reliable.

Good Fit: Appropriateness

The value of a source depends not only on its quality but also on its use to you in a specific writing situation. No matter how weighty and reliable the source may be, if it's not on your topic, it gets the old heave-ho. For example, if you're writing a research paper on current events, you're going to need newspapers and magazines with the most up-to-date information, rather than books, since even the most recent ones are at least six months to a year old. You're probably going to use Web sites and Usenet newsgroups, too. Even though they lack the authority you want, they have the material you need.

Even if a source proves to be of high quality and free from bias, it doesn't necessarily mean that it belongs in your research paper. For a source to make the final cut, it has to fit with your audience, purpose, and tone. It must be *appropriate* to your paper. How can you decide if a source is suitable for inclusion in your research paper? Try these suggestions:

➤ Do you understand the material in the source? If the source is too technical for you to grasp fully, you might not use it correctly in your paper.

➤ Is the source written at a level appropriate to your readers?

➤ Does the source have the information you need?

➤ Does the source suit your purpose in this research paper?

In summary, all sources are *not* equally valid. Be sure to evaluate every source carefully and completely before you decide whether to use it in your research paper. Weak or inaccurate sources can seriously damage your credibility as a writer and thinker.

On the Right Track

There's a lot to be said for the motto "Shop 'Til You Drop," especially when it comes to shoes, sweaters, and reference material. Once you get a nice pile of stuff, it's time to put it in some kind of order. Try these suggestions for your research findings:

➤ See how each source helps you prove your thesis. If the source doesn't help support your point, it's not relevant.

➤ Make sure the material you found is *really* valid and can be verified in more than one source.

➤ Check that you have a variety of perspectives in your source material. This will help protect your paper from bias.

➤ See that you have material that appeals to logic as well as emotion. Remember that an effective research paper is built on logic rather than feelings.

➤ Decide how you will fit each source into your paper. Remember all those gorgeous shoes that pinch? Can't bear to throw them out? If the shoe and source fit, slip them on. If not, set them aside.

Writer's Block

Never force a source to fit. You can tweak your thesis a bit here and there, but never wring or wrench your point to make a source blend in.

A Place for Everything, and Everything in Its Place

Next, create a *working bibliography*, a systematic way to organize all the material that looks promising. For each source, write all the bibliographical material on a 3×5 index card. Here's what you should include:

➤ Author's complete name

➤ Title of source

➤ Printed matter: publisher, place of publication, date of publication, page numbers (for magazines and journals)

➤ Web site: URL, date you accessed the page

If a catalog or index doesn't provide complete bibliographical information, leave blanks you can fill in later.

As you learned earlier, there are several different methods of documentation. For example, research papers in the humanities often use the *Modern Language Association (MLA)* style, while papers in social sciences use the *American Psychological Association (APA)* style. As you write your bibliography cards, follow the documentary style preferred by the discipline in which you are writing.

Write Angles

Cards allow you to keep the most promising sources and discard the irrelevant ones. Also, cards can easily be alphabetized when you create your Bibliography or Works Cited page.

Computer "Cards"

Or, you can make "bibliography cards" on a computer. This is a great technique because you can update, alphabetize, and correct cards as you go along. Make your own cards by drawing a box around each entry or using software especially designed for this purpose.

Writer's Block

Don't rely too heavily on any one source—no matter how good it looks. First, this can lead to bias. Second, what happens if the source turns out to be invalid or dated? Your argument can collapse.

Write Angles

In most cases, you won't be able to tell what's going to make the cut and what won't. As a result, you'll probably end up taking far more notes than you need. Don't worry: Nearly all researchers end up with extra notes. The deeper you dig into your subject, however, the more perceptive you'll become about what you need to prove your point most convincingly.

However, be sure to back up your "bibliography cards" on floppy disks. In addition, print out hard copies as you work. This way, you won't lose your material if your hard drive crashes or the file develops a glitch.

Working the Crowd

You've gathered your sources and prepared a bibliography card for each one. Now it's time to fit everything into place. Here's how to do it:

1. Skim the sources and arrange them according to difficulty.

2. Read the general, introductory sources first. You'll use these to lay the foundation for the more specialized and technical material you'll need.

3. Rank each source to decide how it fits with the other sources you've gathered. Pay close attention to both sides of the issue: It's a great way to test the validity of your thesis.

4. Annotate the source to examine it closely.

5. Rephrase the source to make sure you understand it fully. Take notes on the source, using summaries, paraphrases, and direct quotations.

6. Position the source in your paper by deciding where it fits in the overall thesis and paper organization.

7. Connect the source to what you've already written. Correlate all the information to see what you have already discovered and what you still have to find.

8. Be sure that every source fits with your point and focuses on a key issue in your paper.

During this process, you'll find that you're automatically changing the structure of your paper to accommodate what you're finding. Usually the changes are minor, but you may find yourself designing a radically new organization to fit the focal points and supporting details. If you're including a Web page or brochure as part of your project, these adjustments take on a spatial consideration as well.

In Chapter 20, "In the End Zone," I'll take you step by step through the process of writing your first draft, but while we're here, it's a great idea to prepare your first draft as early as possible. This gives you plenty of time to fill in the gaps, revise, or redesign your text and graphics.

The Least You Need to Know

➤ Evaluate your research material to make sure it's reliable and authoritative.

➤ When you have sufficient material, see how each source helps prove your thesis. Make sure the material is relevant, balanced, and suitable.

➤ Skim, rank, and annotate the sources. Rephrase the material in your own words.

➤ Position the source in your paper, connect the source to what you have already written, and correlate all the information.

➤ Be sure that every source fits with your point and focuses on a key issue in your paper.

➤ If necessary, adjust the organization of your paper to fit your thesis and information.

Chapter 20

In the End Zone

In This Chapter

➤ Going to the source

➤ Stop, thief!: avoiding plagiarism

➤ Sweet endings

➤ Last licks

A thesis doesn't become a fact just because you line up some proof. You could find three or more reasons to support *anything,* from "We need more federal funding for ferrets" to "I *really* should finish off that pint of rocky road right now." (Hmmm ... back later.)

First, you decide which authorities best support your assertions. As you write, you smoothly integrate the most convincing outside proofs with your own words. You present material logically, deal with opposing arguments, qualify generalizations, and address your readers intelligently. You also document your sources to credit their contribution. That's what you'll learn in this chapter.

In addition, I'll show you how to assemble a Bibliography and Works Cited page. Finally, we'll go over paper presentation, including frontmatter, endmatter, and keyboarding. Let the games begin.

Backed by the Best

So, how can you show that the information you're quoting, summarizing, and paraphrasing comes from experts and isn't something you made up yourself? How can you get the most bang for your buck by using expert opinions effectively?

As an example, let's look at an excerpt from a research paper I wrote on Hester Prynne, Nathaniel Hawthorne's heroine from *The Scarlet Letter*. Here's how the paper opens:

Another Possible Source of Hawthorne's Hester Prynne

And, after many, many years, a new grave was delved, near an old and sunken one, in that burial-ground beside which King's Chapel has since been built. It was near that old and sunken grave … on this simple slab of slate—as that curious investigator may still discern, … there appeared … a herald's wording of which might serve for a motto and brief description of our now concluded legend; so somber is it, and relieved only by one ever-glowing point of light gloomier than the shadow: "ON A FIELD, SABLE, THE LETTER A, GULES" (*The Scarlet Letter,* 264).

So ends Nathaniel Hawthorne's *The Scarlet Letter,* and so begins the search for Hester Prynne's grave. Seventeenth-century Boston town officials, meticulous about keeping accurate records, nevertheless failed to record the death—or life, for that matter—of Hester Prynne, adulteress, seamstress, and ministering angel. The town officials must have been too busy surveying chimneys, keeping pigs off the streets, keeping count of the "many Miscarriages [that] are committed by Saylers … immoderate drinking, and other vain expences," and granting widows permission to keep houses of "publique entertainment for the selling of Coffee, Chuchaletto, & sydar by retayle" (Nobel, 113).

The lack of official records notwithstanding, Hester's grave is more often inquired after by visitors to the King's Chapel Burial Grounds than any other, claims the custodian of that historic enclosure in a 1999 interview. Her grave is apparently sought there because Hawthorne's skillful intermingling of real and fictional people and places has led readers to believe that *The Scarlet Letter* is based on a true story. In his essay entitled "The New England Sources for *The Scarlet Letter,*" scholar Charles Ryskamp establishes the fact that the supporting characters in *The Scarlet Letter*—other than Hester, Pearl, Dimmesdale, and Chillingworth, for whom we can find no real historical basis—were actual figures (258). The fictional characters assume solidity in part through their encounters with well-known citizens of colonial Boston. According to Ryskamp, Hawthorne used the most credible history of Boston available to him, Caleb Snow's *History of Boston.* …

In this instance, I started off by citing a primary source, *The Scarlet Letter*. This shows that I know the necessary basis for the discussion. I also integrated the name of the source directly in the body of the paper ("scholar Charles Ryskamp"), used cue words to show how he stood behind his work ("establishes the fact that …"), and gave credit to a source in parenthesis (Nobel, 113). Here's why.

Star Power

When you cite material from a well-respected source, put the author's name directly in the body of your text to get more mileage from it. Readers are impressed—and rightly so—when you cite a recognized authority. Placing the person's name in the text shows that you've done your homework, that you understand who to line up behind your argument. For example:

Write Angles

It's not enough just to slap the information into your paper, even if you *do* surround any exact quotes with quotation marks. The material must be smoothly blended in and used to make a specific point.

➤ In "Notes on the Decline of Naturalism," the well-known scholar Philip Rahv states that …

➤ Testifying before Congress on the issue of unrestricted Internet access, computer wizard Bill Gates argued that …

Cued In

Also use *cue words* and phrases to set off outside material. For example, I used "establishes the fact that" in my example.

Fortunately, you've got a wide variety of cue words at your disposal. For each source, choose the cue word that expresses your exact shade of meaning. Life is difficult enough without having to hunt for cue words, so I've put together a list of the most useful ones:

Writer's Block

Never omit material from a quotation to change its meaning. Also, if you do excerpt a quotation, always be sure it makes grammatical sense after you've cut it.

Cue Words to Integrate Quotations

adds	agrees	argues	concedes
acknowledges	admits	advises	confirms
asks	asserts	believes	concludes
claims	comments	compares	considers
contends	declares	defends	denies
disagrees	disputes	emphasizes	explains
endorses	establishes	hints	hopes
finds	holds	illustrates	implies
insists	maintains	notes	observes
points out	rejects	relates	reports
responds	reveals	says	sees
speculates	shows	speculates	states
suggests	thinks	warns	writes

Credit Given Here

As you weave in expert opinions, facts, examples, and statistics, provide enough information so your readers can easily trace every source. You've just learned two ways to do this: by citing the name of the source and by integrating the source with cue words. There's a third way to give credit as well: by adding the *documentation in parenthesis, footnotes,* or *endnotes.* It's the most important way of all because it provides complete information.

As you learned in Chapter 16, "Writing Across the Curriculum," there are a number of formats you can choose from as you document your sources. These include methods developed by:

➤ The Modern Language Association (MLA)

➤ The American Psychological Association (APA)

➤ *The Chicago Manual of Style* (CMS)

➤ The Council of Biology Editors (CBE)

➤ The Columbia Guide to Online Style (COS)

Each discipline favors a specific documentation style. Research papers written in the business world, for example, usually follow the rules laid down in *The Chicago Manual of Style,* while the humanities favor the MLA style of documentation. Therefore, when you're writing business papers, you might have to use footnotes. When you're writing humanities papers, in contrast, you'll most likely use parenthetical documentation.

Always consult the documentation guide in your field when you prepare internal documentation, footnotes, endnotes, Works Cited pages, and Bibliographies. These guidebooks are all listed in Chapter 16.

Word Watch

Parenthetical documentation, footnotes, and **endnotes** are all ways of giving credit to sources you used in

When you're writing in the humanities (English, history, foreign language, social studies, etc.) you most often use the MLA style of *parenthetical or internal documentation.* Let's check it out now.

MLA Internal Documentation

MLA favors *parenthetical documentation* over the traditional footnotes or endnotes. Parenthetical documentation offers an abbreviated, handy-dandy form of credit right in the body of the paper. For a complete citation, your readers can check the Works Cited page. This is a nifty system because it's easy for you and your readers to use.

So how much bibliographic information must you include in the body of the paper when you use internal documentation? The first time you cite a source in your paper, include as much of the following information as necessary for your reader to figure out the source easily:

Write Angles

Parenthetical or internal documentation places an abbreviated form of the source within the body of the research paper rather than in footnotes or endnotes. Therefore, parenthetical documentation takes the place of traditional footnotes or endnotes.

➤ Title of the source

➤ Writer's name

➤ Writer's affiliation

➤ Page numbers

The following passage shows the first time a source is cited. The author is important, so his name is included in the text of the paper. The parenthetical documentation is underlined.

In addition, many patients on Prozac began to experience personality changes over time. A new study described at the annual meeting of the American Psychiatric Association suggests that Prozac alters aspects of personality as it relieves depression. <u>Ron G. Goldman, a psychiatrist at Columbia University, believes that "Emotional and personality features are intertwined in depression so it's not really surprising that some types of personality change would accompany improvement in this condition" (Bower 359).</u>

Writer's Block

Quotations have to be copied exactly as they appear, so *never* correct an error in one. If a quotation does contain an error, include the error, but add [*sic*] after it to show that you know there's a mistake.

Word Watch

A **footnote** is a complete bibliographical citation indicated by a number in the text. **Endnotes** follow the same format but are listed on a page at the end of the paper. Today's nifty computer programs make them a snap to prepare.

This next example shows a paraphrase from a source also cited for the first time. Since the author isn't important, he or she isn't mentioned. Instead, the focus is on the journal from which the material was taken. The internal documentation is underlined.

It has been reported that some individuals on Prozac have a decreased libido or no desire for sexual activity. <u>A study published in *The Journal of Clinical Psychiatry* in April 1994 found that among 160 patients taking Prozac, 85 reported their sexual desire or response diminished after using the drug (Nichols 36).</u>

Now tell me, isn't internal documentation a sweet system? Easy to use, clear as can be. This isn't to say that footnotes and endnotes don't have their place, however, as you'll see in the next section.

CMS Footnotes and Endnotes

Footnotes and endnotes are another form of documentation used in research papers. The folks over at *The Chicago Manual of Style* set the standard for those who favor footnotes. As always, check the requirements in your field before you hitch your wagon to a footnote style.

A *footnote* is a bibliographical reference indicated by a number in the text. The complete citation is then placed at the bottom ("foot") of the same page. An *endnote* is identical in form to a footnote, but the complete citation is placed at the end of the paper on a separate page labeled "Endnotes."

For example, here's a direct quotation credited with a footnote:

No one supposes that an actual bundle of papers prepared by a surveyor named Jonathan Pue ever existed. However, as Charles Boewe and Murray G. Murphey remarked in their article "Hester Prynne in History," it is nevertheless "far from certain that no real historical basis exists for Hester."[6]

So that you can compare, here's how the same passage looks when credit is given through parenthetical documentation:

No one supposes that an actual bundle of papers prepared by a surveyor named Jonathan Pue ever existed. However, as Charles Boewe and Murray G. Murphey remarked in their article "Hester Prynne in History," it is nevertheless "far from certain that no real historical basis exists for Hester" (203).

Here's how to use a footnote to document how an author constructs an argument or a line of thinking:

Others have tried to find out if Hawthorne based Hester on actual historical facts. The most striking is the case of Hester Craford, punished for "fornication" with John Wedg. She confessed and was ordered severely flogged. The punishment was postponed for a month to six weeks after the birth of her child, and it was left to Mayor William Hawthorn to see it carried out. The woman's first name and the judge's last name—he was, of course, Hawthorne's ancestor, the infamous "hanging judge" of Salem who refused to repent his role in the 1692 witchcraft hysteria, suggests that Hawthorne must have used this case as the basis for his novel.[6]

To once again compare, here's how the same passage looks when credit is given through parenthetical documentation:

Others have tried to find out if Hawthorne based Hester on actual historical facts. The most striking is the case of Hester Craford, punished for "fornication" with John Wedg. She confessed and was ordered severely flogged. The punishment was postponed for a month to six weeks after the birth of her child, and it was left to Mayor William Hawthorn to see it carried out. The woman's first name and the judge's last name—he was, of course, Hawthorne's ancestor, the infamous "hanging judge" of Salem who refused to repent his role in the 1692 witchcraft hysteria, suggests that Hawthorne must have used this case as the basis for his novel (Bell, 61).

Here are the general guidelines for footnote/endnote use:

➤ Choose either endnotes or footnotes. You can't have both. Sorry.

➤ Place each number at the end of the material you wish to credit.

➤ Use superscript Arabic numerals. These are raised a little above the words.

➤ Indent the first line of the footnote or endnote five spaces. All subsequent lines are placed flush left.

➤ Single-space each footnote; double-space between entries. This is done automatically in most software programs.

➤ Number footnotes or endnotes consecutively from the beginning to the end of your paper.

➤ Use a new number for each citation even if several numbers refer to the same source.

➤ Leave two spaces after the number at the end of a sentence. Don't leave any extra space before the number.

Write Angles

Use an **ellipsis** (three evenly spaced periods: ...) to show that you've omitted part of a quotation. Don't use an ellipsis at the beginning of a sentence; just start with the material you wish to quote. If you omit more than one sentence, add a period before the ellipsis to show that the omission occurred at the end of a sentence.

The basic *CMS* footnote/endnote citation for a book looks like the following. You would place this information at the bottom of the page for a footnote or at the end of the entire paper for an endnote.

Footnote number. Author's First Name and Last name, *Book Title* (place of publication: publisher, date of publication), page number.

For example:

[6]Seymour Miles, *The Long and Winding Road* (New York: Traveling Books, 1969), 231.

The basic footnote/endnote citation for a magazine, newspaper, or journal looks like this:

Footnote number. Author's First Name and Last Name, "Article Title," *Periodical Title*, date, page number.

For example:

[3]Wilma Wacca, "Underwater Fire Prevention Made Easy," *Modern Fire Fighter*, 20 May 1999, 123.

The basic footnote/endnote citation for an electronic source looks like this:

[12]*Hamlet*. In <u>MIT Complete Works of Shakespeare.</u> Available from http://mitshakespeare.edu; INTERNET.

Complete coverage of bibliographic formats appears in Appendix B, "Documentation Format."

You can use footnotes or endnotes not only to acknowledge a source but also to add observations and comments that don't fit into the body of your text.

Author! Author!

According to the U.S. copyright law, authors own their own words as soon as they are "fixed in any tangible medium of expression, now known or later developed, from which they can be perceived, reproduced, or otherwise communicated, either directly or with the aid of a machine or device." Under the Fair Use section of the copyright law, copyrighted material can be used in other documents without infringement of the law "for the purposes of criticism, comment, news reporting, teaching (including multiple copies for classroom use), scholarship, or research."

Stop, Thief!

As you learned in Chapter 17, "Paper Chase," you write a research paper to argue a thesis. To do so, you cite other writers' words and ideas, giving full credit. As you write, you honor your moral responsibility to use someone else's ideas ethically and make it easy for readers to check your claims.

What should you document? Give a source for everything that's not *common knowledge,* the information an educated person is expected to know. If you fail to give adequate credit, you can be charged with plagiarism.

Plagiarism means using some else's words without giving adequate credit. Plagiarism is ...

Write Angles

Use square brackets, [ ], to add necessary information to a quotation.

➤ Using someone else's ideas without acknowledging the source.

➤ Paraphrasing someone else's argument as your own.

➤ Presenting an entire paper or a major part of it developed as another writer did.

➤ Arranging your ideas exactly as someone else did—even though you acknowledge the source(s).

275

Word Watch

Plagiarism is representing someone else's words or ideas as your own.

Fortunately, avoiding plagiarism is a piece of cake: you just document your sources correctly. Be especially careful when you create paraphrases. It's not enough to change a few words, rearrange a few sentences, and call it kosher. Here's how to correct the problem with parenthetical documentation:

Original source:

> The story of Hester Prynne, heroine of Nathaniel Hawthorne's The Scarlet Letter, takes place in seventeenth-century Boston. Hawthorne no doubt wandered through the King's Chapel Burial Ground when he worked in the nearby Custom House from 1839 to 1841. Tradition says that the fictional Hester Prynne is based on the original Elizabeth Pain (or Payne), who is buried in that graveyard. There is a big red A with two lions on the upper-left corner of Pain's gravestone. The crest looks amazingly like Hester's gravestone, as described in the last line of *The Scarlet Letter:* "On her stone there appears the semblance of an engraved escutcheon with 'on a field, sable, the letter A gules.'"

Plagiarism:

> Hawthorne set his romance *The Scarlet Letter* in Boston in the 1600s. The story describes characters who could be buried in the King's Chapel Burial Ground. Hawthorne had probably walked through this graveyard when he worked in the nearby Custom House in the nineteenth century. People think that Hawthorne's character Hester Prynne is based on the original Elizabeth Pain (or Payne). The two gravestones are a lot alike, since both have a big red A with two lions on the upper-left corner. Pain's gravestone looks like Hester's, as described in the last sentence in *The Scarlet Letter:* "On her stone there appears the semblance of an engraved escutcheon with 'on a field, sable, the letter A gules.'"

Not plagiarism:

> A granite marker erected in the King's Chapel Burial ground cites another intriguing source for Hester Prynne. According to the information on this marker, Hawthorne drew inspiration for Hester Prynne from the real-life tale of Elizabeth Pain (or Payne). On the surface, the similarities are astonishing: Both gravestones have a big red A with two lions on the upper-left corner. However, Pain was tried and acquitted for the murder of her child, while Prynne was tried and convicted for adultery (Powers, 191). However, Hawthorne had very likely seen Pain's gravestone as he walked through the burial ground on his way to his

job next door at the Custom House. Perhaps Pain's striking marker sparked the idea for Hester's gravestone, which Hawthorne describes this way: "On her stone there appears the semblance of an engraved escutcheon with 'on a field, sable, the letter A gules.'"

As you've already learned in this chapter, to create a footnote or endnotes, just add the subscript number at the end of the sentence or passage in place of the parenthetical citation.

Light at the End of the Tunnel

You're almost there, partner. Just a few more matters to attend to and you'll be ready to hand in your research paper. Now it's time to prepare the endmatter and frontmatter and keyboard your paper. Let's start with the *Works Cited* page or *Bibliography.* You get one or the other, never both.

> **Writer's Block**
>
> NEVER use both parenthetical documentation and footnotes/ endnotes to give credit for the same passage. You get one or the other.

Works Cited or Bibliography Page

A *Works Cited* page provides a complete citation for every work you *cited* in your research paper. A *Bibliography* (or *Works Consulted* list), in contrast, provides a full citation for every work you *consulted* as you wrote your paper. Bibliographies are therefore usually much longer than Works Cited pages.

In most cases, you'll just need a Works Cited page. However, you may be asked to prepare a Bibliography as well. Be sure to check with the Powers That Be so you know which format to follow.

Entries are arranged in alphabetical order according to the author's last name. If the entry doesn't have an author (such as a Web page, encyclopedia entry, or editorial), alphabetize it according to the first word of the title. Here's an overview of the specific MLA formats. Notice that the indentation is the reverse of footnote/endnote form.

➤ **Book citation**

   Author's last name, first name. *Book Title.* Place of publication: publisher, date of publication.

➤ **Article citation**

   Author's last name, first name. "Title of the Article." *Magazine.* Month and year of publication: page numbers.

➤ **Electronic citations**

General:

Author's name (if available), Title, publication date, database, publication medium (*Online*), the name of the computer service, and the date of your access.

Electronic newsgroups and bulletin boards:

Author's name (if available), Title, date the source was posted, the medium (Online posting), the location online, the name of the network, and the date of access.

E-mail:

Sender's name, description of the document, date of the document.

Write Angles

Electronic sources are often missing key information such as the author and date. Use whatever information you can find for your citation.

Writer's Block

Visuals you took from an outside source must be documented the same way you would credit any other source.

Let's talk formatting. Here's how your Works Cited page or Bibliography should look:

➤ **Title.** Center the title (Works Cited or Bibliography) at the top of the page, about an inch from the top. Don't underline, bold, or italicize it.

➤ **Numbering.** Don't. The entries on a Works Cited page aren't numbered.

➤ **Spacing.** Start each entry flush left. Indent all subsequent lines of an entry. As with the rest of your paper, double-space each entry on your Works Cited page.

Endmatter

You may have some endmatter after your Works Cited or Bibliography. Endmatter includes:

➤ **Graphs, charts, maps, figures, and photographs.** Place each graphic at the appropriate place in the text or group them at the end.

➤ **Glossary.** A *glossary* lists and defines technical terms or presents additional information on the subject.

Frontmatter

Depending on the subject of your research paper and the course requirements, you may need to include specific materials before the body of your paper, such as a title page, table of contents, foreword, preface, and abstract. They are arranged in this order. Here's how to prepare each one.

> ➤ **Title page.** At the minimum, include the title, your name, and the date. Depending on your audience, you may also need to include the person for whom the paper was prepared (such as a client or instructor) and a reason the paper was written.

> ➤ **Table of contents.** Lists the paper's main divisions. Be sure to label each section of the paper to match the headings on your table of contents.

> ➤ **Foreword.** In most cases, the *foreword* is written by an expert in the field and serves as an endorsement of the contents. Check out the foreword in this book.

> ➤ **Preface.** The writer's acknowledgment and thank-you page.

> ➤ **Abstract.** A one-paragraph summary of the contents of your paper, most often required in technical or scholarly papers.

Write Angles

Keyboard your table of contents last so you will know the page numbers.

Keyboarding

Use standard 10- or 12-point fonts such as Times Roman, Courier, or Helvetica. Avoid fancy, elaborate fonts, since they're a pain in the neck to read. Also avoid stylistic elements that might distract readers, such as excessive highlighting, boldfacing, or boxes.

Double-space the text and unless specifically requested to do so, don't right-justify (align) your paper. The right margins should be ragged.

The Final Shine: Proofreading

It goes without saying (but I'm saying it anyway) that you'll very carefully proofread your final document. Of course, you've already revised and edited the paper at each stage. I knew I could trust you.

The Least You Need to Know

➤ Integrate source material by mentioning the writer's name and using cue words.

➤ Use parenthetical documentation, footnotes, or endnotes to give credit to your sources.

➤ Each discipline favors a specific documentation style. Use the method of documentation expected in your field.

➤ Avoid plagiarism by documenting quotations, opinions, and paraphrases.

➤ Prepare a Works Cited page or a Bibliography, depending on the requirements in your discipline. Follow the specific format.

➤ Always proofread your research papers carefully.

Part 5
More Big Deals

Rejected Dr. Seuss books: Herbert the Pervert Likes Sherbert, Fox in Detox, The Flesh-Eating Lorax, Aunts in My Pants, Yentil the Lentil, The Cat in the Blender

The moral of the story? If at first you don't succeed, try, try again. This is especially true when it comes to everyday writing tasks, including essay tests, speeches, letters, e-mail, and business documents. It's important to get these everyday writing tasks letter-perfect because they can have such a big impact on your life. It's all here, from the big picture to the itty-bitty details.

Chapter 21

In the Hot Seat: Writing Under Pressure

In This Chapter

➤ Hot under the collar

➤ Questions, questions, questions

➤ When the pressure's on

➤ Red alert

You know you're having a bad day when …

➤ You have a hard time alphabetizing a bag of M&M's.

➤ You try to fax chocolate chip cookies to your child in college.

➤ You have to write under pressure.

That last one's the real dilly, isn't it? Most people regard pressure writing situations as appealing as icky bugs, deep water, and death. In fact, just the mention of the phrase "pressure writing" is enough to set off that sinking feeling in the pit of your stomach. Not to worry; in this chapter, you'll learn to write with grace under pressure.

First, you'll explore your feelings about writing under pressure. Then we'll examine the four most common types of pressure writing essay test situations: *recall, analysis, evaluation,* and *synthesis.* Next, I'll give you some tried-and-true suggestions for writing successfully when the heat's on. You'll learn how to prepare yourself *before* the test and how to deal with stress *during* the test. Finally, I'll show you how to cope with the monster under the bed: panic during the test. Let's start by seeing how you *really* feel about writing when the pressure's on.

What, Me Worry?

How can you tell if pressure writing situations make you nervous? Take this quick quiz to see. Check the items that describe your feelings when you have to write by the clock.

You get the assignment, read it, and start writing.
Within a few minutes ...

❏   You can jump-start your car without cables.

❏   You don't need a hammer to pound in nails.

❏   People get dizzy just watching you.

❏   You can outlast the Energizer bunny.

❏   You haven't blinked since the test started.

❏   You just ate a candy bar. It was still wrapped.

❏   A nurse would need a scientific calculator to take your pulse.

❏   Your nervous twitch registers on the Richter scale.

❏   You're so wired you pick up AM radio.

❏   You just shorted out a motion detector.

❏   You could channel surf faster without a remote.

❏   People can test their batteries in your ears.

Score Yourself

10 to 8 checks   You need me, you really need me.

7 to 5 checks   Stop shaking; the test is over.

4 to 0 checks   Are you alive?

Write Angles

Always be sure you're in the correct room taking the correct test. Every semester, I have several students who wander into the wrong classroom. Test time drifts away as the lost sheep rejoin the flock.

Relax. Feeling nervous in a pressure writing situation (or in *any* tense circumstance) is natural. You wouldn't be human if you didn't get a little hot under the collar when you're put on the spot. Besides, being nervous by itself isn't an issue.

That's because a minor case of the nerves can actually work to your advantage, since it keeps you alert and focused. But too much of anything is bad—especially when it comes to being nervous. Understanding what you'll be called on to write can help you tame your raging tension, so let's look at the types of questions you're most likely to be asked.

What's the Big Idea?

There are more pressure writing situations than ants at a picnic, but odds are that you'll plunge into this particular ring of hell most often if you're enrolled in a class. Whether it's high school, college, graduate school, or any other kind of professional training, the essay test is ubiquitous. Like designer water and people who have no right wearing spandex in public, you can run, but you can't hide.

Why do so many instructors make you show your stuff in a pressure writing situation? Here's what they're looking for:

1. **Recall.** Your instructor wants to find out what's sunk in. Having everyone write en masse in class is the only way the instructor can be reasonably sure that you're dredging up your own learning and not cribbing from some poor sucker. In this situation, you must merely *recall*, to regurgitate facts and summarize them in a cogent essay. For example: "In an essay of 350 to 500 words, trace the primary events of the Russian Revolution."

2. **Analyze.** With these essay questions, your instructor wants to find out how well you've made sense of what you've heard in class and read at home. Did you get the Big Picture? In this case, you're being asked to *analyze* information. When you analyze, you separate something into parts, examine each part, and show how they relate to the whole. For example: "What crops or products have shaped the world? In what ways? You have one hour in which to write."

3. **Evaluate.** Here's where the teacher says, "Show me the money" by requiring you to make judgments. This is called *evaluation* and involves applying your own value system to the information that's germane to the topic. For example: "Are fathers necessary? Explain why or why not in an essay of no more than 750 words."

4. **Synthesize.** This is the toughest nut of all, because you're being asked to combine several elements to create something new. Synthesizing generally requires the most creativity because it includes all the other tasks—recall, analysis, evaluation—and then some. For example: "Describe a person, real or imaginary. Through the description, reveal something about that person's character."

To do well on essay tests, then, you must first be able to figure out which of these skills the test demands, because each skill requires a different approach to writing. Let's look at each writing situation in turn.

Author! Author!

Analyzing, evaluating, and **synthesizing** are all examples of "critical thinking," along with **hypothesizing, predicting, inferring, drawing conclusions,** and **classifying.** Critical thinking is the ability to solve problems; be flexible, creative, and original; capture and transmit knowledge, and express views and feelings appropriately. Effective critical thinkers use many of these skills simultaneously, and not in any prescribed order. In general, however, the hierarchy moves from recognizing, recalling, distinguishing, and classifying, up the ladder to sequencing, visualizing, predicting, drawing conclusions, inferring, evaluating, analyzing, and synthesizing.

If the Assignment Asks You to Recall ...

The pressure writing assignment changes dramatically depending on whether you're allowed to refer to your text and notes or not. Open-book tests are not likely to be recall tests, for instance, because it would be pretty silly to ask you to recall information if the book was sitting open in front of you. Open-book tests, in contrast, always call for higher-order thinking skills. This means that the teacher isn't generally doing you any favor with an open-book test.

At the very least, every closed-book test will ask you to remember information. How can you tell if the essay focuses on recall?

Read the exam closely to see if it's designed to find out if you've *read* the material or whether you've *thought* about it. If it's the former, then you're dealing with a recall essay. In that case, your essay should be chock-a-block with facts, details, and examples.

It's especially important that you find a solid method of organization for a recall essay. Otherwise, you'll end up with little more than a laundry list of facts. Here are two methods of organization well suited to recall writing tests:

Write Angles

Forewarned is forearmed: Most essay tests in English and literature classes ask you to analyze.

➤ **Order of importance.** Present the facts from most to least significant.

➤ **Chronological order.** Present the information in time order.

If the Assignment Asks You to Analyze ...

Writing tests that focus on *analysis* usually contain one or more of these key words:

➤ analyze	➤ assess
➤ clarify	➤ classify
➤ describe	➤ determine
➤ examine	➤ explain
➤ explore	➤ explicate
➤ interpret	➤ probe
➤ review	➤ scrutinize
➤ show	➤ support

Writer's Block

It's tempting to include a lot of summary in an analysis writing test because it pads the essay so very nicely and seems to fulfill the assignment. It doesn't, so resist the temptation to merely recall when you're supposed to analyze.

Start these essays by stating the analytical position you'll be taking. Then summarize the points that support your analysis. Many analysis essay tests are organized around cause-and-effect or comparison-contrast.

If the Assignment Asks You to Evaluate ...

Questions that ask you to *evaluate* require you to give your opinion, to make a judgment call. This means you can't sit on the fence, partner—you have to take a stand. The stand itself isn't as crucial as the support you muster to back it up. Of course, you're going to consider pandering to the professor, because it seems that professors live to be pandered to.

However, it's often the less obvious opinion that garners the better grade, because it shows the writer put more thought into the evaluation. Here's my advice: Make the judgment that's in line with your value system and the material you have to support it.

If the Assignment Asks You to Synthesize ...

This is the one where you really get to strut your stuff, because you're being asked to pull together everything you've read on your own, heard in discussions, and experienced firsthand. You have to go beyond all three sources to make something new, to reach a conclusion, to show that you're thinking in depth.

Write Angles

Even before you get your writing back from the grader, think about your performance. What could you have done better? For example, did you allocate your time wisely? Did you find the best possible structure and present your points cogently? Depending on how you answer these questions (and others like them), you might wish to approach the next pressure writing test differently.

Synthesis questions never have one "right" answer; what determines success here is the logic and originality of your thinking and how well all the pieces fit with your thesis. Obviously, you must have all the facts at your fingertips, so recall matters. But it's equally crucial that you tie that summary to higher-level thinking: analysis, evaluation, and synthesis.

Consider this organization:

➤ Open with your thesis, an overview of the point you'll be making.

➤ Bring in details to support your thesis, adding summary where necessary.

Write This Way

Here's an excellent essay written under pressure in one hour. The writer was directed to create a well-organized essay of about 350 words that supports his or her viewpoint of the following topic. The essay had to use specific details and examples.

Topic:

Some critics have charged that American cities are dying, victims of neglect, crime, and decay. Others counter that American cities have never been more vital, offering unparalleled cultural, recreational, and social activities. Analyze the issue and decide which side of the argument is more valid.

Sample response:

weighs both sides of issue —

Cities can be the liveliest, most exciting places in which to live, offering the best of our civilization. It's true that cities also have an opposite face, as grimy as the other is shiny. Poverty and despair stalk the cities' streets, claiming many a weak, poor, ill-equipped victim. Nonetheless, cities offer incomparable treasures not available anywhere else. That's because cities are great cultural centers.

thesis —

three main points: libraries, museums, theaters —

The finest libraries, museums, and theaters are located in major cities, because only large population centers have the money to attract such jewels. These institutions allow residents and visitors to enjoy first-class cultural events.

examples of point #1 —

When I was younger, my family often drove from Long Island to New York City to visit the public library, where we would walk through the cool, high-ceilinged halls and select books to read. Since I live in New York City today, I am able to visit the library often and borrow books, magazines, videos, and even photographs. I could not possibly afford to buy these materials on my own.

examples
of point #2

Large cities also contain magnificent museums. New York City, for example, boasts the Metropolitan Museum of Art, the Guggenheim, and the Museum of Folk Art, to mention just three. These museums contain famous paintings by such great painters as Rembrandt, Van Gogh, Monet, Picasso, and Matisse, as well as early American quilts, weathervanes, and even rare household utensils. We often took field trips to these museums when I was in elementary school. I remember my first sight of Picasso's mural *Guernica*. I had never seen anything so stirring.

examples
of point #3

Cities also showcase the greatest stage actors, directors, musicians, and set designers. New York City's Broadway, Off-Broadway, and Off-Off-Broadway, for instance, offer a wide variety of classic and experimental theater. As a child, I saw Carol Channing in *Hello Dolly* and Zero Mostel in *Fiddler on the Roof*. Recently, I sat mesmerized at Brian Dennehy's wrenching performance in *Death of a Salesman*, gasped in awe at the set design of *The Lion King*, and thrilled to Cathy Rigby soaring overhead in *Peter Pan*.

sums up
thesis

Only major cities offer so many libraries, museums, and plays—not to mention concerts, athletic events, and monuments. Don't get me wrong; suburbs and rural areas also have their charm, but for culture, cities can't be beat. They have it *all*.

The Golden Rules

You want to write as well as you can—no mediocre prose for you, partner. If you're taking a test, you want to get the highest possible score; if you're writing something on the job, you want that raise, promotion, and pat on the back. The following suggestions can help you prepare for writing under pressure. Make these hints part of your standard repertoire.

Word Watch

Prose is nonpoetic writing. Essays, stories, and newspaper articles are classified as prose, for example.

Before the Test ...

The following suggestions can help you use your time to best advantage as you prepare for writing tests. Actually, they work great for *any* kind of test!

1. **Study.** Know your stuff. If you're well prepared, not only will you stand a better chance of answering the questions correctly, but you'll also be less likely to panic during the test. Set up a study schedule well in advance of the exam date.

2. **Get a good night's sleep.** Yes, I know you've heard it before, but it really works. A solid eight hours of zzzz's can recharge your batteries and get you freebee extra points on *any* test.

Writer's Block

Avoid sleeping medication the night before, because there's the chance it will leave you groggy.

3. **Be sure to eat.** Yes, I know you'll get sick if you eat. Eat anyway; you need the nourishment. And stick with your normal foods—this isn't the time to go for the super-size Enchilada Grande with a side of squid.

4. **Go easy on the caffeine.** Too much coffee or cola can give you the jitters, the last thing you want.

5. **Avoid all alcohol.** Even if you feel that a drink will relax you and take the edge off, steer clear of demon rum. The booze will just blunt your brain and prevent you from seeing the test as clearly as you must to succeed.

6. **Relax the day before.** If you relieve the pressure the day before, you're less likely to shift into panic mode while you're writing. So take your mind off the test by doing something you enjoy.

7. **Get your ducks in a row.** The night before, lay out your clothing, writing implements, watch, and other necessaries. For example, to take nationwide standardized tests such as the SAT, you need identification to get into the test room. Be sure to have a valid driver's license, school ID, or passport or you won't even be admitted to the test.

Author! Author!

Today, many tests that were traditionally short-answer formats, such as the Scholastic Aptitude Test (SAT), contain an essay. More and more standardized tests are moving in this direction, too. That's because essay tests assess the higher-order critical thinking skills you need to succeed, such as analysis, evaluation, and explication. Short-answer tests hit only the facts, not how you express them.

8. **Make sure you know where you're going.** If you haven't been to the test site before, make sure you have good directions. It's not a bad idea to take a dry run to the site a day or two before the actual test, so you'll know how to get there when it really matters. This is especially important for directionally challenged people like me.

9. **Leave enough time in the morning.** Figure out how much time you need in the morning to get ready—and then leave yourself an extra 30 minutes. If an emergency arises, you'll have time to deal with it. If everything goes smoothly, you can linger over your juice and toast.

10. **Put on a happy face.** Getting upset the day before a pressure writing situation does more than make you feel lousy; it can also rob you of the confidence you need to succeed. This is called a *self-fulfilling prophecy.* Thinking the good thoughts can help you keep your focus, so do your best to remain upbeat.

Word Watch

A **self-fulfilling prophecy** occurs when you talk yourself into something. So why not talk yourself into writing well under pressure?

When the Meter's Running

So here you are, sitting in front of a crisp exam book and an equally crisp exam question. What to do? It's a piece of cake—if you follow these suggestions.

1. **Read the entire test before you start to write.** If you have to write similar documents under pressure all the time, become familiar with the directions. This can save you valuable time you can apply to the writing itself. But when you're in a new writing situation, it's imperative that you *read all the directions all the way through before you begin to write anything*—even your name.

   Here's what you want to know:

   ➤ *Audience.* Who will be reading your writing? What do they expect from you?

   ➤ *Purpose.* Are you writing to persuade or inform? (It's very rare that pressure writing situations involve extensive description or narration.)

   ➤ *Length.* How long should your writing be? You're usually expected to write 350 to 500 words in an hour.

   ➤ *Time.* How long do you have to write? If you have a choice of test questions, determine which one(s) you're best qualified to answer. Go for the one(s) you know the most about, the one(s) you can most fully answer in the time you have.

2. **Figure out how to budget your time.** Decide how much time you can spend prewriting, drafting, and revising. Don't gnaw your fingernails to the quick trying to stick to your schedule, but do have an idea where this experience is going, and how fast. For a one-hour writing exam, for instance, you can allocate your time this way:

Step in the Writing Process	Time
prewriting	10 minutes
drafting	30 minutes
revising and editing	15 minutes
proofreading	5 minutes

3. **Find key words.** Writers under pressure often forget to answer an important part of a question. You can safeguard against this by underlining key words in the question. For example, if the question asks: "Summarize the key events in the French Revolution," underline *summarize* and *French Revolution*.

4. **Outline.** Before you begin to draft, take a few minutes to decide how you'll arrange the details in your essay. Set them down in outline form.

5. **Keep moving.** Try not to get bogged down in details or rough patches. The single biggest time-waster (and therefore the single biggest point-stealer) is getting hung up on one aspect of the assignment. If you do get stuck, leave some spaces and keep writing. With pressure writing situations, time is key.

Pace yourself by taking a deep breath every five minutes, putting down your pen for a moment every 10 minutes, and so on. You want to work at a slow, steady pace. (Yes, slow and steady *does* win the race.)

6. **But don't rush!** In your haste to answer everything, don't write so quickly that you make silly mistakes—or even worse, that you misinterpret the entire question. In the anxiety of pressure writing, it's easy to lose your way and misconstrue something you really know very well. You might misread a word; even skipping over a prefix can throw an entire question off kilter. Pace yourself, just as you would when running a race or boogying the night away.

Write Angles

Be sure to use a writing style with sufficient complexity to handle the subject matter. In general, adopt a style suitable for educated adults.

7. **Cover all the bases.** Make sure that your essay really *does* answer the question fully and completely. Have you addressed all the key points? Have you shown that you fully understand the material?

8. **Stay on topic.** When you're under pressure, it's tempting to remake the topic into something you feel more comfortable answering. Stand strong. You're not going to get any points for answering your own question when you've been asked to answer someone else's.

9. **Go for brownie points.** Even with recall questions, add some insight of your own, no matter how small. This not only shows that you've done some serious thinking about the issues, but also sets your paper (and you!) apart from the teaming multitudes.

10. **Use *all* your time; *never* leave early.** Unless you're about to give birth to a child (and maybe even then), there's no excuse for leaving a pressure writing test situation early. For 11 years, I taught an English class that culminated in a three-hour test, complete with two major essays. Students had to pass this test to graduate high school. An astonishing number of students left the test early. Guess what—the students who stayed the full time *always* did better. Why? They had time to rethink and rewrite so they caught their errors and polished their writing.

11. **Proofread.** So you've made some startling insights. So you've had some original thoughts. Maybe you've even been genuinely creative. To paraphrase the song, "That don't impress me none"—if your paper is riddled with errors. Instructors really do give writers some latitude when it comes to pressure writing; no one expects a *perfect* paper in these situations. But neither does anyone expect egregious errors. Sloppiness will undercut the best thinking and shatter the most original argument.

Panic in the Streets

What happens if you have an anxiety attack during a pressure writing situation?

➤ Stop writing.

➤ Close your eyes for a moment.

➤ Take several slow, deep breaths.

➤ Tell yourself that you're addressing one issue at a time.

➤ Tell yourself that every part of the question you answer is a point in your pocket.

➤ Open your eyes and keep writing.

➤ Take it step by step.

Writer's Block

Never try to snow your reader. If you don't know the answer, don't make one up. You're not writing fiction, ladies and gentlemen, you're writing fact.

Last Licks

The most successful essays always fulfill their purpose, address their audience, and have a logical organization, whether they're written at your leisure or under the gun. Good writing is complete and logical—even when it's written under pressure.

Create a checklist like this one to use when you have to write under pressure.

Pressure Writing Checklist

Preparation

- ❏ Am I well prepared for this test?
- ❏ Did I get enough sleep?
- ❏ Have I eaten?
- ❏ Am I in the right place taking the correct test?

Prewriting

- ❏ Have I read the directions? Do I understand the task?
- ❏ Did I read the entire test before I started to write?
- ❏ Have I analyzed my audience and purpose?
- ❏ If I have a choice, have I selected the question I can answer most fully?
- ❏ Do I understand the question? Have I found the key words?
- ❏ Have I budgeted my time well?
- ❏ Did I select a logical and suitable method of organization?
- ❏ Have I made a simple outline?

Writing

- ❏ As I write, am I pacing myself well?
- ❏ Is my answer complete?
- ❏ Did I select vivid, specific words?
- ❏ Do my paragraphs contain sufficient detail?
- ❏ Are my facts correct?
- ❏ Have I included some original insight?

Postwriting

- ❏ Did I edit and revise my essay?
- ❏ Did I proofread carefully to eliminate distracting and careless errors?
- ❏ Have I used all my time?
- ❏ Have I labeled every part of my response with my name and other necessary information?
- ❏ Did I hand in everything required, such as scrap paper and the test booklet as well as the finished essay?

The Least You Need to Know

➤ Essay tests ask you to recall facts, analyze a topic, evaluate an issue, or synthesize information. Each task requires its own organization and content.

➤ Excellent essays are well organized and address the topic with vivid details and examples.

➤ Prepare for an essay test by studying, getting a good night's sleep, eating, and avoiding caffeine and alcohol. Relax the day before and lay out what you'll need.

➤ During the test, read directions and the entire test before you start to write, figure out how to budget your time, find key words, outline, and pace yourself.

➤ Stay on topic, answer the question fully, use all your time, and edit, revise, and proofread.

➤ There are effective ways to deal with panic.

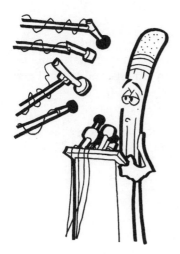

All the World's a Stage: Writing Speeches

Jerry Seinfeld once made the following observation: "According to most studies, people's No. 1 fear is public speaking. Death is No. 2. Does that seem right? That means that to the average person, if you have to go to a funeral, you're better off in the casket than delivering the eulogy." Jerry has a point, but you *can* lessen much of your fear of public speaking by writing a stupendous speech. In this chapter, you'll learn how to craft a speech that will suit the audience, occasion, and your own personal style.

First, we'll survey the three types of speeches: speeches that *inform,* speeches that *persuade,* and speeches that *entertain.* Then we'll explore each speech in depth, so you'll be able to write the speeches you need. Finally, I've included sample speeches so you'll have models as you write.

The Big Three

Some people can stand in front of a crowd and have them spellbound within minutes. What's the magic? Surprisingly, there's no magic at all. In large part, public speakers shine because they're completely prepared. They understand the different speeches they're called upon to deliver in public. They know how various speeches are organized, so they can write speeches that *work*. Now, so can you.

All speeches fall into one of three categories: speeches that *inform*, speeches that *persuade*, or speeches that *entertain*. These correspond to the four modes of discourse you learned in Part 3, "Write for Success." Here's the shakedown:

Speech Mode	Writing Mode
speeches that inform	expository writing
speeches that persuade	persuasive writing
speeches that entertain	narrative/descriptive writing

Let's look at each type of speech more closely.

Author! Author!

Here's another reason why it's so important to write a solid speech: Many speeches are printed after they have been delivered. In some cases, they're even printed *before* the fact. Speeches delivered at many different types of events, such as academic conferences, graduations, stockholders' meetings, and state funerals, become part of the public record. So even if you're addressing a small group, there's a good chance that your remarks might become part of the conference proceedings—and history.

Before we continue, it's important to emphasize that the lines between genres blur when it comes to speeches. For example, even the most persuasive speech can be quite entertaining. Further, any persuasive speech *must* inform in order to achieve its purpose.

Speeches That Inform

This type of speech explains, reports, describes, clarifies, defines, and demonstrates. These speeches include …

➤ Court testimony

➤ Incident reports

➤ Job training sessions

➤ Presentations

➤ Process analysis ("how to") speeches

Speeches That Persuade

Speeches that persuade are designed to move your audience to action or belief. When your goal is to influence your listener, you're speaking to persuade. You can approach a persuasive speech from different angles. For example, you can use your own credibility to strengthen your argument. Or, you can appeal to your audience's emotions, reason, or ethics—exactly as you do in any persuasive writing. Persuasive speeches include …

➤ Appeals for funds

➤ Campaign speeches

➤ Eulogies

➤ Job interviews

➤ Nominations

➤ Sales presentations

Speeches That Entertain

Here, you're speaking to fulfill a social need, often to draw people together for a shared occasion. To accomplish your goal, you include the same vivid details and examples you would in any narrative/descriptive essay. Speeches that entertain include …

➤ Address of welcome

➤ Award presentations

➤ Closing remarks

➤ Dedicating imposing structures (buildings, ships, etc.)

➤ Introducing a speaker

➤ Retirement speeches

➤ Toasts and roasts

Writer's Block

Don't make the mistake of thinking that entertaining speeches have to be funny. These speeches *can* be amusing, and indeed many of them are. But they don't have to be humorous at all. Match the amount of humor to the audience, occasion, and your own personal style.

Word Watch

A speech's **theme** is its thesis, the main idea.

Since each type of speech requires its own approach, it's time well-spent learning how to write in all three modes. Besides, you're more than halfway there, since you've already learned all about the four types of writing earlier in this book. So put your feet up, relax, and learn how to write effective speeches that will have the audience eating out of *your* hand.

Information, Please: Speeches That Inform

As you've already learned, informative speeches show, clarify, and inform. To give the audience the information they've come for, you need to learn how to focus on a topic, decide on an effective method of organization, and include sufficient details, examples, and facts. Always start with the topic.

Sweet Themes Are Made of This

Said the after-dinner speaker: "I feel like Roseanne's fourth husband. I know what I'm supposed to do, but I'm at a loss how to make it different." You won't feel like Roseanne's fourth husband if you start writing an informative speech by choosing a central *theme,* the main idea or thesis.

As you plan your informative speech, ask yourself, "What is the one idea that I want to convey to my listeners?" That's your theme. First of all, effective themes should appeal to you as well as your audience, because your speech will be more interesting if you're interested in the topic. It will also be easier to write. In addition, effective themes ...

➤ Have some genuine merit; they are worth the time to research, write, and deliver.

➤ Meet the audience's expectations.

➤ Hold the audience's attention.

➤ Never cause anyone embarrassment.

➤ Fit the time constraints.

➤ Blend with the overall theme of a conference (if you're speaking with others).

Once you've settled on a theme, it's time to select a method of organization that fits with your audience, purpose, and topic.

Crystal Clear

Remember that an informational speech is designed to convey the speaker's ideas to the audience. The best-written speeches concentrate on helping listeners grasp and remember the essential ideas the speaker presents. To make sure your speech conveys its purpose, select a clear method of organization. Possibilities include …

➤ Alphabetical order

➤ Cause and effect

➤ Chronological order

➤ Numerical order

➤ Problem and solution

➤ Spatial (the order of space)

➤ Topical (subject order)

In addition, keep your points to a minimum. Three or four main points are usually the most an audience can absorb at one sitting. This is exactly the same as the five-paragraph essay structure you learned in Part 3 (introduction, three main points, conclusion). Also, be sure to link your points clearly and logically. This is crucial with speeches, because you're dealing with an oral medium: Unlike readers, listeners can't go back and reread a confusing passage.

Writer's Block

Never forget the implied contract between speaker and audience: They must sit still and listen politely. In exchange, you must have something of value to say.

Write Angles

It's especially important with speeches to include clues to help your readers follow your method of organization. Possibilities include numbers (such as 1, 2, 3 or the words "first," "second," "third," etc.) and transitions ("in contrast," "on the other hand," "however," and so on).

Detail-Oriented

Informational speeches are content-oriented—but that doesn't mean they're dull or dry. Just the opposite is true! As with all effective writing, good speeches are compelling because they include tantalizing facts, delicious details, and succulent examples.

Specific facts are the backbone of any informational speech, because that's what your listeners are going to remember. To get the facts to back up your point, read widely

Writer's Block

Never include material that's off the topic, cannot be verified, is boring, or might insult your audience.

on your topic. Check reference books, the Internet, and experts in the field—the exact same techniques you use when you're writing an expository essay.

Model Informative Speech

On February 12, 1959, the 150th anniversary of Abraham Lincoln's birth, the poet Carl Sandburg delivered a speech to a special joint session of Congress. The author of a Pulitzer Prize–winning biography of Lincoln, Sandburg included copious detail to make his subject spring to life. Here is an excerpt from that historic speech.

Address on the Anniversary of Lincoln's Birth

—Carl Sandburg

Not often in the history of mankind does a man arrive on earth who is both steel and velvet, who is hard as rock and soft as drifting fog, who holds in his heart and mind the paradox of terrible storm and peace unspeakable and perfect. Here and there across centuries come reports of men alleged to have these contrasts. And the incomparable Abraham Lincoln, born 150 years ago this day, is an approach if not a perfect realization of this character.

In the time of the April lilacs in the year 1865, on his death, the casket with his body was carried north and west a thousand miles; and the American people wept as never before; bells sobbed, cities wore crepe; people stood in tears and with hats off as the railroad burial car paused in the leading cities of seven states, ending its journey at Springfield, Illinois, the home town.

During the four years he was President he at times, especially in the first three months, took to himself the powers of a dictator; he commanded the most powerful armies till then assembled in modern warfare; he enforced conscription of soldiers for the first time in American history; under imperative necessity he abolished the right of habeas corpus; he directed politically and spiritually the wild, massive, turbulent forces let loose in civil war.

He argued and pleaded for compensated emancipation of the slaves. The slaves were property; they were on the tax books along with horses and cattle, the valuation of each slave next to his name on the tax assessor's books. Failing to get action on compensated emancipation, as a Chief Executive having war powers he issued the paper by which he declared the slaves to be freed under "military necessity." In the end nearly $4,000,000 worth of property was taken away by those who were legal owners of it, property confiscated, wiped out as by fire and turned to ashes, at his instigation and executive direction. Chattel property recognized and lawful for 300 years was expropriated, seized without payment …

Point Counterpoint: Speeches That Persuade

Question: What's a great way to stop an argument?

Answer: Drop a hard fact on it.

As you learned in Chapter 14, "Why Not See It My Way?: Persuasion and Argumentation," persuasive essays appeal to reason, ethics, and/or emotion. Persuasive speeches are no different. Like their cousin the persuasive essay, persuasive speeches rely on accurate logic and facts (as well as emotion) to move their listeners to action or belief. Here's how to do it.

Write Angles

When you write a speech, use punctuation not only to indicate the usual sentence breaks, but also to allow you to pause for emphasis when necessary.

As Easy as One, Two, Three

There are three basic types of persuasive speeches:

1. **Speeches of fact.** Here, you try to prove that something is or is not so, or that something did or did not happen. "Our candidate has always supported more money for education" would be a thesis for a persuasive speech of fact.

2. **Speeches of value.** In this type of persuasive speech, you try to prove good or bad, better or worse. "This movie is superior to its sequel" would be a thesis for a persuasive speech of value.

3. **Speeches of policy.** In this case, you try to prove that something should or should not be done. "You should buy only American-made goods" would be a suitable thesis for a speech of policy.

As you decide which type of persuasive speech best suits your audience and purpose, ask yourself these questions:

1. What do I want my listeners to do?
2. What objections, if any, will they have?
3. How strong a case can I make?
4. What type of persuasion does my organization or audience value (fact, value, or policy)?

Writer's Block

Don't forget that your speech is being written to be heard, not read, so write for the ear, not the eye. Speech is straightforward and conversational, so it calls for short, familiar words; action verbs; personal pronouns; contractions; and subject-verb-object sentence order. You can even use incomplete sentences if they convey your meaning well.

Vote Early and Often

Election addresses, for example, are speeches of policy. As a result, they always try to prove that something should or should not be done. The password is *should*.

Savvy candidates follow these three caveats:

1. **Be factual.** Don't stretch the truth—not even a little.
2. **Be specific.** Give details to support your claims.
3. **Be reliable.** Don't promise what you can't deliver.

Nearly all candidates attempt to create dissatisfaction with existing conditions to convince the audience that these conditions need to be changed—and they're the ones to do it. Candidates craft speeches that point out flaws and failure. Follow these steps when you write and deliver a campaign speech:

Direct Appeal	Election Campaign
1. Tell the audience what you want.	"Elect me."
2. Give them the information they need to act on your request.	"We're paying too much in taxes. I can lower taxes."
3. Tell the audience what you want.	"Vote for me."

But people don't make decisions based on logic alone. Emotional appeals make the audience want to do what you ask. When combined with direct requests, emotional appeals make surprisingly strong election campaigns.

Model Persuasive Speech

As a first baseman for the New York Yankees, Lou Gehrig played in 2,130 consecutive games from 1925 to 1939, setting a major league record. On July 4, 1939, he stood before 60,000 fans at Yankee Stadium and confirmed what everyone seemed to know, that the "Pride of the Yankees" had been diagnosed with a deadly disease. Less than two years later, on June 2, 1941, he died in Riverdale, New York. Here is his famous farewell speech.

> Fans, for the past two weeks you have been reading about a bad break I got. Yet today I consider myself the luckiest man on the face of the earth. I have been in ballparks for seventeen years and have never received anything but kindness and encouragement from you fans.

Look at these grand men. Which of you wouldn't consider it the highlight of his career to associate with them for even one day?

Sure, I'm lucky. Who wouldn't consider it an honor to have known Jacob Ruppert—also the builder of baseball's greatest empire, Ed Barrow—to have spent six years with that wonderful little fellow, Miller Huggins—then to have spent the next nine years with that outstanding leader, that smart student of psychology—the best manager in baseball today, Joe McCarthy?

Sure, I'm lucky. When the New York Giants, a team you would give your right arm to beat, and vice versa, sends you a gift, that's something! When everybody down to the groundskeepers and those boys in white coats remember you with trophies, that's something.

When you have a wonderful mother-in-law who takes sides with you in squabbles against her own daughter, that's something. When you have a father and mother who work all their lives so that you can have an education and build your body, it's a blessing! When you have a wife who has been a tower of strength and shown more courage than you dreamed existed, that's the finest I know.

So I close in saying that I might have had a tough break—but I have an awful lot to live for!

Author! Author!

When it comes to writing models, study the best. For a great persuasive speech, try Abraham Lincoln's "House Divided" address (1858). Lincoln delivered this speech when he was nominated for the Senate. It was probably Lincoln's most radical statement about the implications of the slavery issue, as he predicted that "this government cannot endure permanently half slave and half free."

Life of the Party: Speeches That Entertain

Speaking to the Young People's Society in Greepoint, Brooklyn, in 1901, Mark Twain advised, "Always do right. This will gratify some people and astonish the rest."

For centuries, speakers have been called upon to "say a few words" at various social events. These include club meetings, dinners, parties, graduations, holidays, weddings, and ribbon cuttings—all our social functions. Sometimes these speeches help create greater unity within an organization. Other times, they honor individuals or fulfill part of a social ritual or special ceremony.

What makes these speeches different from the other forms I've described so far is their purpose: They don't inform or persuade. Instead, they entertain. Here's how to write speeches that weave the social fabric a bit tighter.

Crowd Pleaser

When it comes to speeches that entertain, if you can't be brief, at least be memorable. Write a speech that's easy to remember and tantalizing for the press to quote. For example, Winston Churchill was once asked to give the commencement address at Oxford University. Following his introduction, he walked to the podium, said "Never, never give up," and took his seat.

> ### Writer's Block
>
> Speeches that entertain can have a more profound effect on your life than speeches that inform or persuade. That's because entertaining speeches are delivered at social occasions that give you the opportunity to ingratiate yourself with your audience. This often results in promotions, new employment opportunities, business contacts, and other goodies.

When you write a speech that entertains, *always* start by assessing your audience. You know that audience analysis is a crucial component in *every* writing situation, but it's especially vital when you're writing an entertaining speech because here, your listeners are gathered to have a good time. They don't have to stay to gather information or to listen to your viewpoint (so they can later rebut it). As a result, always start by thinking how you can make sure the audience gets what they came for. Consider their likes and dislikes and their level of sophistication.

> ### Author! Author!
>
> President Woodrow Wilson's Declaration of War Against Germany speech (1917) contains the famous line: "The world must be made safe for democracy." The speech is also remarkable for Wilson's insistence that "we have no quarrel with the German people ... We fight without rancor and without selfish object." Such self-restraint and Wilson's promise that victory would result in "a universal dominion of right" helped win liberal support for the war effort.

Come on Baby, Let the Good Times Roll

After you complete your audience analysis, select a central theme, just as you did with informative and persuasive speeches. But here, remember that your audience just wants to have fun. Your topic should be genial, good-natured, and suited to you: after all, if you're not having fun, how can anyone else party hearty?

Your overall theme should be ...

➤ **Optimistic.** This is not the time to unburden your soul and let it all hang out. Keep it light.

➤ **Uncomplicated.** Don't make your audience do any heavy lifting to get your point. Instead, develop your speech around one or two points that your listeners can grasp easily.

➤ **Lively.** Select a theme that can be illustrated by pertinent anecdotes and humorous stories (if humor works with your comfort zone).

But wait! Every entertaining speech, no matter how light and amusing, should have at least one serious point. A speech that's all sweetness and light can border on empty. Including one serious point serves as an anchor, so people feel like their getting their money's worth, like the prize in the Cracker Jack box.

The Line-Up

Here's my favorite way to organize an entertaining speech:

1. Open with an anecdote. Select one that directly relates to your audience or purpose.

2. Explain the point of the anecdote. Describe how your speech will be organized around this point.

3. Beef up your theme with additional anecdotes. Remember to spread your anecdotes evenly through your speech so the really good stuff isn't all bunched in the beginning, middle, or end.

4. Conclude by restating your central point.

5. Finish with a great anecdote to ensure a memorable ending.

Write Angles

Open with your strongest anecdote and close with your second strongest one. Your listeners (just like your readers) will remember the beginning and end of your speech most clearly.

Model Entertaining Speech #1

The following entertaining speech is by Mark Twain (1835–1910), one of the most captivating writers and speakers to ever grace a podium. Mark Twain, the pen name of Samuel Langhorne Clemens, rocketed to fame with humorous local-color tales of the West; he became a media darling by transforming stories of his childhood into American myth. Twain was extraordinarily popular on the lecture circuit, a popular venue for public entertainment before movies, television, radio, and Madonna. Here's his speech:

> My heart goes out in sympathy to anyone who is making his first appearance before an audience of human beings. By a direct process of memory I go back forty years, less one month—for I'm older than I look.
>
> I recall the occasion of my first appearance. San Francisco knew me then only as a reporter, and I was to make my bow to San Francisco as a lecturer. I knew that nothing short of compulsion would get me to the theater. So I bound myself by a hard-and-fast contract so that I could not escape. I got to the theater forty-five minutes before the hour set for the lecture. My knees were shaking so that I didn't know whether I could stand up. If there is an awful, horrible malady in the world, it is stage fright—and seasickness. They are a pair. I had stage fright then for the first and last time. I was only seasick once, too. I was on a little ship on which there were two hundred other passengers. I—was—sick. I was so sick that there wasn't any left for those other two hundred passengers.
>
> It was dark and lonely behind the scenes in that theater, and I peeked through the little peek holes they have in theater curtains and looked into the big auditorium. That was dark and empty, too. By and by it lighted up, and the audience began to arrive.
>
> I had a number of friends of mine, stalwart men, to sprinkle themselves throughout the audience armed with clubs. Every time I said anything they could possibly guess I intended to be funny, they were to pound those clubs on the floor. Then there was a kind lady in a box up there, also a good friend of mine, the wife of the governor. She was to watch me intently, and whenever I glanced toward her she was going to deliver a gubernatorial laugh that would lead the whole audience into applause.
>
> At last I began. I had the manuscript tucked under a United States flag in front of me where I could get at it in case of need. But I managed to get started without it. I walked up and down—I was young in those days and needed the exercise—and talked and talked.
>
> Right in the middle of the speech I had placed a gem. I had put in a moving, pathetic part which was to get at the hearts and souls of my hearers. When I

delivered it, they did just what I hoped and expected. They sat silent and awed. I had touched them. Then I happened to glance up at the box where the governor's wife was—you know what happened.

Well, after the first agonizing five minutes, my stage fright left me, never to return. I know if I was going to be hanged I could get up and make a good showing, and I intend to. But I shall never forget my feelings just before the agony left me, and I got up here to thank you for helping my daughter, by your kindness, to live through her first appearance. And I want to thank you for your appreciation of her singing, which is, by the way, hereditary.

Author! Author!

On May 13, 1940, Prime Minister Winston Churchill prepared England to battle the Nazis with these famous words:

... I have nothing to offer but blood, toil, tears, and sweat. ... You ask, what is our policy? I say it is to wage war by land, sea, and air. War with all our might and with all the strength God has given us, and to wage war against a monstrous tyranny never surpassed in the dark and lamentable catalogue of human crime. That is our policy.

You ask, what is our aim? I can answer in one word. It is victory. Victory at all costs—Victory in spite of all terrors—Victory, however long and hard the road may be, for without victory there is no survival.

Model Entertaining Speech #2

Since odds are that you'll be writing and delivering more entertaining speeches than any other kind (and sweating more over them), here's another model you can use. This is an outstanding graduation speech delivered on May 21, 1998, by Jennifer L. Joyner-Lebling, the valedictorian of the graduating class at the State University of New York College of Technology at Farmingdale. Notice how Ms. Joyner-Lebling graciously credits others.

Voyage of Discovery

Chairman Mastroianni, Dr. Cipriani, honored members of the college council, faculty, staff, fellow classmates, family, and friends, I am honored to have been selected Valedictorian of the graduating class of 1998. I am honored to represent your commitment, dedication, and accomplishment in achieving your goal to be here today.

Congratulations to all of you. As our celebrations end later today, consider tomorrow and realize that graduation is just one giant step in a very important direction. For some of us, this step has been a struggle full of obstacles, barriers, and distractions—for others it has not been that easy. However, through our struggles we have still accomplished our goal, and we are here today to celebrate our achievements. This awesome achievement we have made together, as well as the individual achievements of our team members.

Like Karen Conner, the Valedictorian for the Associates degree, who was awarded the National Scholarship from the Institute of Management Accountants.

And like Michael Rodriquez of the Aerospace program, the recipient of the John L. Godwin Memorial Flight Scholarship awarded by the National Air Transportation Association Foundation. Each are receiving Chancellor's Awards for Student Excellence.

And like Ornamental Horticulture graduates Pat Haugen, Elizabeth Boruke, Melissa Rigo, Steve Langella, Jessica Bottcher, Matt McFadden, and Steve Noone, who were members of a team which took first place at the Mid-Atlantic Horticultural Field Day at Suffolk Community College.

Today is the culmination of a lot of work, a lot of sweat, a lot of tears, and a lot of money ... but we are not finished. This is not final. It is, however, a significant milestone in our voyage of discovery. We have just emerged on a whole new level. You are all outstanding representatives of our graduating class. But none of us accomplished these feats alone. We had our families, partners, and friends—and we had the tutelage and guidance of some pretty incredible teachers. Before you leave today, be sure to thank at least one teacher from whom you have learned while at SUNY Farmingdale, and let them know that they are appreciated.

Thank you Dr. Gary Brown for your enthusiasm and passion for your subjects and for your interest in and concern for your students.

Thank you Dr. Richard Iversen for your never-ending support, encouragement, and mentoring. You have both made a substantial impact on my education and on my future.

Thank you Gary, Fred, Debbie, and Danielle for your guidance and friendship.

French novelist Marcel Proust once said, "The real voyage of discovery consists not in seeking new landscapes but in having new eyes." In receiving our diplomas today, we are receiving "new eyes." Use what you have learned here at SUNY Farmingdale to see things in ways in which you have never noticed before. Continue to learn. Open your minds to new ideas and concepts. We leave here with the ability to make a change, the capability to make a difference, and the responsibility to make a contribution. Congratulations to you, my fellow graduates, and good luck to you as you continue on your voyage of discovery.

The Least You Need to Know

➤ You can reduce your fear of public speaking by writing a great speech that suits the audience, occasion, and your own personal style.

➤ All speeches fall into one of three categories: speeches that inform, speeches that persuade, or speeches that entertain.

➤ When you write a speech that informs, focus on a topic, select an effective method of organization, and include sufficient details, examples, and facts.

➤ When you write a speech that persuades, use logic, ethics, and/or emotion.

➤ When you write a speech that entertains, focus on audience, select a central theme, and be optimistic, uncomplicated, lively, and brief.

➤ For more information on writing speeches, see my book, *The Complete Idiot's Guide to Public Speaking* (Alpha Books, 1999).

Chapter 23

Letter Perfect

In This Chapter

➤ Letters as historical documents

➤ Why people write letters

➤ Hints for writing personal letters

➤ Zip codes and place abbreviations

➤ Thank-you notes

➤ Condolence letters

➤ Party invitations

➤ Letters of opinion

As much as we use the telephone to reach out and touch someone, there are times when only a letter will do. *Personal letters* share feelings and information among friends and family, while *social notes* relay an invitation or refuse one. These letters also express our gratitude, congratulations, or condolences. We also have *letters of opinion,* sent to newspapers, businesses, and the media. In this chapter, you'll learn how to write these important and useful types of letters.

Drop Me a Line

Letters are a testimony to the enduring attempts of human beings to bridge the communication gap between themselves and others. Letters pack an astonishingly big wallop for their size. In some cases, they even become the stuff of history.

"Of course," you say, "all those letters the bigwigs write to each other get into the history books." That's certainly true, but even personal letters can influence the course of events. For example, Abigail Adams (1744–1818), the wife of John Adams, America's second president, was an untiring letter writer. After John left their Massachusetts home to serve in the First Continental Congress in Philadelphia, the couple saw each other only intermittently for the next 10 years. While raising the children and managing the family's business affairs, Abigail also became an untiring advocate for women's rights. From her letter of March 31, 1776, came the famous phrase "Remember the ladies!":

> Remember the Ladies, and be more generous and favourable to them than your ancestors. Do not put such unlimited power into the hands of the Husbands. Remember all Men would be tyrants if they could. If particular care and attention is not paid to the Ladies we are determined to foment a Rebellion, and will not hold ourselves bound by any Laws in which we have no voice, or Representation.

Keep this in mind the next time you write a letter to your spouse or lover. You could be making history.

Dear Mr. Postman

September 28, 1909

Dear Mrs. Coney,

Your second card just reached me and I am plumb glad because, although I answered your other, I was wishing I could write to you, for I have had the most charming adventure.

I was awakened by a pebble striking my cheek. Something prowling on the bluff above us had dislodged it and it struck me. It was four o'clock, so I arose and spitted my rabbit. The logs had left such a big bed of coals, but some ends were still burning in such a manner that the heat would go both under and over my rabbit. So I put plenty of bacon grease over him and hung him up to roast. Then I went back to bed. I didn't want to start early because the air is too keen for comfort early in the morning ....

—Elinore Rupert Stewart

Personal letters are written for several important and intriguing reasons. These include an urge to record an experience, the desire to respond to a situation, the craving to maintain contact, a wish to offer congratulations or comfort, and the longing to be creative. Elinore Rupert Stewart, a pioneer trekking west at the turn of the century, wrote for all these reasons. Today, letters such as hers offer us a fascinating record of the westward expansion.

Signed, Sealed, Delivered

Let's look a little more closely at the reasons why people write personal letters. See which items match *your* reasons for writing letters to friends and family. (Or why you should start writing them!)

➤ **Letters as travelogue.** People often write letters to record their experiences and share them with one or more friends. Novelist E.M. Forster, for instance, wrote a series of letters to his mother to document his first trip to India, the country that was to play such an important role in his future writings.

Author! Author!

E.M. Forester (1879–1970) is most famous for his novels *A Passage to India, A Room with a View,* and *Howard's End.* Forster's letters, published in 1980, "provided greater insight into the relationship between his life and art," one critic noted. (Nearly all his novels have been filmed in luscious if languid versions by the cinematic duo Merchant/Ivory.)

➤ **Letters as statements.** Letters can also be sparked by a need to respond to a specific situation, public as well as private. Martin Luther King Jr., for example, wrote his famous "Letter from Birmingham Jail" to answer criticism from eight fellow clergymen. Perhaps you wrote a letter to a friend or colleague to explain your position on a key issue.

➤ **Letters as social cement.** People also write letters because they want to make or maintain a connection with another person. When her big-game hunter husband brought her to Africa, Isak Dinesen sent letter after letter home to her family in Denmark to relieve her loneliness and maintain contact with her kin. We also write to congratulate or console, crow and comfort.

➤ **Letters as creative outlet.** Personal letters are also a way to be creative, especially for people who have a keen interest in writing but are afraid to risk publication or are having difficulty getting published. Letters give us the chance to share our personal feelings. Perhaps you write letters for this reason.

With telephones and e-mail, you'd think the personal letter was as dead as a dodo. It's actually flourishing, thank you very much. Let's review the generally accepted conventions of letter writing.

Stamp of Approval

Because personal letters express your own ideas, you generally have a far wider choice of content with them than you do with business letters. However, an effective personal letter must still be clearly organized and carefully thought out. The following tips should make your task easier.

Ten Tips for Writing Great Personal Letters

1. Never apologize for not having written or for running out of ideas. You're not on trial here.

2. Reread any recent letters you received from the person to whom you are writing. This will help you answer the person's questions and include items of interest to the reader.

3. To make your ideas come alive, use vivid sensory impressions, descriptions that appeal to sight, hearing, smell, and so on.

4. Also include figures of speech, such as *similes* and *metaphors*.

5. Dialogue makes your writing more specific and interesting, too.

6. Never assume that your reader knows the complete cast of characters in your life, especially newcomers like your daughter's boyfriend (the one with the ring in his navel and hole in his head). Identify all unfamiliar people and places you mention.

7. Check your grammar and usage carefully. Even though your letter is informal, you want to get it right and prevent misunderstandings.

8. Reread for errors in spelling, punctuation, capitalization, and logic.

9. Make your letter easy to read by typing or writing clearly.

10. Try to end your letter on a positive note. Avoid lame endings like, "Well, that's all I have to say" or "It's late so I'll end this letter." A strong ending leaves your readers thinking the good thoughts—and thinking well of you.

Return to Sender, Address Unknown

When you address the envelope, follow the style you used in the letter. Here are a few more guidelines:

➤ If you typed the letter, type the address on the envelope. The style should match.

➤ If you wrote the letter longhand, write the envelope longhand. Be sure your writing is legible: Don't make the post office play 20 Questions.

➤ Addresses are electronically scanned, so center the recipient's name and address in the lower middle quadrant.

➤ Don't use *Mr., Mrs.,* or *Ms.* when you write your own name on the return address.

➤ Use only standard abbreviations for streets, states, and countries.

➤ To insure speedy delivery or return, include the zip code in both the recipient's address and your return address.

➤ Be sure the envelope is large enough to meet postal service regulations. Otherwise, they won't accept it.

➤ Use sufficient postage. If in doubt, have the letter weighed at the post office.

Zip It Up

Following are the standard US Post Office abbreviations for the 50 states, the District of Columbia, Puerto Rico, the Virgin Islands, American Samoa, Guam, and a few other handy places. Notice that the zip code abbreviations for states aren't followed by periods.

State	Zip Code Abbreviation
Alabama	AL
Alaska	AK

State	Zip Code Abbreviation
American Samoa	AS
Arizona	AZ
Arkansas	AR
California	CA
Colorado	CO
Connecticut	CT
Delaware	DE
District of Columbia	DC
Florida	FL
Georgia	GA
Guam	GU
Hawaii	HI
Idaho	ID
Illinois	IL
Indiana	IN
Iowa	IA
Kansas	KS
Kentucky	KY
Louisiana	LA
Maine	ME
Marshall Islands	MH
Maryland	MD
Massachusetts	MA
Michigan	MI
Minnesota	MN
Mississippi	MS
Missouri	MO
Montana	MT

State	Zip Code Abbreviation
Nebraska	NE
Nevada	NV
New Hampshire	NH
New Jersey	NJ
New Mexico	NM
New York	NY
North Carolina	NC
North Dakota	ND
Ohio	OH
Oklahoma	OK
Oregon	OR
Pennsylvania	PA
Puerto Rico	PR
Rhode Island	RI
South Carolina	SC
South Dakota	SD
Tennessee	TN
Texas	TX
Utah	UT
Vermont	VT
Virgin Islands	VI
Virginia	VA
Washington	WA
West Virginia	WV
Wisconsin	WI
Wyoming	WY

Never use any abbreviation if there is the slightest chance of a misdelivery or mis-understanding. In that case, write out the full place name.

Short and Sweet

The following list gives some of the most common abbreviations for geographical terms. Notice that unlike zip codes, these are true abbreviations, since each one ends with a period.

Place	Abbreviation
Avenue	Ave.
Building	Bldg.
Boulevard	Blvd.
County	Co.
District	Dist.
Drive	Dr.
Fort	Ft.
Highway	Hwy.
Island	Is.
Mountain	Mt.
National	Natl.
Peninsula	Pen.
Point	Pt.
Province	Prov.
Road	Rd.
Route	Rte.
Square	Sq.
Street	St.
Territory	Terr.

Now, let's turn to a specific type of personal letter: the social note.

People Who Like People: Social Notes

Unlike personal letters, social notes generally serve a single purpose. Personal letters dish the dirt; social notes may express thanks, offer condolences, or invite someone to a party, for example. As a key part of good manners, social notes are the glue that holds the fabric of society together. Because social notes have a specific purpose, they have to be organized more carefully than personal letters. Here's how:

Thanks a Bunch: Bread-and-Butter Notes

Remember how your mother used to force you to write thank-you letters to Cousin Bertha for those ugly, itchy sweaters? "Aw, Ma," you whined, "Cousin Bertha won't care. I bet she doesn't even read my stupid letters." Guess again. It's not only your relatives who are impressed by your good manners; it's friends, neighbors, and social acquaintances as well.

Follow these guidelines when you write a thank-you note:

➤ Mention the specific gift or act of kindness.

➤ Explain why the gift or kindness was appreciated. Be as specific as possible.

➤ Send the letter promptly, since this can help avoid misunderstandings and family feuds, as well as show your appreciation.

What happens if you get a gift you detest, a real stinker? No matter how stinky the gift, it still deserves acknowledgment. Don't lie and gush about the gift. Instead, be polite and more general in your thanks. Remember: A gift is just that—a present rather than an obligation.

Write Angles

B&B notes are crucial in the business world as well. It's never a bad idea to send a thank-you letter after a phone interview with someone at a company about employment, an actual job interview, or when you've been offered a job and declined it.

Writer's Block

"Your check is your receipt" doesn't cut it as a thank-you note. Never assume that since you've endorsed the check, your obligation to write a thank-you note is discharged. It's not.

I Feel Your Pain: Letters of Condolence

No, you don't, and don't even try. But a letter of condolence is more appreciated than a phone call because it's tangible proof that the person cared enough to write. Many people keep meaningful letters of condolence and reread them in times of pain.

Letters of condolence must be written with tact and sincerity. While it's always best to write promptly after the person's loss, a letter of condolence is the rare situation

Write Angles

Unless you have a handicap that prevents you from handwriting, letters of condolence should *always* be handwritten.

where "better late than never" holds true. If you put off writing the note because you couldn't think of appropriate words of comfort, it's not too late to do it now. Here are some ideas to get you started:

Do ...

➤ Show the person that you care and you have been affected by the loss.

➤ Keep the letter sincere. Write from the heart.

➤ Use a compassionate and sorrowful tone.

➤ Offer friendship or love, whatever the relationship.

➤ Include specific details about the person's admirable traits. Tell a brief story about the time the person picked you up from the airport at midnight, for example.

Don't ...

➤ Try to show that your loss is greater than the person's loss. It isn't.

➤ Rehash the tragedy and the gory details.

➤ Tell them their loved one is in a better place. They may not share your value system.

➤ Offer something you can't deliver.

➤ Fall back on stock phrases from greeting cards.

Abraham Lincoln wrote the following letter to a woman who had suffered an unimaginable loss during the Civil War. Notice how he uses a comforting, compassionate, and reverent tone. He doesn't pretend to have known the woman's sons; nor does he offer anything he can't deliver.

Executive Mansion, Washington

November 21, 1864

Dear Madam,

I have been shown in the files of the War Department a statement of the Adjutant-General of Massachusetts that you are the mother of five sons who have died gloriously on the field of battle. I feel how weak and fruitless must be any words of mine which should attempt to beguile you from the grief of a loss so overwhelming. But I cannot refrain from tendering you the consolation that may be found in the thanks of the Republic they died to save. I pray that our Heavenly Father may assuage the anguish of your bereavement, and leave you only the cherished memory of the loved and lost, and the solemn pride that must be yours to have laid so costly a sacrifice upon the altar of freedom.

Yours very sincerely and respectfully,

Abraham Lincoln

Author! Author!

Abraham Lincoln was a superb writer, stating his ideas with elegance and precision. In his professional correspondence and documents, Lincoln drew on the cadence and diction of Shakespeare and the Bible. In his personal notes, however, Lincoln was known to use phrases as plain and homespun as he himself was. For example, a woman once asked Lincoln to intercede on her behalf at the War Department. Lincoln declined, saying he could not be of any help in the situation because "they do things their own way there, and I don't amount to pig tracks in the War Department."

It's My Party, and I'll Cry If I Want To

All invitations must include the social occasion (birthday, anniversary, and so on), time, date, or place. You may also wish to include information about what to wear. Here are some additional guidelines:

Word Watch

RSVP is French for *Répondez-vous, s'il vous plaît,* meaning "please answer."

➤ **RSVP.** Want to know how many people are coming to your shindig? Write the abbreviation "RSVP" in the lower-left corner of the invitation to request that the person respond.

➤ **Reply date.** Always include a specific date by which the person must answer "yes" or "no" or you'll be getting calls months after the party has ended.

➤ **Regrets only.** Don't want to hear from everyone? Write "regrets only," which means that only those people who can't attend must call and respond.

Writer's Block

For fancy parties, it's common-place to have the invitations printed. If you go this route, be sure to proofread the invitation *before* it's printed. We're still laughing over the wedding invitation that had the bride's name misspelled.

Traditionally, all invitations were handwritten in the form of a personal letter. Today, however, many people use preprinted invitations and fill in the relevant information. Whatever method you use, be sure to include all the information the reader needs.

Letters of Opinion

How about those Mets? Everybody's got an opinion, and few of us are shy about expressing it. That's where letters of opinion come in. By stating our point of view in writing, letters of opinion give legitimacy to our feelings.

Letters of opinion are like telephone books: They have a wide variety of uses. Here are some of the most common ones:

➤ To praise or criticize a company

➤ To register your viewpoint on a community issue

➤ To comment on public policy

➤ To respond to an editorial or article

➤ To support a candidate or other elected official

All letters of opinion state your opinions clearly and provide reasons to support them. Here's how it works with a letter of complaint.

I Can't Get No Satisfaction

The washing machine ate your socks; the hair dryer has more hot air than your local Senator. You're mad as hell, and you're not going to take it anymore. What to do? Why not write a letter of complaint? "Ah, they never work," you scoff. Actually, they do—and quite well. Here's how to lodge a consumer complaint and accomplish more than just venting your spleen.

1. Gather up all the paperwork related to the product or service in question—which you saved, like the careful consumer you are, rather than throwing away with the box. Here's the proof you'll need to make your case:

   ➤ Sales receipts

   ➤ Work orders

   ➤ Canceled checks

   ➤ Charge slips

   ➤ Warranty booklets

2. Contact the company by letter. The letter approach allows you time to frame your complaint more carefully and completely than a phone call. It also provides tangible proof of dissatisfaction in the form of a "paper trail."

3. Follow these guidelines as you write:

   ➤ Address the letter to the company president or the consumer complaint department.

   ➤ Explain your problem with the product or service.

   ➤ Include the model number, serial number, and any receipts.

   ➤ State what you want. Be specific but reasonable. If the toaster broke after a month, a replacement is another toaster or a refund, not a side-by-side refrigerator/freezer or a week in Barbados.

   ➤ Be sure to include your return address and a daytime telephone number.

   ➤ Keep the letter brief.

4. Give the company sufficient time to respond to your complaint.

5. If you haven't received satisfaction after what you judge to be a reasonable length of time, you can take the following steps:

   ➤ Assume the letter was misplaced and write again.

   ➤ Contact your locate consumer affairs office or regulatory agencies.

Write Angles

You can often find a company's phone number or address through toll-free customer service numbers or on the Web.

Writer's Block

Never throw out any response you get from the company, and keep a record of any phone calls, too. Of course, you'll keep a copy of all the correspondence *you* send.

Kudos!

A letter of opinion can state a positive viewpoint as well as a negative one. For example, you might write to a store to praise a helpful clerk or to a company to applaud a product or service. Or, your letter of opinion might state a dissenting viewpoint, a different way of looking at the same issue. You might write to a newspaper, magazine, or television station about their editorial viewpoint. Whatever your purpose or audience, here are some suggestions to consider as you write.

1. **For letters of praise:**
   - ➤ State exactly who or what you are praising.
   - ➤ Give dates of exemplary service.
   - ➤ Identify outstanding employees by name and title (e.g., Jimmy Joe Johnson, clerk).
   - ➤ Include your name, address, and telephone number.

2. **For letters of dissent:**
   - ➤ State what editorial, article, or so on prompted your response.
   - ➤ Keep your cool; name-calling works against you.
   - ➤ Stay on the issue; avoid pointless digressions.
   - ➤ Include your name, address, and telephone number.

The Least You Need to Know

➤ Personal letters share personal feelings and information among friends and family, while social notes express gratitude or condolences, or relay an invitation.

➤ Effective personal letters are well-organized, descriptive, complete, correct, and easy to read.

➤ Envelopes are correctly addressed, including the right zip code and other abbreviations.

➤ Thank-you notes mention the specific gift or act of kindness and describe why it was appreciated.

➤ Condolence letters are written with tact and sincerity, showing the bereaved that you care about their loss.

➤ Letters of opinion offer praise or criticism of a person, place, thing, or idea.

Chapter 24

The Professional Edge: Writing on the Job

In This Chapter

➤ What makes a boffo business letter?

➤ Good-news, bad-news letters

➤ Getting your foot in the door

Tech Support:	"What does the screen say now?"
Person:	"It says, 'Hit ENTER when ready.'"
Tech Support:	"Well?"
Person:	"How do I know when it's ready?"

Ready or not, it's time you mastered the basics of business writing: letters and resumés. First, we'll review the characteristics, different purposes, and formats of business letters. Then, I'll teach you how to write the most important kinds of business letters, including good-news letters, bad-news letters, resumés, and cover letters.

The Desk Set

Say there's an improvement in the company's billing policy—and you're the lucky employee who gets to write the letter about it. Perhaps you need to announce a smaller holiday party or a limit to "Dress-Down Fridays," or reject a would-be employee. Or it's time to move on and you need to send a cover letter and resumé. Whatever the task, successful professionals know how to write winning letters and resumés. Now you can, too! Here are their secrets.

While no two kinds of business letters are exactly the same, they *do* share certain features besides their format.

➤ They are brief but complete.

➤ They state the writer's purpose clearly and concisely.

➤ The language is *always* polite.

➤ The tone matches the occasion. A letter to a colleague, for example, is appropriately friendly, but business correspondence in general is formal.

➤ The relationship between the writer and reader is established in the beginning of the letter.

➤ The writer provides any necessary background information.

➤ If the reader is required to take action, the writer states the action outright.

➤ If the letter is a response to a letter, phone call, or personal visit, the writer mentions the date of the previous contact.

➤ Business letters are always typed, never handwritten.

➤ They follow a set format, explained in the following sections.

Author! Author!

Along with good interpersonal skills, the ability to write well is the single most important factor in promotions and job security. The ability to communicate effectively in writing can also be the decisive factor in a candidate getting a position. Ben Ordover, a division president at CBS, notes, "Many people climbing the corporate ladder are very good. When faced with a hard choice between candidates, I use writing ability as the deciding factor. Sometimes a candidate's writing was the only skill that separated him or her from the competition."

Style and Substance

Business letters are single-spaced on 8½ × 11-inch letterhead. There are three different formats you can use: the block style, the modified block style, and the semiblock style. The differences among the three styles depends on paragraph indentations and the placement of headings and closes. Here's the run-down:

Write Angles

Pick one letter style—the **block style,** the **modified block style,** or the **semiblock style**—and stick with it. You're less likely to make mistakes if you're consistent.

1. The *block style* has all parts of the letter flush left.

2. The *modified block style* places the heading on the upper-right corner and the close and signature on the lower-right corner, parallel to the heading. The paragraphs *are not* indented.

3. The *semiblock style* places the heading on the upper-right corner and the close and signature on the lower-right corner, parallel to the heading. The paragraphs *are* indented.

Which format should you use for letters you write on the job? The block format is becoming more popular with business communication, while the semiblock format is more commonly used for personal letters or letters that don't carry a company letterhead. In general, match your letter style to the company's letter style.

Block Head

Here are the guidelines for the block style. Vary them as previously explained if you wish to use the modified block or semiblock style instead.

Date	Month (spelled out), day (followed by a comma), year.
Inside address	The recipient's address. Place two lines after the date.
Salutation	Recipient's title, last name, colon (for example: Dear Ms. Rozakis:).
Body	Short, single-spaced paragraphs stating the information.
Close	Capitalize the first word, conclude with a comma (for example: Yours truly,). Place two lines after the last line of the letter.
Signature	Sign your name in blue or black ink. Leave three lines after the close for your signature.

Initials	If the letter is typed by someone other than the writer, insert the typist's initials below the typed name of the signatory. Capitalize the writer's initials; use lowercase for the typist's (for example: LR:st or LR/st).
Enclosures	"Enclosures" or "Enc." indicate that additional material is included with the letter.
Copies	List other recipients alphabetically or by rank. Write cc: before their name to show they are receiving a copy of the letter (for example: cc: Jill Aron, Ben Carson).

If you don't know the gender of the person you're addressing, use the person's full name and omit the title. Avoid "Gentlemen" and "Dear Sir," since they are considered biased language. If you don't have a clue who will be receiving the letter, fall back on the traditional "To Whom It May Concern."

Appearance Is Reality

Good letter design is more than a matter of looks: It also saves time and money. Letters that are hard to read waste time and create extra work for the recipient. Well-designed letters create customer satisfaction and show that you value the people both inside and outside your organization. Good letter design is just plain good business.

Here's how to make your letters look as professional as they read:

Word Watch

White space is the empty space on a page. It is a key element in all document design.

1. Leave 1½-inch margins all around your message. In nearly all cases, the side margins will be preset on your word processing program. With very brief letters, center the text by increasing the top margin.

2. Use *white space* (space without writing) to separate and emphasize key points within the letter. Provide sufficient white space around paragraphs, too.

3. To help readers locate key elements, use *headers* (words or phrases that group points). You can also use indented lists, bullets, or numbers—just as this book does!

4. To get maximum impact, put key elements such as a chart in the upper-left and lower-right quadrants of the page. Since we read from left to right, top to bottom, these quadrants attract our interest most.

5. Go easy on highlighting, decorative devices, fonts, and color. Keep it simple and professional.

6. Decide whether to *justify* the right margin (line up the type), based on the situation and audience. Justified margins let you add about 20 percent more text on the page. However, use them only with proportional type to avoid distracting wide spaces between words.

7. For letters of application and resumés, use good-quality, heavy, white bond paper and matching envelopes. Today's fonts make it easy to create your own attractive and professional-looking personal letterhead. Use company letterhead for official company business.

8. When possible, limit your letters and resumés to one page. No one wants to read any more than that.

9. Consider your audience's needs and expectations. Show that you understand the reason for the business communication and the context in which it takes place.

10. Use conventional letter formats, as explained earlier.

Now that you've got the basics, let's explore some of the most common letter-writing situations you're likely to encounter in your professional life, starting with good-news and bad-news letters.

Write Angles

Courier is a "proportional" font, so-called because every letter is the same size. Times New Roman is not a proportional font, because each letter is a different size. Both of the previous sentences are written in a 12-point font, but notice how much larger Courier appears than Times New Roman.

Write Angles

Good-quality letterhead paper is the writing equivalent of the power suit; it always makes a great impression. Traditionally, local printers typeset letterhead, but a good-quality laser printer and software package can create fine letterhead as well.

Have I Got News for You!

"I'd rather write a good-news letter than a bad-news letter any day," you say. "No way!" counters your better half. "Bad-news letters are actually easier to write than good-news letters." Stop arguing: You're both right—and wrong.

The difficulty you have writing a message depends on your familiarity with the situation and the information you must convey. Even good news can be hard to deliver when you don't know enough about the situation or have a lot of information to include. Let's do some special deliveries now.

When the News Is Good

Compared to some of the horrible situations we face every day at work, delivering good news seems to be the least of our problems. But even such a seemingly pleasant task as giving welcome news has its sandtraps. To avoid getting bogged down, try these guidelines.

First, recognize that good-news letters provide information as they build a positive image of the writer. They also cement a good relationship between the writer and reader and reduce the need to send any further correspondence. This way, you can finally get to the bottom of the pile of paper on your desk.

Good-news letters are written this way:

1. Start with the good news.
2. Summarize the main points of the message.
3. Provide details and any needed background information.
4. Present any negative elements as positively as you can.
5. End on a positive note.

The following is a model good-news letter.

Writer's Block

Never go overboard when you're delivering good news. For example, if you praise someone in print for a job well done, never mislead them into thinking the letter will lead to anything more—such as a promotion or raise. If you promise more than you can deliver, you're opening the way for potential litigation. Your letter can later be used as proof of intent.

WHATSAMATTER U
Rte. 453 and Cowplop Road
Glassy Point, Idaho 67819

May 2, 2000

Professor Schmendrick
Department of College Studies
Solid Community College
Kneejerk, Nevada 98761

Dear Professor Schmendrick:

good news — We are pleased to offer you a term appointment as an Assistant Professor of Self-Actualization, effective August 31, 2000. You will be teaching two classes in Barefoot Aluminum Foil Dancing, one class in Underwater Fire Prevention, and one class in Advanced Quantum Physics. In addition, you will mentor six undergraduate students in the "I'm Okay, You're Okay" department.

summarize main points

background — Whatsamatter U is a select liberal arts college on the cutting edge of the twenty-first century. We pride ourselves on our wide and eclectic course offerings, focus on self-awareness, and high tuition costs. This year we are especially excited about our new major, "Fen Shu and You," which already has three enrollees.

negative elements Your salary will be $20,000, and you will be considered for a tenure-track position at the end of your five-year probationary period. This is the standard procedure at our university.

positive ending Please send your written acceptance as soon as possible and let me know if you need any software or supplies. On August 31, please report to the personnel office, located on the second floor of Cheez Whiz Hall. Please stop by my office at noon, and I'll take you out to lunch at the Dew Drop Inn.

Welcome to Whatsamatter U!

Sincerely,

Seymour Miles, Dean

333

When the News Is Bad

You should live and be well, but into each life a little trouble always comes. And when it does, you'll probably have to be the one to write the letter about it.

Word Watch

A **buffer** is a neutral or positive statement that allows you to soften a negative message. **Buffer statements** can provide good news, state a fact, provide the order of events, refer to enclosures in the letter, thank the reader for something he or she has done, or state a general principle. Naturally, whatever method you select will suit your audience and purpose and directly relate to the contents of the letter.

Bad-news letters deliver the lousy news and help readers accept it. They also build a good image of the writer and his or her organization. To be effective, bad-news letters leave readers feeling that the decision was reasonable and that even if they were in the writer's position, they would make the same decision. Bad-news letters accomplish this by using the following pattern:

1. Open with a *buffer,* a statement that allows you to soften the negative message to come.

2. Give reasons for the action.

3. Present the negative news. Don't over-stress the downside, but be very clear. You don't want your reader to miss your message. If that happens, you'll just have to deliver the bad news all over again.

4. Present an alternative or compromise, if one is possible.

5. End with a positive statement.

The following is a model bad-news letter.

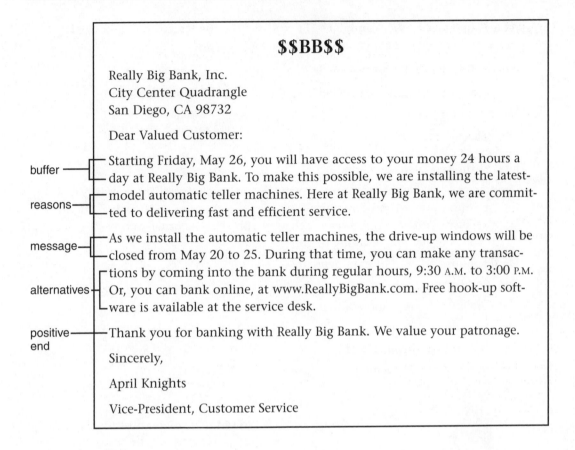

$$BB$$

Really Big Bank, Inc.
City Center Quadrangle
San Diego, CA 98732

Dear Valued Customer:

buffer — Starting Friday, May 26, you will have access to your money 24 hours a day at Really Big Bank. To make this possible, we are installing the latest-

reasons — model automatic teller machines. Here at Really Big Bank, we are committed to delivering fast and efficient service.

message — As we install the automatic teller machines, the drive-up windows will be closed from May 20 to 25. During that time, you can make any transac-

alternatives — tions by coming into the bank during regular hours, 9:30 A.M. to 3:00 P.M. Or, you can bank online, at www.ReallyBigBank.com. Free hook-up software is available at the service desk.

positive end — Thank you for banking with Really Big Bank. We value your patronage.

Sincerely,

April Knights

Vice-President, Customer Service

Onward and Upward: Resumés and Cover Letters

A *resumé* is a persuasive summary of your qualifications for employment. It's designed to entice an employer into calling you for an interview. Of course, when they see your smiling face, they'll give you the job.

A resumé is always accompanied by a *cover letter*. They're a team, like Ben and Jerry or spaghetti and meatballs. Effective resumés and cover letters are neat and accurate, free from any writing errors, and usually no more than one page long.

As you write your resumé, emphasize the things you've done that are most relevant to the position for which you are applying and show how

Word Watch

A **resumé** is a written presentation of your educational background, job experience, and related talents and abilities. A **cover letter** is the letter that accompanies a resumé when you apply for a job.

335

you are superior to other candidates. Be realistic, use the layout to emphasize key points, and relate your experience to the job you want.

Here are the facts you *must* include:

➤ Name, address, phone number, and e-mail address (if you have one)

➤ Education

➤ Relevant experience

Here are the facts you *can* include:

➤ Career objective line to zero in on the position you want. Think of this as a "position wanted" ad for yourself. It's placed right after the heading. For an executive moving up, however, the career objective is usually omitted, since it's obvious where you're trying to go.

➤ Previous and current employment.

➤ Promotions.

➤ Foreign languages and computer language proficiency.

➤ Volunteer positions held.

➤ Education and course work.

➤ Honors and achievements.

➤ References.

Writer's Block

Questions about your age, marital status, race, sex, and health are illegal. If you include any of this information, large companies will delete it from your resumé so they cannot be accused of discriminating. Include height information only if the job has a minimum height requirement.

You're expected to put your accomplishments in the best possible light, but *always* tell the truth. Background checks are a hot topic in personnel circles today. Experts say a decade of litigation has nervous employers turning more and more to professional background checkers, who report that caseloads are growing at 30 percent a year. Investigators find discrepancies or outright lies in about one third of the resumés they check. Yours won't be among them.

An effective cover letter and resumé aren't like sweat pants: One size doesn't fit all. A successful cover letter and resumé are tailored to suit the employer's needs and your qualifications as closely as possible. For that reason, savvy people have several different versions of their resumé, depending on the specific job for which they are applying. There are two basic types of resumés, the *work history resumé* and the *functional (skills) resumé*. Here's each type of resumé in detail:

Work History Resumé

The *work history resumé* summarizes your accomplishments in reverse chronological order (starting with the most recent accomplishments and working backward). It stresses academic degrees, job titles, and dates. Use a work history resumé when …

➤ Your education and experience are logical preparation for the job you want.

➤ You have an impressive education or job history.

Academics, such as scientists and scholars, create a work history resumé that contains every relevant accomplishment, not just the high points. This type of resumé, called a *curriculum vitae (CV)*, can run more than 10 pages.

Word Watch

A **Curriculum Vitae (CV)** is the Goodyear Blimp of resumés: It contains every relevant thing you've ever done. Scholars use CVs instead of resumés to include all their publications, conferences, and professional affiliations. My CV is 22 pages long.

Functional (Skills) Resumé

A *functional resumé* emphasizes your skills. Use this type of resumé when …

➤ Your education and experience are not the usual preparation for the job you want.

➤ You lack an impressive education or job history.

➤ Arranging your recent work history in reverse chronological order would create the wrong impression (perhaps because you have been demoted, fired, or hopped from job to job).

Cover Letters

Like a resumé, the purpose of a cover letter is to get an interview. Although a resumé and a cover letter do overlap in certain areas, there are three crucial differences:

➤ A *cover letter* is adapted to the needs of a particular organization; a *resumé* is usually adapted to a position.

➤ A *cover letter* shows how your qualifications can help the organization meet its needs; a *resumé* summarizes all your relevant qualifications.

➤ A *cover letter* uses complete sentences and paragraphs; a *resumé* uses short phrases.

Writer's Block

If you decide to drop some names in your cover letter, only use the names of people who will speak well of you. Be sure to get prior permission from the person to mention his or her name.

Tailor each cover letter to the specific company or organization. If you can substitute another inside address and salutation and send out the letter without any further changes, it isn't specific enough. Here's what to include:

1. The major requirements for the job.
2. Facts and examples that show how you can do the job.
3. Details that prove your knowledge of the company.
4. Qualities that employers seek: the ability to read and write well, think critically, speak effectively, and get along with others.

Some people find it difficult to write effective cover letters because they don't want to sing their own praises. My advice? Sing away. Good work rarely speaks for itself—it usually needs a microphone to be heard. Studies have shown that successful executives spend about half of their time on their job ... and the other half on self-promotion and office politics.

To increase your chances for success ...

1. **Do your homework.** Take the time to know the company or organization you're contacting.
2. **Know thyself.** Be aware of what you have to offer. Analyze your strengths and weaknesses. Be prepared to show the employer that you can do the job—and do it well.
3. **Be real.** Focus on your readers' needs, not yours. Make your qualifications clear and emphasize how you can use them to help their organization.
4. **Get a name.** Call the company and find out the name and title of the person to whom to address your letter. Addressing a letter to an individual shows initiative and resourcefulness. It also helps make sure your letter lands on the right desk. (It can also help make sure the recipient keeps his or her mouth shut that you're looking for a different job!)
5. **Get it right.** Your letter will end up in the circular file if it contains writing errors or mistakes about the job or company. Have a trusted friend review your resumé. Be sure to pick someone who is attentive to details, can effectively critique your writing, and will give an honest and objective opinion. Seriously consider the advice. Get a third and fourth opinion if you can.

6. **Be classy and professional.** Make your resumé look as good as you are, so laser-print it on plain, white paper. Typing and dot matrix printing can look cheesy.

I can't overestimate the impact a professional, individually tailored cover letter can create on prospective employers. It shows that you're a member of the inner circle: an intelligent, competent individual. Writing a brilliant cover letter can help you convince employers that you're someone worth hiring.

The Least You Need to Know

➤ All business letters are brief, complete, clear, and polite.

➤ Business letters always contain the date, inside address (recipient's address), salutation, body, close, and signature. They may contain initials, enclosures, and cc: for copies.

➤ Good-news letters start with the good news, present the main points and details, present any negative elements, and end on a positive note.

➤ Bad-news letters open with a buffer, give reasons for the action, present the bad news, offer an alternative, and end with a positive statement.

➤ A resumé is a persuasive summary of your educational background, job experience, and related talents and abilities. A cover letter is the letter that accompanies a resumé when you apply for a job.

➤ A work history resumé summarizes your accomplishments in reverse chronological order, stressing academic degrees, job titles, and dates. A functional (skills) resumé emphasizes your skills.

Chapter 25

You've Got Mail!

In This Chapter

➤ Jump aboard the information superhighway!

➤ E-mail like a pro

➤ Walk this way in cyberspace

➤ E-mail and privacy

➤ Mind your manners, with a little help from netiquette

Reason #173 to fear technology:

```
o  o  o  o  o  o  <o  <o>
^|\  ^|^  v|^  v|v  |/v |X|  \|  |
/\  >\ /<  >\ /<  >\ /<  >\
o>  o  o  o  o  o  o
\  x  </  <|>  </>  <\>  <)>  |\
/<  >\ /<  >\ /<  >\  >>  L
```

Mr. E-Mail does the Funky Chicken.

You're not afraid of technology—especially not of Mr. E-Mail. Stick with me, baby, and soon you and Mr. E-Mail will be best buddies.

E-mail *can* be a little scary because it's relatively new. But e-mail is actually a lot easier to use than you think. As with other forms of everyday writing, once you've learned the ropes, you'll find that e-mail is easy, effective, and enjoyable.

Writing.com

Did you know that …

➤ About one third of all Americans send messages over the Internet. (*1999 World Almanac*)

➤ E-mail is currently the most popular and widely used resource on the Internet. (*1999 World Almanac*)

➤ Americans now send 2.2 billion e-mail messages a day, compared with 292 million pieces of first-class mail. (*U.S. News and World Report*)

➤ Traffic on the Internet doubles every 100 days. (UUNET, Internet backbone)

➤ Around the world, about 100 million people use the Internet. (*1999 World Almanac*)

➤ The number of e-mail participants increases by 15 percent a month.

➤ It is estimated that by the year 2005, about one billion people will be connected to the Internet. That's a lot of e-mail! (*1999 World Almanac*)

Word Watch

E-mail, or **electronic mail,** lets you exchange messages with others via the Internet.

Radio existed nearly 40 years before 50 million people tuned in. It took television 13 years to reach 50 million viewers. It took 16 years before 50 million people used personal computers. *But it took only four years for 50 million people to use the Internet.*

How does this affect you, Gentle Reader? It means that e-mail is becoming a critical means of written communication. You need to learn how to write e-mail, because more and more people and businesses are using it. Here's how to become an e-mail pro.

Author! Author!

Want more fascinating facts about the Internet to dazzle your friends and family? *The Emerging Digital Economy*, a study released by the U.S. Department of Commerce, is packed with information. The entire text is available at www.ecommerce.gov. As with all government documents, it's a freebie (your tax dollars at work).

Welcome to the Future

The *Internet* is a vast computer network of computer networks. It's composed of people, hardware, and software. With the proper equipment, you can sit at your computer and communicate with someone at any place in the world as long as that person also has the proper equipment. Let's focus first on *equipment*.

Word Watch

A **modem** is a communication device that enables a computer to transmit information over a standard telephone line.

Basic Internet access is possible with any computer that has a modem connected to a telephone line. However, it's recommended that unless you want to spend days cooling your heels as you get online, you have the following basics:

➤ At least 8 megabytes of RAM

➤ A 250-megabyte hard drive

➤ A 14.4 *modem* (28.8 or faster is better, because the speed of your modem is critical to your ability to get on the Internet)

An *Internet Service Provider* (*ISP*) is a company that provides access to the Internet. The best-known ISPs are the commercial online services such as America Online, CompuServe, Prodigy, and MSN. However, many national companies such as AT&T and MCI, as well as regional and local companies, provide Internet access. ISPs usually charge a monthly subscription rate and offer unlimited access to e-mail.

Check with your public library, too, because many offer free Internet access from your own home, through their own ISPs. Professional organizations such as IEEE (an engineering group) also provide Internet access for little or no fee.

What's Your Address?

Internet mail uses a hierarchical system of names to make sense of the millions of computers served. The name of each computer (or "domain") contains at least two words or abbreviations and at most five, separated by periods, with the top of the hierarchy at the right. Here's the Internet address of the president:

president@whitehouse.gov

Here's what it means:

➤ "**president**" is the recipient's personal mailbox.

➤ "**whitehouse**" is the organization, company, and so on.

➤ "**.gov**" shows the type of organization. For example, .gov is government, .com is commercial, .edu is education, .int is an international organization, .mil is the military, and .org is a nonprofit organization (see Chapter 19, "Cast a Critical Eye," for a list of suffixes).

Writer's Block

Avoid cute or silly e-mail addresses. Not only are they unprofessional, but they also invite so-called cyberstalkers to target you. There are creeps in cyberspace, too.

To send or receive e-mail, you need an address of your own and your recipient's address. You establish your e-mail address when you sign on with an Internet Service Provider. You can get your recipient's e-mail address by asking the person for it or by looking in an e-mail phone book. There are many different ones available. *E-Mail Addresses of the Rich and Famous* (Addison-Wesley, 1997), for example, lists media darlings, the world's movers and shakers, and people we wouldn't throw out of bed for eating crackers.

The Password Is Swordfish

You'll need a password to access your e-mail account. Think of something clever and obscure, but also easy for you to remember. Your password should NEVER be the same as your e-mail address. Neither should it be anything easy to research, such as your maiden name. *Hackers* are wise to these gambits.

Word Watch

Hackers are people who use their computer knowledge for illicit purposes, such as gaining access to computer systems without permission and tampering with programs and data.

Super Model

For those of you who have yet to cruise the Information Superhighway, here's a model e-mail message:

subject line	**Subj:**	**Record Label Employment Opportunity**
date	Date:	8/3/99 6:08:51 PM Eastern Daylight Time
sender	From:	record-resumes@fastweb.com
recipient	To:	CFChan@aol.com

FastWeb is pleased to bring the following employment opportunity to your attention on behalf of one of our marketing partners.

Position: Coordinator, New Media

A Major Record Label in Los Angeles seeks a hard-working and energetic person for full-time work in the New Media department. Qualified applicants will be proficient with HTML, PhotoShop, and e-mail as everyday working tools. Responsibilities will include updating existing Web sites, creating new ones, overseeing servers, working with ongoing PR and marketing efforts, and developing new promotions. Persons should have working knowledge of Word, Excel, Access, Eudora, UNIX, CGI, Dreamweaver, Quark, PhotoShop, Windows Media, and RealAudio/Video.

E-mail resumes to record-resumes@fastweb.com. The deadline for application is August 13, 1999.

(label on left: message)

Now it's time to write some e-mail.

Bits and Bytes

Since writers using e-mail feel as if they're speaking, they tend to be less concerned with spelling, grammar, usage, and punctuation. However, readers judge e-mail as they would any written document. Careless errors reflect badly on the writer. Further, e-mail can be sent to others online or printed and passed around the office, house, or community. This magnifies any errors in the document.

In addition to style, the informal nature of e-mail leads some people to write things that are better left undocumented. This can cause embarrassment—and worse.

To prevent such errors, follow these guidelines:

Boot Up

First of all, don't be seduced by the seeming informality of the medium: Write all e-mail as you would any important written communication. Follow the steps in the writing process, drafting offline so you can reread your message at least once before you send it.

345

This process can help you prevent misunderstandings, misprints, and misery. So before you start writing any e-mail, define your purpose, audience, and style by asking yourself these questions:

➤ Why am I writing this e-mail? What do I expect from my reader?

➤ Who will read the e-mail?

➤ What words and attitude will help me accomplish my purpose?

Follow these steps as you write the e-mail:

1. **Brainstorm ideas.** Write offline; gather your ideas, just as you do with any document you write.

2. **Underline or circle the key points.** Decide which elements to include—and which ones to ax.

3. **Organize the points into categories and put a heading on each.** Create an outline to order your ideas in a logical way. Remember: Your aim is to make your e-mail clear and easy to read.

4. **Draft the e-mail.** Still working offline, write one or more rough drafts. Resist the temptation to toss off a quick note. Once you push that "send" button, you've lost the chance to revise.

   As with all types of writing, your audience's expectations determine your tone and diction. For example, when using e-mail or real-time communication ("instant messages"), you may be tempted to write informally, overlooking some of the accepted conventions of grammar, usage, spelling, and punctuation. Resist the temptation. If I had a dime for every e-mail that contained a crucial typo, I'd be sitting on a tropical isle right now, enjoying one of those drinks that comes with a little umbrella.

5. **Write a subject line.** The *subject line* is a brief description of the message. An effective subject line grabs your reader's attention and summarizes the content of the e-mail. When you're in a hurry, it's tempting to type something quick like "re" in the box. Instead, take the time to provide a brief description of the contents of your message or the main point you wish to convey.

   As an added courtesy, if your message doesn't require a reply, type FYI (For Your Information) at the beginning of the subject line.

Write Angles

If you respond to an e-mail message, delete the first message's header (all the routing information) so your correspondent doesn't have to scroll through it.

And while we're here, if necessary, change the subject line when you reply. Any change in topic requires a change in the subject line. This helps your reader identify your purpose and topic at a glance.

6. **Use order of importance.** Place the most important facts first. These might include results or recommendations, for example. Busy readers will appreciate your consideration—and you'll get better results.

7. **Be brief.** Write concise messages and make your point quickly. In general, make your sentences and paragraphs shorter than you would in a letter, memo, or other offline communication.

    In addition, place blank lines between paragraphs rather than indenting to make your e-mail easier to read.

8. **Make your purpose clear.** Be very clear why you're sending the e-mail. Are you just saying hello to an old friend? Do you want the reader to make a decision? Do you expect a telephone call? Don't make the reader hunt for the message.

9. **Edit and proofread.** As with any written communication, e-mail can become a legal document. Therefore, before you send your message, review it carefully to make sure it conveys your precise meaning and is free of errors in grammar, spelling, punctuation, and usage.

10. **Always sign your e-mail.** Never assume that your recipient knows your identity from your screen name.

Word Watch

Snail mail is a scornful term for traditional letters, a slam at their lack of speed.

Special Delivery

While the writing process for e-mail is the same as that for *snail mail* there *are* some special conventions for e-mail not used in other forms of written communication.

First of all, most e-mail is sent in ASCII unformatted text. As a result, you can't use italics or boldface to show emphasis. To show that a text should be italicized or boldfaced, surround the word(s) with underscore marks or asterisks. For example:

Write Angles

Double-check the address before you click that "send" button. To prevent misdirected e-mail, enter frequently used addresses in your address book. Or, copy and paste an address from a previous message into your address book.

➤ Men are from Earth. Women are from Earth. __Deal with it.__

➤ Shakespeare invented the words *assassination* and *bump.*

Second, before you send any attached file, ask your correspondents if they can accept it. If not, you can copy the attachment and paste it into your e-mail, provided that it isn't too long.

Private Eyes

When you send e-mail, remember that its content is harder to keep private than traditional mail. You can make an online communication secure by encryption (coding), but once your recipients decode the document, they might forward it to anyone else on the Internet. This can happen accidentally as well as intentionally.

As a result, consider every e-mail message—even private ones—as potentially public documents that can be accessed by anyone. Therefore, never e-mail any message that you wouldn't want everyone to read. Consider this a variation of your mother's sage advice, "If you can't say anything nice, don't say anything at all."

Word Watch

Netiquette is the system of appropriate behavior that governs the Internet.

Word Watch

Flaming is sending abusive or personally insulting e-mail. **Spam** is unsolicited e-mail sent to many recipients simultaneously.

Now, let's explore the "culture" of cyberspace and the system of manners that governs it.

Johnny B Good: "Netiquette"

E-mail has its own system of manners that has come to be called "netiquette"—*network etiquette.* It's the code of appropriate online conduct that *netizens* (Internet citizens) observe in virtual communities. Follow these simple guidelines to make it easier for you to navigate your way through cyberspace.

1. **Don't flame.** A *flame* is a personal attack on someone. Flaming involves capital letters as well as invective. Using all capital letters, LIKE THIS, is considered the Web equivalent of shouting. It's rude, so avoid it.

2. **Don't spam.** Spam is unsolicited e-mail, the junk mail of the Internet. *Spamming* is sending the same message to hundreds or thousands of e-mail addresses in the hope of hitting a few interested people. Spam is even worse than junk snail mail, because you can throw away junk mail unread, but you often have to read spam to find out that it's junk. Spam clutters your mailbox, wastes time, and is annoying.

3. **Respect others' time.** Remember that your readers value their time. When you send e-mail, you're taking up other people's time. It's your responsibility to ensure that the time they spend reading your mail isn't wasted.

   Since it's easy to copy practically anyone on your e-mail, people often send unnecessary e-mail. Before you copy people on your messages, ask yourself whether they really need to know. If the answer is no, don't waste their time. If the answer is maybe, think twice before you hit the "send" key.

Write Angles

If you disagree with someone publicly online, be tactful. If you're really annoyed, send a private correspondence through a traditional letter.

4. **Watch e-breviations.** In a quest to make e-mail even quicker, a whole crop of e-breviations—some already common IRL (in real life)—have sprung up. How many of these have you seen?

E-Mail Abbreviation	Meaning
afaik	as far as I know
afk	away from keyboard
atm	at the moment
b	be
b4	before
bbiaf	be back in a few (minutes)
bcnu	be seeing you
brb	be right back
btw	by the way
c	see
cul	see you later
f2f	face to face
focl	falling off the chair laughing
fwd	forwarded
fwiw	for what it's worth
gg	got to go

E-Mail Abbreviation	Meaning
hhoj	Ha! Ha! Only joking!
imho	in my humble opinion
imnsho	in my not-so-humble opinion
j/k	just kidding
oic	oh, I see!
r	are
rotfl	rolling on the floor with laughter
ttyl	talk to you later
ttfn	ta-ta for now
u	you
y	why

Never assume that Internet slang, jargon, and abbreviations are understood by everyone. Reserve these expressions for informal e-mail.

5. **Avoid smileys.** Smileys (also known as "emoticons") are cute little symbols that have become common in e-mail communication. Here are some of the most well-known ones. Read them sideways, left-to-right.

:-)	happy face	;-)	winky face
:-(	sad face	:-D	laughing face
:-X	lips are sealed	%-)	bleary-eyed

Smileys are fun when it comes to personal e-mail, but they are inappropriate for professional e-mail.

The Least You Need to Know

➤ E-mail is an easy and convenient means of written communication.

➤ To send or receive e-mail, you need some basic equipment, an address of your own, your recipient's address, and a password.

➤ Follow the writing process when you compose e-mail.

➤ Include a subject line and be brief, clear, and careful.

➤ *Always* assume that any e-mail message is a public document that can be accessed by anyone.

➤ Observe netiquette, the rules of cyberspace. Don't flame or spam. Respect others' time and watch e-breviations and smileys.

Part 6

Picture Perfect

An engineer had an exceptional gift for fixing all things mechanical. After serving his company loyally for over 30 years, he happily retired. Several years later his company contacted him regarding a seemingly impossible problem they were having with one of their multi-million-dollar machines.

The engineer reluctantly took the challenge. He spent a day studying the huge machine. At the end of the day he marked a small x in chalk on a particular component of the machine and said, "This is where your problem is." The part was replaced and the machine worked perfectly again. The company received a bill for $50,000 from the engineer for his service. They demanded an itemized accounting of his charges. The engineer responded briefly:

| One chalk mark | $1 |
| Knowing where to put it | $49,999 |

In these chapters, you'll learn where to put all those "chalk marks" in your writing—the commas, periods, semicolons, and colons. You'll also brush up on your grammar, usage, spelling, and capitalization.

Chapter 26

Grammar 101

In This Chapter

➤ Grammar and usage quiz

➤ Writing correct sentences

➤ Correcting common punctuation errors

➤ Dealing with common grammar errors

➤ Avoiding annoying usage errors

A linguistics professor was lecturing to his class one day. "In English," he said, "A double negative forms a positive. In some languages, however, such as Russian, a double negative is still a negative. However, there is no language wherein a double positive can form a negative."

A voice from the back of the room piped up, "Yeah, right."

Double negatives. Misplaced modifiers. Dangling participles.

What *is* all this stuff? When most people complain that they "can't write," they're referring to problems with grammar and usage. If you fell asleep while Ms. Flysmacker was explaining agreement of subjects and verbs or can't remember if you're suppose to split an infinitive or not, then this chapter is for you. Here's where we review the most common grammar and usage dilemmas. By the end of the chapter, you'll no longer worry about making embarrassing mistakes in writing. Then you can deal with that tooth that's been bothering you for a month ...

To get the most from this chapter, read it all the way through. Then track your errors to see which ones you make most often. Concentrate on learning those specific rules. You'll retain more if you focus on specific writing problems rather than trying to master all the rules of grammar and usage at once.

Woe Is I

Read each of the following grammar and usage guidelines and identify each error (hint: It's mentioned in the rule). Then correct each sentence. Don't panic if you can't identify or correct every error. Just do the best you can. Everything is explained later in the chapter, and I'm not grading you.

1. Any sentence fragments, if you want to be clearly understood.

   Error: _____

   Correction: _____

2. Avoid run-on sentences, they are hard to understand.

   Error: _____

   Correction: _____

3. Save the apostrophe for its' proper use and omit it where its not needed.

   Error: _____

   Correction: _____

4. Avoid commas, that are not, required in a, sentence.

   Error: _____

   Correction: _____

5. Use the semicolon correctly, always use it where it is appropriate; and never where it is not suitable.

   Error: _____

   Correction: _____

6. Never overuse exclamation marks!!!!

   Error: _____

   Correction: _____

7. Verbs has to agree with their subjects.

   Error: _____

   Correction: _____

8. Everyone should be careful to use a singular pronoun in their writing.

   Error: _____

   Correction: _____

9. Write all adverbs correct.

    Error: _____

    Correction: _____

10. Place pronouns as close as possible, especially in long sentences, as of 10 or more words, to their antecedents to avoid confusion.

    Error: _____

    Correction: _____

11. Never use no double negatives.

    Error: _____

    Correction: _____

12. Writing carefully, dangling participles must be avoided.

    Error: _____

    Correction: _____

13. The passive voice should never be used.

    Error: _____

    Correction: _____

14. This is a sentence that some people would not put up with.

    Error: _____

    Correction: _____

15. Remember to never split an infinitive (even if you want to boldly go where no man has gone before).

    Error: _____

    Correction: _____

16. You're capable to using the correct idiom.

    Error: _____

    Correction: _____

17. If you reread your work, you will find upon serious reconsideration that a great deal of repetition can be avoided by careful proofreading, attentive reevaluating, and scrupulous editing.

    Error: _____

    Correction: _____

18. If you reach a crosswalk on the ocean of life, avoid mixed metaphors.

    Error: _____

    Correction: _____

You're reviewing *Standard Written English,* the level of usage based on conventional punctuation, standard grammar and usage, and the vocabulary used by educated professionals.

Write Angles

If you want to review grammar and usage in greater depth, consider taking an English class given through a local community college. Increasingly, such courses are offered "offsite" on public transportation routes, making it easier for busy commuters to attend class. Some colleges also offer grammar classes online.

Sentence Errors

As you learned in Chapter 6, "Sentence Sense," to be a sentence, a group of words must ...

➤ Have a *subject* (noun or pronoun).

➤ Have a *predicate* (verb or verb phrase).

➤ Express a *complete thought*.

In all but one type of writing, you should always create complete sentences. Complete sentences not only express your ideas clearly but also fulfill your reader's expectations. The exception is dialogue: There, fragments are acceptable because they express the way people really speak. Fragments can also be used in resumés, personal letters, and dialogue. Fragments have a place in some social notes, advertising, speeches, and strong persuasive pieces, too. It's knowing how to use fragments for emphasis that matters. Now, let's look at the problems with items 1 and 2.

1. Any sentence fragments, if you want to be clearly understood.

   Error: <u>Incomplete sentence.</u>

   Correction: <u>You should not write any sentence fragments if you want to be clearly understood.</u>

   Remember that a word group must have both a subject and a verb to be considered a sentence. In this example, both the subject—*you*—and the verb—*write*—were missing.

2. Avoid run-on sentences, they are hard to understand.

   Error: <u>Run-on sentence.</u>

   Correction: <u>Avoid run-on sentences; they are hard to understand. Or: Avoid run-on sentences because they are hard to understand.</u>

   A run-on sentence occurs when two complete sentences ("independent clauses") are incorrectly joined. Two complete sentences can only be joined with a coordinating conjunction or semicolon—a comma doesn't cut the mustard. Review Chapter 6 for a complete discussion of sentences.

Punctuation Errors

As you'll learn in Chapter 28, "Mark Me: Punctuation," punctuation is a crucial aspect of all good writing because it helps determine meaning. Those itty-bity marks provide important visual clues to readers, showing where sentences begin and end, telling readers where to pause, and so on. The following sentences contain errors in punctuation.

Write Angles

Remember that a *command* is often missing the subject. This is okay because the subject is understood. For example: [You] Buckle your seatbelt. Or: [You] Extinguish all cigarettes.

3. Save the apostrophe for its' proper use and omit it where its not needed.

   Error: <u>Apostrophe error.</u>

   Correction: <u>Save the apostrophe for its proper use and omit it where it's not needed.</u>

   The apostrophe (') is used three ways:

   ➤ To show possession (ownership)

   ➤ To show plural forms

   ➤ To show contractions (where a letter or number has been omitted)

   The following chart shows how *it's, its,* and *its'* are used:

Word	Part of Speech	Meaning
it's	contraction	it is
its	possessive pronoun	belonging to it
its'	is not a word	none

   Capitalization is covered in Chapter 29, "A Capital Affair."

4. Avoid commas, that are not, required in a, sentence.

   Error: <u>Comma overkill.</u>

   Correction: <u>Avoid commas that are not required in a sentence.</u>

   You can't be too rich or too thin—but you *can* have too many commas. There are very specific rules governing comma use. Fortunately, they're both easy and logical. See Chapter 29 for the whole enchilada.

5. Use the semicolon correctly, always use it where it is appropriate; and never where it is not suitable.

   Error: <u>Misused semicolon.</u>

   Correction: <u>Use the semicolon correctly; always use it where it is appropriate, and never where it is not suitable.</u>

359

Writer's Block

Avoid the old saw "add commas where you would take a breath." Sometimes it works, but sometimes it doesn't. It's especially dangerous when you've reread and reread your writing and *everything* looks wrong. To avoid confusion and frustration, learn the standard punctuation rules.

Word Watch

Grammar is a branch of linguistics that deals with the form and structure of words.

A semicolon has two main uses:

➤ To separate two complete sentences whose ideas are closely related

➤ To separate clauses that contain a comma

In this example, you're working with the first rule, since "Always use the semicolon correctly" is a complete sentence.

6. Never overuse exclamation marks!!!!

Error: Unnecessary exclamation marks.

Correction: Never overuse exclamation marks.

In general, steer clear of exclamation marks in formal writing. They're best saved for teenagers' love letters, romance novels, and other over-heated prose. Convey emphasis through careful, vivid word choice. To check that I've put my money where my mouth is, skim this book. How many exclamation marks do you see? (I'll bet not more than one or two.)

Grammar Errors

What is *grammar?* According to the famous grammar maven Henry Fowler, it's "a poor despised branch of learning" (*Dictionary of Modern English Usage,* 1926). Okay, so Henry got a bit grumpy from correcting all those student papers. To the rest of us, grammar is a branch of linguistics that deals with the form and structure of words. It's an attempt to make explicit and conscious what the skilled writer and speaker of English does intuitively and unconsciously. Here are some of the most common grammar errors.

7. Verbs has to agree with their subjects.

Error: Agreement of subject and verb.

Correction: Verbs *have* to agree with their subjects.

Agreement means that sentence parts match, singular to singular and plural to plural. Since the subject "verbs" is plural, it takes a plural verb, "agree."

This is confusing because we add -s or -es to make the third person *singular* form of most <u>verbs</u> but add -s or -es to make the *plural* form of most <u>nouns.</u> For example, *she walk<u>s</u>* is singular but *six room<u>s</u>* is plural—yet both end in *s.*

Author! Author!

What is considered "correct" grammar varies from era to era and location to location. For example, people who speak British English follow different rules concerning the agreement of subjects and verbs. They might say, "The family *are* eating dinner early," while American English speakers would say, "The family *is* eating dinner early." We consider collective nouns such as "family" as singular, since they treat an entire group as one unit. Our cousins across the pond obviously don't agree.

8. Everyone should be careful to use a singular pronoun in their writing.

   Error: <u>Pronoun agreement.</u>

   Correction: <u>Everyone should be careful to use a singular pronoun in his or her writing.</u>

   In the previous guideline, you learned that subjects and verbs must *agree* or match by having the same number (singular or plural). Therefore, a singular subject takes a singular verb, a plural subject takes a plural verb, and a singular indefinite pronoun takes a singular verb. Since "everyone" is a singular antecedent, it takes a singular pronoun, "his or her."

   Indefinite pronouns that end in *-one* are always singular. These include:

Singular Indefinite Pronouns

one	everybody	anything
each	anyone	nobody
everything	much	everyone
somebody	nothing	other
someone	something	either
no one	neither	

Some pronouns can be either singular or plural, depending on how they are used in a sentence. For example:

Singular: *Some* of the catch *is* sold to restaurants.

Plural: *Some* of the ports *are* located near my home.

The following chart shows these pronouns:

Pronouns That Can Be Singular or Plural

some	any	all	more	most

To avoid biased language, we now get into constructions like this: "Everyone bring *his or her* lunch." Rather than grappling with the clumsy construction "his or her," make the whole sentence plural: "*People* should bring their own lunch." This helps you sidestep the issue of agreement while you keep everyone happy.

9. Write all adverbs correct.

Error: <u>Incorrect adverb use.</u>

Correction: <u>Write all adverbs correct*ly*.</u>

Adverbs are words that describe verbs, adjectives, or other adverbs. Adverbs answer the questions:

How? When? Where? or *To what extent?* For example: climbed <u>slowly,</u> quit <u>abruptly,</u> stepped <u>carefully,</u> <u>nearly</u> done.

As you can see from these examples, many adverbs are formed by adding *-ly* to an adjective. A common error involves using an adjective (such as "correct") for an adverb (such as "correctly"). This isn't acceptable usage in standard written English.

The matter is complicated because many useful adverbs *don't* end in *-ly*. Here are a few of the most common ones you'll likely use in your writing:

Word Watch

Adverbs are modifiers, words that describe verbs, adjectives, or other adverbs.

Adverbs

afterward	already	hard	never
today	low	rather	tomorrow
then	yesterday	late	often
almost	back	long	soon
when	here	next	still
where	far	too	near

Usage Errors

Usage is the customary way we use language in speech and writing. There are different levels of usage to suit different audiences. Here's the run-down:

Formal Usage	Informal Usage	Nonstandard Usage
educated forums	everyday speech	Don't go there.

For example, someone writing or speaking formal English might say, "They have not done anything." Note the elevated diction and lack of contractions. Informal usage, in contrast, would be "They've done nothing." Nonstandard would be something like "They ain't done nuttin'." Nonstandard usage, which includes slang, weird spelling and punctuation, and inappropriate verbs, is never acceptable in educated speech and writing.

Here are some expressions to avoid:

Unacceptable	Acceptable
irregardless	regardless
being that	since
had ought	ought
this here	this
hisself (etc.)	himself (etc.)
like I told you	as I told you
off of	off
real good	really good
that there	that
kind of	sort of

Word Watch

Usage is the customary way we use language in speech and writing.

Now let's turn to some other usage issues:

10. Place pronouns as close as possible, especially in long sentences, as of 10 or more words, to their antecedents to avoid confusion.

    Error: <u>The pronouns are placed too far from their *antecedents*, the words to which they refer. This makes the sentence difficult to follow and may also result in confusion or misunderstanding.</u>

Correction: <u>Place pronouns as close as possible to their antecedents, especially in long sentences, as of 10 or more words.</u>

The revision corrects the error, but it's still not an effective sentence because it's hard to follow. To convey your meaning clearly and forcefully, break the long sentence into smaller sentences, as in the following example:

Place pronouns as close as possible to their antecedents. This is especially important in long sentences that have 10 or more words.

11. Never use no double negatives.

    Error: <u>Double negative.</u>

    Correction: <u>Don't use any double negatives.</u>

    A *double negative* is a sentence that contains two negative words. The two words effectively cancel each other out. Along the way, they confuse the reader. To avoid this error, review the following negative words—and then remember you get one per sentence:

    Negative Words

no	never
none	nothing
scarcely	barely
not or n't (couldn't, didn't …)	hardly

12. Writing carefully, dangling participles must be avoided.

    Error: <u>Dangling modifier.</u>

    Correction: <u>When you write carefully, you must avoid dangling participles.</u>

    A *modifier* is a word or phrase that describes a subject, verb, or object. (To "modify" is to describe.) The modifier is said to "dangle" when the word it modifies has been left out of the sentence. Dangling modifiers confuse your readers and obscure your meaning because the sentence doesn't make sense.

Correct a dangling modifier by adding the word or words that have been left out of the sentence. Here, I added the subject: "When *you* write carefully …" and changed "writing" to "write" so the sentence makes sense.

And while we're dangling, let's look at another mangled construction, *dangling participles*. A *participle* is a verb ending in *-ing*. It's *dangling* when the subject of the *-ing* verb and the subject of the sentence don't agree. For example:

Word Watch

Modifiers are words or phrases that describe a subject, verb, or object. Adjectives and adverbs are modifiers.

Incorrect: Sailing up the harbor, the Statue of Liberty was seen.

The subject is the Statue of Liberty, but it better not be sailing.

Correct: While we were sailing up the harbor, we saw the Statue of Liberty.

or

We saw the Statue of Liberty as we sailed up the harbor.

13. The passive voice should never be used.

    Error: <u>Passive voice.</u>

    Correction: <u>You should never use the passive voice.</u>

Writer's Block

Warning: Not all words that end in *-ing* are participles. For example: "Finishing the cake by Sunday is your assignment, Mr. Phelps." The word "finishing" functions as a noun, not a verb. Nouns ending in *-ing* are called *gerunds*.

As you learned in Chapter 6, English has two voices: *active* and *passive*. A verb is *active* when the subject performs the action. A verb is *passive* when its action is performed upon the subject. The active voice is usually preferable over the passive voice because it's less wordy and clearer.

However, the passive voice has its uses, and they're pretty darned useful. Use the passive voice to avoid placing blame and when you don't know the subject's identity.

14. This is a sentence that some people would not put up with.

    Error: <u>Ending with a preposition.</u>

    Correction: <u>None.</u>

Yes, this is one of those trick questions. (Hey, a girl's gotta have *some* fun.) Traditionalists argue that writers should never end a sentence with a preposition; modernists argue that traditionalists should get a life already.

Here's the Rozakis Rule: If a sentence is more logical and elegant with a final preposition, let it stand. Remember that a sentence becomes unnecessarily obscure when it's cluttered with "from whoms" and "with whiches."

Author! Author!

When reprimanded by his assistant for ending a sentence with a preposition, Winston Churchill said, "This is the sort of thing up with which I will not put." Obviously, Churchill's original end-with-a-preposition version—"This is the sort of thing which I will not put up with"—was a better sentence because it was less stilted.

15. Remember to never split an infinitive (even if you want to boldly go where no man has gone before).

    Error: <u>Split infinitive.</u>

    Correction: <u>Remember never to split an infinitive (even if you want to go boldly where no man has gone before). Or None.</u>

    An *infinitive* is the base form of the verb, before it has been *conjugated,* changed to show time. You can recognize infinitives by their buddies "to," which can be stated or implied. This is another one of those hotly contested usage rules. Traditionalists would rather split hairs than infinitives. Modernists, in contrast, go for sound as well as sense. Traditionalists have their way in the first instance—"to split"—but the second sentence sounds downright silly—"to go boldly."

    My rule: Always consider your audience and purpose when deciding whether to split an infinitive. If you know you're writing for a grammar stickler, mind your p's, q's, and split infinitives.

16. You're capable to using the correct idiom.

    Error*:* <u>Incorrect idiom.</u>

    Correction: <u>You're capable *of* using the correct idiom.</u>

    Idioms are expressions that mean something beyond the sum of their parts. An idiom such as "raining cats and dogs," for example, means it's raining very hard, not that felines and canines are dropping from the sky. Here are some common idioms and their meanings:

Idiom	Meaning
buy the farm	die
be under the weather	be sick
live high on the hog	live beyond your means
the old college try	try hard
fresh as a daisy	fresh and new
be in the driver's seat	be in control

If you decide to use idioms in your writing, be sure to use the correct phrase. For instance, it's idiomatic to say, "Never <u>pick on</u> people smaller than you are." It's not idiomatic to say, "Never <u>pick at</u> people smaller than you are."

17. If you reread your work, you will find upon serious reconsideration that a great deal of repetition can be avoided by careful proof-reading, attentive reevaluating, and scrupulous editing.

    Error: <u>Redundancy.</u>

    Correction: <u>If you reread your work, you will find that a great deal of repetition can be avoided by careful editing.</u>

    Here's your motto: short and sweet. If your writing is concise, people will be more likely to make it to the end.

18. If you reach a crosswalk on the ocean of life, avoid mixed metaphors.

    Error: <u>A mixed metaphor.</u>

    Correction: <u>If you reach a crosswalk on the road of life, avoid mixed metaphors.</u>

Metaphors are figures of speech that compare two unlike things to explain the less-familiar object. When used correctly, metaphors make your writing more descriptive and precise. For a metaphor to convey meaning, however, it must compare images or objects that go together. Here, we're matching "crosswalk" and "road."

Writer's Block

In general, avoid idioms when you're writing for a multicultural audience, since idioms are culturally linked.

Word Watch

Redundancy is using unnecessary words.

The Least You Need to Know

➤ Write complete sentences. (A sentence is a group of words with a subject and predicate that expresses a complete thought.)

➤ Punctuation is important because it helps determine meaning. The most common errors occur with apostrophes, commas, semicolons, and exclamation marks.

➤ Correct errors in agreement, pronouns, and adverbs.

➤ Place pronouns close to their antecedents, don't use double negatives, and avoid dangling participles.

➤ Consider your audience when you use the passive voice, end a sentence with a preposition, and split an infinitive.

➤ Use the correct idioms, delete unnecessary words, and correct mixed metaphors.

Chapter 27

Spelling Ace

In This Chapter

➤ Follow the (spelling) rules!

➤ Contractions, possessives, and plurals

➤ See and say

➤ Out of sight—but not out of mind!

➤ Naughty words

A young Puritan was having great difficulty remembering the rules of conduct in his community. No matter how hard he tried, he constantly committed social blunders. Desperate, he asked an elder to teach him proper manners. The older man's patience grew thin as he repeatedly chastised the younger man's awkward ways.

One Sunday, the younger man again entered the church ahead of the older man. The elder man collared him and allowed a lady to enter ahead of both of them. The older man then yelled, "Canst thou remember nothing? How much easier can it become?" Pointing at the woman he said, "It is I before Thee, except after She!"

Remember that old spelling jingle "i before e, except after c"? It still holds, too. You can remember how to spell many common and confusing words by learning a few simple rules. Unfortunately, a whole bunch of words refuse to fall into line, but not to worry: I've got some easy ways for you to learn how to spell those rogue words, too.

Even though there's little evidence to suggest that spelling aptitude has anything to do with intelligence, people are nonetheless judged on their ability to spell. Even one little misspelled word can destroy the effect of an entire document—especially if it's a resumé, cover letter, or personal note. For this reason, it's well worth the time to learn to spell correctly. That's what this chapter is all about.

Spelling Bee

How good a speller are you? Take the following spelling test to see which words present the most problems for you. In each of the following groups of words, only one word is misspelled. Find the misspelled word, spell it correctly, and write your answer in the space provided. Then you can make the most of your study time by focusing your attention on the words you have the most difficulty spelling.

_____	1.	argueing knives	baggy shepherd
_____	2.	achieve piece	cheif siege
_____	3.	succeed ceiling	intercede deciet
_____	4.	monotonous eigth	superintendent surprise
_____	5.	Arctic Febrary	diamond schedule
_____	6.	fourty symptom	library pronunciation
_____	7.	supoena scissors	ascertain diaphragm
_____	8.	shepherd autumn	amond condemn
_____	9.	pneumonia bankrupcy	ptomaine mortgage
_____	10.	Caribbean meteor	hideous Mediterranen
_____	11.	biscut buoy	brooch Connecticut
_____	12.	suite forfiet	lieutenant hiccough

Breaking compound words into their parts can help you spell them correctly. For example, breaking *bookkeeper* into its two words—*book* and *keeper*—can help you remember to keep that double *k* in the middle.

Answers

1. arguing

2. chief

3. deceit

4. eighth

5. February

6. forty

7. subpoena

8. almond

9. bankruptcy

10. Mediterranean

11. biscuit

12. forfeit

Score Yourself

If you missed #1 to #3, concentrate on words that conform to spelling rules.

If you missed #4 to #6, concentrate on words that are misspelled because they're often mispronounced.

If you missed #7 to #9, concentrate on words that are difficult to spell because they contain a silent letter.

If you missed #10 to #12, concentrate on words that require special study because they don't follow *any* rules. These are the bad boys in the back of the room.

Author! Author!

The Roman alphabet has always been inadequate for the phonetic representation of the English language. For example, we have only five vowels, *a, e, i, o,* and *u,* and it's not enough for all the vowel sounds we have. For example, the vowel *a* can have as many as six different sounds, as in *cat, came, calm, any, call,* and *was.*

Spelling Rules!

By and large, spelling rules work. Okay, so they're not perfect, but what is? Here are some of my favorites:

➤ *i* before *e* except after *c*.

➤ Don't drop or add letters when you add a prefix.

➤ Keep all the letters when you add a suffix, unless the word ends in a *y* or a silent *e*.

➤ Don't drop or add letters in compound words.

Learning these rules can make it easier for you to spell the words you encounter in your everyday writing tasks, such as letters, notes, and reports.

i *Before* e *Except After* c ...

This rule has been around forever—because it works.

i before *e* except after *c*

or as sounded as *a* as in *neighbor* and *weigh*

Here are some commonly used words that follow the rule:

i Before e	Except After c	Sounded as a
piece	receive	eight
chief	deceive	vein
fierce	perceive	weight
siege	receive	freight
relief	conceive	reign
achieve	conceit	neighbor
believe	ceiling	weigh
grief	deceit	sleigh
piece	receipt	beige
shriek		heir
yield		surveillance
relieve		veil

In most cases, when the *c* sounds like *sh,* the order of the letters is *ie,* not *ei.* Words that fit this rule include *ancient, efficient, coefficient, conscientious,* and *prescience.*

Nothing's foolproof, so here are the common exceptions:

height	leisure	neither	seize
codeine	counterfeit	either	Fahrenheit
fiery	financier	foreign	glacier

What can we conclude from this section, Gentle Reader? Here's the inside skinny: Learning a few simple spelling rules can help you master an astonishingly large number of words. And when you can spell 'em, you'll be much more likely to use 'em.

Word Watch

A **prefix** is a word part added at the beginning of a word to change its meaning; a **suffix** does the same at the end of a word.

The Prefix Rule

Remember that a *prefix* is a group of letters put at the beginning of a word to change its meaning. The rule here is simple: Don't add or omit a letter when you attach a prefix. Keep all the letters. Every one of them. Here are some examples:

Prefix	+	Root Word	=	New Word
dis	+	satisfied	=	dissatisfied
mis	+	spell	=	misspell
re	+	election	=	reelection
inter	+	related	=	interrelated

The Suffix Rules

Remember that a *suffix* is a group of letters put at the end of a word to change its meaning. The rules for attaching suffixes aren't quite as simple as the rule for attaching prefixes, however. Read on to learn how to deal with these handy word endings.

1. Keep all the letters when you add a suffix, unless the word ends in a *y* or a silent *e*. Here are some examples of the first part of the rule. (The "*y* or a silent *e*" part follows.)

Word	+	Suffix	=	New Word
drunken	+	ness	=	drunkenness
ski	+	ing	=	skiing
foresee	+	able	=	foreseeable

2. If the letter before the final *y* is a consonant, change the *y* to *i* and add the suffix. For example:

Word	+	Suffix	=	New Word
hurry	+	ed	=	hurried
greedy	+	ly	=	greedily
pony	+	es	=	ponies

3. If the letter before the final *y* is a vowel, don't change the *y* before adding the suffix. (Exceptions: *laid, paid, said, daily.*)

Word	+	Suffix	=	New Word
destroy	+	ed	=	destroyed
play	+	ed	=	played

How about some double trouble? Why is the *r* in *defer* doubled when *-ed* is added, but the *r* is *differ* is not (*differed*)? Why is the *n* in *plan* doubled (*planning*) when *-ing* is added, but the *n* in *burn* isn't (*burning*)? Here are some rules about doubling final consonants when a suffix is added.

4. In a one-syllable word, double the final consonant before a suffix beginning with a vowel.

Word	+	Suffix	=	New Word
plan	+	er	=	planner
big	+	est	=	biggest
stop	+	ed	=	stopped

5. Don't double the final consonant if it comes after two vowels or another consonant. For example: *failed, stooped, warmer, lasting.*

6. Don't double the final consonant if the accent shifts back to the first syllable, as in *reference, preference,* and *conference.*

7. In a word of two or more syllables, double the final consonant when it's in an accented syllable before a suffix beginning with a vowel, as in *deferred* and *resubmitting*.

8. *-ify* or *-efy?*

   In most cases, the suffix will be spelled *-ify* rather than *-efy*. Exceptions include *rarefy, liquefy,* and *putrefy.*

9. *-ise* or *-ize?*

   After the letter v, the suffix is always *-ise*, never *-ize*. Here are some examples: *supervise, revise, advise.*

Word Watch

Just when you thought it was safe ... someone creates a new word by joining two or more familiar words. And you have to learn how to spell it. The process of creating new words this way is called **agglutination.** *Web* site, *supertwin,* and *egosurfing* are all examples.

Joined at the Hip: Compound Words

Compound words fall into three categories: *open compounds, closed compounds, hyphenated compounds.* Here are the definitions and examples:

1. **Open compounds** are written as two words: cedar shingles, night shift.

2. **Closed compounds** are written as one word: handbook, northeast.

3. **Hyphenated compounds** have a hyphen: comparison-contrast, nurse-practitioner.

The rule: Don't drop or add letters in compound words.

Author! Author!

The only 15-letter word that can be spelled without repeating a letter is *uncopyrightable.* *Facetious* and *abstemious* contain all the vowels in the correct order, as does *arsenious,* meaning "containing arsenic."

Good Things Come in Small Packages: Contractions

Contractions, such as *can't, don't,* and *didn't,* add an informal tone to your writing, which helps you achieve your purpose and meet your audience's needs. Contractions are especially useful when you're writing dialogue, so your characters don't all sound like fake British nobles.

To combine two words, insert an apostrophe in the space where the letter or letters have been omitted. For example:

Word #1	+	Word #2	=	Contraction
does	+	not	=	doesn't
can	+	not	=	can't
could	+	not	=	couldn't
has	+	not	=	hasn't
he	+	is	=	he's
he	+	will	=	he'll
I	+	am	=	I'm
I	+	have	=	I've
it	+	is	=	it's
she	+	would	=	she'd
she	+	will	=	she'll
there	+	is	=	there's
they	+	are	=	they're
was	+	not	=	wasn't
we	+	will	=	we'll
were	+	not	=	weren't
who	+	is	=	who's
would	+	not	=	wouldn't
you	+	are	=	you're
you	+	have	=	you've

Note: *Will* + *not* = *won't* (not *willn't*) is an exception to the contraction rule.

9/10th of the Law: Possessives

Which sentence is better?

1. The eye of an ostrich is bigger than its brain.
2. An ostrich's eye is bigger than its brain.

It's door number two, you lucky contestant, because that sentence is less wordy. Notice that the second sentence uses an *apostrophe* (') to show possession (ownership). In this case, the possession involves the ownership of an eye, but possession can involve the ownership of any item, idea, or personality traits.

Follow these rules to create possessive nouns.

1. With singular nouns, add an apostrophe and an *s*.

   Examples: Bozo, Bozo's nose

2. With plural nouns ending is *s*, add an apostrophe after the *s*.

   Examples: swimmers, swimmers' ears

3. With plural nouns not ending in *s*, add an apostrophe and an *s*.

   Examples: children, children's tempers

4. To form the possessive of a compound noun, put an apostrophe and an *s* after the last word.

   Examples: brother-in-law's snazzy new car

5. Don't confuse contractions with possessive pronouns. Here's the run-down:

Contraction	Possessive Pronoun
it's (it is)	its
you're (you are)	your
they're (they are)	their
who's (who is)	whose

Word Watch

An **apostrophe** is used to show possession or ownership in nouns.

Write Angles

Remember that possessive pronouns do not require an apostrophe. The possessive pronouns are *yours, hers, its, ours, theirs,* and *whose.*

Since possessives are important in writing, go back over this section several times, Gentle Reader. Make sure you've got these rules down cold. Why? A misused apostrophe is a real sore thumb in an otherwise fine passage.

Crowd Control: Plurals

Plural nouns name more than one person, place, or thing. There are regular plurals and irregular ones. The regular plurals rarely result in spelling errors, but irregular plurals are nasty creatures indeed. Follow these guidelines to form the plural of nouns:

1. Most regular plurals are formed by adding *s* to the end of the word.

   Examples: clown, clowns

   Add *es* if the noun ends in *s, sh, ch,* or *x.*

   Examples: circus, circuses, dish, dishes, church, churches, box, boxes

   If the noun ends in *o* preceded by a *consonant*, the noun can take *es, s,* or either *s* or *es.*

   Examples: echo, echoes, piano, pianos

2. Irregular nouns don't follow this rule (or any rule, for that matter). Some change their spelling when they become plural.

   Examples:

Singular	Plural
ox	oxen
crisis	crises
tooth	teeth
alumnus	alumni (female)
alumna	alumnae (male)
criterion	criteria
index	index, indices
memorandum	memorandums, memoranda
parenthesis	parentheses
phenomenon	phenomena

   Others have the same singular and plural form.

   Examples: series, species, Portuguese, deer

Author! Author!

The Marquis of Queensberry made his way to the Albemarle Club, where he left his card, upon which he had written: "To Oscar Wilde posing as a somodmite"—a misspelling which was to become famous. The porter, with wise discretion, put the card in an envelope. As the porter handed the card over to Wilde, he calmly assured the recipient he had not understood what it meant.

How's That Again?: Pronunciation

Then we have words whose spellings get mangled because they're mispronounced. You may drop letters, add unnecessary letters, or simply mispronounce a word and so spell it the way you hear it—the wrong way. Pronouncing a word correctly is an easy way to learn to spell it correctly.

Here are 24 words often misspelled because they're mispronounced:

➤ grievous

➤ disastrous

➤ calisthenics

➤ library

➤ temperature

➤ cemetery

➤ laboratory

➤ accompaniment

➤ incidentally

➤ disassemble

➤ government

➤ accidentally

➤ characteristic

➤ Wednesday

➤ asked

➤ valuable

➤ plaintiff

➤ asterisk

➤ separate

➤ representative

➤ environment

➤ quantity

➤ category

➤ acreage

Silent but Deadly: Silent Letters

There are times when silence is golden ... but not when it comes to spelling words with silent letters. Say the silent letter to yourself to remember to include it, as in *dumb*, *gnaw*, and *empty*.

Many words contain silent letters, such as the *k* and *w* in *know* or the *b* in *dumb*. What do you want first, the good news or the bad news? Here's the bad news: The easiest way to learn these words is to commit them to memory. Want the good news? See the bad news.

Each of the following words contains a silent letter. Since the letter is seen but not heard, you must be extra careful to include it when you spell the word.

1. **Silent b:** The silent *b* is small but deadly. Here are some of the most common words in which the *b* hides:

   - plumber
   - redoubtable
   - thumb
   - doubt
   - crumb

   - dumb
   - debt
   - undoubtedly
   - subpoena
   - subtle

2. **Silent c:** The silent *c* can be even harder to find than the silent *b* because it doesn't tend to stick out as much. Here are some words that contain the silent *c*.

   - scissors
   - fascinate
   - muscle

   - acquire
   - scent
   - acquaint

3. **Silent g:** This one is sneaky. How many of these words pose problems for you?

   - diaphragm
   - design

   - gnarled
   - align

4. **Silent h:** *Rhyme* and *rhythm* are very often misspelled because of their silent *h;* only the bold tackle such silent *h* words as *rheumatism, exhilaration,* and *gingham*. After this lesson, however, you'll sneer at such spelling wimps.

   - ghost
   - ghetto
   - exhaust

   - spaghetti
   - shepherd
   - rhetoric

Author! Author!

The unphonetic spellings in English, such as *reign* and *light,* have inspired many attempts at spelling reform. The last major attempt at spelling reform, around 1900, resulted in at least two real changes: *music* for *musick* and *catalog* for *catalogue.*

5. **Silent p:** Watch for hidden *p*'s all through words, because they don't follow a pattern. Here are some examples:

➤ empty

➤ psychology

➤ pneumonia

➤ psalm

➤ corps (the s is silent)

➤ pseudonym

Spelling Demons

How do you spell any one of the denizens of the deep, such as a flounder, bass, trout, sturgeon, carp, or even the lowly gold? This is a snap, you're thinking. It's "f-i-s-h." Not so fast, friend. Did you know that fish can also be spelled *ghotti?* Here's how.

Take the ...
gh as in *tough;*
o as in *women;*
ti as in *action* ...
and you get "f-i-s-h"
(or *ghotti,* as it's also spelled)

Unfortunately, some words just refuse to be spelled the way they sound or look. These are often called "spelling demons," no doubt reflecting the trouble that generations of spellers have had with them. In these instances, you're working without a net. There are no rules to lead you through this thicket. With unphonetic words, only spelling techniques like memorization, visualization, and study techniques can help you spell the words correctly.

Word Watch

The spelling of a word as it appears within parentheses in a dictionary is called its **phonetic** spelling. In the **phonetic alphabet,** letters and symbols represent the sound of the word as you say it.

The following study procedure can help you learn how to spell difficult words, such as unphonetic ones.

1. Pronounce the word. Use it in a sentence.
2. Visualize the word, syllable by syllable. Say the letters in order.
3. Close your eyes and spell the word. Check your answer.
4. Write the word. Check your answer.
5. Write the word several times.

Here are my favorite 125 most difficult words to spell. Feel free to add your own personal favorites.

125 Toughest Spelling Demons

abbreviate	abhor	abscess
absence	abundant	achievement
acquire	across	address
adjacent	bachelor	badminton
balloon	banal	banana
bigamy	bizarre	bourgeois
Britain	broccoli	bruise
brusque	budget	bureau
burglar	cafeteria	caffeine
calendar	camouflage	campaign
candidate	doctor	draught
dachshund	daughter	deceive
defer	delicious	devastate
diagnose	ecstasy	edible
embarrass	existence	enumerate
envelope	enzyme	euphemism
exacerbate	expel	frivolous
forfeit	furlough	Fahrenheit

feminine	gaseous	gasoline
gauge	gorgeous	gorilla
hiccough	hypocrisy	heir
headache	hygiene	icing
illegible	incident	innuendo
island	janitor	jeopardy
journal	juvenile	khaki
kindergarten	laid	leisure
laboratory	lieutenant	martial
medieval	memento	midget
misspell	naive	narrate
niece	ninety	nuclear
origin	odyssey	pastime
parliament	pigeon	privilege
quay	racism	ravioli
revolt	relieve	repel
reminisce	renaissance	sedate
sergeant	sieve	sponsor
sovereign	suite	surgeon
taxable	through	traitor
turquoise	until	ukulele
vacation	vague	vicious
vacuum	Wednesday	waist
wear	worrisome	

Some languages, such as Spanish and German, are spelled with a high degree of phonetic accuracy. English, on the other hand, is known for markedly unphonetic spellings for about 25 percent of its words.

The Least You Need to Know

➤ Learning a few simple spelling rules can help you spell many different words correctly.

➤ Don't add or drop letters when you spell compound words.

➤ To create a contraction, insert an apostrophe in the space where the letter or letters have been omitted.

➤ Most regular plurals are formed by adding *s* to the end of the word. Irregular plural nouns are tricky to spell.

➤ One of the easiest and most effective ways to become a good speller is to pronounce words correctly. Be on the lookout for words with silent letters, especially b's, c's, g's, h's, p's.

➤ Bad spellers of the world—untie!

Mark Me: Punctuation

The wrong punctuation can be costly. In the 1890s, a Congressional clerk was supposed to write, "All foreign fruit-plants are free from duty" in transcribing a recent bill. Unfortunately, he changed the hyphen to a comma and wrote, "All foreign fruit, plants are free from duty." Before Congress could correct his error with a new law, the government lost over $2 million in taxes. All those duty-free plants add up fast.

Errors in punctuation can also have serious legal repercussions. For example, a district attorney introduced an unpunctuated confession taken down by a police officer that read: "Mangan said he never robbed but twice said it was Crawford." The prosecution contended the confession should have been punctuated this way: "Mangan said he never robbed but twice. Said it was Crawford." The defense claimed the sentence should read: "Mangan said he never robbed; but twice said it was Crawford." The last version introduced reasonable doubt and the accused went free.

Punctuation *is* a crucial aspect of all good writing, because it helps convey meaning. But you already knew that—you just want to know where you put all those little marks. So settle down, put your feet up, and get ready to review periods, commas, semicolons, and the rest of the gang.

End Runs: Period, Question Mark, and Exclamation Mark

The period, question mark, and exclamation mark may appear different, but they have important similarities. These include …

➤ **Position.** They are all placed at the end of a sentence.

➤ **Function.** They all indicate a full stop.

➤ **Purpose.** They all show that a specific thought is complete.

Here's how these three marks of punctuation are used.

Word Watch

Punctuation is the use of standard marks in written language to clarify meaning.

The Period

Here are the rules that govern the use of that cute little tike, the period.

➤ Use a period after a complete sentence (one complete thought).

Example: Age is the outrageous price paid for maturity.

➤ Use a period after a command.

Example: Buckle your seatbelts.

➤ Use a period after most abbreviations. If an abbreviation comes at the end of a sentence, don't add another period.

Examples: Dr.; Ms.; Jr.

➤ Use a period after an initial.

Example: J.F. Kennedy

Writer's Block

Don't use a period after acronyms, such as SCUBA, CNN, and NATO.

➤ Use a period after each Roman numeral, letter, or number in an outline.

Example: I.

    A.

    B.

      1.

      2.

➤ Always place a period inside a quotation mark that ends a sentence.

Example: The sign read, "The IRS—Be audit you can be."

End marks aren't difficult to use—but they *are* important. Every time you write a sentence, select the end mark you need to convey your exact meaning.

The Question Mark

Walk this way when you use question marks at the end of your sentences.

➤ Use a question mark after a question.

Example: If police arrest a mime, do they tell him he has the right to remain silent?

➤ Place the question mark *inside* closing quotation marks if it *is* part of the quotation.

Example: "If a parsley farmer is sued, can they garnish his wages?" she asked.

➤ Place the question mark *outside* the closing quotation marks if it *is not* part of the quotation.

Example: Was it your candidate who said, "No president of the United States was an only child"?

The Exclamation Mark

In speech, exclamations are used freely, especially in moment of high passion as when the sink overflows during a dinner party. In writing, however, it is far more convincing to create emphasis by the force of your words rather than the force of your punctuation.

Author! Author!

"!" goes by a number of names. In America it's usually called an **exclamation mark** or **exclamation point.** The British, however, call it an **exclamation** or a **note of exclamation.** No matter what it's called, the ! has had few friends through history. The famous dictionary maker Dr. Johnson defined it as "a note by which a pathetical sentence is marked thus!" The poet Spenser said, "The lowest form of language is the exclamation, by which an entire idea is vaguely conveyed though a single sound." Tradition says that the mark derives from the Latin *io* (exclamation of joy), written vertically as *I*, which became ! in time.

If by some odd chance you do have to use an exclamation mark, it goes after an exclamatory sentence.

For example: Wear short sleeves! Support your right to bare arms!

Don't combine an exclamation mark with a period, comma, or question mark. None of this stuff—?! or !.

Writer's Block

Never use a comma to separate two complete sentences. Doing so creates a type of run-on called a "comma splice."

Big Man on Campus: The Comma

Punctuation helps readers identify clusters of words between and within sentences. *Between sentences,* the most common mark of punctuation is the period; *within sentences,* the most common mark of punctuation is the comma.

Commas tell us how to read and understand sentences because they tell us where to pause. A correctly placed comma helps move readers from the beginning of a sentence to the end. Here are the guidelines that govern comma use:

In the Beginning

Commas are often necessary in the beginning of sentences. Follow these guidelines:

➤ Use a comma with names and titles.

Examples: Idi Amin, Dictator; Elmer Fatpockets, County Legislator

➤ Use a comma after introductory expressions, any group of words that opens a sentence. Possibilities include introductory prepositional phrases, introductory participal phrases, and introductory subordinate clauses.

Examples: On average, people fear spiders more than they do death.

In the Arctic, the sun sometimes appears to be square.

If you find yourself in a hole, first stop digging.

In the Middle

➤ Use a comma before a coordinating conjunction in a compound sentence.

Example: The early bird gets the worm, but the second mouse gets the cheese.

You can omit the comma if the clauses are short.

Example: I don't have a solution but I admire your problem.

➤ Use a comma after interrupting words and expressions.

Example: Yes, every time Beethoven sat down to write music, he poured ice water over his head.

➤ Use a comma to set off a direct quotation.

Examples:

Rodney Dangerfield's best one-liners:

A girl phoned me the other day and said, "Come on over, there's nobody home." I went over. Nobody was home.

"I could tell that my parents hated me," he said. "My bath toys were a toaster and a radio."

Write Angles

Remember that the coordinating conjunctions are *and, but, for, nor, or, so, yet.*

➤ Use a comma to set off *appositives*. (The words in apposition are underlined in these examples.)

Examples: There are over three million lakes in Alaska. The largest, <u>Lake Iliamna,</u> is the size of Connecticut.

The brightest star in the sky, <u>Sirius,</u> gives out 26 times as much light as the sun.

Word Watch

Appositives are words that give additional information by renaming the noun or pronoun.

➤ Use a comma to separate items in a series.

Example: A little song, a little dance, a little seltzer down your pants.

➤ Use a comma to set off words of direct address.

Examples: Herman, did you know that some toothpastes contain antifreeze?

There are more plastic flamingos in America than real ones, Nick.

Wait! There's More!

Following are some additional uses of the comma.

➤ Use a comma after the greeting of an informal letter.

Examples: Dear Sweetcakes, Dear Pudding Puss,

➤ Use a comma at the close of any letter.

Examples: Yours truly, Sincerely,

➤ Use a comma to separate the parts of an address.

Example: 15 Main Street, Huntington, New York 11746

➤ Use a comma with names and titles.

Example: Margery Brown, Ph.D.

➤ Use a comma between the day of the month and the year.

Example: July 4, 1776

➤ Use commas to show thousands, millions, and so on.

Examples: 1,000; 10,000; 100,000

Author! Author!

Numbering systems throughout the world differ in the way they use punctuation. Some numbering systems use a period to mark a division of thousands, so ten thousand would be written 10.000. In the United States, commas are used to mark divisions of thousands.

As you can tell, the comma is a very handy mark of punctuation. However, that doesn't give you permission to sprinkle it willy-nilly throughout your writing. Instead, use the comma where it's needed—and nowhere else.

Hot Shot: The Semicolon

Now what about the semicolon? Many people are confused—even scared—about using the semicolon. Fortunately, the semicolon is actually an easy mark of punctuation to use—and a surprisingly useful one.

A semicolon has two primary uses: to separate two complete sentences ("independent clauses") whose ideas are closely related or to separate clauses that contain a comma. Let's look at each use more closely.

➤ Use a semicolon between closely related independent clauses.

Examples: Never raise your hands to your kids; it leaves your groin unprotected. (Red Buttons)

Don't sweat the petty things; don't pet the sweaty things.

➤ Use a semicolon to join independent clauses when one or both clauses contain a comma.

Example: If you toss a penny 10,000 times, it will not be heads 5,000 times, but more like 4,950 times; the heads picture weighs more, so it ends up on the bottom.

➤ Use a semicolon between main clauses connected by conjunctive adverbs such as *however, nevertheless, moreover, for example,* and *consequently.*

Example: She planned to run away with the circus; however, she was allergic to elephants so she took an MBA instead.

Now that I've cured your fear of semicolons, you're free to use them as needed to make your writing clear and graceful. A semicolon may not be the greatest thing since rocky-road ice cream, but it can help you craft your unique writing style.

With Great Power Comes Great Responsibility: The Colon

Like Mick Jagger and Liza Minelli, the semicolon and the colon are often confused. But unlike our stars, the colon and the semicolon are not interchangeable. Here's how to use the colon.

➤ Use a colon before a long, formal quotation. Figure that five lines or more qualifies as "long":

Example: In his famous speech on the steps of the Lincoln Memorial on August 23, 1963, the Reverend Martin Luther King Jr. said: "I say to you today, my friends, that in spite of the difficulties and frustrations of the moment I still have a dream. It is a dream deeply rooted in the American dream. I have a dream that one day this nation will rise up and live out the true meaning of its creed: 'We hold these truths to be self-evident; that all men are created equal.' I have a dream that one day on the red hills of Georgia the sons of former slaves and the sons of former slave owners will be able to sit down together at the table of brotherhood."

➤ Use a colon before a list.

Example: Today's hottest restaurants include the following eateries: *Fu's Rush In, Taste of Greece,* and *International House of Tofu.*

Write Angles

What to do if you have a quotation within a quotation? Use single quotation marks (') to set off the inside quotation, as the accompanying example shows.

➤ Use a colon before part of a sentence that explains what has just been stated.

Examples: There are three kinds of people: those who can count and those who can't.

For people who like peace and quiet: a phoneless cord.

➤ Use a colon after the salutation of a business letter.

Examples: Dear Mr. Featherbrain:; To Whom It May Concern:

➤ Use a colon to set off hours from minutes, titles from subtitles, chapter from verse in Biblical citations.

Examples: 1:15 P.M., *Enemies: A Love Story*, Genesis 1:3

Author! Author!

Punctuation varies from language to language and preference for specific marks vary from writer to writer, but within any given document, all writers favor stylistic constancy. Today, the trend is toward a minimum of punctuation, with clarity as the main criterion for use.

The Dynamic Duo: Quotation Marks

As you've already learned, dialogue is a great way to provide specific examples and add a dash of style to your writing. Here's how to use these adorable twins:

➤ Use quotation marks to set off a speaker's exact words.

Example: A grasshopper walks into a bar and the bartender says, "Hey, we got a drink named after you."

The grasshopper answers, "You got a drink named Bob?"

➤ Use quotation marks to set off a definition.

Example: *Procrastination* means "keeping up with yesterday."

➤ Use quotation marks to set off the title of a short work, such as a poem, essay, song, short story, or magazine article.

Examples: "The Raven," "America the Beautiful," "The Tell-Tale Heart"

Wild Things: The Hyphen, Dash, and Ellipsis

John Benlow of the *Oxford University Style Book* once claimed, "If you take hyphens seriously, you will surely go mad." Well, you could apply that statement to *all* our punctuation rules, but I don't think the hyphen per se is all that maddening. Now teenagers … that's another kettle of fish entirely.

Here's the basic rules:

1. A *hyphen* is used to show a break in *words*.

2. A *dash* is used to show a break between *phrases and clauses*.

3. *Ellipses* are used to show a break in *continuity*.

Let's look at each mark of punctuation in detail.

Word Watch

A **hyphen** is one click of the key -, a **dash** is two clicks of the key —, and ellipses are three spaced periods ….

The Hyphen

The following guidelines show how to use a hyphen, a small but necessary mark of punctuation.

➤ Use a hyphen to show a word break at the end of a line of type. This is silly, because today we can so easily wrap around type, thanks to computers and variable-spaced fonts. Nonetheless, the rule stands.

➤ Use a hyphen specific compound nouns and adjectives.

Examples: half-price, well-known

➤ Use a hyphen in fractions and in compound numbers from twenty-one to ninety-nine.

Examples: one-half, sixty-six

Write Angles

Hyphenate compound adjectives when they are used together before the noun they modify, as in *the well-known person.* Don't hyphenate compound adjectives if they follow the noun: *The person was well known.*

The Dash

The dash isn't a common mark of punctuation like the comma or the period, but when you need it, nothing else will do. Here's how to use the dash:

➤ Use a dash to show emphasis, such as a sudden change of thought.

Example: Late one night a mugger wearing a ski mask jumped into the path of a well-dressed man and stuck a gun in his ribs. "Give me your money," he demanded.

Indignant, the affluent man replied, "You can't do this—I'm a U.S. Congressman!"

"In that case," replied the robber, "give me MY money."

➤ Use a dash before a summary of what is stated in the sentence.

Example: IRS—Be audit you can be.

The Ellipsis

These three little dots aren't a very common mark of punctuation, but when you need them, nothing else will fit the bill. Use them this way:

➤ Use ellipsis to show that you have deleted words or sentences from a passage you're quoting.

Example: Abraham Lincoln said: "Fourscore and seven years ago ... a new nation, conceived in liberty and dedicated to the proposition that all men are created equal."

➤ Use ellipsis to show a pause or interruption in dialogue.

Example: "No," she said. "It's not your breath ... or your clothes ... or your hair."

Pair Off and Square Off: Parentheses and Brackets

According to Mark Twain, "Parentheses in literature and dentistry are in bad taste. Parenthetical expressions are like dentists who grab a tooth and launch into a tedious anecdote before giving the painful jerk." Hmmm .... I think Twain managed to bash both a useful form of punctuation and my favorite health-care provider.

Parentheses

Parentheses are a pair of curved braces, like this: ( ). *Brackets,* in contrast, are a pair of squared braces, like this: [ ]. Parentheses are a much more common form of punctuation than brackets.

➤ Use parentheses to set off nonessential information in a sentence.

Example: Is it true that a cockroach can live for several weeks without its head? (See Figure 1, page xx.)

➤ Use parentheses to enclose numbers or letters.

Examples: Coca-Cola has many uses: (1) it removes rust from the toilet bowl; (2) it cleans rust and paint from a car; and (3) it's also a beverage.

Word Watch

These are **parentheses:** ( ).
These are **brackets:** [ ].

Brackets

Use brackets for editorial clarification. And that's all, folks.

➤ Use brackets to enclose a comment that interrupts a direct quotation.

Examples: Steven Spielberg said, "He [George Lucas] reminded me a little of Walt Disney's version of a mad scientist."

➤ Use brackets and the abbreviation *sic* to acknowledge an error that originated in quoted material.

Example: Thomas Paine said, "These are the times that try mens [sic] souls."

Writer's Block

Never correct an error in quoted material; just point it out. Use the word **sic.** in parentheses to indicate the error. For example: Abraham Lincoln was assassinated in 1965 (sic).

A Triple Threat: The Apostrophe

The apostrophe (') is used three ways: to show possession (ownership), to show plural forms, and to show contractions (where a letter or number has been omitted).

Use an Apostrophe to Show Possession

Here's how to use the apostrophe, the little comma that hangs in the air:

➤ With singular nouns *not* ending in *s*, add an apostrophe and an *s*.

Examples: Nancy, Nancy's nose

Write Angles

If the new word is hard to say, leave off the "s," as in *Rozakis'* book and *Charles'* menu.

➤ With singular nouns ending in *s*, add an apostrophe and an *s*.

Examples: Rozakis, Rozakis's nose, Charles, Charles's car

➤ With plural nouns ending is *s*, add an apostrophe after the *s*.

Examples: students, students' writing

➤ With plural nouns *not* ending in *s*, add an apostrophe and an *s*.

Examples: children, children's games

Use an Apostrophe to Show Plural Forms

➤ Use an apostrophe and *s* to show the plural of a letter.

Example: Mind your p's and q's.

➤ Use an apostrophe and *s* to show the plural of a number.

Example: In the late 1990s, some people started stockpiling water and freeze-dried rations in anticipation of the Y2K crash.

➤ Use an apostrophe and *s* to show the plural of a word referred to as a word.

Example: There are too many distracting like's and huh's in his speech.

Word Watch

Contractions are two words combined.

Use an Apostrophe to Show Contractions

When you contract words, add an apostrophe in the space where the letters have been taken out, as in *does + not = doesn't*.

➤ Use an apostrophe to show letters have been left out of *contractions*.

Examples: did not, didn't, she will, she'll

➤ Use an apostrophe to show numbers have been left out of a date.

Examples: the '60s, the '90s

The Least You Need to Know

➤ Between sentences, the most common mark of punctuation is the period; within sentences, the most common mark is the comma.

➤ Semicolons separate complete sentences; colons show lists.

➤ Use quotation marks to set off a speaker's exact words or a definition.

➤ A hyphen (-) shows a break in words, a dash (—) shows emphasis, and an ellipsis (...) shows a deletion from a direct quotation.

➤ Use parentheses ( ) to set off nonessential information and brackets [ ] for editorial clarification.

➤ The apostrophe (') shows possession (ownership), plural forms, and contractions (where a letter or number has been omitted).

Chapter 29

A Capital Affair

In This Chapter

➤ Capitalization quiz

➤ Rules of capitalization

➤ Rules for using abbreviations

➤ Rules for using numbers in writing

According to the famous Irish wit Oscar Wilde, "Experience is the name everyone gives their mistakes." This chapter covers the rules of capitalization, abbreviations, and numbers. That way, you'll have all the experience without having to make the mistakes!

Capital Punishment

"Capitalization," you moan. "Just one more thing to review." Don't fret; I'll bet you know more about capitalization than you realize. Prove me right by taking this little quiz. Just correct all the errors in capitalization. Some words will need capital letters; other words will need them removed.

1. a woman asked Harvey the artist to paint her in the nude.

2. "No," he said. "i don't do that sort of thing."

3. "i'll double your fee," she said.

4. "No, no thanks!" harvey replied.

5. "I'll give you five times as much as you normally get," She said.

6. "Okay," said the Artist, "but you have to let me at least wear my socks ... I need somewhere to hold my brushes."

Answers

Error	Explanation
1. a woman	Capitalize the first word of a sentence.
2. i	Capitalize I.
3. "i'll ..."	Capitalize a quotation, if it is a complete sentence.
4. harvey	Capitalize proper nouns.
5. She said	Don't capitalize speaker's tags.
6. Artist	Don't capitalize common nouns.

Now that you've gotten your feet wet, let's review the rules of capitalization.

A Tall Order: Capitalization

Here are the guidelines for capitalizing correctly.

Write Angles

Capital letters provide important visual clues to readers, showing where sentences begin and pointing out proper nouns within sentences. As a result, capital letters help determine meaning.

1. **Capitalize sentences.**

   ➤ Capitalize the first word of a sentence.

   Example: <u>T</u>he longest recorded flight of a chicken is 13 seconds.

   ➤ Capitalize the first word in a complete sentence after a colon.

   Example: Standing on the golf course, we all realized the same astonishing fact: <u>M</u>ost people play golf to wear clothes they would not be caught dead in otherwise.

   ➤ Capitalize the first word in a quotation, if it is a complete sentence.

   Example: In *Casablanca,* Humphrey Bogart never did say "Play it again, Sam."

2. **Capitalize names and titles.**

   ➤ Capitalize each part of a person's name.

   Examples: <u>F</u>ranklin <u>D</u>elano <u>R</u>oosevelt

   ➤ If a last name begins with *Mc, O',* or *St.,* capitalize the next letter as well.

   Examples: <u>McM</u>ann, <u>O'R</u>eilly, <u>St. S</u>tephens.

➤ If the name begins with *la, le, Mac, van, von, de,* or *D',* the capitalization varies: *le Blanc* and *Le Blanc* are both correct, for example. Ask the person for clarification.

➤ Capitalize "President" when you refer to the President of the United States, but no cap if you refer to all the presidents of the United States. The presidents of corporations don't warrant caps unless you're using "president" as a title. Go figure.

➤ Capitalize titles before a person's name.

   Examples: <u>D</u>r. Levitan, <u>M</u>s. Loren

➤ Capitalize the names of specific animals.

   Example: <u>R</u>in <u>T</u>in <u>T</u>in

➤ Capitalize titles used in direct address.

   Example: "<u>D</u>octor, I have a toothache."

➤ Capitalize abbreviations that appear after a person's name.

   Examples: Martin Luther King <u>J</u>r., Betsy Sullivan, <u>P</u>h.D.

➤ Capitalize the titles of books, plays, newspapers, and magazines. Capitalize the main words, not articles (*a, an, the*) or prepositions (*of, for, to,* etc.).

   Example: *The <u>C</u>omplete <u>I</u>diot's <u>G</u>uide to <u>W</u>riting <u>W</u>ell*

➤ Capitalize the names of specific historical events, eras, and documents.

   Examples: The Gulf War, The Constitution

3. **Capitalize the names of languages, nationalities, and races.**

   Examples: languages: <u>E</u>nglish, <u>F</u>rench; nationalities: <u>G</u>erman, <u>P</u>olish; races: <u>A</u>frican-<u>A</u>merican, <u>A</u>sian

4. **Capitalize proper nouns and proper adjectives.**

   Examples: <u>C</u>alifornia, <u>C</u>alifornian, <u>C</u>hina, <u>C</u>hinese

   ➤ In a hyphenated proper adjective, capitalize only the adjective.

      Example: <u>E</u>nglish-speaking tourists

Writer's Block

When you quote a word or phrase, don't capitalize it, as this example shows: The phrase "rule of thumb" is derived from an old English law which stated you couldn't beat your wife with anything wider than your thumb.

Write Angles

Is it *Spanish omelet* or *spanish omelet? french fries* or *French Fries?* Dictionaries vary on this point, so pick one style and stick with it.

➤ Capitalize brand names and trademarks.

Examples: Saran Wrap, Kellogg's Rice Krispies

➤ Capitalize the names of organizations, institutions, businesses, and famous.

Examples: The United Way, The Boy Scouts of America, Paramount Corporation, The Empire State Building

5. **Capitalize the name of courses, but not subjects.**

Examples: Psychology 1, psychology, Math 203, math

Writer's Block

Don't capitalize a compass point when it refers to direction. For example: The wind came from the north.

6. **Capitalize geographical places.**

➤ Capitalize countries, places, and sections of the country.

Examples: France, Italy, Lake George, Mars

➤ Capitalize a compass point when it identifies a specific area of the country.

Example: The big ball of twine is in the West.

7. **Capitalize days, months, and holidays.**

Examples: Tuesday, Friday, January, July, Thanksgiving, Independence Day

8. **Capitalize parts of a letter.**

➤ Capitalize the greeting of a letter.

Examples: Dear Mr. Smithers:, Dear Lover,

➤ Capitalize only the first word in the complimentary close of a letter.

Examples: Yours very truly, As ever,

9. **Capitalize each item in an outline.**

Examples: I. Reasons to write well

      A. Express yourself clearly

      B. Feel pleasure

      C. Gain respect

10. **Capitalize I and O.**

Examples: I can't believe I ate the whole thing! O what a rogue and peasant slave am I.

Short and Sweet: Abbreviations

An *abbreviation* is a shortened form of an *existing* word or phrase. Note the word "existing"—it means that you can't make up your own abbreviations, no matter how strong the temptation. Remember that abbreviations start with a capital letter and end with a period. Here's how to use abbreviations correctly.

Word Watch

An **abbreviation** is a shortened form of an *existing* word or phrase.

1. **Abbreviate names and titles.**

   ➤ Abbreviate social titles.

   Examples: Mister, Mr.; Mistress, Mrs.; Doctor, Dr. (always abbreviated)

   Technically, *Ms.* isn't an abbreviation because it isn't a shortened form of an existing word. Nonetheless, it's treated as an abbreviation. Hence, Ms.

   ➤ Abbreviate title of rank. When only the surname is given, the title is usually written out.

   Examples: Col. Hawkeye, Maj. Hot Lips, Colonel Pierce, Major Hoolihan

The following list shows some of the most common titles of rank and their abbreviations.

Title	Abbreviation
Ambassador	Amb.
Captain	Capt.
Colonel	Col.
General	Gen.
Governor	Gov.
Honorable	Hon.
Lieutenant	Lt.
Lieutenant Colonel	Lt. Col.
Lieutenant General	Lt. Gen.
Major	Maj.

Write Angles

People work hard to earn titles and often feel very strongly about them. When you use a person's title, be sure to get it right.

Title	Abbreviation
President	Pres.
Professor	Prof.
Representative	Rep.
Secretary	Sec.
Senator	Sen.
Sergeant	Sgt.
Superintendent	Supt.
Treasurer	Treas.

2. **Abbreviate earned degrees.**

Examples: Russell Wohl, O.D., Ira Rosoff, D.D.S.

Because of their Latin roots, abbreviations for many degrees can be written in either direction: M.A. or A.M. for Masters of Arts, for instance. The following chart shows some of the most commonly abbreviated degrees:

Degree	Abbreviation
Associate's Degree	A.A.
Bachelor of Arts	B.A. or A.B.
Bachelor of Business Administration	B.B.A.
Bachelor of Science	B.S.
Doctor of Divinity	D.D.
Doctor of Dental Surgery	D.D.S.
Doctor of Philosophy	Ph.D.
Masters of Arts	M.A. or A.M.
Masters of Business Administration	M.B.A.
Masters of Science	M.S. or S.M.
Medical Doctor	M.D.
Registered Nurse	R.N.

Writer's Block

Never combine the abbreviations *Mr., Mrs.,* or *Ms.* with the abbreviation for a professional or academic title. For example: Laurie Rozakis, Ph.D., *not* Ms. Laurie Rozakis, Ph.D.

3. **Abbreviate time and dates.**

Use these abbreviations when time is shown in numbers.

Examples: The sale starts at 9:00 A.M. Let's get there at 6:00 A.M.

You can use either capital letters or lowercase letters.

Examples: A.M. or a.m.; P.M. or p.m.

4. **Abbreviate some historical periods.** In some cases, the abbreviation is placed after the date; in other cases, it comes before it.

Examples: B.C. (before the birth of Christ) and B.C.E. (before the common era) always follow the number, as in *409 B.C.* (or *B.C.E.*)

C.E. (common era) comes after the number; A.D. (*Anno Domini*) may come before or after it, as in *A.D. 14* (or *C.E.*). If the century is spelled out, A.D. must come after it, as in the *sixth century A.D.*

Word Watch

A.M. stands for before noon; **ante meridian. P.M.** stands for afternoon; **post meridian.**

5. **Abbreviate geographical terms.**

Examples: Their new house is on the corner of Main St. and Pine Tree Ave., near Lois La.

The following chart lists some of the most common abbreviations for geographical terms. If there's the slightest chance of a misdelivery or misunderstanding, write out the full place name.

Place	Abbreviation
Avenue	Ave.
Building	Bldg.
Boulevard	Blvd.
County	Co.
District	Dist.
Drive	Dr.
Fort	Ft.
Highway	Hwy.
Island	Is.
Mountain	Mt.
National	Natl.
Peninsula	Pen.
Point	Pt.
Province	Prov.

Place	Abbreviation
Road	Rd.
Route	Rte.
Square	Sq.
Street	St.
Territory	Terr.

6. **Abbreviate states.**

Use the official US Post Office Zip Code abbreviations, not the traditional abbreviations for states (N. Mex. vs. NM for New Mexico, for example). See Chapter 23, "Letter Perfect," for the complete list of zip code abbreviations.

7. **Abbreviate measurements.**

Examples: in. (inches), ft. (feet)

Here are some of the most common abbreviations for measurements. Notice that metric abbreviations aren't followed by a period.

Item	Abbreviation
Celsius	C
centimeters	cm
Fahrenheit	F
grams	g
kilograms	kg
kilometers	km
liters	L
meters	m
miles	mi.
millimeters	mm
ounce	oz.
pint	pt.
pound	lb.
quart	qt.
tablespoon	tbs.
teaspoon	tsp.
yards	yd.

You Can Count On It: Numbers

Everyday writing often involves numbers. The rules for using numbers vary according to the discipline. Here's the run-down:

1. **In scientific and technical writing, most numbers are written in figures.** This is especially true for statistics and measurements.

   Examples: The pressure dropped by 5 kilometers per square centimeter.

   Fewer than ½ of those polled responded.

2. **In nontechnical writing, fractions and numbers 100 and under are usually written out.**

   Examples: five trapeze artists, one-half of the clowns

3. **For numbers over 100, write out round numbers if they can be expressed in two words.** Otherwise, use figures.

   Examples: five hundred books, 471 books, more than sixty thousand, 66,131

   If in doubt, use the most logical method.

   Example: The Census Bureau calculates that the U.S. population exceeds 250 million.

4. **Use numbers consistently.**

   Weak: Last year, twenty-three clowns and 12 lion tamers were hired.

   Boffo: Last year, 23 clowns and 12 lion tamers were hired.

   or

   Last year, twenty-three clowns and twelve lion tamers were hired.

5. **Use figures in dates and addresses and with abbreviations and symbols.**

   Examples: April 15, 1999; 1234 Terra Mar Street, Apt. 11A; 41%; 32c; $21.11

6. **Numbers used with *o'clock, past, to, till*, and *until* are generally written out as words.**

   Examples: at seven o'clock, twenty past one

The Least You Need to Know

➤ Capitalize the first word of a sentence and a quotation.

➤ Capitalize names and titles, proper nouns, proper adjectives, geographical places, days, months, holidays, and the greeting and complimentary close of a letter.

➤ Abbreviate social titles, titles of rank, earned degrees, time, dates, and some historical periods. Abbreviate geographical terms, states, and measurements.

➤ In scientific and technical writing, most numbers are written in figures.

➤ In nontechnical writing, fractions and numbers one hundred and under are usually written out.

Sample Term Papers

Term Paper #1

Felix Mendelssohn

by Charles Rozakis

Jakob Ludwig Felix Mendelssohn-Bartholdy was born on February 3, 1809, to Abraham and Lea Mendelssohn in Hamburg, Germany (Oxford Companion 1162). He was the second of four children, but he was closer to his older sister Fanny than any of his other siblings. The two of them studied music and played together for many years, and Fanny also composed. Several of the Songs Without Words were her works, published under Felix's name because of the family's feeling that it was unbecoming for a woman to engage in public life (Harris 1368).

The family moved to Berlin in 1812, where Felix, at the age of four, began to receive regular piano lessons from his mother. In 1816, Abraham Mendelssohn went to Paris on business and brought his family with him. Throughout their stay, Felix and Fanny had piano lessons with Madame Marie Bigot, who was highly esteemed by both Haydn and Beethoven (*Grove Dictionary* 135). When they returned to Berlin, Abraham put into effect a systematic plan of education for his children.

Under this plan, Karl Wilhelm Ludwig Heyse (father of poet and short story writer Paul Heyse) taught the children general subjects and classical languages; Johann Gottlob Samuel Rosel taught drawing; Ludwig Berger taught piano; Carl Wilhelm Henning taught violin; and Carl Zelter gave lessons in musical theory and composition. The children were up at 5 A.M. and began their lessons right after breakfast. Abraham Mendelssohn never considered his children too old for his discipline and correction, and Felix could not consider himself his own master until he was twenty-five years old (Harris 1368).

Felix made his first public appearance as a pianist at the age of nine. He debuted with a *Concert militaire* by F. X. Dusek and was met with great success (*Grove*

Dictionary 135). On April 11, 1819, he entered the Singakademie as an alto, and on September 10 of that year they performed his setting of the Nineteenth Psalm. He remained a member for many years, even after he became a tenor at age sixteen (Harris 1368).

On March 7, 1820, Felix's piano piece *Recitativo* was published. It is his oldest surviving work. From then until he was thirteen, Felix entered a phase of composing in which he mastered counterpoint and classical forms of music, especially in sonata form (*Grove Dictionary* 135–136).

In November of 1821, Zelter took Felix to Weimar to meet his friend Goethe. Between 1821 and 1830, Felix visited Goethe five more times. During one of these visits, Felix wrote home: "Every afternoon Goethe opens the piano with these words, 'I have not heard you at all today, so you must make a little noise for me.'" Goethe's philosophical emphasis on the dynamic and productive aspects of art provided an enriching experience for Felix, while Felix increased Goethe's understanding of the music of the Classical period (Harris 1369).

In 1824, Ignaz Moscheles, one of the greatest pianists of his time, visited Berlin and formed a lifelong friendship with Felix. He gave piano lessons to Fanny and Felix during his stay, but he wrote that he never lost sight of the fact he was sitting beside a master, not a pupil. Abraham, not certain that a musical career was right for Felix, took him to Paris in March of 1825 to consult the great Cherubini, who was then the director of the Paris Conservatoire. Cherubini was so taken with the boy that not only did he approve of a career in music, he offered to undertake the boy's further training. Abraham, however, thought the home atmosphere was better suited, and so declined the offer (Harris 1369).

Felix composed the overture to Shakespeare's *A Midsummer Night's Dream* when he was only seventeen years old. From then on, he was composing constantly. He studied at the University of Berlin in 1826 after attending for three years. He did not earn a degree, but he received a far better general education than most musical composers of his time. It was only in 1829 that he definitely decided upon music as a profession (*Grove Dictionary* 137–139).

Starting in April of that year, Felix went on a three-year tour planned by his father. First he went to England, where he was greeted whole-heartedly, then to South Germany, Austria, Italy, Switzerland, France, then back to London, and finally back home (Harris 1369). He conducted a number of concerts and was the city music director for Düsseldorf for three years (*Grove Dictionary* 138).

In 1834 he was elected a member of the Berlin Academy of Fine Arts. He became conductor of the famous Gewandhaus Orchestra of Leipzig in June of 1835, and in 1836 he received an honorary Ph.D. from the University. That summer, he met Cecile Charlotte Sophie Jeanrenaud. They were engaged in September and married on March 28, 1837 (Harris 1370–1371).

In 1841, King Frederick William IV invited Felix back to Berlin to become director of a proposed music department of the Academy of Arts. When he finally accepted, he found the attitude of the Court, the musicians, and even the public was nothing less than openly hostile. By command of the king he began a series of concerts in Berlin in January of 1842, but by October he wished to resign. He did remain, at the king's request, long enough to organize music at the cathedral. For this, he received the title of Royal General Music Director, but he then moved back to Leipzig (Harris 1371).

After another five years of conducting and composing, he resigned the Gewandhaus Orchestra due to overwork and extreme fatigue. He retired to Frankfort to rest, but received his death blow when he heard of his sister Fanny's death. He returned to Leipzig with his family in September and died on November 4, 1847 (Harris 1372).

Behind every great man … lies many influential people. Many different events and people lead to the man Mendelssohn became and the music he wrote. Of these, the most important musical influences were Carl Zelter and Johann Sebastian Bach.

Carl Friedrich Zelter (1758–1832), a German composer and conductor, was one of Mendelssohn's first teachers. He began Mendelssohn's instruction in music theory and composition in 1819 (*Encyclopedia Britannica* vol. X: 871). Of the thirteen early symphonies Mendelssohn wrote for string orchestra, the first ten were composed as exercises for Zelter.

Zelter introduced Mendelssohn to Goethe in November of 1821. Zelter's friendship with Goethe had begun in 1796 when Zelter published his first collection of lieder. This collection included settings of poems by Goethe, and Goethe wrote Zelter to tell him he was pleased with the settings. After the suicide of Zelter's stepson, Goethe's letter of condolence showed the depth of his feelings in the use of the pronoun "du." This established their close relations for the rest of their lives, and inspired Zelter's continued work on the lied (*Grove Dictionary* 663–664). Given Zelter's close relationship with Mendelssohn, it was inevitable that the young composer would also be inspired by Goethe. Mendelssohn's *Die erste Walpurgisnacht,* one of his greatest cantatas, was based on Goethe's *Faust,* and on Goethe's personal interpretation of the scene (*Grove Dictionary* 146). Mendelssohn's friendship with the poet lasted for a great many years, up until Goethe's death in 1832.

Mendelssohn's cantatas also show Bach's influence. While some critics comment that the settings Mendelssohn wrote of the psalms for liturgical use show a decline in musical quality from his highly dramatic work, they do recall the form and structure of Bach's cantatas (*Grove Dictionary* 146).

In 1784, When Zelter became interested in serious composing, he went to Carl Fasch, a leading musician, who accepted him as a pupil. Zelter joined Fasch's Singakademie in 1791. After Fasch's death in 1800, Zelter took over the Singakademie. Zelter also continued Fasch's practice of having the Singakademie perform works by J.S. Bach (*Grove Dictionary* 663–664).

Bach was Mendelssohn's idol. As a boy, Mendelssohn copied out Bach's music, and his early compositions were greatly influenced by it (*Grove Dictionary* 143). Zelter was quite zealous in his training of strict contrapuntal style. Also, many of Mendelssohn's works follow the contrapuntal style, in particular the fugal technique, of Bach (*Grove*

411

Dictionary 663–664). After all, Bach was, for a time, known as the supreme master of counterpoint (*Funk & Wagnalls* vol. 3: 180–181).

Mendelssohn's first six string symphonies, the work of a very talented twelve-year-old, clearly show the influence of the Viennese Classical style. Of these, the first movements of the third and fourth bear the contrapuntal imprint of Bach and Handel. The influences of Bach and Handel, and the Viennese Classics, are even more clear in Mendelssohn's later string symphonies. The first movement of the seventh contains a great deal of emphasis on counterpoint, as does the introduction to the eighth. Also, the second theme of the eighth is constructed within the limitations of a fugue subject (*Grove Dictionary* 146–147).

This all comes together in Mendelssohn's twelfth early string symphony. Here, he used a complex, chromatically descending fugue subject. This works to develop his symphonic form from Bach's contrapuntal influence to his own, personal mode of expression (*Grove Dictionary* 147).

Further, Mendelssohn's early concertos of 1822–1823 are, like most of the string symphonies, similar to the Viennese Classical models. The form, structure, and even thematic material resemble these models quite closely. However, Mendelssohn's two double piano concertos (1823–1824) show his work matured very quickly from this theme (*Grove Dictionary* 149–150).

After Mendelssohn joined the Singakademie in April of 1819, he often performed small pieces of Bach's works. Zelter discovered an almost forgotten manuscript copy of Bach's *St. Matthew Passion* and Mendelssohn and his peers soon came into possession of the piece (*Encyclopedia Britannica* vol. X: 871). Soon after, Mendelssohn and Eduard Devrient, a fellow member of the Singakademie, proposed a performance of the piece on the 100th anniversary of its first performance. In their plan, Mendelssohn would conduct, and Devrient would sing the part of Christ. At first, Zelter thought that the public would not accept such an extended work by Bach because large-scale works were considered impossible to perform at the time. *St. Matthew Passion* was performed, however, on March 11, 1829 (Harris 1369–1370). The performance was a great success and in years to come, *St. Matthew Passion* became, according to Wohlfarth, "the universal possession of humankind" (96).

This also led to a great revival of Bach's music, which was one the greatest achievements in musical history. This event ushered in the modern cultivation of Bach and its success further inspired Mendelssohn to use Bach's work as a model for his own.

Without Bach's work as his model, or Zelter to teach him the basics of it, Mendelssohn's music would have been radically different from what we know today. But then again, without Mendelssohn, Zelter's role in history would have been much smaller, and Bach's greater works may have been lost to time. So, in effect, this relationship was beneficial to all of them, not just Mendelssohn himself.

Felix Mendelssohn is classified as a Romantic composer, but this classification only fits his works somewhat. While Mendelssohn's Romantic influences and his own comments about his music would make him and Romantic, his affiliations with the eighteenth century, especially the music of Mozart, make him a neo-classicist more than anything else (*Grove Dictionary* 143).

According to the *Encyclopedia Britannica,* the Romantic period in music took place from around 1800 to around 1910. It was "most markedly characterized by emphasis on the expression of individualized or subjective emotion, as well as by a sense of the transcendental, exotic, mythical, and supernatural" (vol. VIII: 655). In part, Mendelssohn is called a Romantic composer because he lived during this period.

In addition, some of his compositions also have some very strong literary influences. For example, the *Grove Dictionary* points out a definite connection between Mendelssohn's *Octet* and lines from the *Walpurgisnacht* scene in the first part of Goethe's *Faust* (143). Mendelssohn's work shows some even stronger Romantic influences. These other influences include Schlegel's Shakespeare translations, Goethe's other poetry, and, mostly in the Italian Symphony, art and nature. Also the lieder and choruses of the Italian Symphony show the influence of emotions from personal human relationships (*Grove Dictionary* 143). Mendelssohn himself stated that the *Elijah* expressed his feelings of acquiescence and strong protest after his disappointments in Berlin. This is an "expression of individualized or subjective emotion" which is most definitely Romantic.

However, Mendelssohn's work also shows many Classical influences. According to the *Encyclopedia Britannica,* the Classical period in music took place from approximately 1750 to 1820. It was "full of changing emotions, fragmented, sighing phrases, and sudden changes of key and musical texture ... [the] melodies were composed of small fragments, or motives, rather than spun out endlessly" (vol. II: 972). Mendelssohn's music fits well into a later version of this period because of its great influence on his work. For example, the classical emphasis on clarity and tradition are very strong in many of his compositions. Harris, in his entry in *The International Cyclopedia of Music and Musicians,* commented that, "[The] range of feeling and expression [in Mendelssohn's music] is limited. It is filled with perfect order and neatness" (1372). As a youth, Mendelssohn was guided by classical and pre-classical techniques. He was especially fond of Bach's works, which he copied out as a boy. Mendelssohn's early work also demonstrates an intensive study of Handel's instrumental techniques. In the introductions of the string symphonies, he used typically Handelian rhythms and harmonic progressions (*Grove Dictionary* 143).

Other Classical composers had an effect on Mendelssohn's music as well. Mendelssohn quoted Mozart's "Jupiter" Symphony in the ending of his *Die bieden Padagogen.* Beethoven's instrumental technique was a powerful influence on Mendelsssohn's works for a full symphony orchestra. And Mendelssohn's personal stylistic traits show a freer adaptation of many other classical forms (*Grove Dictionary* 143–147).

So how can we classify Felix Mendelssohn's work? His style is somewhat Romantic, fairly neo-Classical, and wholly his own. Harris referred to him as a "Romantic Classicist" (1372). This melding of styles is what made his music what it is.

413

Works Cited

"Bach, Johann Sebastian." *Encyclopedia Britannica*. vol I. 15 ed.

"Bach, Johann Sebastian." *Funk & Wagnalls New Encyclopedia*. vol 3. 1983 ed.

Barr, R. "Zelter, Carl Friedrich." *The New Grove Dictionary of Music and Musicians*. vol 20. Ed. Stanley Sadie. London: Macmillan Publishers Limited, 1980.

"Goethe, Johann Wolfgang von." *Encyclopedia Britannica*. vol IV. 15 ed.

Harris, G.W. "Felix Mendelssohn." *The International Cyclopedia of Music and Musicians*. Ed. Oscar Thompson. New York: Dodd, Mead Inc., 1985.

Kohler, Karl-Heinz. "Mendelssohn, Felix." *The New Grove Dictionary of Music and Musicians*. vol 12. Ed. Stanley Sadie. London: Macmillan Publishers Limited, 1980.

"Mendelssohn, Felix." *Encyclopedia Britannica*. vol 11. 15 ed.

"Mendelssohn, Felix." *Funk & Wagnalls New Encyclopedia*. vol 3. 1983 ed.

Wohlfarth, Hannsdieter. *Johann Sebastian Bach*. Philadelphia: Fortress Press, 1984.

"Zelter, Carl Friedrich." *Encyclopedia Britannica*. vol X. 15 ed.

Term Paper #2

The Effects of Calorie Restriction on Aging

by Jessica Swantek

Introduction

For ages, humans have been searching for ways to counteract the aging process. The legendary fountain of youth generated much attention in the past, and more recently, thousands of dollars have been spent each year on creams, pills, plastic surgery, and various forms of therapy designed to make one look and feel younger. So far nothing has been proven to reverse or even retard human aging, but scientists are finally catching a glimpse as to a dietary manipulation technique that might work.

Preliminary Experimentation

In the 1930s, Clive McCay, a scientist at the laboratories at Cornell University, experimented on his rats by feeding them less than they would ordinarily take for themselves, but without depriving them of nutrition to the point of starvation. He found that the food-deprived rats lived considerably longer than expected for a standard rat's life span, and about 33 percent longer than his control group of rats, which were fed as much as they wanted to eat (Weindruch 46). McCay didn't fully understand his results, and although published, they were generally disregarded by the science world (*Man Immortal*).

Years later, Roy Walford, a nutritionist working at the University of California at Los Angeles Medical Center, came across the documentation of McCay's experiments, and, using modern technology and mice instead of rats, picked up where McCay had left off (*Man Immortal*).

Walford found that for the best results to achieve the longest life extension in his mice with the fewest negative side effects, calories should be restricted by 30 percent of what would be taken freely by the mice, and essential nutrients must still be consumed (Mlot 162). Dietary reduction of other things, such as fat intake, may be beneficial to health, but it does nothing to extend life span (Whitlock). Mice usually live anywhere from 38 to 40 months. When calories were restricted by 30 percent, they lived from 56 to 57 months, which is roughly equivalent to 147 years old in human terms (*Man Immortal*).

Among his findings, Walford discovered that the mice lived about 30 percent longer than average, weighed about 30 percent less than usual, had lower blood pressure, lower levels of serum cholesterol, lower concentrations of circulating glucose, lower triglyceride concentrations, lower insulin levels, and greater insulin sensitivity. In short, their bodies were becoming extremely efficient at utilizing the few calories that were put into it (Weindruch 49). The animals had stronger immune systems, and the onset of common late-life diseases, such as certain cancers, were held off as well (Weindruch 48).

Why It Works

Walford knew that reducing calories was slowing metabolism in the mice and improving their health in general, but he was unaware of exactly what was causing the slowing of the metabolism, and why it caused the extension of life span in the mice. In order to explain what was triggering the results, we first look at worms.

Nematodes have an average life span of 14 days. However, at times when food is scarce, such as when overpopulation occurs, the seemingly simple worms have the ability to switch into a state of suspended animation known as the Dauer phase, "dauer" being the German word for "durable," during which they can live for two months or more, which is over four times longer than usual. Scientists such as Cynthia Kenyon at the University of California at San Francisco are studying the nematodes and their connection with humans (Roush 897).

Kenyon and her colleagues have found that there is a gene responsible for the worms changing into their Dauer phase. It is called DAF-2, for Dauer-formation defect 2. The gene senses when there is not enough glucose present, and then acts as a switch to begin the Dauer phase. More recently it has been found that the DAF-2 gene shares 35 percent of its amino acid sequence with the human insulin receptor, making it the worm equivalent of our insulin receptor (Roush 897). So when there is insufficient glucose in the human body, there is less insulin secreted in response, and the human insulin receptor detects that there is not enough insulin, and acts as a switch to slow our metabolism and cellular respiration.

Metabolism is defined as the energy-releasing breakdown of molecules. Energy is created through cellular respiration. Cellular respiration takes place in the mitochondria of the cell, and uses oxygen to make energy in the form of ATP. During ATP synthesis, an electron is removed from an oxygen molecule during the electron transport chain, leaving an unpaired electron. These molecules with one unpaired electron are known as free radicals (Kotulak and Gomer).

Free radicals are very unstable molecules. The byproduct of burning oxygen in cells, they severely damage essential enzymes, molecules, organelles, and DNA (Weindruch 49). The molecule wants to have a complete pair of electrons, so it steals an electron from another molecule so that it becomes stable. However, then the second molecule has an incomplete set of electrons, and must rip an electron off of a third molecule, thus causing a very destructive chain reaction that eventually ends when two free radicals come together, but wreaks cellular havoc in the meantime (Kotulak and Gomer).

Our bodies produce antioxidants which combat free radicals and repair free radical damage, and antioxidants are also present in certain foods, especially vitamins C, E, and A (*Dietary Manipulation*). However, after a point the antioxidants simply cannot keep up with the amount of free radical damage inflicted. When cells become irreparably fractured by free radicals, they die, which results in human aging (*Man Immortal*). Free-radical damage is also responsible for diseases such as cataracts, heart disease, and some cancers (Kotulak and Gomer).

Caloric restriction counteracts these age-causing processes. So, if fewer calories are ingested, which causes a gene to tell the metabolism and respiration to slow down, fewer free radicals will be produced in the mitochondria, so cells will undergo less oxidative damage, and life will be extended, which is how caloric restriction treatment works.

Ongoing Experimentation

Calorie restriction experiments have now been performed on organisms ranging from water fleas to guppies to monkeys (Weindruch 46). One ongoing experiment that seems significant is currently being done on rhesus monkeys at the University of Wisconsin at Madison with funding from the National Institute on Aging. Since the monkeys ordinarily live to be around 40 years old, it will be some time before end results are seen, but scientists already observe the effects of calorie restriction in blood pressure, cholesterol, and basic observed markers of aging in the 17-year-old monkeys (Mlot 162). This experiment is considered to be particularly important because of the primates' close relation to humans. Scientists will be able to more accurately predict what results of calorie restriction on humans could be by observing the rhesus monkeys over the next few decades. A similar experiment using squirrel monkeys has also been underway since 1987 in Baltimore, Maryland (*Dietary Manipulation*).

Application in Humans

When Roy Walford finished his preliminary experiments on mice, he knew that he had stumbled across some very important information, and wondered if a parallel extension of life could be observed in humans under similar conditions. As it turned out, he was able to conduct his experiments on humans sooner than he had expected. Walford was one of eight human subjects sealed inside Biosphere 2 in September of 1991. The team produced far less agriculturally than had been anticipated and were therefore forced to cut back on their food intake. Walford, being a nutritionist, put himself and the seven other Biospherians on a diet that closely reflected the 30 percent calorie reduction that he used on his mice, also making sure that essential nutrients were not cut out of the diet. As expected, Walford recorded parallel results in the humans (Walford).

Walford has since published several books on caloric restriction as a means for human life extension, such as *The 120 Year Diet: How to Double Your Vital Years,* and has even designed a computer program for the purpose of constructing what he considers an appropriate diet for this purpose (*Dietary Manipulation*). He has also experimented on himself: He has been on a calorie-restricted diet for the past ten years, and at age 72, believes that he has added five or six years to his life already (*Man Immortal*). Most scientists, however, agree that it is too soon to accurately conclude that caloric restriction would be safe and successful for humans.

Even if caloric restriction is approved as a feasible means for life extension in the future, there will probably not be many people willing to use it. Reducing one's calorie intake by 30 percent is a big dietary change, and ensuring that essential nutrients are still ingested requires careful planning. It is not necessarily easy to get used to. Subjects do feel hunger, and because of the reduced calorie intake, they have less energy and are not able to have extremely active lifestyles (*Man Immortal*). It's hard to imagine many people adopting such a drastic diet change, when even seemingly simple health improving measures, for example consuming five servings of fruit and vegetables a day, have had few takers (Mlot 163). And risks must be taken into consideration, such as the inability to reproduce when one's body processes are focused solely on survival (Weindruch 52).

What the Future May Hold

Although surprising to some, what may come to the forefront of life extension research is Cynthia Kenyon and her UCSF nematodes. The scientists there have been tinkering with the DAF-2 gene and have been able to get the worms to go into the Dauer phase without being first deprived of food. This indicates that perhaps in the future, we will be able to manipulate the human insulin receptor to slow respiration to the point of significant life extension without changing our diet very much (*Man Immortal*).

There will undoubtedly be more caloric-restriction experiments on human subjects in the future, but no matter what the means, with scientists learning more every day about how basic life processes work and how to change them, plus the tremendous advances in medicine both recently and soon to come, the future of the human race might live to see more birthdays than its ancestors ever dreamed of.

Works Cited

Delaney, Brian Manning."Calorie Restriction FAQ." *Calorie Restriction for the Purpose of Retarding Aging.* 30 March 1998. <www.infinitefaculty.org/sci/cr/cr/htm> (23 May 1998).

"Dietary Manipulation of Aging." *Life Extension* Magazine June 1995. <www.lef.org/shop/95jun1.htm> (23 May 1998).

Kotulak, Ronald and Peter Gomer. "Scientists Try to Tame Molecular Sharks." *Chicago Tribune* 11 December 1991. <tular.nist.gov/week0/ch0731/news/aging/aging6.htm> (20 May 1998).

"Man Immortal." Dir. Howard Reay. Prod. Joanne Reay. *TLC.* New York. 1997.

Mlot, Christine. "Running on One-Third Empty." *Science News* 15 March 1997: 162–163.

Roush, Wade. "Worm Longevity Gene Cloned." *Science* 15 August 1997: 897–898.

"Slowing the Process of Aging." *Fact Sheet: Normal Changes of Aging.* <www.biorap.org/rg/rgageslowp.html> (23 May 1998).

Walford, R. L. "Abstract: Biosphere 2." 1992. <www.walford.com/abstrct2.htm> (23 May 1998).

Weindruch, Richard. "Caloric Restriction and Aging." *Scientific American* January 1996: 46–52.

Whitlock, Kelli. "Researchers Find a Low-Fat Diet Does Not Prevent Age-Related Memory Loss." 15 November 1996. <www.cats.ohiou.edu/~univnews/months/nov96/125.html> (23 May 1998).

Term Paper #3

Irish Step Dancing and Appalachian Clogging:
The Roots of American Dance

by Jessica Swantek

My curiosity about clogging and step dancing began about a year ago, when I read a newspaper article about the success of the Irish dancing show *Riverdance*. The author stated that Irish step dancing had a major influence on Appalachian clogging, a form of American folk dancing. I'd never heard of clogging before, and my knowledge of step dancing was limited as well. The article sparked my interest, which led to my decision to choose step dancing and clogging as the topic of my final presentation and paper.

I had several questions in mind. Did Irish step dancing actually affect Appalachian clogging, and if so, how much? How did the evolution from one dance to the other occur? And were there other influences as well? I was also interested in the two dances as separate entities. I wanted to find out more about each one, compare and contrast them, and examine each dance's place in contemporary America, especially with regard to issues such as cultural identity and authenticity.

As the semester and my research progressed, I found the most helpful resources to be encyclopedias, Web pages, and the assistance of two dancers who patiently answered the questions I threw at them and provided me with some insight that I couldn't get from books. In addition to learning a great deal about the two dances, I found the answers to some of my guiding questions and came up with new questions for further research. What follows is a chronological account of the history of Irish step dancing and Appalachian clogging, and a discussion of the two dances as they exist today.

Early Irish History: Conflict and Conquest

Somewhere between 350 and 250 B.C.E., the Celts (also known as the Gaels), settled in Ireland ("Irish" 84). Their feisianna date from the early 1000s. A feis was a big Gaelic festival, which served as a combination of a trade fair, political gathering, and cultural event, complete with music, storytelling, sporting events, and crafts. According to Ann Richens and Don Haurin, these festivals still exist today.

Ireland was home almost exclusively to the Celts and their successive generations until the middle of the twelfth century. In 1169, Ireland was invaded and conquered by the Norman knights of Henry II of England, beginning a long history of conflict between the British and Irish. This event was known as the Anglo-Norman conquest, and King Henry partially controlled the land for the next 400 years (*Encyclopedia of Multiculturalism* 291).

In 1366, the Statute of Kilkenny was passed, which excommunicated or placed heavy penalties on those who allied with the native Irish or followed their customs. Pipers were routinely banned and arrested in the mid-1500s (Richens and Haurin). In the seventeenth century, Ireland became a British colony, and the Scottish and English people were forceably resettled to Northern Ireland. The Penal Laws, enacted by the British Parliament in the late seventeenth and early eighteenth century, limited the Catholics' religious and civil rights, banned their education, and set Irish commerce and industries into ruin. By 1750, the original Irish controlled only five percent of all Irish land. Some of the Irish left the homeland due to the severity of the conflicts, but most couldn't afford to ("Irish" 84).

The Creation of Irish Step Dancing

Irish step dancing had its beginnings in the early 1700s during the turmoil of British oppression. The Irish wanted to learn upscale dances like those done in France and England. To accommodate their demands, dance masters invented Irish step dancing by adapting the French and English dances to fit with traditional Irish music (Harrison <www.inx.net/~mardidom/rcidance.htm>).

This led to the distinctive foot percussion seen in Irish step dancing, known as *battering*. The new dance style was named "step dancing," because each dance sequence executed within eight bars of music was called a step (Richens and Haurin).

A dance master would travel within a county, staying in each village for about six weeks and teaching step dancing to boys. A local family provided room and board, and it was considered an honor to have a prominent dance master stay in one's home.

Ever since St. Patrick introduced Christianity to Ireland in the fifth century, the Catholic Church played a very important role in the lives of the Irish. By the mid-1700s the Church had condemned dancing, so this expression of Irish culture was practiced with some secrecy. Step dance was taught in kitchens, barns, and other fairly private indoor locations. Sometimes a stage was as small as a tabletop or a half door. Because of the lack of adequate dancing space, early step dancing was rather stationary in style. Step dancers tried their best to stay in one place while doing quick footwork (Richens and Haurin).

Men often wore black shoes with elevated heels and large front buckles, so they were ready to dance. The dancers inserted coins between the sole and toe of the shoe and hammer nail heads into the heels to increase the volume of their battering. The dancers usually wore their everyday clothes, and would don their Sunday best, typically swallowtail coats and knee breeches, when performing at a competition. Competitive dancing took place at feisianna, and competition eventually became, for most dancers, the primary reason for learning to step dance. The winner of a competition was the dancer who knew the most steps, not necessarily the one who performed them the best (Richens and Haurin).

There were several different step dances that the dance masters taught, all of which are still done today. The *jig* is perhaps the most recognizably Irish dance that is still in existence. It is performed to music played in a 6/8 time signature. The *reel* originated in Scotland, but was perfected by Irish dance masters. It is a relatively fast dance in 4/4 time. The *hornpipe* evolved from an English dance in the mid-1700s. It is done in 4/4 time, and has a distinct triple rhythm in the music: one-and-a-two-and-a-three-and-a-four-and-a. *Set dances* are performed to a specific tune that remains set over time. It has two parts, the lead around, which is danced as an introduction during the first eight

421

to sixteen measures, and the set, which usually begins at the twelfth to sixteenth measure. Set dances are done in jig or hornpipe time, and greater interpretation of the dance is expected in comparison with other step dances (Richens and Haurin).

The First Irish-American Immigrants

Technically, St. Brendan's voyage just after 500 C.E. brought the first Irish to what would later become the United States of America. The first substantial number of early Irish settlers, however, were those in the mid-1700s who desired an escape from the British-Irish conflicts in their homeland, and could afford to leave Ireland. These immigrants traveled down along the Appalachian mountain range, some going as far as Florida and New Orleans (Cullinane 125).

Most of these immigrants settled during the eighteenth century in the Appalachian mountain region, in what is now Pennsylvania, Virginia, West Virginia, and North and South Carolina. By the first U.S. census of 1790, there was a 12 percent Scotch-Irish population (*Gale Encyclopedia of Multicultural America* 62).

The Irish, like most other immigrant groups, brought their music and dance with them to America, and incorporated it into their new lives. Irish settlers contributed largely to the making of folk music of America (Cullinane 125).

Of all the traditional instruments used by the Irish, their style of fiddle playing had the greatest effect on what was to become American music. Irish fiddle tunes influenced American country music, while their ballads had an impact on American folk songs (*Gale Encyclopedia of Multicultural America* 62). Similarly, Irish dance had an effect on new kinds of American dancing that were soon to come about.

The Creation of Appalachian Clogging

The first official record of a dance master in the United States was recorded in 1789. Based in Philadelphia, he taught reels, jigs, and hornpipes. Irish step dancing, especially the heavy jig and hornpipe, was sometimes referred to as "clog dancing," so it follows logically that when a new form of dance, influenced by Irish step dancing, came into being, it would be called *clogging* (Cullinane 125).

Clogging was influenced not only by the step dancing from Ireland, but also by dances brought to America by other settlers from the British Isles, as well as Native American traditional dances, and solo buck and wing dances of the African American slaves (Mangin, Julie <www.access.digex.net/~jmangin/clogging.htm>).

Clogging began as a very social dance, which was a far cry from the competitive nature of Irish step dancing. The inhabitants of the Appalachians were part of a rural society, and they worked hard during the day, many in the coal mines or on the farm. After sundown, for special occasions or just for enjoyment, families and neighbors would gather together in a barn or on a porch to play music and dance (Charlton 23).

Although the dance has become somewhat rare in comparison to its popularity a century or two ago, a few "old timers" can still be seen flatfooting at Appalachian music festivals today. In Angela Charlton's Associated Press article, she quotes Jane

George, a clogging instructor from West Virginia: "Clogging is … more structured. Flatfooting is freer. You can watch a bunch of people flatfooting and they'll all be doing something different." Dancers who flatfoot have no specific style of dress, but simply wear whatever they've already got on at the time, including everyday shoes.

Traditional clogging has been described as the most energetic form of step dance and is characterized by a relaxed upper body and fast-moving, percussive footwork ("Stepdance/Clogging in Nova Scotia" <fox.nstn.ca/~blee/dans/stepindex.html>).

It is a mobile, informal dance whose steps have become somewhat standardized only within the past century. Distinct steps and their names used to vary from region to region, and West Virginia is one of the last places to retain those differences (Charlton 23). The two most basic steps, which are the foundation for most other clogging steps, are called the shuffle and the buck, and are very similar, if not exactly the same, as some dance steps seen in modern tap dancing.

Subsequent Irish Immigrants: The First Great Wave

In 1800, the British passed the Act of Union. England had tight control over Ireland at this point, and the Irish couldn't have their own parliament or government. All Irish government agencies were moved to London (*Encyclopedia of Multiculturalism* 291). The infamous Irish potato famine occurred in the mid-1800s as well. About a quarter of the Irish population died of starvation and disease, and many of the remaining Irish fled their homeland, bound for the United States.

The First Great Wave of Immigration to America lasted from 1841 until 1890. Included in the approximately eight million foreigners who immigrated to the United States were three million Irish and British (*Encyclopedia of Multiculturalism* 291).

The Irish moved primarily to large American cities like Boston, New York, and Philadelphia. Mostly Catholic unskilled peasants, they often faced job discrimination and were generally disliked in the United States (*Gale Encyclopedia of Multicultural America* 62). Due to these circumstances, they often lived in more or less isolated ethnic communities, such as the Hell's Kitchen area of New York City (*American Immigrant Cultures: Builders of a Nation* 76).

The Evolution of Modern Irish Step Dancing

In 1893, the Gaelic League was founded, which encouraged the revival of Irish culture (Richens and Haurin). This finally brought Irish dancing out into the open and began a chain of events that would result in the worldwide awareness and recognition of step dancing. The 1921 treaty that established the Irish Free State in the south and Northern Ireland as two separate countries also helped to stir up enthusiasm for the outward expression of Irish culture (*American Immigrant Cultures: Builders of a Nation* 76).

In 1929, the Irish Dancing Commission was founded. Its purpose was to standardize Irish dance by establishing universal rules regarding teaching, judging, and competitions. The commission established a 100 mark judging system. The points were distributed evenly among four categories: timing, deportment/style, construction of steps, and execution/method (Richens and Haurin).

423

Starting near the turn of the twentieth century, women began to step dance. They had most likely been doing so privately for quite some time, but it was considered indecent by the Church for women to dance, so any such displays in public were previously unacceptable. However, the gender dynamic had completely reversed itself by the 1930s. Because of the influx of female dancers, a new, more feminine dance was invented specifically for women, called a slip jig. Danced to music in 9/8 time, a slip jig's steps consist of graceful skipping, hopping, and toe pointing. Soft shoes were introduced around 1924 for use during slip jigs. They are soft leather shoes with flexible soles, much like Western ballet shoes, and they lace up the front and tie around the dancer's ankle (Richens and Haurin).

The prevalence of female dancers also led to the unique posturing of Irish step dancing that is its trademark today. Parish priests felt that women dancing with loose arms were far too provocative, so in order to increase their self-control, Irish step dancers must dance with their torso rigid, arms firmly at their sides, and faces expressionless (Richens and Haurin).

Costuming for Irish step dancing changed over the years as well. In 1893, the Gaelic League went on a quest for a traditional Irish costume, and as a result, feis rules made by the Irish Dancing Commission now call for "authentic Gaelic dress." Boys wear white button-down shirts and dark pants, or kilts for older boys and men. Girls and women wear elaborately embroidered dresses with a shawl draped from the left shoulder to the right side of the waist, as well as black stockings, or white knee socks for younger dancers. There are even rules regarding hairstyles at a feis. A female dancer must curl her hair in ringlets for a competition, and keep it away from her face with a headband. Footwear has been through some significant improvements over the years as well. The old men's "buckle shoes" were replaced by what are known as hard shoes. They have fiberglass tips and hollow heels, making them much lighter and louder (Richens and Haurin).

Clogging Evolves

Around the onset of World War II, a new style of clogging emerged, called "pitter pat." The older clogging style was referred to as "traditional style or mountain style." Pitter pat is synchronized clogging, with a group of dancers all doing the same step at the same time. Dancers form precision teams and perform choreographed clogging dances to a variety of recorded music of any genre, some of it modern or popular music (Mangin, Julie <www.access.digex.net/~jmangin/clogging.htm>).

Pitter pat is more static than mountain-style clogging, and teams often assemble themselves in a line formation on stage. The clogging steps are executed more quickly than in mountain style clogging, and modern dance steps as well as arm and hand movements are used. Some precision teams wear leotards or spandex dance costumes, just like any other modern dance group, and clogging shoes are usually worn. Pitter pat has become the current most popular clogging style, and teams can be found all across the United States (Earnhardt, Brooke, "Brooke's Clogging Page" <www. geocities.com/Nashville/Opry/2891>).

Clogging and Step Dancing in Present Day America

Competition has always been an integral part of step dancing, and the Irish dance infrastructure continued to expand until just a few decades ago. In 1964, the Irish Dance Teachers Association was founded, and there are currently more than 300 certified Irish dance instructors in North America. The North American Feis Commission was founded in 1968 to regulate competitions in the United States and Canada, and an annual North American championship competition started in 1969. Current feisianna focus primarily on Irish culture, and have crafts for sale, as well as vocal, instrumental, dance, and Gaelic language competitions. An *oireachtas* is a "super feis," organized by region since 1976 (Richens and Haurin). The Oireachtas na Cruinne is the official title of the World Championship held annually in Ireland. The step dancing competition scene is remarkably organized, in part due to the assistance of these new organizations.

I learned from step dancer Brooke Earnhardt that many organizations hold independent clogging competitions, such as the Showstoppers National Talent Competition, the National Clogging and Hoe-down Championships, and the Clogging Champions of America Competition. However, none of these organizations is affiliated with one another or overseen by a higher establishment. In accordance, there is no set teaching or judging criteria. Some judges look for precision, some judge the choreography, some watch for the dancers' ability to stay with the music, and some pay attention to the costumes. Usually a group will be rated numerically, though the number range varies from one competition to the next, on some combination of the above categories.

Identity/Community

So who are these dancers? Is Irish step dancing still just the dance of the Irish? Is clogging only done by white descendents of settlers from the British Isles? I asked Brooke and Katie about their family backgrounds in order to see if there was a predictable pattern. Interestingly, while both dancers fit the historic description of their respective dances—Katie is 100 percent Irish and Brooke has Scottish and English ancestors—both denied that their heritage had anything to do with their choice of dance. Also, neither Brooke nor Katie had any history of family members who were involved in their dance, so they were both firstp-generation dancers, so to speak. Apparently for Brooke and Katie, any ethnic link was purely coincidental. I concluded that in order to accurately and more completely explore this issue, I'd need to ask more than one person from each dancing community. It would be an interesting topic for further research.

Authenticity

We spent a great deal of time discussing authenticity in class, so it seemed natural for me to incorporate it into my research. While watching *Riverdance,* I realized that while the footwork was beautifully executed, the dancing as a whole was not necessarily "authentic" Irish step dancing. For one thing, the costuming was wrong. The dancers in the show wear more modern clothes, which look great on stage but would never be permitted at a feis. The dancers don't keep their arms at their sides either. These two observations among others left me wondering what a real Irish dancer would think if I, in my relative ignorance, had noticed all these discrepancies. Perhaps surprisingly, the Irish dancers don't seem to mind. As of yet, I have read and heard only positive things from Irish dancers about the step dancing that takes place in *Riverdance* or *Lord of the Dance*. In general, they seem to be delighted that their dance and culture is so positively received by the public. Katie's comment was, "The two shows have increased public awareness of Irish dancing and made it distinct. Before the shows, few people would have known what step dancing was …. Since the shows, there has been a huge swell in the number of new dancers of all ages who enroll in dance classes. I think the shows have … helped to promote Irish step dancing as being fun and modern" (E-mail to the author, 10 November 1998). What may be the greatest effect of *Riverdance* and *Lord of the Dance* is the realization that there is a life for Irish dancers outside of competition (Cullinane 125).

Media Attention

Irish step dancing has obviously received a lot of media attention lately, largely due to the huge commercial successes of the step dancing shows *Riverdance* and *Lord of the Dance*. Clogging, however, remains fairly unknown as an old Appalachian mountain tradition and is familiar only to those who clog and those who live in rural communities where clogging is common. Or is it? Interest in Appalachian dance was somewhat revived along with the folk movement in the late 1970s. The Green Grass Cloggers often performed publicly to live music and apparently had quite a following (Mangin, Julie <www.access.digex.net/~jmangin/clogging.htm>).

Perhaps at the height of clogging's visibility, the Leather 'N' Lace Cloggers, a precision team from Leicester, North Carolina, performed at the opening ceremonies of the 1996 Summer Olympics in Atlanta before an audience of thousands and broadcast via television to millions worldwide (Mangin, Julie. <www.access.digex.net/~jmangin/clogging.htm>). So while clogging may not have the fame that step dancing currently enjoys, it seems to be quietly holding its own.

In conclusion, Appalachian clogging and Irish step dancing are two dynamic dance forms, each with a rich history, that are thriving quite well and becoming ever more popular as we reach the turn of the twenty-first century. While I've found the answers to the original questions I asked about the dances, I've also come up with even more questions over the course of my research. More important, I've grown to genuinely like the two dances. For the time being I can only enjoy watching them, but I just might take a clogging or step dancing class sometime in the future. It will be interesting to see what the future holds for step dancing and clogging, whether step dancing falls back out of vogue or clogging undergoes a surge of popularity and takes the limelight once and for all. Either way, both dances have proven to stand the test of time, and almost certainly will be around in some form for the enjoyment of many generations to come.

Works Cited

"Banjo." *The New Grove Dictionary of Musical Instruments,* vol. 1. 1984 ed.

Charlton, Angela. "Cloggers Shuffle and Skip to Save Appalachian Tradition." The Associated Press. June 1997.

Cullinane, Dr. John. *Aspects of the History of Irish Dancing in North America.* Cork City, Ireland: Dr. John P. Cullinane, 1997.

Earnhardt, Brooke. "Brooke's Clogging Page." <www.geocities.com/Nashville/ Opry/2891> (9 October 1998).

Earnhardt, Brooke. E-mail to the author. 9 November 1998.

"Fiddle." *The New Grove Dictionary of Musical Instruments,* vol. 1. 1984 ed.

Harrison, Bill. "A Brief Overview of Irish Dance." 27 December 1997. <www.inx.net/~mardidom/rcidance.htm> (16 October 1998).

"Introduction." *Gale Encyclopedia of Multicultural America,* vol. 1. 1995 ed.

"Ireland." *Compton's Interactive Encyclopedia.* 1998 ed.

"Irish." *American Immigrant Cultures: Builders of a Nation,* vol. 1. 1997 ed.

"Irish Americans." *Encyclopedia of Multiculturalism,* vol. 4. 1994 ed.

"Irish Americans." *Gale Encyclopedia of Multicultural America,* vol. 2. 1995 ed.

The Irish Emigrant, Ltd. "The IE Glossary." January 1997. <www.emigrant.ie/ emigrant/glossary.html> (18 November 1998).

The JVC/Smithsonian Folkways *Video Anthology of Music and Dance of the Americas,* vol. 1: Canada and the United States. Dir. Hiroaki Ohta. Prod. Stephen McArthur and Multicultural Media. Victor Company of Japan, Ltd., 1995.

The JVC/Smithsonian Folkways *Video Anthology of Music and Dance of the Americas,* vol. 2: United States. Dir. Hiroaki Ohta. Prod. Stephen McArthur and Multicultural Media. Victor Company of Japan, Ltd., 1995.

The JVC Video *Anthology of World Music and Dance,* vol. 20: Europe I. Dir. Nakagawa Kunihiko. Prod. Ichikawa Katsumori. Victor Company of Japan, Ltd.

Live Performance: October 10, 1998 at Hofstra University's John Cranford Adams
    Playhouse. Scotch/Irish-Canadian performers, the Leahy family, musicians &
    step dancers.

Mangin, Julie. "The Clogging Page." 9 October 1998. <www.access.digex.net/
    ~jmangin/clogging.htm> (14 October 1998).

Matthews, Gail. "Movement and Dance: Nonverbal Clues About Culture and
    Worldview." *The Emergence of Folklore in Everyday Life: a Fieldguide and Sourcebook*.
    Ed. George H. Schoemaker. Bloomington, Indiana: Trickster Press, 1992.
    101–105.

Mullen, Katie. E-mail to the author. 10 November 1998.

O'Connor, Barbara. "Safe Sets: Women, Dance, and 'Communitas.'" *Dance in the City*.
    Ed. Helen Thomas. New York: St. Martin's Press, 1997. 149–172.

Richens, Ann, and Don Haurin. "Irish Step Dancing: A Brief History." February 1996.
    <HYPERLINK "tigger.cc.uic.edu/~aerobin/irhist.html" tigger.cc.uic.edu/
    ~aerobin/irhist.htm> (17 October 1998).

Riverdance. Dir. John McColgan. With Jean Butler and Colin Dunne. Composer Bill
    Whelan. Columbia Tristar, 1997.

"Stepdance/Clogging in Nova Scotia." <fox.nstn.ca/~blee/dans/stepindex. html>
    (17 October 1998)

Times Ain't Like They Used to Be: Early Rural and Popular American Music, 1828–1935.
    Prod: Sherwin Dunner and Richard Nevins. Yazoo Video of Shanachie
    Entertainment Corp., 1992.

Documentation Format

MLA Documentation

The Modern Language Association (MLA) uses internal documentation in place of foot-notes and endnotes, embedding the reference in the text of the paper. As you learned in Part 4, "Just Shoot Me Now: Research Papers and Term Papers," you usually need to include only the author's last name (or the title, if the source does not have a credited author) and the page number in an internal documentation.

Following are the standard MLA formats for a Works Cited page. Remember to use MLA style-formatting for papers in the humanities (English, literature, composition, and rhetoric).

Citing Books

The basic citation for a book looks like this:

Author's last name, first name. *Book Title*. Place of publication: publisher, date of publication.

Here are some models to show you how the variations are written:

➤ **A book with one author.**

Orwell, George. *1984*. New York: Penguin, 1989.

➤ **A book with two or more authors.** Notice that the first author's name is inverted for alphabetical order.

Rozakis, Laurie, and Bob Rozakis. *The Complete Idiot's Guide to Office Politics*. New York: Alpha Books, 1998.

➤ **A book with four or more authors.** You can cite all the authors listed or only the first one and then write *et. al.* ("and others") for the rest of the authors.

    Baym, Nina, et. al. *The Norton Anthology of American Literature,* 2nd edition. New York: W.W. Norton, 1989.

➤ **A corporation.** Give the name of the corporation as the author, even if it's the publisher as well.

    IBM. *Know Your Computer.* New York: IBM, 1999.

➤ **An author and an editor.** Be sure to include the author's name, the title of the book, and then the editor. Use the abbreviation ed. whether there is one editor or many.

    Faulkner, William. *The Portable Faulkner.* Ed. Malcolm Cowley. New York: The Viking Press, 1978.

➤ **An editor.** Give the name of the editor or editors, followed by *ed.* (if one editor) or *eds.* (if more than one editor).

    Baker, Russell, ed. *The Norton Book of Light Verse.* New York: W.W. Norton & Company, Inc., 1986.

➤ **A book in a series.** After the title, include the name of the series and series number.

    Horatio, Leon. *Phillip Roth.* Twayne's United States Authors Series 54. Boston: Twayne, 1999.

➤ **A translation.** After the title, write *Trans.* ("translated by") and the name of the translator.

    Cervantes. *Don Quixote.* Trans. Vilma Sanchez. New York: Holt, Rinehart and Winston, 1999.

➤ **A selection reprinted in an anthology.** First give the name of the author and the title of selection, then the title of the book, the editor, the edition, and the publication information.

    King, Martin Luther. "I Have a Dream." *Lend Me Your Ears: Great Speeches in History.* Ed. William Safire. New York: W.W. Norton & Company, Inc., 1992.

Citing Periodicals

The basic citation for an article looks like this:

Author's last name, first name. "Title of the Article." *Magazine.* Month and year of publication: page numbers.

Notice that the date in a bibliographic citation is written in European style, with the date *before* the month, rather than *after.* For example: 12 September 1989.

If the page numbers in an article are not consecutive, cite the first page number followed by a plus sign (+).

Here are some variations on periodical citations:

➤ **Signed article in a monthly magazine.**

Mallory, Jane. "Sing Your Way to Happiness." *American Educator* May 1999: 49–50.

➤ **Signed article in a weekly magazine.**

Losi, Jennifer. "Art and Architecture." *Time* 20 August 1998: 11–12.

➤ **Unsigned article.**

"Beanie Babies May Be a Rotten Nest Egg." *Chicago Tribune* 21 June 1989: 12.

➤ **Editorial.** Show that the article is an editorial by writing *Editorial* after the title._
"Nassau Country Bailout." Editorial. *Newsday* 12

➤ **Review.** To indicate that an article is a book, movie, or play review, write "Rev. of" before the work being reviewed. Use the abbreviation "dir." for the director.

Goldish, Meish. "The Karen Ziemba Story" Rev. of *Steel Pier*, dir. Chaya Rosen. *The New York Times* 1 August 1998: 1.

Citing Electronic Sources and CD-ROMs

Electronic sources are often missing key information such as the author and date. Use whatever information you can find for your citation. Given the staggering variety of sites on the Internet, you will have to adapt your documentation to a particular source. Include the information your reader would need to access the source.

Warning: Electronic sources can change without notice. Get the most up-to-date information but recognize that this may not always be possible.

➤ **Periodicals available on both CD-ROM and in print.** Include in your citation all the information you would for a print magazine, as well as the publication medium (CD-ROM); the name of the distributor or vendor; and the electronic publication date.

Engel, Diane. "Midwest Realities." *Time* 1 December 1998: 34+. Midwest Voices. CD-ROM. InfoTrak. March 1999.

➤ **Periodicals available only on CD-ROM.** Include the author, title, edition, publication medium (CD-ROM), distributor or vendor, city of publication, publisher, and date of publication.

"Rocks and Gems." *Compton's Interactive Encyclopedia*. 1999 ed. CD-ROM. Cambridge, Massachusetts, 1999.

431

➤ **Online sources.** Give the author's name (if available), the title of the source, the posting date, the identity of the group sponsoring the site (if known), the date of your access, and the Web site in angle brackets < >.

"Holes in Space." <u>Space Science Institute.</u> 5 January 1999. NASA 10 January 1999. <http://oposite.stcsi.edu/pubinfo/RP/35/>

➤ **E-mail.** Give the sender's name, a description of the document, and the date of the communication.

Cunningham, Tom. "Hawaii 5-0." E-mail to Carol Lash. 17 August 1999.

Citing Pamphlets

Cite a pamphlet the same way you would a book.

Gordon, Marla Meg. "You and the Law." *Consumer Affairs Pamphlet 511* (September 1999): 23–45.

Citing Government Documents

The format varies with the information available. The basic citation for a government document looks like this:

Government agency. Subsidiary agency. *Title of Document.* Publication information.

For example:

United States Congressional House Subcommittee on Workfare. *Federal Statement on Workfare.* 99th Congress. Washington, DC: GPO, 1999.

Citing Interviews

Name the subject of the interview, followed by *Personal interview* or *Telephone interview.* Then comes the date.

Lichtenstein, Ellen. Personal interview. 1 September 1999.

Citing Speeches or Lectures

Name the speaker, the title of the speech, the name of the occasion or sponsoring organization, the location, and the date. If you can't get all this information, provide as much as possible.

Bernback, Linda. "Golf for the Beginner" New England Regional Golf Association Yearly Meeting. Burlington, New Hampshire 3 May, 1999.

Citing Radio Shows and TV Shows

Identify significant people involved with the production, followed by their role: Writ. (writer), Dir. (director), Perf. (performer), Narr. (narrator), Prod. (producer).

"Collectibles, Antiques, and Desirables." *Home Matters*. Narr. Vivian Herterford. Prod. Linda Softy. Fox News, New York, 4 February 1999.

APA Documentation

American Psychological Association (APA) documentation is used in social sciences, including anthropology, education, home economics, linguistics, political science, sociology, and, of course, psychology.

Like MLA documentation, APA documentation uses internal references (Smith 1999) in place of footnotes and endnotes. However, the alphabetical list of sources at the end of the paper is called "References" rather than "Works Cited." There are also significant difference between the two formats.

Citing Books

The typical APA reference for a book includes the author's last name, followed by initials rather than the first and middle names. The date is placed in parentheses, followed by the title of the book, underlined, and a period. Then comes the place of publication, colon, publisher, and a period. The second and all subsequent lines are indented, as with the MLA citations. For example:

Rozakis, L. (1999). The Complete Idiot's Guide to Shakespeare. New York: Alpha.

Citing Periodicals

APA periodical references look like this:

Mallory, J. (1999, May). Sing your way to happiness. American Educator, pp. 49–50.

Notice how the name, date format, title, and page numbers differ in APA and MLA formats.

Citing Electronic Sources and CD-ROMs

Give the author's name (if available), the posting date (year, month, day), title of the work, information about the form of the information (On line, CD-ROM, Computer software, in brackets), electronic address.

Note: *On line* is spelled as two words in APA format, one word in MLA format.

Cardillo, L. (1999, January). Holes in Space. <u>Space Science Institute</u> [Web site]. Retrieved 10 January 1999 from the World Wide Web http://oposite.stcsi.edu/pubinfo/RP/35/.

Sixty Word Groups Most Often Confused, Misused, and Abused Words

1. accept—take
   except—leave out, exclude
2. advise—give counsel
   advice—counsel (noun)
3. air—atmosphere
   err—make a mistake
4. affect—influence (verb); a particular psychological state (noun)
   effect—impact and purpose
5. a lot—many
   allot—divide
6. altar—a platform upon which religious rites are performed
   alter—change
7. allowed—given permission
   aloud—out loud, verbally
8. all together—all at one time
   altogether—completely
9. allude—refer to
   elude—escape (verb)
10. already—previously
    all ready—completely prepared
11. allusion—a reference to a well-known place, event, person, work of art, or piece of literary work
    illusion—a misleading appearance or a deception
12. among—three or more people, places, or things
    between—two people, places, or things
13. amount—things that can't be counted
    number—things that can be counted
14. arc—part of the circumference of a circle; curved line
    ark—boat
15. are—plural verb
    our—belonging to us
16. ascent—move up
    assent—agree
17. bare—undressed or unadorned, plain
    bear—fuzzy-wuzzy animal (noun); carry, hold (verb)
18. base—the bottom part of an object; the plate in baseball; morally low
    bass—the lowest male voice; a type of fish; a musical instrument
19. beau—sweetheart
    bow—to bend from the waist; a device used to propel arrows; loops of ribbon; the forward end of a ship
20. berth—a sleeping area in a ship
    birth—being born
21. board—a thin piece of wood; a group of directors
    bored—not interested
22. born—native, brought forth by birth
    borne—endured (past participle of "to bear")
23. bore—tiresome person
    boar—male pig
24. brake—a device for slowing a vehicle
    break—crack or destroy
25. bread—baked goods
    bred—cause to be born

26. breadth—the side-to-side dimension
breath—inhalation and exhalation
27. bridal—pertaining to a bride or a wedding
bridle—part of a horse's harness
28. buy—purchase
by—near or next to
29. capital—the city or town that is the official seat of government; highly important; net worth of a business
capitol—the building in Washington, D.C., where the U.S. Congress meets
30. conscience—moral sense
conscious—awake
31. cell—a small room, as in a convent or a prison
sell—trade
32. cent—a penny
scent—aroma
33. cheep—what a bird says
cheap—not expensive
34. deer—an animal
dear—beloved
35. do—act or make (verb)
due—caused by (adjective)
36. dye—alter or change color of something
die—cease living
37. emigrate—move away from one's country
immigrate—move to another country
38. eminent—distinguished
imminent—expected momentarily
immanent—inborn, inherent
39. fare—price charged for transporting a passenger
fair—not biased; moderately large; moderately good
40. faze—stun
phase—a stage
41. for—because
four—the number 4
42. gorilla—ape
guerrilla—soldier
43. grate—irritate; reduce to small pieces
great—big; wonderful
44. hair—the stuff on your head
heir—beneficiary
45. here—in this place
hear—listen
46. hours—60-minute periods
ours—belonging to us
47. it's—contraction for "it is"
its—possessive pronoun
48. lay—put down
lie—be flat
49. lead—conduct (verb)
lead—bluish-gray metal
led—past tense of "to lead"
50. loose—not tight, not fastened (noun); untighten, or to let go (verb)
lose—misplace (verb)
51. meat—animal flesh
meet—encounter (verb)
52. peace—calm
piece—section
53. plain—not beautiful; obvious
plane—airplane
54. presence—company; closeness
presents—gifts
55. principal—head of a school (noun); main (adjective)
principle—rule
56. reed—a kind of plant
read—interpret the written word
57. right—correct
write—to form letters
58. than—comparison
then—at that time
59. their—belonging to them
they're—contraction for "they are"
there—place
60. Add words that you often confuse, misuse, or abuse:

_____ _____
_____ _____
_____ _____
_____ _____
_____ _____
_____ _____
_____ _____

Index

D

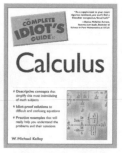